The Structure of
SOCIAL SYSTEMS

The Structure of
SOCIAL SYSTEMS

By Frederick L. Bates
University of Georgia

Clyde C. Harvey
Fort Valley State College

GARDNER PRESS, Inc., New York

Distributed by HALSTED PRESS

A Division of JOHN WILEY & SONS, Inc.

New York • Toronto • London • Sydney

GARDNER PRESS, INC.
32 Washington Square West
New York, New York 10011

Distributed solely by the HALSTED PRESS Division of
John Wiley & Sons, Inc., New York

Library of Congress Cataloging in Publication Data

Bates, Frederick L.
    The structure of social systems.
    1. Social structure. 2. Social systems.
3. Social role. I. Harvey, Clyde C., joint author.
II. Title.
HM24.B364   301.1   75–19150
ISBN 0–470–05649–5 (Halsted)

Printed in the United States of America

1   2   3   4   5   6   7   8   9

To Our Sons

JAMES
ROBERT
QUENTIN
BERTRAM
and
PATRICK

May they, together, work toward a better world.

Preface

Although books are regarded as the creations of the persons whose names appear on their covers, they are actually the products of the social systems in which they are published and read. This is true not only in the sense that, as physical objects, they are the output of publishing companies and printing firms, but also in the sense that the thoughts that appear as words and sentences in their pages are the products of a complex system of human behavior.

The author of a book is like a medium, in that he serves as the mouthpiece through which the society speaks, transmitting its words to the public. Every book is truly produced by a multitude of "authors" functioning together as a system of interrelated influences that accounts for the book's form and content. If one compares books written on the same subject at widely separated times, one sees that the sentence structure, vocabulary, punctuation, and printing style all reflect the prevailing tastes of the different generations. But what is true of language style is also true of intellectual content. A book's content reflects the social and intellectual climate within which it is produced, and by doing so, proves the statement that books, like the personalities of their authors, are the products of the society in which they are published.

An author usually translates this fact into a form more acceptable to our egocentric culture by enumerating the intellectual influences that have shaped his thoughts, and by acknowledging his debt to other writers in prefaces and footnotes. But these conventions tend to preserve intact a greater degree of personal credit or blame than we prefer to claim here. If any consistent thread runs through this volume, it is the notion that all human behavior is part of a general social process in which the actions of the individual form a part of a system of behavior.

We contend throughout that this system explains or accounts for individual actions, whether they be emotions, thoughts, or overt acts. Since books are written by people, and writing is a human behavior, then like all behavior, it must be the output of the system in which it takes place. This book, therefore, was "written" by the social system in which the authors play only a part.

More specifically, this book is the output of a system in which at least four categories of people have contributed heavily to the outcome. First, our intellectual ancestors, whose brain children were the forebears of our ideas. Second, our teachers, who introduced us to these brain children and guided us through our intellectual infancy and childhood. Third, our colleagues and contemporaries with whom we have interacted directly or indirectly. And last, our students, on whom we have tried out our own ideas, and by whom those ideas have been sharpened and refined.

In the category of intellectual ancestors, we acknowledge we owe most to Ralph Linton, E. T. Hiller, Georg Simmel, Charles Cooley, George H. Mead, Max Weber, Bronislaw Malinowski, A. R. Radcliffe-Brown, N. S. Nadel, and Pitirim Sorokin. It was from these writers that we got our basic ideas of role theory and of social structure.

The senior author is particularly indebted to his teachers, both graduate and undergraduate, who set his thoughts on the track that this book follows. In particular, he is indebted to the late Harold L. Geisert of The George Washington University who was his mentor through his undergraduate and early graduate career. Professor Geisert was both a great teacher and a great friend.

Nicholas J. Demerath, at Washington University in Saint Louis, deserves much credit for the shape that this book has taken. He, E. William Noland of the University of North Carolina at Greensboro, and Gordon W. Blackwell, now President of Furman University, took a group of young graduate students and exposed them to field research in complex social systems in such a way as to maximize the joys and intellectual rewards of graduate study. Other students who were members of that group will be able to recognize in these pages thoughts and problems we thrashed out together as members of the Air Force Base Project staff. These individuals include the late James D. Thompson of Vanderbilt University; George S. Tracy of Louisiana State University; Raymond W. Mack, Provost of Northwestern University; Richard L. Simpson of the University of North Carolina; Richard W. Stephens of The George Washington University; Jack L. Dyer of California State College, Stanislaus; Kenneth Wagner of Jackson, Mississippi; Fred E. Katz of the University of Tel Aviv; and Paul H. Minton of the University of Richmond. Also included in our group was a young faculty member, John J. Honigmann of the University of North Carolina, who was an inspiration to us all.

There are others who have also shaped this work in its later development, some known personally, others only through their writings. The greatest intellectual debt is owed to Talcott Parsons and Robert K. Merton. Harold L. Nix and H. Max Miller have profoundly affected the way we think about human communities. Charles J. Dudley helped shape our ideas concerning person-centered analysis. J. Drenan Kelley contributed substantially to our perspective on social stratification, and A. P. Garbin to our view of occupations and work positions. We owe a debt of gratitude also to Vernon L. Parenton and Roland J. Pellegrin, both of whom contributed substantially to the intellectual content of this book. Finally, our thanks go to Alvin L. Bertrand of Louisiana State University, who encouraged us to persist in completing this volume.

This book is not only the product of all these professional sociologists and anthropologists—it also owes more than can be put into words to our wives, Hettie and Inez. It would not been written or published without the inspiration, encouragement, and constant assistance of Hettie Dowtin Bates, who typed and edited the manuscript several times, and who suffered through the writing process with the authors. We also wish to acknowledge the editorial assistance of Barbara Fried of Gardner Press, who put the manuscript in final form, and whose efforts made it eminently more readable.

F. L. BATES
C. C. HARVEY

Athens, Georgia
June, 1975

Contents

Part IV
The Actor As
a Participant
in Social Systems

Part V
Dimensional Analysis
and Change

Part VI
A General
Assessment

PART I

PHILOSOPHICAL
FOUNDATIONS

CHAPTER 1   *GENERAL ORIENTATION*

The object of this book is to present a conceptual scheme or structural model useful for describing and analyzing the organization and operation of human social systems, varying in size and complexity from a small group to an entire society. It is not our intention to offer a summary of current knowledge gained from empirical research. Nor do we intend to review the principal theories or conceptual schemes related to social systems. Rather, we shall present, as clearly and as logically as possible, a single integrated set of concepts designed to enable sociologists to describe and analyze both large and small social systems.

Sociology shares with all other branches of science the need for a set of clearly defined and logically interrelated concepts. Through the use of concepts, scientists create intellectual images of some part of the natural world. These images serve as models for that part of the world the scientist is attempting to understand. They furnish him with a set of symbolic tools that may be manipulated logically to formulate theories and hypotheses for empirical testing, and to guide observation.

Although conceptual clarity and precision are among the prime requisites of a science, until now sociology has been characterized by a diversity of conceptual schemes that employ loosely defined terms whose definitions vary according to the person using them. We need, therefore, to examine and redefine basic sociological concepts and their logical interrelationships so that they can be used more precisely and logically to state sociological propositions and generalizations. Such redefinitions should place all of the elementary sociological terms deemed necessary for building a conception of society and its operation in a single, logically integrated, symbolic model or set of models.

This book will therefore attempt to build a set of structural models for various types of social entities. These models will be created by combining and, where necessary, reformulating existing sociological perspectives and terminology. We will combine the viewpoints of the general systems approach and the so-called "role theory" approach, and adapt certain assumptions from the symbolic interactionists, the conflict theorists, and from behavioral psychology. In combining these various elements, we will use a structural approach to defining social elements and their interrelationships, and integrate the essentially static spatial perspective of structuralism with a time dimension, thereby creating models for social systems that allow for change and process by visualizing structures as they progress through time. But the scheme presented herein is more than a set of concepts. Each concept used will be integrated into an internally consistent, logically related configuration which taken as a whole offers a paradigm, or model, useful for identifying and formulating new research problems, and also for evaluating the significance of old ones.

By creating an integrated symbolic model which employs a systematic structural approach, we are presenting a new sociological problematic. "A problematic, or a thought structure is a particular way of looking at the world, defined by the fundamental questions asked," according to Glucksmann. It includes not only the basic question or questions regarded as important, but also the concepts, methods, and theories implied by the question (1).

The fundamental query underlying our particular problematic is the question asked by most modern structuralists: What are the underlying principles or laws which govern the structure or form of human social systems, and thereby produce and maintain order, regularity, and change in human affairs? The kind of structuralism we present, however, differs considerably from that of Levi-Strauss and his adherents (2). The main difference is that we believe the search for underlying principles of social structure, order, and change must rest on solid empirical grounds, which in turn must be based on detailed morphological studies of concrete, ongoing social systems. Before seeking the deep structure of human social behavior, especially as it is exemplified in complex social systems, we believe that it is necessary to be less general and more exact in dealing with structure at the first level of abstraction than Levi-Strauss is apparently willing to be. For instance, we think we have to describe and measure the structure of particular real families, or particular real factories, before we can realistically hope to formulate any underlying principles which might govern these, or all other, structures.

The problematic presented here, therefore, lies more toward the descriptive or sociographic end of the epistomological scale than does the work of Claude Levi-Strauss, Noam Chomsky, or Louis Althusser. It more nearly approaches our idea of the problematics of such British social anthropologists as Edmund Leach, Raymond Firth, and S. F. Nadel, or of the American sociologists Talcott Parsons and Robert Merton.

In a sense, this book builds upon the foundation laid by Talcott Parsons and Robert Merton. But it departs from the structure-function tradition in that its major concerns are with the principles of social structure themselves, and with the problem of how best to describe the organization of social systems as it relates to their operation as systems. Again we feel that we are operating at a level of abstraction different from the Parsonians' or Mertonians'. We wish to know *in detail* how social systems are put together and how they change along the time dimension. We are, therefore, more concerned with the exact anatomy or morphology of systems than with abstract structural or functional problems. Our problematic dictates that we ask ourselves such a question as, "What are the precise structural mechanisms through which one particular group is articulated with another particular group to form a part of a larger whole?" rather than asking, as Parsons does (3), "By what general principles are social systems integrated?"

Our problematic contains a scientific program for sociology which, in brief, calls first for painstaking observations made of real social systems while they are actually operating. Then it demands a detailed analysis of these observations from a structural perspective, which means an emphasis on analyzing how these real social systems are organized internally and linked externally to other systems. The last part of the program involves examining our morphological analyses to determine what principles or laws of structure might underlie what we have found in the empirical world. It is in this final step that we join intellectual forces with other modern structuralists.

Our program for sociology is based on a belief that sociologists and social anthropologists have not as yet come to grips in their research with their object of study, society. Both sociological and anthropological research has so far been so unstructured and unsystematic that it has produced only very general and inexact information about the nature of human societies and the principles by which they are structured and by which they operate.

For the most part sociological research has centered on social psychological problems, and has neglected the direct study of functioning social systems. Sociology has succeeded in avoiding the study of society and its component parts by exploiting a simple social-psychological paradigm (4):

1. Human beings as members in society become social actors through a process of socialization by which they acquire their culture, form attitudes and beliefs, and acquire information and unique personality traits.

2. How the individual is shaped by socialization depends on the biological characteristics of the individual—that is, sex, age, or race; and on the social characteristics associated with the individual's birth and socialization.

3. Individuals as well as categories of individuals fit into society differently; as a consequence of that fit and their previous molding by society, they will behave differently.

4. Therefore: if we wish to discover how any form of behavior can be accounted for, we must search for whatever combination of social and personal characteristics are associated with the actors who engage in the behavior we wish to explain. For example, if we wish to understand crime, voting behavior, mate selection, divorce, fertility, migration, success in school, social mobility, occupational choice, leadership, and so forth, we need only treat these phenomena as forms of behavior which are amenable to explanation through our formula.

In following this paradigm a sociologist may learn something about certain social psychological aspects of human behavior, but he will not be forced to face functioning social systems as real operating entities in the actual process of occurring. He will, in short, learn more about the *consequences* of the operation of social systems than about the systems themselves.

This failure of sociologists to come to grips with real functioning social systems is both evidence and consequence of the fact that sociology lacks a truly sociological paradigm. With respect to our stated object of study, society, we are in what Thomas S. Kuhn calls the pre-paradigmatic stage (5). The research which is being generated in sociology at present either follows the general social psychological paradigm outlined above, or reflects the very general orientation passed down to us from our founders.

Kuhn (6) says that "In the absence of a paradigm or some candidate for paradigm, all of the facts that could possibly pertain to the development of a given science are likely to seem equally relevant. As a result, early fact-gathering is far more nearly random activity than the one that subsequent scientific development makes familiar. Furthermore, in the absence of a reason for seeking some particular form of more recondite information, early fact-gathering is usually restricted to the wealth of data that lie ready to hand." What statement could more accurately describe the present state of affairs in sociology than this!

During the past thirty-five years there have been some notable attempts to develop a truly sociological problematic, one which focuses on society and its component parts as the object of study (7). These attempts have, however, failed to produce any great impact on sociological research. The result is that a curious separation now exists between the major sociological schools of thought, which are based on quasi-paradigms, and the research that is being performed by sociologists on a largely nonparadigmatic basis.

In our view, the problematic that comes closest to paradigmatic status is the Parsonian-based structure-functional approach. Its claim to this status rests not only on its stated central concern with social systems, and in particular with societies as the object of study, but also on its gradual evolution into modern systems theory. Parsons and his students and their students have kept alive an interest in society, in groups, and in organizations as social entities during a period when most other American sociologists have only been interested in social-psychological or demographic phenomena. Further, only such sociologists and anthropologists as Radcliffe-Brown, Malinowski, Firth, Nadel, Levi-Strauss, Parsons, and Merton have come close to developing a conceptual scheme joined to a theoretical perspective that aims to comprehend whole societies.

Two other approaches—"conflict theory" and "symbolic interactionism"—may be viewed as problematics on the way to becoming paradigms, but they seem to us to be not well articulated or especially sociological in their outlook. Symbolic interactionism is a basically psycho-linguistic problematic which offers a foundation for a social-psychological paradigm for dealing with small group behavior (8). However, it is difficult to see how, at least in its present form, it could offer a paradigm for the sociological investigation of complex social systems, unless it is absorbed into a larger paradigm such as that proposed by Parsons. Actually, the Parsonian conception of social action and the Blumer conception of symbolic interactionism seem to resemble each other more than they differ. The critical comments of the symbolic interactionists about structure functionalism seem to be based on their own ideological commitment to humanism; they apparently find structure functionalism deficient in this respect, but otherwise there seems to be no basic difference in the way they explain social behavior.

Conflict theory can barely be called a theory at all, nor can it be called a paradigm (9). Instead, it appears to represent a problematic which emphasizes the importance of conflict and change as underlying phenomena to be accounted for, and which may be able to explain morphogenic processes in social systems. But unless conflict theory is integrated with some form of structural systems analysis, as indeed it was by Marx himself, it represents an incomplete problematic—one which can develop into a paradigm only by taking over much of the perspective attributed to structure functionalists by conflict theorists.

Pure structuralism, as it is emerging from the work of Levi-Strauss and his associates, offers, according to Glucksmann, a new problematic for the social sciences (10). However, its emphasis on discovering the underlying structural principles by which the human psyche operates hardly qualifies it as a basis for a future sociological paradigm. The search for deeper structures in the organization of society which appears to be taking hold among the British social anthropologists, if it joins with more traditional functionalism and is cross-fertilized by modern systems theory and the Parsonian-Mertonian perspectives, may develop into the first truly sociological paradigm.

It is instructive to ask, why hasn't the Parsonian systems perspective (11), produced more research on social systems? and, why didn't Merton's paradigm for functional analysis (12) immediately stimulate a flowering of truly structure-functional research on real social systems? The answer to these questions is that neither Parsons' general model, nor Merton's paradigm for functional analysis is supported by a conceptual scheme sufficiently detailed and exact to permit systematic empirical research. Neither provides a means of describing, with a scientifically exact terminology, the parts or elements of social systems, and of relating these parts to each other in larger structural patterns. As a consequence, one does not know what to look for when performing structure-functional analysis; nor does one know how to categorize or assemble observations in a way that will lead to functional interpretations. Both Parsons and Merton tell us approximately what to do *after we have performed a structural analysis* and have arrived at a morphological image of the system we are studying. But the question is, how do we get to this point?

The British and French social anthropologists have not solved these problems any better than Americans. Neither American nor European sociology offers a detailed and exact system of morphological concepts that would permit precise structural analysis of even small social systems, much less large organizations or entire societies.* All that is available is a grab-bag of structural concepts, each of which is inexact in and of itself, and more or less independent from most other concepts. This means that structural analysis at present is more an art than a science. As a consequence, the structural pictures that have emerged from the

---

*This is true with the possible exception of anthropological work on kinship systems, which has achieved a degree of structural precision that is lacking in research on other aspects of society. Even here the kinship systems are not often viewed as functioning social systems comprised of groups which have a distinct internal structure.

small amount of structural research tend to be more influenced by the theoretical and philosophical orientation of the artist than by the characteristics of the objects he intends to represent.

What sociology needs to move it toward the paradigmatic stage of its development is a clearly defined, integrated set of structural concepts that will permit us to do comparable research and to communicate with each other. The act of formulating these concepts will make it possible to identify the important elements, properties, and relationships upon which structural research and functional analysis should be performed. It will also make it possible for us to formulate theories that let us test critical hypotheses concerning the social organization of society.

This book is intended to be a starting point for this all-important undertaking. It does not present a true sociological paradigm; but it does offer a road on which we may proceed toward one. We believe that research on society and on its parts is the central concern of sociology, and that until we can agree upon a terminology to describe societies, we cannot hope to progress to the stage of sociologically productive paradigms in the Kuhn sense. Essentially, therefore, this book represents an attempt to build a single integrated conceptual model of human society and of its various subparts.

Since the discipline began, sociologists have claimed that society is their object of study. Yet it has always been apparent that even the smallest societies are so large and complex, and exist over such a long time-span, that whole societies can neither be observed as total objects nor studied exhaustively by a single scientist or group of scientists in a short length of time. Sociologists share certain problems with geologists and astronomers: as observers, we are in the position of trying to understand objects whose scale and duration are immense. No matter what our method of data collecting, we can only observe a small portion of a society, measured either temporally or spatially, at one time.

In a way, we are like scientific ants attempting to formulate some idea of an elephant. Let us imagine that one day an elephant walks by an ant hill, and an ant is sent to find out what kind of object has created the destructive rumblings in the earth. He has ant-size vision, and therefore can only see a few feet ahead. He climbs on to the left hind foot of the elephant, and looks upward into a hazy distance, over a craggy grey surface that extends beyond the limits of his eyesight. He is able to change directions, sometimes running upside down, sometimes vertically, and sometimes horizontally. He feels movement in the surface, perhaps warmth; but wherever he runs he sees the same grey surface.

The point is, if he runs for a whole ant lifetime he can never cover the entire surface of the elephant, much less invade its subsurface and explore its internal organs. Furthermore, his senses do not allow him to get far enough away to see the whole of the elephant at once. Nor can he observe the elephant long enough to gain any information about its growth, maturation, or reproduction.

A big part of our ant's problem is that he started exploring without a plan. The only hope he might have had of being able to add something accurate to the ant hill's knowledge of elephants would have lain in his using some predetermined set of rules to order his observations. He needed some systematic way to map or chart his observations, put them into relatively precise temporal and spatial relationships to one another, and thereby achieve some notion of what some parts of the elephant looked like. Other ants making similar systematic observations could then have added their bits of information to his; and perhaps eventually they would have gained a mosiac-like image of an elephant.

If we are ever to understand what an entire society is like as an object, we too must have some systematic plan for drawing sociological maps or charts of societies. We need accurate models that will enable us to grasp intellectually both the structure or "anatomy" of the system we are trying to understand, and the processes or "physiology" which occur within its structure. We must formulate our concepts to include categories into which we can place our observations, interrelating them in temporal and spatial patterns that will then enable us to build models of larger entities.

The kinds of concepts we need are those which will define in detail the parts and subparts of social systems, which can be logically linked into larger patterns according to a geometric plan. This means we must start by specifying the smallest particles of societies we expect to observe, and then relate our ideas about these parts to one another; thus we will be able to conceive of the next larger and then the next larger part, until we reach the boundaries of the system we are attempting to describe.

This is the plan this book will follow. We will start at the micro level, defining concepts and establishing the rules for their use; then we will pyramid these into larger and larger concepts that are logically consistent with one another. In the end we will have a conceptual model for society in the abstract sense. It will not tell us what any given society is like. Rather, it will supply us with a way to build descriptive models of empirical societies by combining our observations with our concepts.

The system of concepts that will be presented in this book, then, will represent a general abstract model for society—society here being a name for the largest, most complex system to which men belong. This conceptual model serves two uses. First and foremost, it is a way to order empirical observations made on real societies, so that descriptive models can be built that are based on actual social systems or some of their component parts. Secondly, because its logically consistent nature and its basis in easily observed phenomena give it a certain degree of face validity, it can be used to formulate theories both about social systems in general and also about particular systems for which empirically-based descriptive models have been built. It can, in other words, serve to identify critical variables and to state hypothetical relationships among them. A brief discussion of each of these uses and its implications is in order.

Building Descriptive Models

Any science, including sociology, must begin its work by acquiring a detailed knowledge of the structure and characteristics of the objects or phenomena it is attempting to understand through painstaking, orderly observation. Until these observations are made, it is premature to theorize about origins or development, let alone causative relationships or alterations through time. Without a thorough descriptive knowledge of the object of study, theories are meaningless, no matter how elegant or logical. Since theoretical assumptions and logic work equally well with both imaginary and real phenomena, we need to have a body of empirical data against which to check our theories. But random observations are also not enough by themselves; for when our conceptual scheme is faulty, observations may be misleading, for they will not be interpreted correctly. For example, doctors once observed a positive correlation between the rate of malaria and living near swamps, which they then interpreted as meaning that miasmas from the swamps were responsible for the disease.

There is the chance, of course, that exceptional insight may lead some research sociologist to formulate a set of hypotheses about society or some part of it which turn out in the long run to be relatively accurate. But if each sociologist is to work independently, without a clear picture of the object he is trying to understand, and without a set of symbols he shares with others in his field, we are as unlikely to achieve a systematic understanding of the whole system as separate ants each trying to perceive an elephant (13). Furthermore, sociology can ill afford the amount of effort we now waste on collecting and analyzing data to test hypotheses about spurious or imaginary phenomena. Painstaking data collection and elegantly sophisticated analysis procedures are useless if the original conception of the problem is so poor that it dooms the research to insignificance before it is even begun.

We must do the basic work of examining and describing the objects we are attempting to understand. Like the biologist, we need to dissect and examine our organism; or like the astronomer, we need to gaze painstakingly for hours on end through our sociological telescopes and carefully chart what we see. Then our theories and hypotheses can be formulated on the basis of what we *have* observed, rather than what we think we *might* observe.

It would be wrong to say that sociologists have not made observational studies, or have not described accurately what some parts of society "look like," although it may be true that anthropologists have made a better and more extensive start on this job. But even those few really excellent descriptive studies that do exist have not been constructed within the framework of precise or internally consistent conceptual schemes. Therefore we cannot easily add them together to furnish an image of a larger segment of a society, nor can they be compared or used to crosscheck each other. Similarly, the statistical analyses like those made by demographers may reveal certain gross characteristics of society; but they are not part of a conceptual scheme which is essentially sociological or scientific. Demographers are forced to accept the politically-based categories of those who generate the data and proceed from there; as a result they have no conceptual framework that can help them gain any detailed insight into what the society is like as a functioning system.

Societies as Real Systems

It is clear from the discussion so far that we view societies and their parts as real entities, susceptible to being described. Our problematic assumes that societies are real in the same sense that any object or phenomena studied by any branch of science is assumed to be real, subject to observation—that is, to any and all methods of collecting sense impressions through the use of any method—and through such observation subject to systematic description. We also assume that society as an object exists independent of the observer; and that as an object it serves as a source of sense impressions which can become data for the scientist (14).

Furthermore, society as an object consists of behavior. It is therefore to be defined as a complex system of human activities. In assuming it to be real, we thereby assume behavior to be real and observable, for if human behavior is real, then systems, small and large, comprised of behavior are also real.

Some scientists and many laymen tend to believe that individual human beings are real because they are tangible, biological objects who can be weighed on a scale, measured by a yardstick, and otherwise subjected to physical and chemical analysis; but that their behavior, being "intangible," is either less real or "unreal," and therefore not subject to scientific analysis in the same sense as the physical organism. It is true that behavior as a phenomenon has some peculiar characteristics which make it appear almost illusory to the casual observer, mostly because it consists of not one single action or event but a process, which takes place over time. An action is performed, recedes into the past, and is gone from the purview of the observer, to be followed immediately by another action and another. Behavior is thus a series of events or happenings which are perishable in the sense that they occur over a given time interval and then recede from view. Because action is so perishable and transitory, at times it appears unreal. Apart from any physical record, such as a motion picture, behavior exists, once it has occurred, only as a memory in the mind of the observer; or as a set of displacements or consequences in the environment.

Society at any given time is a series of simultaneously occurring and unfolding events; like the actions of its individual participants, it is constantly fading into the past and unfolding into the future. Can such an object, which is apparently so intangible and illusory, be regarded as real? Most behavioral scientists assume that it can; and so do we.

In actuality, all so-called "objects" in nature are systems of movement. Viewed from the process perspective, and at the proper speed, they are all fleeting and temporary. A mountain viewed in fast motion over a period of an eon is merely an event which is present for a brief moment and is gone. It is only the time-space limitations of our unaided senses, which are essentially adapted to instantaneous adjustment to the behavioral events occurring within and around us, that make us conclude that behavior is more fleeting and temporary than the organism performing it or the physical objects that surround it. Our senses operate at a speed and at a spatial level adapted to behavioral adjustment. In order to "see society" as a real object, we must find some way to alter the time-space limitations of our senses so that we can perceive both faster and slower than is natural. Likewise, we must develop methods that will allow us to record both smaller particles and larger systems of action than we can perceive as actors involved in the living process of social behavior.

In short, behavior is real because it is observable. It is observable because it occupies space, occurs over time, and can be demonstrated to have lasting effects on objects declared on the same grounds to be real. Human behavior is a factor in producing a building, a highway, a forest fire, and pollution in a stream or in the air. A building exists for a long period of time as an entity that appears stable and relatively slow changing. It is therefore generally regarded as a real object. But if something is unreal—behavior—it cannot produce anything real—a building; nor can the unreal alter or modify the real.

On the other hand, something real, such as an organism, cannot produce anything unreal. This last point needs careful examination. Part of the argument over the reality of human society centers on the fact that people, as thinking beings, are able to and do imagine or concoct ideas which postulate the existence of things or phenomena which are not real. But when we say that a real object, such as a human being, cannot produce anything or have any consequence which is not real, we are saying that ideas, thoughts, and concepts are as real as are the minds or personalities that produce them, in the sense that they are events occurring in the organisms that produce them. They occupy space, transpire in time, utilize energy, and are to be viewed as biochemical processes; therefore they are real. This is not the same as saying that a belief in ghosts makes ghosts themselves a reality. The act of believing in ghosts, however, consists of an as-yet imperfectly understood mental process which is itself real. Being real, as a belief or idea, it has the power to affect behavior. This is what W. I. Thomas meant by saying that things defined as real are real in their consequences (15). It is the conception of ghosts which is real, not ghosts themselves.

Like believing, which we regard as a behavior of the organism, perceiving is a behavior or type of behavior. It is therefore possible for a belief in ghosts, in combination with a set of other circumstances, to result in the "perception" of ghosts. Again, it is the act of perceiving a ghost which is real, because it involves the behavior of a real, observable object—a perceiving person—and not the ghost itself. And the act of perceiving a ghost will result in actions which are themselves real; for example, flight from the apparition.

It is apparent that the scientific observer faces the same problem in knowing reality that any human being faces. This problem is essentially no different with respect to the study of human behavior than it is with respect to understanding other natural phenomena. What men define as *real* is a function of their concepts, combined with the processes used to observe the world and what exists in the environment being observed.

Thus, there are several factors involved in the process of defining objects in nature as real, and in isolating and conceiving of their interrelated characteristics: (1) The system of concepts or symbolic representations used to guide thought and to order perception; (2) the method of making observations and relating them to those concepts; and (3) the combination of events and objects which constitute the situation in which the observations are made, and which are regarded as phenomena to be observed and understood (16).

The art of the scientific enterprise consists of devising strategies which will make the second factor (data gathering) as independent as possible of the first (conceptualization) and the third (the objects being observed), in such a way that scientists will not perceive and define as real merely what they conceived to be real prior to observation—in short, of devising means to prevent the belief in ghosts from inevitably resulting in the perception of ghosts, regardless of whether they are there or not; and at the same time to prevent a disbelief in ghosts from inevitably leading to the conclusion that they do not exist.

In general, these goals are achieved by using two rather simple but powerful tactics. The first and more important may be called the strategy of doubt, and the second the strategy of logical inference, which extends the logical argument so as to permit doubt to operate as a corrective to preconceptions.

The strategy of doubt amounts to approaching the process of perception of the real world with the objective of disproving rather than proving that that which is assumed to exist, is real. We look for weaknesses and inadequacy in our arguments, seek exceptions to our rules, and proceed by eliminating possibilities rather than by seeking to confirm our pre-existing beliefs. Concepts are regarded as tentative and hypothetical, not as fixed beliefs to be accepted as guides to perception.

The strategy of logical inference stretches an argument to the point of saying that if a given thing is true, other things whose conception is independent of the original assumption must also be true. Thus, no concept or belief is allowed to stand independent of others which must logically follow. It is assumed that nothing in nature stands independent of its context and that all things are a part of a system of interdependent phenomena. If a given thing is true because it is a part of a system, it therefore follows that other related things must also be true. If ghosts are real, then as phenomena they must be related to other phenomena which are observable. By observing these other phenomena, we are able to test our beliefs in ghosts, and, if they are real, expand our knowledge of them.

When this deductive hypothetical strategy is combined with the strategy of doubt, it corrects the tendency to see as real what we would like to see in order to confirm our preconceptions.

Theoretical Statements and Models

Concepts are a vital part of science, as they are indeed of the behavior process for everyone, scientist or not. After all, science is no more than human behavior carried on in accordance with a particular set of rules. But scientific concepts must have certain characteristics. They must be defined in terms which make them amenable to observation (operationalization). They must also be defined in logical relation to one another, so that they can be fitted into larger theoretical statements. And in order to allow one scientist to crosscheck another's results, scientific concepts must have a stable meaning commonly accepted by all who are using them.

Because of their vital role in the scientific process, no more important task exists for the scientist than to formulate concepts and conceptual schemes. Such work should not be confused with theorizing. Theories consist of logical arguments about relationships deduced from conceptual schemes. Theories employ concepts, and use their defined interrelationships in stating propositions. Theories attempt to explain something. Conceptual schemes explain nothing. They only furnish the basis for categorizing information, and for building descriptive models of the objects or phenomena needing explanation. In other words, concepts permit us to conceive of the elements about which theory may be constructed.

This book, therefore, presents a conceptual model of social organization from which theories can be constructed (17), rather than a theory of social organization. Essentially, it is an exercise in conceptual clarification, and not an exercise in theory building. It will be necessary, however, at the beginning to review some theoretical matters of a very general sort, and to make explicit certain theoretical and philosophical points that underlie the particular problematic used in building a conceptual model for society. The next two chapters, therefore, will set the metaphysical stage for the main enterprise of the book.

The plan of the remainder of the book is to begin by discussing the smallest elements or particles of society, and, by defining concepts, to deal with them. Then these small elements will be combined into larger and larger ones, until, having defined its components in an orderly and systematic fashion, we are finally able to conceive of an entire society. It is the equivalent in chemistry of proceeding from electron and proton to atom, to crystals, and finally to compounds. And in proceeding systematically from the smallest particle of behavior to the largest system of behavior we can imagine, we shall state how they are linked together as systems and subsystems.

CHAPTER 2   *GUIDING ASSUMPTIONS AND PERSPECTIVES*

In the following chapters we intend to build a structural model of society by defining, or, more properly, redefining a set of concepts that will allow us to conceive in the abstract what societies are like as systems. Since this is our intention, it is proper that we specify in detail, before we begin, what we mean by such words as "structure" and "social system," and furthermore what our general orientation is as far as the nature and causation of human behavior are concerned. We are assuming certain things to be true about the object, "society," and about its various parts. Our model will rest on these assumptions, and therefore the reader must be familiar with them before he can evaluate fairly what follows.

The Idea of Structure

Structure, wherever it is used as a concept, involves certain notions (1). First and foremost, it employs the notion of space. Structures exist in and occupy space. Indeed, structures themselves define space, since without structure, space cannot easily be delimited. Structure furthermore implies an ordering of parts, particles, or units in space—units that need not be tangible or material objects, but can be forces or intangible factors. Before we can define structure, therefore, we have to understand what we mean by *space,* and by a *part, particle,* or *unit.* And finally, we must define some relationship through which the ordering of particles in space can be described.

The notion of structure also implies that a boundary to the unit whose structure is being described must exist. That is to say, a set of parts located in space, in relationship to each other, is regarded as forming some whole, which is distinguishable from other wholes comprised of other parts in relationship to one another. For instance, the structure of a solar system is described in terms of parts called the planets and the sun; and the relationship of each of these parts to one another is described in terms of orbits and gravitational systems. The larger whole, the solar system, when it is regarded as separate from other possible units in space, is said to have a structure consisting of the parts (planets and the sun) which are in relationship to each other (orbits and gravitational interrelations). To apply the concept of structure to social phenomena, we will have to describe them in the same way. Social systems of varying levels of complexity will be the larger wholes. The parts out of which these larger systems are made must be identified, and their properties and relationships defined.

As we have already said, the sociologist who deals with the structure of large complex human social systems, such as societies or human communities, faces a basic problem of scale or size. Even the smallest human communities consist of hundreds of actors organized into even more hundreds of groups, which together form many complex organizational systems. With whole societies the problem is even greater. Action within these systems takes place continuously and unevenly, and occurs in many parts of the system simultaneously. A human observer cannot see all of the system at once, so that he is forced to conceive of the structure of the larger system on the basis of having observed only small parts of it. For this reason, he must be very careful in selecting his observation point, and in deciding on which concepts he will use to order his observations into an image or model of the larger structure.

His first task is simple description and definition. He must be able to describe the system, in terms of its parts and their interrelationships, on the basis of a few strategic observations at key points within the system. And he must define the parts, elements, particles, or ingredients out of which the more complex structure of the object called the social system is made. For before he can specify what a large object, such as a social system is like, he has to specify as unambiguously as possible its smaller, component parts. Sociologists have variously chosen as parts or particles out of which to contruct their image of social structure the following things: (1) actors or people; (2) strata, such as social classes, castes, and estates; (3) social institutions; (4) social groups, organizations, and communities; and (5) social actions.

Awareness of the problem of scale should strongly influence a sociologist's choice of which parts or particles he will use to construct his model of the larger whole. Human observers can only observe certain kinds of objects directly, and the parts chosen as units of structure should be small enough so they can be seen directly by an observer. Otherwise, the concept of structure will not be anchored in objective reality. If, for example, a sociologist starts out by saying that the structure of society consists of social institutions, and he then defines social institutions as being gigantic entities like economic, political, and educational systems, he will not be able to observe them as a whole. Instead, he will only be able to observe small parts of them directly, and thus he will not be able to make any meaningful empirical observations. Similarly, if he defines the structure of society as consisting of a series of interrelated communities, he will be unable to observe entire communities, and again, his image of structure cannot be based on empirical observations.

Therefore, in choosing the parts or particles out of which the concept of structure will be forged, observability must be a criterion. This also implies that the parts be of such a scale that they can be adequately described within a reasonable amount of time, using a reasonable amount of resources, and within the limitations of the state of the art of data collection.

Once the sociologist has chosen the parts he will observe he must go on to make explicit and exact statements about how these smaller elements and units are linked or joined to form a society. And then he has to state how these parts function, operate, or behave in relation to each other. In other words, his image of structure should not only identify linkages among parts, but should give, at a minimum, a general notion of the dynamic relationships among them. For, in describing function, he describes the nature of the linkage among parts in terms of the behavior of the system, which is to say, its *meaning*. This point will become clear if we illustrate it with an organic analogy. If we are defining the structure of the human organism, we have to go beyond the statement that the heart is connected to a system of veins and arteries, which in turn are linked to the lungs, kidneys, liver, and brain. We will have to describe how the various parts of this system *function* with respect to one another—what the heart does in relation to the arteries and veins; what the lungs do in relation to the heart. Similarly, we can say that society consists of people, or, more properly, persons. We can then say that these persons are linked together through interaction, or perhaps through complementary role relationships, into families and other groups. But then we still have to say how the people who form families and other groups *function* in relation to each other to produce the operations or behavior of the larger system called society.

Once a discipline is advanced in concept building and model construction, its scientists are able to convey a world of meaning with only a very few words. Simply by saying that man is a primate, a biologist has specified much about human organic structure and functioning, because this accumulated knowledge is already implicit in the word *primate.* Sociological theory, however, is only beginning, and does not yet have available a body of commonly-recognized concepts on which we can draw. It behooves us, therefore, to amass as much descriptive detail as possible, and to remain close to the empirical level in defining the structure of social systems. In choosing relational concepts, we should be particularly careful to employ ideas that are easily checked against empirical reality; it is all too easy to invent magnificent abstractions which can be manipulated with logical grace, but which have no valid basis in objective common sense.

After we have selected the parts or particles out of which our image or model of structure will be constructed; defined the relationships among the parts; and specified the functions that they perform in relation to each other and their environment, we still cannot say how the social system evolves and changes. The concept *function* implies time, it is true, but time in the short run. It does not permit us to deal with change in functions, or change in the character of parts, or change in the relationship among parts over longer periods of real time (2). We cannot describe, in terms of function alone, growth and development, decline and decay, or even simple transition from one stage to another in the development of a social system. Especially we cannot deal with change in function itself.

To enable us to deal with these problems, we have to specify how our object, the social system, relates to its environment, and further, how it appears in relation to this environment with respect to different segments of time. To do this, we have to specify what other objects exist in the environment of the social system; how they relate to each other in that environment; and how they relate to the social system whose structure we are describing. We must be able to describe how our social system operates as a system in relation to these objects in the environment. This means that our concept of the structure of the social system must contain some clearly identifiable concepts of *boundaries,* which allow us to deal with internal processes as they relate to the environment of the system (3). This environmental concept, added to our conception of the internal structure and functioning of the system, will enable us to deal with the dynamics of change, development, growth, and transition within the system.* This will necessitate defining the mechanisms through which inputs are received from the environment and outputs are transferred to it.

---

*Social systems are "open systems." They are therefore subject in a peculiar way to influence by the environment with which they interact.

The Utility of the Structural Approach

Sociologists seek scientific explanations for human behavior. Like any other science, sociology aims beyond mere description of what exists in the world of social behavior to the statement of principles, perhaps even laws, of cause and effect.* Conceptual models which utilize the structural approach are useful in this pursuit. There are four ways in which such models aid the sociologist in his search for causative relationships. First, they furnish a framework through which systematic description of social objects and events can be carried out. Through structural concepts, the parts of social systems may be isolated and identified, their relationships to one another described, and their functions defined, using a systematic approach to description. Indeed the description of any object is incomplete, perhaps even impossible, without at least an implicit statement concerning its structure.

The second way in which structural models are useful is that they provide a frame of reference that focuses the perceptions of the scientist who is observing social phenomena. It is obviously true that no observer or group of observers can perceive and record all of the facts about any phenomena they are observing. Their perception is inevitably selective, and organized in terms of some frame of reference, either conscious or unconscious. The structural frame of reference provides guidelines for this organizing process, so that the observer can select from among the myriad possible perceptions those which are pertinent to scientific generalization. Specifically, the structural framework focuses the observer's attention on the notion of parts, relationship, and function; and it draws his attention to certain forms of regularity or order in whatever he is studying. In short, it provides the basis of a plan or strategy through which sociological ants can order their observation of society, the sociological elephant.

The third way in which structural models are useful is in furnishing a category of variables which can be utilized either as independent or dependent variables in statements of causative relationships. In other words, social structure variables, as opposed to other variables, such as personality, for example, can be examined as independent variables with respect to human behavior as a dependent variable. Selected aspects of social structure, such as structural distance, the forms of structural relationships, or structural complexity can then be used to state hypotheses relating to human behavior.

There is a fourth way in which structural models are extremely

---

*Later we will discuss the idea of causation and modify the traditional view held toward it. For the present, we will use the concept "cause" to allow us to discuss other problems.

important. They make it possible to deal with the study of social change. Social change amounts to alteration in the structure of a social system. Without a means of describing structure and analyzing it in terms of its parts, relationships, and functions, it is impossible to conceive of change, since change constitutes an alteration in the parts of a system, or in the relationships among the parts, or in the functioning of that system in some way.

Order and Structure

When we say that the sociologist seeks causative explanation for human behavior, we are saying that he is seeking to discover order and regularity in human affairs (4). He assumes that social behavior is a natural phenomenon, and like everything else in nature operates in an orderly and predictable fashion. Therefore, the tasks of the sociologist could be described as follows: (1) to discover ways of perceiving the order and regularity in human affairs; (2) to describe that order in the most precise terms possible; and (3) to explain how that order is produced, maintained, and changed (5).

The concept of *order* may be defined in terms of two dimensions: replication and persistence. Order amounts to the replication or persistence of the same structural forms. By replication we mean that the same phenomenon repeats itself over and over in the same time interval. It is replicated when it contains the same elements in the same structural and functional relationship to each other. In terms of human behavior, the same system of action is observed to replicate itself with minor variations over and over again within the social system at the same moment. Every morning in American society millions of people brush their teeth using a similar set of implements. In other words, toothbrushing behavior is repeated across individuals, with many different actors within the same social system performing the same behavior at roughly the same time.

The notion of persistence in time uses the idea of repetition over and over again, but longitudinally. If we were to observe people on successive days throughout their adult lives, we would observe that the pattern of toothbrushing recurs day after day, and persists over a long period of time in roughly the same form. Replication and persistence can also be illustrated with respect to family organization and structure. In the same society at a given time, the same family pattern or structure occurs over and over again, so that most families are alike in certain specific respects. For example, husband-wife, parent-child relationships involve roughly the same role behavior, which produces similar interaction patterns. Similarly, the family pattern or structure remains relatively stable in given families over a period of time.

At first glance, it appears that the concepts of order and structure are almost synonymous, but there is an important difference. For the concept of structure to be applied to an object or series of events, one needs simply to be able to identify parts, describe their relationship to each other, and indicate their function with respect to one another and towards their environment. For a thing to be structured, it does not have to be replicated or persist. Structure is a way of describing or perceiving objects; it is not the same thing as order. A structure may be unique; that is, there may be no coexisting case that displays similar parts, relationships, and functions.

The concept of structure can be applied to absolutely unique cases where no similarity exists between them and any other object known. In making this statement, we are going beyond the notion that no two objects or events are ever exactly alike, and therefore cannot in any case have duplicate structures. In society, for example, a group may have a structure which is entirely unique, and not found in any other within the society.

Sociologists in the past have made a mistake by confusing the idea of structure with order (6). For example, to study family structure, they have examined a number of families, sampling from the universe of families; then they have tried to describe the structure of the family system by extracting common elements from the sample. Such a scheme merely allows the sociologists to describe what common elements exist in the structures of different families, but it does not allow them to describe the structure of a family—since structure does not depend on replication. Instead, we must regard replication as variable with respect to structure. Some structures are replicated over and over again, while others are unique. In between these two extremes lies a range of points on a scale. There is no reason to say that the recurrent or virtually universal structures are more important to study scientifically than those that are unique.

It is also true that structures need not persist through time; they can have only an instantaneous existence. Structures can vary in their persistence, in other words, from an instant to an eon, and the length of time that they persist is not a necessary condition to the idea of structure. If it is possible to identify parts, relationships, and functions with respect to that instant in time, it is possible to describe the event occurring in that short span in terms of structure. The span of time through which a given structural arrangement persists is variable with respect to structure, rather than a part of the definition of it. And again, there is no philosophical or scientific basis for saying that structures which persist over long periods of time are more important for the scientist to study and understand than those that persist for shorter periods. A revolution may take a day, while the social structures that it destroys or alters may have persisted for a thousand years. The structure of the revolutionary behavior may be as important to study and understand as the structure of the nonrevolutionary or conformist behavior during the longer span of time.

It can be seen now that the concept of structure is quite different from the concept of order. Order is defined in terms of the replication and persistence of structure. It is order in human affairs that sociologists are most interested in; we seek to discover and describe it, and explain its existence. We wish to know how order is produced and maintained, how it breaks down, and how, in the process, new structures emerge to become a part of new orders. Since order amounts to the persistence and replication of structure, the concept of structure is essential to understanding order. It supplies a conceptual framework through which order and regularity in the system can be described and analyzed.

Structural Dynamics

There is a tendency for sociologists to regard structure as a static concept, and to use the concept of process to deal with movement or change within structural systems (7). In actuality, however, whether or not structure is static or dynamic depends on what concepts of parts, relationships, and functions have been chosen to define it. An astronomer who defines the structure of the solar system as consisting of the sun, planets, and their satellites, which are related to each other in terms of orbital movement maintained by the counterbalancing of forces of gravitational pull and centrifugal force, is using a dynamic concept of structure. Here the concepts of relationship are essentially of a dynamic nature. Relationships are described in terms of orbits, which imply movement; and in terms of gravitational pull and centrifugal force, which imply counterbalancing functions within the system. Similarly, the concepts used to describe the structure of atoms and molecules are essentially dynamic structural concepts.

The choice of the concept of relationship determines whether a structure is visualized as static or dynamic. Too many sociologists conceive of the structure of society in architectural or geological terms, as though it were made of fixed parts serving static functions. Instead, even casual observation tells us that the model for society must be conceptualized in terms of relationships that are based on movement and change. We have not fully described the structure of an automobile engine if we have simply listed the parts that go into making up the system, and outlined their relationship to each other in space at one instant of time. That approach produces what amounts to a single instantaneous slice of time, a still photograph of the engine parts in strictly spatial relationship to each other.

But a larger slice than an instant of time can be used in describing the structure. We may go on to say that pistons move up and down the cylinders in a certain pattern, that the crankshaft rotates within bearings, and that the transmission, which functions in a particular way, connects them to the drive shaft. This kind of description of the relationship among these parts allows us to take into account the full cycle or sequence of positional relationships among them, so that a dynamic rather than a static structural conception emerges (8), and the pattern of the movement is incorporated into the definition of structure.

When using such a dynamic structural concept, the word *process* does not mean the routine movement of a system in time; instead it refers to the *transition* or change in structure from one form to another. In other words, the parts of a structure may pass through cyclical movements or repetitive actions. These cyclical movements and repetitive actions may be properly regarded as a part of the description of structure; so that *process* then refers to a change in the nature of the cycles. However, if all movement or behavior of parts is ruled out of the concept of *structure*, and structure is taken to refer to a frozen slice of an entity, then *process* will amount to movement or behavior itself—a view that ignores the dynamic tensions or relationships among parts that exist even in a single instant of time.

Actually, time would have to be sliced into infinitely small segments to eliminate movement; and even then the dynamic imbalances among parts that produce movement would be present. It seems preferable, therefore, to include a long enough span of time in our definitions to allow the dynamic relationships to function to produce their patterned or ordered movement, and to incorporate this pattern of movement in our concept of structure. If no change takes place in the relationships among parts, then the pattern remains repetitive. Thus *process* describes the way in which structures are built, altered, or changed.

Given this point of view, structure and process are not two sides of the same coin; nor are they the antithesis of each other, one being dynamic, and the other static. Instead, process becomes the conceptual tool for understanding how structures are built or put together, how they evolve or are changed, how they break down, or disintegrate and decay. Processes alter structures, or represent descriptions of the alteration of such structures. They do not represent simple movement of the parts within the structure that does not constitute change.

We must now distinguish between static and dynamic structural conceptions. One way to conceive of an entity is to freeze it in time and space, and describe its parts and their relationships to one another in strictly spatial or mechanical terms. This yields a static structural conception. The other way is to allow the entity to operate, and then describe the repetitive features of its operation as part of our understanding of how the parts that comprise it relate to each other. This procedure yields a dynamic conception of the entity's structure.

Two important issues are raised by the conception of dynamic structure. First, can we postulate the existence of two types of entities, one characterized by static structures and the other characterized by dynamic structures? Second, if dynamic structures include routine repetitive movement, then what becomes of the distinctions among order, structure, and process formulated earlier?

The two questions must be answered simultaneously, because the distinctions between structure and order, and between structure and process, are formulated in such a way as to be closely interrelated. Obviously, entities which we conceive of as having static structures can experience change, and such change would ordinarily result in the gradual emergence of a different static structure. The parts do not move or behave in relationship to one another in static structures, except in an irreversible but nonrepetitive fashion. That is, the movement of parts in a static structure amount to "permanent" alterations in the relationship system. They are, in other words, noncyclical or nonrepetitive. This kind of change is exemplified in phenomena like growth or shrinkage in size, or in breakdowns.

A building is an entity whose structure is static. The bricks and mortar, the beams and pillars are placed in relationships to one another which are fixed, except that as time passes they may decay and eventually collapse. They do not "behave," "act," or "move" with respect to each other in such a way that the pattern of movement is routine and reducible to structural terms. In the case of static structures, such as buildings, the pattern of movement (decay) never routinely returns the parts to a relationship to one another that existed at a previous time: once the static structure decays or disintegrates, it does not return to its original form to repeatedly decay again. Static structures change, but they do not embody patterned movement or behavior.

Dynamic structures are those objects or entities in which the parts routinely move, act, or behave with respect to each other. Obviously such objects can also undergo change. When change occurs in such objects, it not only alters the relationship of parts in the formation of the whole, but it also alters the routine pattern of their movement or behavior. An organism, a clock, a solar system, an ecosystem, and a social system are all dynamic structures. They have moving parts; and change in the pattern of movement occurs within them and between them and their environment.

Some, though not all, dynamic systems grow, shrink, speed up, slow down, become more differentiated, or less complex; and through a combination of such alteration, their structures may evolve or change. These changes are called *processes* to distinguish them from the simple routine movement of parts in an entity with a dynamic structure.

Order, which can be observed in both dynamic and static entities, is defined as the replication or persistence of the structure of the entity. Thus, if we observe that the same kind of entity, be it static or dynamic, occurs over and over again, or persists, we are led to postulate the existence of order. With respect to dynamic entities this amounts to saying that we perceive the same sort of moving structure repeating itself.

If this is true, can we say that change is the destroyer of order? Obviously, if change occurs, the "same" object cannot be observed over and over again through time. Because change alters the original object, it therefore appears to be the antithesis of order. On the other hand, change itself can be orderly. Therefore, in a more general sense, processes can be repetitive or they can lack this quality; which lets us say that some processes exhibit or undergo "ordered change."

If we can demonstrate, for example, that a given type of entity which has a given dynamic structure, when combined with certain other ingredients undergoes a transformation in structure, such that the new or transformed structure is the same for all entities undergoing the process, then we have ordered change. Metamorphosis in insects is a prime example. By such a process, a given dynamic structure, barring external interference, is transformed into another dynamic structure in an orderly and predictable or repetitive fashion: a larva transformed into a butterfly. If it were to be shown that there were definite repetitive processes through which societies evolve from simple tribal societies to complex urban industrial societies, and that the stages were alike in many instances, then we would be justified in describing this as ordered social change.

Order, therefore, can be observed in both structure and process. It is different from either as a concept. Its essential ingredient is the repetition of the same process or structure over and over again in time and space, so that each object and process is perceived not as unique, but as similar to other objects or processes found at other times or places. Ordered change is different from dynamic structure; there are no repeated cycles or recurrences with respect to the entity undergoing change in ordered change; and in dynamic structures, patterns of movement are repetitious with respect to the same object.

Social systems may be viewed utilizing all three concepts—structure, process, and order. But these three ways of viewing things are not, as is quite often said, two or, more properly, three, sides of the same coin. They are more like three different coins that are able to buy us different kinds of scientific understanding. Each may be spent together with others or separately. We cannot here debate the value of each; but it does seem that it is much easier to come by structural knowledge than process knowledge, and easier to come by either of these than knowledge concerning order.

Structure and Causality

Even dynamic concepts of structure and process only permit the scientist to describe the phenomenon he has studied. They let him identify the elements or parts that make up the system, and define relationships and functions through time; but they do not supply him with a theory of causation. He is left with questions such as: What produced this structure to begin with? What maintains it? What accounts for the movement of parts within the system? What accounts for the repetition of the same structure over and over again within the same society? What produces decay, breakdown, or change in structures?

Before we can use the concepts of structure and process in answering these kinds of questions, we will have to devise theories of causation which take structural and processual elements into account.

CHAPTER 3   *THE SYSTEM CONCEPT AND SOCIAL CAUSATION*

In building a conceptual or symbolic model of society, we will assume that human societies are open, morphogenic systems. Like Parsons and his followers, we will, in other words, regard society as a "social system" which is made up of "social subsystems" as parts. It is important to realize however that *social system,* as used in sociology, implies a definite perspective toward the problem of causation, and extends the concepts of structure, order, and process beyond the realm of mere description into the realm of explanation (1).

The systems perspective incorporates as a part of its assumptions a certain view of causation. This view may be understood best by examining the way in which the idea of system differs from the ideas of structure, process, and order. The idea of system and the idea of structure have common elements. Both employ the notion of several parts related to each other within a boundary to form a definite pattern. *System,* however, refers to a certain kind of entity, while *structure* refers to a way of looking at that entity in terms of its internal organization (2). We may say, therefore, that the idea of system as an entity subsumes the notion of structure. However, the systems perspective enlarges the notion of structure to include certain assumptions about how the parts of a structure are related; how they operate with respect to each other; and how the structure relates to its environment.

System Relationships

The systems perspective assumes: (1) that all parts of a structure are linked to each other directly or indirectly; and (2) that the linkage is such that a movement or change in one part will inevitably produce a movement or change in all other parts—provided that enough time passes for the processes which operate in the system to transmit the effect throughout the linkage system, and also provided that the movement or change is large enough to transmit itself through the linkage network. In other words, in the systems perspective all elements of a structure are assumed to be mutually responsive to one another. Of course, systems differ in how closely their parts fit. Some may be so completely integrated that even small changes in one part will affect all other parts. Others may fit so loosely that only large changes will produce these consequences. Movement or change produced as a consequence need not be of the same nature or magnitude as in the original part.

In order for a movement or change in one part to produce a movement or change in another, there must be a linkage or path over which the influence may travel. Most systems analysts assume that the greatest and most immediate movement or change will occur in those parts directly linked to the part originally moving or changing.

A structure also has a pattern of linkage among parts, but these are not necessarily mutually responsive. In contrast, a system must have linkages or relationships that provide for the possibility of mutual responsiveness.

Rule of System Operation

The second modification of the idea of structure added by the systems approach is that each part of the system operates in response to whatever else is occurring within it. This is to say, that a given event in the system is to be accounted for by its relationship to other events occurring within the system.

The words *cause* and *causes* are, in a sense, inappropriate for use in conjunction with the systems approach, since this approach presupposes that there is another way to explain events that is different from the traditional cause and effect (3)—namely, that a systematic set of relationships among the parts of the system, and between the system and its environment account in concert for what occurs within the system, or between it and its environment.* However, for purposes of explanation we will say that the systems perspective takes the view that behavior on the part of one unit or subsystem in a larger system is "caused" by the simultaneous behavior of the other

*When we take a system and its environment and treat them as related we have created a larger system within which this assumption holds.

parts to which it is linked as a part of the system.

In the systems approach there are no dependent and independent variables. There are no causes or sets of causative factors. There is, instead, simultaneous universal responsiveness among parts, so that they act together as an unfolding operation of parts functioning in relation to one another as a whole.

Unfortunately, sociologists sometimes tend to use causal language to express what they claim to be system relationships. This usage should be avoided, since it weakens both approaches by mixing two sets of assumptions about the operation of the entities being described.

In the broadest sense, the systems perspective takes the view that it is the way the elements of a system are organized in relation to each other that accounts for the events occurring within the system, and between it and its environment. This point of view presumes that if we were in some way to alter the organization of the system, we would change the events which take place within it. As a result, systems analysts are inevitably interested in the laws, principles, or mechanisms of organization, and strive especially to discover the laws that govern how social systems are structured. They ask: Are there any natural laws which limit or govern the way power may be organized and distributed within a system? Are there any natural limits to the way the division of labor among positions, roles, and group structures may be accomplished? Are there underlying variables which stand in such a relationship to one another as to produce only certain types of power structure, ruling out all other real possibilities?

An equivalent approach in the field of chemistry would be for chemists to ask what are the rules that govern the way chemical elements can be combined into compounds? Or, in biology, what are the rules that govern the way in which cells in an organism may be combined into higher order systems? For we know that in both chemical compounds and organisms, it is the way elements or parts are organized in relation to one another that produces their behavior as entities; and this being true, it becomes critical to understand the rules that govern the process of organizing. In social systems, too, those questions are critical which relate to how systems are put together, and how the organization of parts operates to limit or determine the behavior occurring in the system. From this perspective, asking questions about causation means asking questions about the mechanisms which operate through the organization of the system to produce its behavior.

This is quite different from searching for statistical relationships among variables. A systems analyst considers that the demonstration of the probable existence of any such relationship is merely a beginning point for the search for mechanism, rather than a final result. Suppose it can be demonstrated statistically that there is a relationship between the division of labor in a bureaucratic organization and the number of steps in the hierarchy of its power structure. The questions of significance for a systems analyst are then: How do the division of labor and the power structure operate so that as one is varied the other varies also? What is the mechanism which is involved in the relationship? Given such a relationship, how do power and the division of labor operate as behavior within the system, and how is this behavior associated with other behavior within it?

Another way of putting it is to say that the systems perspective focuses on trying to isolate the means by which the behavior within the system and between it and its environment are produced, rather than on isolating the variables which will predict or "statistically account for" the variation in one or another variable. It is of little value, to use the example of a home heating system, to know that the outside temperature is an excellent predictor of the amount of time the furnace is observed to be on. What is of value is to know how the elements in the system are linked to each other, and how they operate in terms of the mechanisms that link their operation together into a system.

This concern, in the loosest and broadest sense, is a concern with "causation;" but it is a concern of a particular sort which takes a particular perspective. It is not simply an expanded multidimensional view of causality. It is a different view. It is the view that the way real systems are put together as entities accounts for the way they operate.

Given this perspective, the concept of structure is vital to system analysis. The principles of system organization or structure are one and the same as the "principles of causation," and the essential and overriding task is to find a way to build structural models.

The greatest difficulty with the systems approach arises out of the fact that everything cannot be said at once. We are about to construct a system of concepts; in reality, since it is a system, no single one of the concepts can be defined and understood separately from the others. They must stand or fall as a total system, each being a part of a whole, rather than an independent isolated entity. We cannot, however, communicate like that. Each idea must be developed separately and in a given order. Only after all have been discussed and defined will we be able to comprehend the system of concepts as a whole, and be able to critically evaluate the model as a model.

Because of this semantic difficulty, perhaps we ought at the outset to establish a few guide posts to identify the territory we are going to stay within, and to show that our arguments are based on classical sociological conceptions.

Some Historical Considerations

During the past several generations, sociologists have reached tentative agreement about certain "factors" that must be included in any reasonable explanation of human social behavior. These factors are: (1) culture; (2) personality; (3) situation; and (4) social interaction. They have been treated in a number of differing ways by different sociological theorists.

These four critical factors, it will be noted, do not include the concept "society." Instead, two other concepts are used: situation and social interaction. We hope thereby to avoid a certain amount of semantic difficulty; for one of the most persistent and troublesome problems for all social scientists writing about human behavior systems has always been confusion over the concepts of culture and society. Much of the dispute among social scientists over what *society* and *culture* and *personality* mean probably owes less to rational disagreement than it does to the political need to justify the existences of sociology, psychology, and anthropology as distinct disciplines. If three separate entities—society, culture, and personality—can be posited, then jurisdictional disputes between psychology, sociology, and anthropology can be resolved amicably, and academic fiefs can be protected against encroachment, at least symbolically.

Politics aside, however, sociologists must define culture, personality, and society as distinct ideas within a rigorous conceptual scheme. Talcott Parsons and his followers, for instance, regard culture, personality, and the social system as systems. Parsons' view is that these three separate types of systems are interdependent in two ways: they all are analytically derived from social action, and each influences and is influenced by the others (4). Nevertheless, the cultural system, the personality system, and the social system (society) are each considered by Parsons to be systems in and of themselves. As such, they have boundaries, and are constituted of parts that are related to one another and function as entities in interaction with an environment.

If the Parsonian notion is taken literally, the social system exists outside the boundaries of given personality systems; on the other hand, the personality system of an individual is separate from and external to the boundaries of the social system. This is also true of culture, which as a system is external to society and to given personalities. The Parsonian conception may be diagramed as in Figure 3–1.

If Parsons' idea were taken literally, one would have to assume that each distinct system receives inputs from its environment and produces outputs for it. A personality, for example, receives inputs from the social system and from the culture and is affected by them. Similarly, an impact can be made on the cultural and social systems by a particular personality system. Thus, as far as Parsons is concerned, culture, personality, and the social system are not to be regarded as variables or dimensions pertaining to a single system. At best, they may be regarded as three distinct subsystems, perhaps functioning as a part of a larger system of action.

It is possible, of course, to view culture and personality not as systems at all, but as broad groups or bundles of variables. From this viewpoint, cultural variables operate as factors in producing human action, much as any independent variable operates with respect to any dependent variable. Values, for example, could be regarded as a factor in causing human behavior, operating as independent variables with respect to a dependent variable—in this case, behavior. When values are varied, behavior varies; if values are changed, then phenomena like voting behavior will vary in response. From this point of view, values are not necessarily regarded as constituting a system; instead, they are seen as collections or categories. This is definitely not the Parsonian view. He regards culture and personality not as variables or groups of variables, but as distinct systems, which implies that all of the structural features and processes characteristic of systems are present.

The view of Sorokin is much like that of Parsons. He writes about society, culture, and personality as if they were distinct entities that

Figure 3–1   Parsonian View of the Relationship Among Culture, Personality, and the Social System

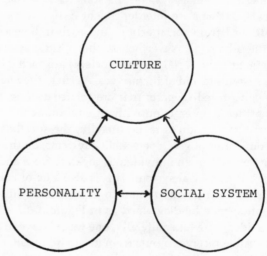

interact with one another. At times, however, both Parsons and Sorokin, as well as the many sociologists and anthropologists who have followed their lead, treat aspects of each of the three as if they were simple or complex independent variables with respect to a dependent variable, human social behavior. In so doing, they ignore the systems perspective in favor of a simpler conception of social causation (5).

In developing our model, we take a position about society, culture, and personality that is different from both Parsons' and Sorokin's. We proceed from the assumption that societies are systems of behavior, comprised of subsystems called communities, organizations, groups, and subgroups. Society and its subsystems are made up of the behavior of individual human actors organized into stable relationship patterns. The individual actor, instead of being seen as a system separate from society, is regarded as a part of society, because the same behavior that constitutes the basic ingredient of society and its subsystems constitutes the individual as an actor. Therefore, if we were to enumerate all the action or behavior comprising all of society, and also enumerate all the behavior for all its individual members, the two enumerations would contain exactly the same quantity and quality of behavior. There can be no behavior on the part of an actor which is not simultaneously part of the society to which he belongs; nor any behavior which is part of the society which is not also behavior performed by an individual member.

Culture, in our view, consists of rules for behavior. These rules constitute a part of society stored as a kind of learned program for action in the memories of individual actors who are, themselves, part of society. Culture is therefore an internal aspect of the personalities of the actors whose behavior forms a part of the total behavior constituting the society. There can be, according to our assumption, no part of culture which is not simultaneously a part of a particular actor's personality. Similarly, there can be no member of society who does not contain a part of what is customarily called the culture of the society to which he belongs. Furthermore, we also assume that no actor contains all of the culture; instead, each contains the fragment of the total culture which pertains to his particular behavior as a member of society. Roughly speaking, then, our conception of the relationship of society, culture, and personality could be diagramed as in Figure 3-2.

Society

As for society, first and foremost we regard it as an on-going system of human behavior or action. As such, its basic ingredient is the behavior performed by its members in relationship to one another. This conception, however, is deceptively simple, because it masks a number of important properties of society, and it is these properties that make the relationship between society and culture understandable. For example, a behavior or an act performed by a member of society is an event which occurs at a particular location in time and space. Once it occurs, other events follow, and then others, and then others. At any given time, therefore, only a few of the events or behaviors constituting a society are actually occurring; and consequently a society must be regarded as a system of recurring events or behaviors that maintain relatively stable temporal and spatial relationships as they change or evolve (6).

Society is not like an organism or a machine. Instead, it is comprised of behavior or action which is continuous, patterned, and recurrent, but whose content is discontinuous and variable. It is more to be compared

Figure 3–2   Relationship Among Culture, Personality, and Society

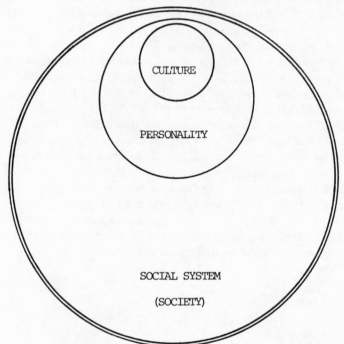

to the behavior of an animal than to the biological organism of the animal.

If behavior is the fundamental ingredient of society, then its parts and subparts must also consist of behavior. It follows, therefore, that the groups, organizations, and communities that constitute subsystems in society are also made up of behavior. Furthermore, it is apparent that the mechanisms that link the parts together to form the whole must also be behavioral mechanisms.

When we say society is made of behavior, we are stating explicitly that the basic stuff or element, or, figuratively, the material, out of which society as an entity is comprised is behavior, and that all parts of whatever magnitude are made up of this same ingredient. The parts may differ in the way their constituents are organized, but their basic ingredients are the same.

Other sociologists are fond of defining society as "the largest group to which a person belongs;" or they will distinguish between society and culture by defining "society" as a very large group and "culture" as its way of life. From this perspective, society consists of people, and culture consists of their customs. We define "society" as the *largest system of behavior* in which all of the actions of an individual actor can be located as parts. When we say an actor belongs to a society, we mean that his behavior constitutes a part of that system.

This same statement may be applied to groups and to organizations, but it must be done cautiously when dealing with anything less than a whole society. All the behavior of an actor is contained within the society to which he belongs, and constitutes a fragment of that system. But when we say a person is a member of a group, we must say that only a portion of his behavior is a part of that group. Other portions of his behavior are parts of other groups. In other words, whole individuals as action systems can be said to belong to societies in the sense that all of their behavior takes place somewhere within the boundaries of the society. However, only a portion of an individual can belong to groups, since only a part of his behavior takes place within the boundaries of the group.

We have made the point that society consists of behavior, and that its various parts also consist of behavior. Let us grant for the moment that, viewed at a certain level of scale, society consists of a large number of groups that are interlocked. Groups themselves are behavior systems that are comprised of certain segments of the actions of their members. It is apparent, if this is true, that at any given time most of the groups constituting a society must be in an inactive state, since the behavior which characterizes them will not be occurring. For example, at 2 A.M. on most days in most cities in the United States, most of the work groups that can be observed in a state of activity during the day are not operating. No behavior by any member is occurring, and we may say, therefore, that most of the social system is shut off or inactive.

It can be seen that if the parts of society are comprised of behavior, and behavior is periodic or noncontinuous with respect to the part, then that part of the system must pass through active and inactive periods. Only a fragment of a society will therefore be active at any given time; the other parts will be inactive. When the part is active, both participants and nonparticipants can observe that actual real behavior—that is, acts performed by members in relation to one another—occur. When the Jones Family is active, its members are performing Jones Family behavior. When they are separated from each other, doing nonfamily things, the Jones Family is inactive or latent.

When we say society is a system of behavior, we mean that it includes all of the real actions of its members which occur, as actions, in real time and real space. However, we do not mean to imply that all of the behavior takes place at once, nor that all of it takes place all of the time; we imply only that the behavior has a persistent form and pattern, so that it recurs. In other words, it displays a degree of order. The Jones Family constitutes a part of the society as a system even when it is not active, but is in its inactive or latent state. Otherwise, no recurrent behavior would take place, and order based on the same sets of actions repeating themselves in time would not be present.

Culture

Because we conceive of the parts of society as existing as parts even while they are in a latent or inactive state, we need the concept of "culture." Very briefly, culture is society in an inactive or latent state —society in storage as it were, between instances of occurrence. It is the family when the family is not happening as behavior. Let us clarify this rather radical conception of culture.

From our perspective, society is described as a complex system of groups; each group consists of actions performed by group members in relation to each other. Thus, groups themselves are behavior subsystems in the larger system, society. It would be wrong to assume, however, that all the groups that make up any given society are simultaneously acting as real, overt behavior systems. Instead, at any given moment within a society, behavior will actually be taking place in only a portion of the groups that constitute its total structure.

For a moment let us consider how a given group would appear as a behavior system if we were to observe it continuously over a relatively long span of time. If, for instance, we were observing a particular family, we would see its members characteristically come together at certain times, perform behavior toward each other, and disperse—later to reappear and perform actions again in relation to one another. Furthermore, most of the time we would observe only some of the family members interacting with each other; and while they were interacting during any given short span of time, we would observe only a few of the actions normally carried out by families. At one moment we might see only the husband and wife interacting, while the children were elsewhere engaged in nonfamily activities. At another time we might observe mother and daughter behavior, while husband-wife, father-daughter, mother-son, and brother-sister behavior would not be taking place. In other words, at any given moment only some of the behavior constituting the family would actually be present. During some other intervals of time, no behavior which constitutes a part of the family being observed would be occurring. Instead, all of the members of the group would be somewhere else in the social system, performing actions that characterize other groups. The father-husband might be at work, exhibiting behavior that belongs to a work group as a behavior system. The children may be at school performing school behavior, and the wife might be at the store acting as a customer.

It can be seen from this example that the behavior constituting a given group is not ordinarily continuous; instead, it is periodic. The behavior which constitutes a group occurs in discrete units of time; that is to say, groups turn on and off. While a group is "on," behavior or action occurs. When it is "off," it exists in a state of storage as a part of the structure of society, but at the moment not as an aspect of what is actually happening in society.

It is clear that, at any given time, most of the groups constituting a society will be in an inactive state, because no part of the behavior which characterizes them is occurring. As we have already remarked, at 2 A.M. on most days in most cities around the world, most of the work groups which constitute parts of the structure of the society are inactive or inoperative. Their members are dispersed, either at home in bed or performing behavior in other nonwork groups; as work groups, they exist in a state of *latency*. If we observe the society for several days, we will see them become active and then latent and then active again, and discover a definite pattern to the behavior which constitutes them.

When we say a society is a system of behavior, we include behavior which occurs routinely, even though at a given moment it may not be in the process of occurring. When the work groups of a society are inactive at 2 A.M. they are nonetheless still part of society. When family members are dispersed performing actions in other nonfamily groups, we still conceive of the family as existing as part of the society. Otherwise, we will have to assume that groups which are nonactive pass out of existence as a part of society and are recreated as they become active again—a somewhat silly position.

We must be able to explain recurrence, and posit a mechanism that can connect two episodes of active family behavior separated by a period during which no family episode is occurring. And that is what our concept of culture is intended to do in our theory of human behavior. Culture is society in a latent state; or if you prefer, in a state of storage or nonactivity. It is society stored in the memories of society's members.

A brief review of some basic ideas and usual concepts of culture will prove that our view is not as far removed from the classical notions as one might think. To begin with, culture is almost invariably defined as consisting of learned behavior patterns, acquired by members of society through processes of socialization. These patterns furnish the person who learns them with a set of customary rules for carrying out behavior in various social situations. Furthermore, the rules supply a person with guidelines for behavior in various groups. A person learns how he is expected to act as a family member, or a work group member, or a member of a religious cult. Once learned, the rules, or behavior expectations, or, if you prefer, customs or norms, are a part of the person's personality, and they make it possible for him to interact in social systems with others who have learned compatible or corresponding rules. The culture of the family, then, constitutes a set of rules for family behavior which specify who will interact with whom under what circumstances, and what kinds of actions they will perform when they interact. Family culture is a kind of crude blueprint for family behavior, or a loose program or script for family action (7).

These statements are relatively commonplace. They add up to saying that culture is the mechanism which allows the family as a group to persist during periods of time when its members are not actually interacting, because it supplies the basis for maintaining the pattern of action in the form of behavior expectations during the interval. During inactive periods, the family exists as expectations or culture. A group called the Jones Family at certain times must therefore be regarded as consisting of the Jones Family culture. This Jones Family culture is the group in its latent or inactive state.

It should be apparent from this argument, and from what we said before, culture *is* society and society *is* culture. These words refer to phases in the behavior process, rather than to different entities. In other words, there is but one entity called the *society* or the *social system*. Its parts at any given time exist in two states, an active state and a latent state.

In the active state, the parts of society are observed as actually engaged in behavior. In the latent state, the parts are perceived as culture—stored, latent behavior patterns awaiting the conditions which will reactivate that portion of the social system.

In order to avoid confusion between the terms *society* and *culture,* which we define as aspects of the same entity in different states at different times, we will follow Raymond Firth's lead and distinguish between *social* or *cultural structure,* and *social organization* (8). *Cultural structure* will refer to the structure of the normative or cultural aspect of social systems: in other words, to the structure of latent behavior. *Social organization* will refer to the structure of actual behavior, that is, the behavior which occurs as real actions performed by real actors, in contrast to the internalized rules for behavior which constitutes cultural structure.

The question immediately arises as to whether culture, or latent behavior, is able fully to account for or explain real behavior. Or, putting it another way, does cultural structure account for or determine social organization? Does latent society simply emerge unchanged or unaltered as active society? If latent behavior in the form of cultural rules simply emerges as real behavior, then we are saying that culture fully determines behavior, and no other explanations are needed. But this obviously cannot be the case. Or, if it is, we have wasted our time in an exercise in circularity which simultaneously explains everything and nothing.

There are a couple of key questions that will help us evaluate this matter. (1) We have stated that culture is stored latent behavior. How is it activated? (2) We have said that culture is stored in the personalities of actors. What else is stored therein, or belongs to the system that accommodates the storage, which is pertinent to the processes of activation of stored elements, or which interacts with them to modify action away from normative expectations?

The Activation of Cultural Elements

As we said above, situation and social interaction are two factors that must be taken into account in explaining the operation of social systems. They offer us a way to describe the activation and modification of cultural elements contained in the personality of an actor, and thereby also allow us to account for the way parts of society turn on and off.

All behavior takes place in a situation, containing certain material and social objects which facilitate or impede that behavior. Rules for behavior are learned in the context of situations which involve particular kinds of social and physical objects. To a large extent, the norms or rules which constitute latent action supply the actor with potential behavior patterns that allow him to adapt his behavior to specific situational elements. In other words, norms are tied to situations. This is true to such an extent that the norms specifying behavior in one situation are not appropriate in a different situational context.

Part of the internalization process for norms, or latent behavior, involves learning when and in what situation these behaviors are appropriate. This means that along with learning the norms, the actor learns a set of cues which tell him when a certain type of action is an adaptive response. These cues act as triggers to bring appropriate parts of the cultural structure into play as an active element in the actor's behavior.

Actors learn cultural prescriptions in a situational context. These prescriptions give meaning to the situation, or as W. I. Thomas put it, they aid in the "definition of the situation"(9). The identity of alter actors,* the presence of certain physical objects such as office furniture, the time of day, and the simultaneously occurring events surrounding an actor serve as triggers for aspects of the culture. These triggers function as elements which define the situation for an actor and define the meaning of the behavior of others, so that he is able to select from his learned repertoire of response patterns the one response which seems most appropriate. This means that as a person moves from one situation to another, the part of the culture he has learned, and which is activated in each situation, will vary. Since this will be true of all actors, group behavior patterns may be activated simultaneously by the co-presence of several actors in the same situation.

The interaction between actors in each other's situation also acts as a triggering mechanism for particular learned response patterns. Ego perceives alter's behavior, which acts as a cue or trigger to activate a learned response on ego's part. Ego's response acts as a signal to alter, and in turn activates an aspect of alter's learned behavioral repertoire. Thus the sequencing and timing of behavior patterns is accomplished by simultaneous and sequential cueing taking place in social interaction. This is made possible by the fact that both ego and alter have learned their response patterns in interaction with others, and, in most cases, have practiced them and had them reinforced in previous interactional episodes.

It should be clear from this brief discussion that situational and interactional factors account for the way latent behavior becomes ac-

---

*Following Parsons, we will use the term *ego actor* for the person who is expected to perform behavior, and *alter actor* for the person toward whom the behavior is supposed to be performed.

tive. They serve as the mechanisms which operate at the interface where society as stored cultural patterns meets society as actual action. Society, the sociological elephant we referred to in the last chapter, is indeed a strange beast. Only some of him is observable as actual living flesh at any given moment. The rest is both invisible and intangible, and to make things even more confusing, what is visible keeps changing. Situational and interactional factors help us explain why some of him can be seen and some not; and also in what state the invisible part exists while it is not observable.

The next question that must be answered is, what else exists as a part of personality other than culture which may be of significance to us? Our position is that culture is an aspect of the personality of particular people; there are other elements in the personality of actors, however, which interact with and influence the cultural aspects; so that the triggering or cueing of some portion of a person's learned cultural repertoire will not necessarily result in the overt behavior prescribed.

A full account of how this process takes place will be undertaken later in this book. At present we will merely note that the personalities of individual actors contain at least the following elements that combine with cultural aspects to produce overt action:

1. Organic capacities, disabilities, drives, or motivations
2. Perception mechanisms and equipment
3. Organic memory, recall, and associational mechanisms
4. Neurological motor control mechanisms
5. Learned memory content other than cultural prescriptions for behavior—for instance, information concerning what has actually been experienced and what is considered factual; and attitudes toward cultural and factual materials acquired by learning, including attitudes toward the self and toward others

Each of these elements of personality will be discussed below as possible modifiers of culturally-prescribed behavior patterns. The point to be made here is that latent behavior or culture exists distributed among personalities of actors, side-by-side with other elements that may function to influence and modify it; and that this fact must be taken into account.

In the foregoing discussion we have emphasized how we conceive of the parts or elements that comprise society in its active and inactive states, and how this conception affects our view of society, personality, and culture. We need now to provide a means of dealing with the relationship among the parts of society which are comprised of the behavior of individual human actors. This is necessary so that we can explain how the parts of the entity, society, are linked together to form the whole. We also have to explain how parts in a latent or inactive state are related to parts in an active or behavioral state.

We will resolve this problem in the following manner. Social interaction will be used as our concept of generic linkage, as is usually done in sociological models; it will be broken down into forms or types of relationships, and considered as being observable in two states, latent and active. *Real social interaction* is defined here as only actually occurring, direct interstimulation and response among actors. *Latent interaction* is defined here as stored patterns of reciprocity, meaning complementary roles that link one actor to another by distributing the culture in such a way that, given certain triggering elements, real interaction occurs between them.

This concept of interaction allows us to introduce the complexity that is added to social behavior by the interplay of all of the personality factors mentioned above. We will therefore be able to understand how a given quirk in a given actor produces a certain response in another that is above and beyond what would be expected if only shared complementary roles were involved.

PART II

THE MICRO STRUCTURE OF SOCIAL SYSTEMS

CHAPTER 4

SOCIAL BEHAVIOR: ACTS, ACTION PRODUCTS, AND FUNCTIONS

In order to examine human behavior using a structural frame of reference, it is necessary to identify some part or particle of behavior which can be used as a basis for a structural concept. These parts can then be described in terms of their relationships to each other and their functions in building a structural model of behavior. *Act* will be used here to identify the smallest particles of human behavior that can be consistently identified.

In order to use the concept of the human act both theoretically and methodologically, it is necessary to arrive at some firm basis for understanding what an act is in terms of total behavior. There is in nature no unit called an act, with easily identifiable boundaries; so we must establish conceptual boundaries, within which we will be able to identify what we will call *unit acts* (1). But first, let us explore what we mean by human social behavior in general.

Social Behavior Defined

Human beings are animals. Like all animals, they are engaged constantly in activity. From birth onward until death, every animal is constantly in a state of action. Indeed, action and life are one and the same thing. As long as life persists, human beings are playing, working, resting, fighting, cooperating, loving, hating, eating, drinking—in other words, constantly active. For purposes of discussion, human activity can be separated into two categories. One is *organic*, physiological activity: the beating of the heart, the operation of the digestive system, the flow of neural impulses, the inhalation and exhalation of air. Human beings share organic activity with all other members of their mammalian order.

It is internal and regulated by life processes, and although the physiologist and perhaps even the physiological psychologist may find organic activity fascinating, it is of no interest to the behavioral scientist.

The second type of activity, roughly speaking, falls into three categories: (1) *muscular actions;* (2) *feelings or emotions;* and (3) *thoughts or cognitions.* All three are expressions of physiological processes, but they must be viewed in a larger context. Feelings, thoughts, and muscular actions are parts of extremely complex systems. They occur in great variety, yet within their variety we can discern certain regularities; and neither the complexity nor the variety can be explained simply in terms of physiological processes. For most of the behavior displayed by human beings seems, as far as we can tell, to be a product of social experience and social learning.

Human Behavior as Action, Feeling, and Thought

Let us assume for a moment that we are invisible observers who can watch human beings behave without their knowing it. Let us also assume that we have extrasensory perception which permits us to know what they are thinking and feeling at the time we are observing them. Let us further assume we begin our observations in the bedroom of a middle-class American couple at about 7:00 on a Monday morning.

When we arrive, we see a middle-aged male, and female fast asleep in a king-sized bed. The man is snoring gently and the wife is sleeping quite soundly. The alarm rings. The wife stirs and her arm reaches out and shuts off the alarm. She settles back again on the pillow for a moment. Finally, with a sigh, she reaches over and shakes her husband's shoulder, saying, "Harry, it's time to get up." He wakes with a start, rising partially in bed and rubbing his eyes. He asks, "What time is it?" "Seven o'clock," she replies. "I'm going to start the coffee. You'd better get moving if you're going to be on time this morning."

The wife leaves, slipping on her robe as she goes toward the kitchen. The man thinks to himself, "Boy, could I use another hour's sleep. But I've got to be at work in time for that meeting at nine." He squirms around and sits up on the side of the bed. He reaches for a pack of cigarettes, and lights his first one of the day. He sits there puffing it slowly, and thinking about the meeting he has to attend that morning.

After about five puffs, he puts the cigarette out, rises, and goes into the bathroom. He looks in the mirror at himself, thinking, "My God, I look tired!" He reaches for the toothbrush and begins to brush his teeth. As he does so, he hears his wife calling the children and telling them it's time to get up and get ready for school. He thinks to himself,

"I hope they're on time this morning. I can't afford to be late today."
He finishes brushing his teeth and gargles with mouthwash before
starting his shaving ritual. He soaps his face, and covers it with shaving
cream, then reaches for the razor and begins to shave. After two or three
strokes, he thinks, "Damn, this is a dull blade. I'd better change it." He
fumbles around through the medicine cabinet looking for a new blade.
There isn't one. He says to himself angrily, "Of all days to run out of
razor blades! Damn it!" And, "I told Mary yesterday to buy some." By
the time he finishes shaving, he's feeling irritated.

He goes back to the bedroom, and his wife arrives with a cup of
coffee. "Thanks," he says. "Say, how about getting me some razor
blades when you go to the store today? I had to pull them out by the
roots this morning." He sips his coffee, then begins to pull on his socks.
As soon as he's fully dressed, he goes to the kitchen, passing by the
children's room on the way. As he goes by, he yells, "Hey kids, you'd
better hurry up this morning. I don't want to be late for work."

When he arrives in the kitchen, he smells bacon frying and knows
that breakfast is about ready. His wife asks, "How're you feeling this
morning, dear?" "Lousy," he answers. "But maybe I'll feel better after
a couple more cups of coffee. I'm really worried about that meeting this
morning with the people from the home office. Our production's been
down the last couple of months, and they're sure as hell going to ask
what's wrong."

"Well, I wouldn't worry about it, dear," she tells him. "Everything
will go all right." He thinks, "Fine advice. How do you follow it?"

The kids arrive and they eat breakfast, talking about various things
as they do. Soon Harry is on his way to work, after having dropped the
kids off at school. Traffic on the freeway is heavier than usual this
morning, and Harry is deep in thought about the meeting. Suddenly a
car darts out of one of the freeway entrances in front of him, and he
jams on the brakes. Sudden fear stabs in his stomach, followed by anger.
He shouts, "You damn fool, you almost killed us both!" After a few
miles, though, he's forgotten his narrow escape and is back to thinking
about his work. He gets to his office at 8:30. As soon as he walks in, he
asks his secretary, "Have Mr. Jones and Mr. Smith arrived yet from New
York?" "Yes," she answers, "They got in last night. They called to say
they'll be here at nine." "Good," he says, "Bring me the file on the last
two months' production." He goes into his office and closes the door,
where we will leave him to return to our discussions of the categories
of human behavior.

Harry engaged in three types of behavior, feeling, thought, and
action, which occurred almost simultaneously, as they do in all human
beings. *Action* consists of muscular behavior—the movement of the

limbs and other parts of the body, and the saying of words out loud. Harry got out of bed, brushed his teeth, shaved, ate breakfast, drove his car, walked into his office, and closed the office door. These are all actions.

And while he was engaged in this behavior, as well as in between actions, he was also thinking about what he was going to do during the day, and planning ahead. These thoughts could not be seen or heard by the other actors in his situation, but nevertheless they amounted to active behavior within his own personality. He thought about his meeting for the day. He thought about needing razor blades. He thought about how dangerous it was for people to drive in a given way on the highway. All represent active mental behavior on the part of an actor.

While Harry was in the process of thinking and acting, he also had feelings or emotions. He got irritated. He was mad. He showed anxiety. He was afraid. In other words, his actions and thoughts were accompanied by various kinds of feelings. These feelings were unobserved behavior as far as other actors were concerned, but they were real to Harry. Since they affected his overt behavior, they could be inferred from the tone of his voice, his mode of expression, the way he looked and moved.

At least during their waking hours, all human beings are constantly in a process of feeling, thinking, and acting. It is probably true, but somewhat difficult to prove, that even during sleep these three forms of activity continue. Together they constitute the total behavior of the individual. Behavior thus is more than simply what is observable to the outside observer. It is also that which occurs internally as thought and feeling. Overt action partially flows from thought and feeling, and is affected by it.

Like society, human behavior has active and latent states. Active behavior is those actions, feelings, and thoughts which are actually in the process of occurring. When someone is in the midst of brushing his teeth, toothbrushing behavior is active. When he is actually feeling the emotion of love toward his children, the emotion of love is active. When he is thinking a thought, such as seven times six is forty-two, this thought is actually occurring and is active. Latent behavior is stored in the organism as capacity and memory. Harry knew how to shave before he got up that morning; the knowledge was stored somewhere in his memory bank. He knew that it involved soaping his face, moistening the whiskers, using a razor, and washing his face when he was through. This knowledge was in the latent state while he was asleep, and became active only when it was time for him to perform the behavior.

Latent behavior emerges when the proper set of stimuli in the environment bring it into a state of activity. Thoughts and feelings, as well as actions, occur in the latent state. Harry may have learned to love his children; however, during his work day, when he is in conference with his boss, he is not actively feeling the emotion of love with respect to his children. Other emotions such as fear, anticipation, and anger dominate his behavior toward other people, and love remains in a latent state until it is called into activity by a set of stimuli in the environment. Similarly, the actor potentially can think thousands upon thousands of thoughts, any one of which can become active given the correct set of circumstances. The knowledge that six times seven equals forty-two, for example, may be stored in Harry's memory bank; but he does not go around all day every day thinking six times seven equals forty-two. Instead, this thought remains in a latent state until a set of circumstances arises to call it forth to activity.

In the sense that the individual represents a bundle or collection of interrelated potential or latent behavior, he has a personality; he is like a computer that contains a program for processing data supplied by its environment. The program is in storage, ready to influence the activity of the computer once data begin to flow into it from the outside.

In another sense, the individual may be viewed as a system of real overt behavior, which actually occurs—in other words, as a set of active feelings, thoughts, and actions which occur in real time and space. These actions, feelings, and thoughts form sequences or series, which occur over time and can be described as more or less linear progressions. One act follows another act through time, one emotion follows another emotion through time, and one thought follows another thought through time. The individual therefore consists of all of the behavior that he performs, and as such he becomes an unfolding or emerging entity. That is to say, the total individual consists of all the behavior performed between birth and death; and at any given time in between he consists of a series of those behaviors performed in the past, those being performed in the present, and those latent or potential behaviors he will perform in the future.

Levels of Complexity in Social Behavior

Individual human beings perform all of the action which takes place within society, feel all of the emotions, and think all of the thoughts (2). As we said before, these feelings, thoughts, and actions occur in behavior streams or sequences which flow through time and space. At the microscopic level, these sequences consist of particles of behavior: small acts, discrete feelings or emotions, individual thoughts which occur more or less one at a time, but in a temporal-spatial order with respect to each other. For the sake of simplicity, we will use *act* to mean a unit of real behavior, whether it is an emotion, a thought, or an overt action. The capital letter A will be used to signify an act, and a subscript will be used to signify whether the act is a thought, an emotion, or an overt behavior. Thus, A_t will refer to a thought, A_e to an emotion, and A_a to muscular action (3).

The behavior of a human being could be diagrammed as shown in Figure 4-1. From left to right on the diagram, the arrows indicate the passage of time. There are three parallel arrows indicating the stream of thought, the stream of emotion, and the stream of overt action, which together make up the total behavior of the individual. As can be seen from the diagram, each particle of thought, feeling, or action is seen occurring as a unit, and one act follows another in a sequence. The diagram also indicates that a person can engage in all three types of action simultaneously. That is, he can perform a muscular action, think a thought, and feel an emotion all within the same unit of time. As for the progression of action, feelings, and emotions, they occur within their own sequences one at a time; one act follows another, one emotion follows another, one thought follows another, together making up a total stream of behavior.

Also shown in the diagram is the fact that behavior not only occurs at definite points in time, but in definite locations in physical space. These are *situations*. A certain part of the feeling, thought, and action of a given individual occurs in Situation 1; another part in Situation 2; a third part in Situation 3. The individual is shown returning to Situation 2, where another part of his behavior occurs.

Human behavior is definitely locatable in both time and space. Within the behavior stream of an individual, acts recur in definite patterns or sequences. The same act is performed over and over again; the same series of acts recur in time and space. If we observed Harry over a long period of time, a year for example, we would see him repeat the same actions on numerous occasions. He would shave virtually every morning, dress, eat breakfast, drive to the office, drop his children off on the way, and greet his secretary over and over again. Not only would the same individual acts recur, but they would do so in similar sequences.

Although all behavior is performed by individual human beings, we cannot explain social behavior by examining only the individual and what he does. The reason is that social interaction takes place in groups, so that the individual's sequences or streams of behavior are tied to those of other individuals to form complex interrelated streams. We may say that *human groups* consist of the behavior of several individuals linked together through a process of social interaction; that is, the be-

	SITUATION 1	SITUATION 2	SITUATION 3	SITUATION 2	
T_1	$A_tA_tA_t$..............	...$A_tA_tA_tA_tA_t$	......A_tA_t.. $A_tA_tA_tA_t$.	.$A_tA_tA_tA_tA_t$..A_tA_t.	T_n
T_1	$A_fA_fA_fA_f$.A_fA_f..	.$A_fA_fA_f$.....$A_fA_fA_f$.	...A_fA_f.$A_fA_fA_fA_f$......	$A_fA_fA_fA_f$...A_fA_f.A_f	T_n
T_1	$A_aA_aA_a$....$A_aA_aA_a$....	. A_aA_a....$A_aA_aA_a$...	..$A_aA_aA_aA_aA_aA_a$....A_aA_a	....$A_aA_aA_aA_aA_aA_aA_a$.	T_n
	A_t = thought, A_f = feeling, A_a = overt action				

Figure 4–1 Streams of Feeling, Thought, and Overt Action

havior of one individual functions as a stimulus for the behavior of the other in complex interwoven and intertwined sequences or sets.

The simplest of these sets of interwoven human actions will be labeled *group behavior.* We mean here only that the acts of individual human beings interact to form stable sets of behavior called groups; we do not imply that an entity called a "group" behaves or acts. Figure 4-2 illustrates the group as an action system. Groups neither feel, think, nor act; but within situations and in the context of the organization of society, the behavior of individual human beings coalesce into sets of behavior which constitute a system of action called a group.

Groups are relatively complex behavior systems compared to the

Figure 4–2   The Group as Converging Action Streams

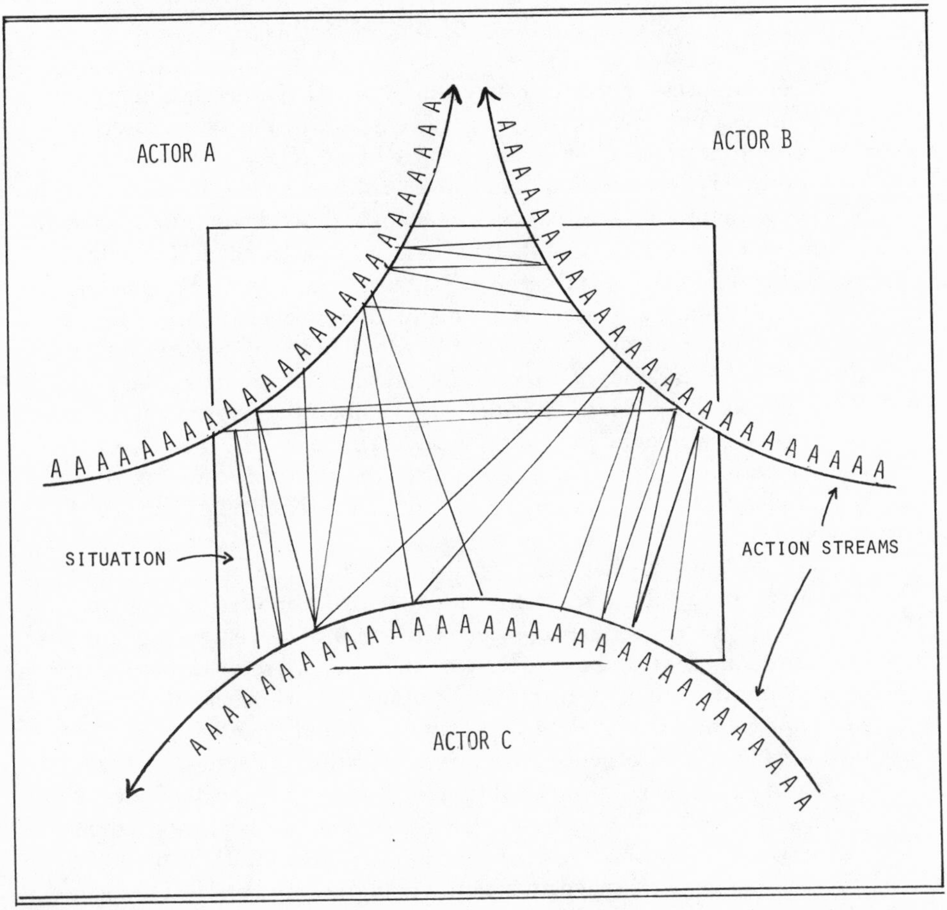

actions of an individual human being; but society is made up of infinitely more complex systems of behavior. Groups combine to form organizational systems; organizations combine to form communities; communities form societies. At the most complex level, that of the society, the behavior of a multitude of human beings is intertwined into a complex set of networks of interlocking behavior sequences, which together form the total system of behavior which is society. When we talk about human behavior, therefore, remember that its complexity rises from that of individuals through a number of human beings in group situations, organizations, and communities, to societies. Each of these systems, however, consists of the actions of human beings, and includes their thoughts, feelings, and overt muscular activity.

Acts as Particles of Social Behavior

While we were observing Harry, our mythical middle-class man, we saw him get out of bed, shave, eat breakfast, drive the children to school, go to work, and give instructions to his secretary. In other words, he performed a stream of action.

How shall we break this large stream of activity down into units of action? In other words, how shall we define "an act?" Shall we characterize shaving as an act, and eating breakfast as another act? But shaving is a rather complex activity with many components of behavior. Is shaving, then, to be used as the unit of action? or shall we use smaller things like face soaping, face washing, and razor stroking as acts?

To make things more difficult, it is possible to move up a level in complexity and regard grooming behavior as an act. In that case, we could regard toothbrushing, shaving, dressing, and hair combing all as one family of activity, that together form a single unit, a single act of grooming.

The problem is that since one activity flows into another, it is difficult to find a natural separation of one act from another (4). It is true, however, that some sequences of behavior require movement from one location to another; and therefore we can use space to distinguish one set of activities from another. Also, certain actions occur together in time, one following the other in a sequence. When these sequences are separated from each other by time, we can use that to distinguish them. Time and space, then, can be used to separate one unit of behavior from another, and thus allow us to identify separate acts. Therefore, actions performed within a short span of time in a common location should be grouped together and called an act, provided they are observed to recur more or less in the same sequence within this time-space context. An act, we may say, is like a word in a sentence: a small unit out of which a larger, meaningful whole is composed. The sentence, paragraph, and narrative are made up of words that come in definite sequences and sets. And like acts, words are made up of smaller parts—syllables and individual sounds. In acts such as shaving, smaller parts like soaping the face and scraping the blade across the whiskers are equivalent to the syllables in words; and when each one of these is broken down into its smaller parts, we are at the linguistic level of individual sounds, or at the time-motion study level of individual muscular movements.

In trying to identify unit acts, we are in the same position as the linguist who attempts to determine the words that make up a language (5). Let us say, therefore, that like a word, an act is the smallest part of behavior that has meaning. That is, it is the smallest part of human action that is understood by the ego actor and his alter actors in the situation to be a completed and unitary performance that makes sense, or has meaning which is comprehensible to the persons involved. It can be argued that in written language, letters as letters (not as words like *a* or *I*) have no meaning that is comprehensible to anyone. Similarly, syllables have no meaning alone. They must be combined with other syllables into a larger whole before they make sense. Furthermore, only when they are combined in a certain order do they take on meaning. Similarly, the unit *act* is the smallest part of behavior which has a symbolically understood meaning to the actor performing it and the person toward whom it is performed.

On this basis, shaving is a unit act that has meaning and significance. Putting soap on the face, however, is not such an act, because to have meaning it must be combined with other actions. When combined with one set of other bodily movements, it becomes shaving. With a different set, it becomes face washing. With still another, it becomes medication. These smaller particles of behavior are like syllables: they may be used in many different acts, and their meanings depend on the combinations. Furthermore, and again like syllables, their combinations always recur in roughly the same sequence within a unit act.

Acts, Products, and Functions

Action or behavior is real. It is observable either directly or indirectly, and is in no sense an abstraction. Thought and feeling are also objective phenomena, in the sense that they occur in the environment of the observer, are not imaginary, and even though covert, can be observed indirectly. When we say that thought and feeling are subjective, the statement is true only from the point of view of the person performing the behavior. From the observer's viewpoint, both thought and feeling occur as phenomena in the environment of the observer; they are no more subjective or unreal than are electricity, magnetism, gravity, and radiation—all of which cannot be observed directly with the unaided senses.

The behavior of the organism, its feelings, thoughts, and actions, are as real as the organism which performs them. Action is transitory, but that does not make it less real than tangible objects which persist unchanged through longer periods of time. An act is performed, and when it has been completed, it is no longer directly observable. It is a happening that, once over, is supplanted by another act, which itself fades into the past and is gone. The organism is a solid, persisting entity whose structure exists through time and can be examined and re-examined repeatedly. Behavior is more like a flash of lightning, or an explosion, or a sound that occurs and is gone.

Again, because behavior is so tied to a given instant in time, it may appear less real than solid objects which endure. But if time could be speeded up so that a millenium became a second, even the phenomena and objects that we think are permanent, like mountains, would appear to be transitory and fleeting. Because behavior is closely tied to a small segment of time, one should not assume that it is somehow less real or less objective or less subject to study than more permanent phenomena.

Although acts have the quality of occurring and receding into the past, actions produce certain outputs or results which persist through time. These outputs we will call the *products of action*. They are the objective results of behavior.

An act, whether a feeling, thought, or overt behavior produces some alteration in the environment in which it occurs. This alteration is the product of the act in combination with its environment. Shaving as an act, for example, results in products: a beardless face, used shaving cream, a worn blade, dirty water. A thought on the part of a human being, coupled with an overt muscular behavior, may result in a sentence on a piece of paper, written lines observable by other human beings. The emotion of fear may result in a rise in blood pressure, an increased heart beat, and an outcry which is heard by others and registered in their memories. In other words, acts performed by human beings leave a kind of footprint or fingerprint in the environment in which they occur, a product which is the result of their occurring. They also have an effect or series of effects on the actor himself.

A series of complex acts on the part of an organized system of human beings may result in the production of automobiles, a city, or a rocket. This means that an object such as an automobile is a product of human behavior. Viewed from the perspective of an archaeologist, the automobile is a kind of fingerprint of the behavior of an organized group of human beings. The behavior which produced it no longer exists in time and space, but the product produced by the behavior does. The cities that we live in, the houses that we build, the factories that make the artifacts of our culture are like the products any animal produces through its behavior. They are directly comparable to the dam built by the beaver, the nest of the bird, the game trail in the wilderness. They are the products of behavior, the leftovers of action. Phenomena such as air and water pollution and erosion are also the products of human behavior. They are the physical output of action.

It is important to realize that behavior is different from its product or consequences. Products or consequences persist after the behavior has receded into the past. Because human behavior leaves traces in its environment, as well as in the organism which produces it, it is possible to examine human behavior through examining its products. It is this fact that makes the science of archaeology possible. Archaeologists infer behavior as well as the nature of the social organization from their surviving products. Obviously, they can only draw inferences about the class of behavior directly related to the product. A pyramid is evidence of organized human action, but gives no clue to the emotions and thoughts that occurred during its planning and building.

One particular form of behavior product is of a special interest to the behavioral sciences, and that is, a memory. Acts performed by ego are registered in ego's and alter's memories as information. Information stored in the form of memory is as much a product of behavior as is a tangible object produced by muscular activity. Without it, the process of socialization and personality formation would be impossible. Only because acts performed by human beings are registered in memory are human beings able to learn their culture and become members of society; and indeed, culture exists only because humans can remember. By observing the action of others, human beings learn behavior patterns; and these too are the products of behavior in the same sense that a footprint on the beach is a product of the passage of a human being across the sand.

We must be careful, however, not to confuse memory, the product of behavior, with behavior itself. Memory is influenced by perception and by internal mental processes, such as rationalization, that may produce distortion. It must be regarded as a product produced by behavior in interaction with the organism in which the memory is registered. In other words, memory, like the footprint on the beach, is as much a product of the beach as of the individual who walked across it; it is merely evidence that behavior has occurred, and incomplete evidence at that. Moreover, one real act—shaving—may occur, and as the result of the interaction between personality and events occurring in the environment, several different memory products may be registered. Several people may observe this act and perceive it differently, so that a single act may produce multiple kinds of memories, each one biased by the process of perception and other mental processes occurring in conjunction with it.

The Concept of Function

Actions not only produce outcomes in the form of products; they also perform functions. The product of an act is directly or indirectly observable. It can be seen, touched, heard, or directly inferred from some measuring instrument. It has a real existence, although that existence may sometimes be extremely transitory. Functions, however, are not directly observable. They do not have a real existence in the sense that they can be measured or observed through the senses. Functions are inferences about what meaning acts have for the operation of the larger system of which they are a part.* They relate acts to the larger system of behavior in terms of the contribution that they make to the maintenance and operation of that system. In this sense, the idea of function refers to a kind of second order outcome of behavior. The products of behavior may be directly observed and exist at the lowest level of abstraction. The functions of behavior refer to an inference drawn about the meaning of behavior products for the operation of the system, and thus represent a second order abstraction (6).

The distinction between product and function can be illustrated by the following incident. Let us suppose that we observe a small child playing with a cat. The child's mother is sitting nearby, talking over the telephone, not paying much attention to what he is doing. He picks the cat up by the tail, and begins to swing it around through the air. The cat yowls, and the mother drops the telephone and dashes across the room, shouting as she goes, "Put that cat down!" The child looks startled and drops the cat, who takes off for parts unknown. The mother grabs the child by the shoulders, and shakes him, saying, "Don't you know better than to mistreat a cat like that? Don't ever let me see you do that again!" The child's face flushes, and he begins to cry.

*We think we are talking about function as Merton does, but it is possible that Merton combines under the heading of function, which he defines as the consequences for the system, both the idea of product and what we are calling function. Like Merton we mean to exclude from the idea of function the notions of purpose, intention, goal, and motive. See Robert K. Merton, *Social Theory and Social Structure* (Revised Edition). New York: The Free Press, 1965, 50–54.

The tears rolling down his face may be regarded, at least partially, as a result of the mother's behavior in relation to his own. The memory of his mother's words, his emotional state, his painful shoulder muscles, and one missing cat are all to be considered as products of the behavior which took place. In a real sense they are a product of interaction between two actors in a situation—but they are products, nevertheless.

If we ask what function the mother's behavior in respect to the child served in the larger system of behavior which makes up society, the answer will probably be something like, "She was socializing the child by teaching him how to treat animals. She was disciplining him to maintain some kind of orderliness in his behavior." In other words, conclusions about the function of her behavior, in terms of its larger meaning for society, are based on inferences about its relationship to the question of how order and pattern are established in human action. The memories, the tears, the sore muscles contribute, either positively or negatively, to the performance of this function of socialization.

We cannot observe socialization directly; we can only observe behavior and its immediate products. After observing a number of instances of a particular behavior, and observing its products and relating them to a larger system of behavior, we can infer the functions that are involved, and then classify the behavior as socialization. It is the act of classification, in terms of function, that identifies the function. The function itself cannot be directly observed. However, the idea of function does allow us to judge what significance or meaning an act has for keeping the larger system operating. This is a judgment made by an analyst who is trying to understand the operation of a system. To answer a question such as, "What keeps the system operating?" he has to try to understand the role or function of the behavior in maintaining the system in an operating state.

As pointed out by Merton, one must not confuse function with motive or purpose (7). The idea of function is not an inference an observer makes about the purpose or motive of an actor in performing a behavior. It is an inference he draws about the part that the behavior plays in relation to the whole. Human beings may perform the same act for a variety of reasons. For example, we could observe thousands upon thousands of instances of human beings being introduced to each other and shaking hands. If we were to delve into the motivations involved in handshaking, we might find that many different motives are involved. One may shake hands to impress someone; because he is too embarrassed not to; to express sympathy or understanding. But whatever the immediate personal motivation, the behavior itself serves a variety of different functions not necessarily related to the purpose or motivation of the actor performing the act.

The idea of function should also not be confused with the notion of effect, as in cause-and-effect reasoning. An effect or outcome of a system of variables is the product of the system of variables, and can be observed directly. The idea of effect is more like the idea of the product of behavior than the idea of function. Function is like the effect of an effect on the system. It is not the direct consequence of behavior, but the consequences of behavior for the system in which the behavior exists and takes place.

Function is an analytical concept rather than an empirical one, and is to be used in analysis rather than in observation. It requires a judgment or insight on the part of the analyst about what meaning what he observes has in terms of a larger system. The concept of function therefore demands some theoretical underpinning, so that the observer will know how to take observations made concerning behavior, and fit them into a theory of what the larger system looks like and how it functions. We will discuss this matter below.

CHAPTER 5

SOCIAL NORMS AND
BEHAVIOR:
THE CULTURAL VARIABLE

Behavior, the larger phenomenon of which acts are the units, is the outcome or product of a system of four interacting factors—culture, personality, situation, and interaction. We must now identify and define particles or parts of these phenomena that correspond in size and level of abstraction to acts. For it will do us little good to say that a certain specific act, such as shaving, is the product of these highly complex phenomena. We must be able to describe those parts or particles of each which actually operate to produce the act of shaving on the part of a particular real actor.

We will begin the task of examining each independent variable and defining its relationship to behavior by identifying the units out of which culture as a larger phenomena is comprised. What particles of culture operate in combination with aspects of personality, situation, and interaction to produce specific acts on the part of real human beings? And how do these particles operate in the process of behavior determination?

Let us begin to answer these questions by returning to our model of behavior as streams of actions in turn made up of acts occurring at specific locations in time and space. Figure 5-1 shows the action streams of several individuals. In ego's action stream, the set of acts $A_x A_y A_z$ occurs three different times. Let us suppose that this set of acts represents breakfast cooking behavior on the part of a housewife. The set therefore represents a progression of action: removing eggs from the refrigerator, placing a frying pan on the stove, turning on the stove, melting butter in the pan, breaking the eggs into the pan, and other activities associated with breakfast cooking.

The same set—$A_x A_y A_z$—also occurs in the action streams of three other actors. How can we explain these two forms of recurrence? In ego's action stream, what connects instances one and two of the occurrence of $A_x A_y A_z$? What accounts for the recurrence of $A_x A_y A_z$ in the behavior of three different actors? These two questions amount to asking why the distributions of acts in time and space aren't random—that is, why do certain permutations and combinations of acts recur with greater frequency than would be expected by chance? In short, how can we account for order in social behavior?

There are two possible explanations for the recurrence of similar or identical action in the action streams of actors. The explanations are based on the classical notions of culture and personality: acts could recur in ego's action stream as a result of the internal operation of ego's bio-personality system; or they could recur as a result of the operation of ego's culture.

If we choose the personality explanation and say that ego's repetition of behavior is accounted for by his personal characteristics which

Figure 5–1   Recurrence of Behaviors

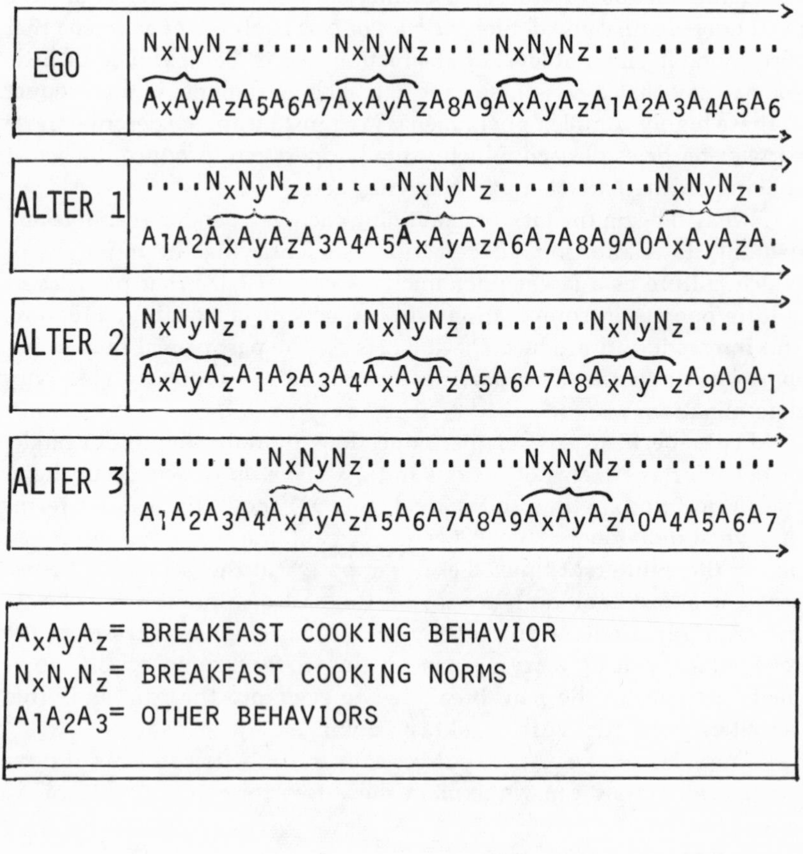

| EGO | $N_x N_y N_z \cdots\cdots N_x N_y N_z \cdots\cdots N_x N_y N_z \cdots\cdots\cdots$ |
| | $A_x A_y A_z A_5 A_6 A_7 A_x A_y A_z A_8 A_9 A_x A_y A_z A_1 A_2 A_3 A_4 A_5 A_6$ |

| ALTER 1 | $\cdots\cdots N_x N_y N_z \cdots\cdots\cdots N_x N_y N_z \cdots\cdots\cdots\cdots N_x N_y N_z \cdots\cdots$ |
| | $A_1 A_2 A_x A_y A_z A_3 A_4 A_5 A_x A_y A_z A_6 A_7 A_8 A_9 A_0 A_x A_y A_z A \cdot$ |

| ALTER 2 | $N_x N_y N_z \cdots\cdots\cdots N_x N_y N_z \cdots\cdots\cdots N_x N_y N_z \cdots\cdots$ |
| | $A_x A_y A_z A_1 A_2 A_3 A_4 A_x A_y A_z A_5 A_6 A_7 A_8 A_x A_y A_z A_9 A_0 A_1$ |

| ALTER 3 | $\cdots\cdots\cdots N_x N_y N_z \cdots\cdots\cdots N_x N_y N_z \cdots\cdots\cdots$ |
| | $A_1 A_2 A_3 A_4 A_x A_y A_z A_5 A_6 A_7 A_8 A_9 A_x A_y A_z A_0 A_4 A_5 A_6 A_7$ |

$A_x A_y A_z$ = BREAKFAST COOKING BEHAVIOR
$N_x N_y N_z$ = BREAKFAST COOKING NORMS
$A_1 A_2 A_3$ = OTHER BEHAVIORS

remain relatively constant through time, then we face the problem of explaining the recurrence of the same behavior among many different actors at the same time. We could contend that actors who act alike *are* alike in their personality structures; however, we would still be faced with explaining the observation that although some actors perform the same behavior at the same time, other actors perform entirely different behaviors. We could explain this difference again on the basis of personality, and claim that the set of actors who behave in fashion A are alike, but are different from those who perform in fashion B; and those performing in fashion B also are similar to each other. Following this line of reasoning, however, forces us to speculate on the sources of similarity and differences in personality, and eventually to take a stand on the issue of heredity versus learning.

Similar behavior could be produced by similar hereditary predispositions. This would account for ego repeating the same behavior over and over, or for many actors displaying the same behavior simultaneously. Differences among actors would then be accounted for by differences in heredity. But this explanation must be rejected on the basis of what we now know of human heredity and learning. We are forced to choose a learning explanation for both forms of recurrence, and to specify what it is that is learned which accounts for the recurrence. The concept of culture will serve this purpose for us. Sets of people who perform similar behavior under similar circumstances are said to have learned the same culture. They share a common set of learned behavior patterns, and therefore perform similar actions.

At any given moment in our society, a large number of people are performing similar behavior. For example, between the hours of seven and eight A.M., several million men simultaneously engage in the activity of shaving. Between the hours of nine and ten A.M., millions of women engage in grocery shopping behavior. Biological predispositions cannot account for either of these activities. Nor could accidental similarities produce in so many personality structures independent decisions to perform similar behaviors. Only the concept of culture can explain this phenomenal ordering of the activities of millions of individuals.

Furthermore, culture must be considered a part of the personality system. Otherwise it could not be an active ingredient in the behavior determination for individual actors. For this reason, we say that culture is learned or internalized by the actor. Thus, we place *some* of the total culture of the society inside the personality of the individual actor, but not all. For if all the culture were internalized by every actor, then it would follow that every actor would behave alike, except for the influence of noncultural personality content. If this were true, we could not deal with the variety of actions which are characteristic of the division of labor in the social system.

Culture thus explains both the recurrence of acts by different actors, and recurrence through time with respect to the same actor. In order to account for particular real acts, however, we must break the concept of culture into small particles which themselves can be distributed in time and space. We will call such a particle of culture a *norm*, and consider it to be the same size as the act it prescribes. By this we mean that the particle of culture will occupy the same location in social space that the act occupies with which it is associated.

A norm, N_x, corresponding to the act A_x, shown in Figure 5-1, exists both prior to and following A_x, and connects A_x to its next appearance. Norms, then, are acts in a state of storage or latency. During the period that is covered by A_5 to A_9 in Figure 5-1, for example, the behavior $A_x A_y A_z$ is in storage in the form of norms or latent acts.

Once a norm is learned, it becomes a part of the personality of the actor learning it, and exists as a part of that personality from that time on, although it may change as the actor continues to learn. A norm is considered to exist through time, as is shown in Figure 5-2, where N_x $N_y N_z$ exist as part of the personality of the actor from time 1 through time 4. Why is it, then, that norms directly affect behavior only at particular times? They are triggered out of a state of inactive storage into a state of active influence by situational and interactional influences; exactly how this happens will be discussed later on.

Norms, then, as particles of culture correspond in size and level of abstraction to acts. A norm is a program or blueprint for action which is learned by an individual actor, and becomes part of his personality. In the sense that a norm is a kind of instruction for behavior, it represents a causative influence with respect to action. The breakfast-cooking behavior described is not invented by the actor as she performs it; instead, it was acquired prior to the performance. The learned imprint of the behavior in the personality of the individual is the behavioral norm. It is an idea of how to act rather than an action itself.

This view of norms allows us to describe the structure of culture, just as the notion of act as a particle lets us conceive the structure of real behavior—that is, by identifying the particle, stating the relationships that exist among the particles, and relating the particles to each other in terms of function.

What we are saying, of course, is that both culture and behavior have a structure. The structure of culture produces the structure of behavior in the same sense that a particular norm produces a particular act. Let us assume, for example, that American society has an identifiable and definable structure. That is, the action patterns that make it up can be described in terms of relationships and functions. Let us further

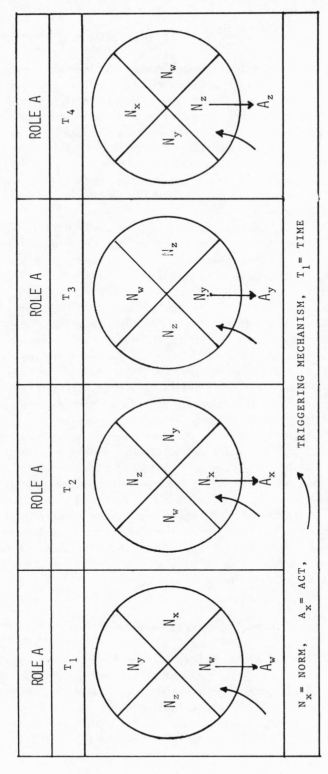

Figure 5–2 The Activization of Norms Comprising a Role

assume that the structure persists through an observable amount of time. We may then state that the structure of the behavior observed in American society is partially a product of the culture of American society, and that that culture contains a kind of blueprint for orderly or structured action. It defines the acts which should take place, and how they should be related to each other in terms of interaction. In so doing, it establishes what their functions are likely to be in terms of the larger system. In this sense, we can say that the structure observed in behavior in society is partially a product of the structure which exists within the culture of the society.

It's like saying that if we see several houses with the same number and arrangement of rooms, that look alike inside and out, we are justified in assuming that the same kind of behavior must have gone into producing all the houses. We may further assume that the several houses all had a common construction blueprint. This blueprint is the pattern; the behavior of the workers—of carpenters, brick layers, contractors—is human action; and each house is the product of human action guided by a blueprint, affected by the personal characteristics of the workers, the situation in which they were working, and the materials they worked with, all interacting as a system.

Culture in its largest sense, then, furnishes a blueprint for behavior in society. In computer terminology, it furnishes a program for human action. At its lowest level of generality, this program consists of norms that are the particles out of which the program is built. They are the individual instructions which, added together, make up the program.

Of course, norms as particles of culture do not alone determine the form that real behavior will take. Norms interact with other sources of influence—personality, situational, and interpersonal interaction—and the behavior which actually occurs will vary, sometimes conforming to norms, sometimes deviating from them. The structure of society as a behavior system therefore is not a direct and invariable outcome of cultural structure. Instead, cultural structure operates as one of the determinants of social organization.

Some Problems in Defining Norms

The concept of norm has been used in sociology for a very long time. It has been associated with a number of other concepts such as customs, beliefs, values, folkways, and mores. The usual definition for norms is that they constitute commonly-held behavior expectations. By *commonly held,* the sociologist usually means "shared by a number of individuals," or "held in common by members of a group." Traditionally, sociologists and anthropologists have said that for a thing to be normative or customary, many members of society must share the same definition of what is right and proper. Family norms, on this basis, become generally held concepts of how various members of the family should or ought to behave (1).

Norm Sharing

This traditional concept of norm needs careful examination, however, especially the idea of commonality or sharing. In order for a thing to be a norm in a group, we must ask, "How many people in the group need to hold the concept? For shaving to be normative, how many people must have the idea that shaving is a proper, correct, right, wise, or intelligent thing to do? How much sharing or commonality does there have to be in customs, beliefs, values, and norms, before we are warranted in saying that they are a part of the culture of a society?"

For a long time sociologists have begged these questions (2). Sometimes we have been willing to say that the norm must be shared by the majority of people in society, or by a significant number of people. But we have not faced up to the methodological and theoretical problems involved in defining norms.

It is a well-known fact that within society certain norms apply to a very limited number of people, and are known only to a few individuals. For example, there are norms which are related to the behavior of the President of the United States, or the National Security Council, which are known only to members of that group. There are other norms related to the functioning of the presidency that are known to and practiced by even a smaller number of individuals. Even though only a few members of the society know these norms and hold them as behavior expectations, most sociologists would not deny that they are norms. Otherwise, we would be able to use norm only to refer to those behaviors most commonly practiced in society—so small a part of the culture that the word would lose its power and meaning (3).

Let us suppose that we are anthropologists observing behavior in a preliterate society. Assume we discover that every year at the vernal equinox the high priest of the society goes into a sacred cave, and remains there for a period of three days. It is known to members of the society that while he is there he is performing a secret ritual connected with fertility. We learn that he is the only one in the society who knows how to perform the ritual. Let us further suppose that we are able to hide ourselves in the cave and watch what he does, and that we are able to do this for a number of years. Each time we observe him enter the cave, he performs the same ritual set of acts, says the same words, and dresses the same way. We learn that the custom in the society is that when the high priest reaches a certain age, he selects a young man from among members of the tribe to whom he passes on this ritual. This young man is told that if he ever reveals the contents of the ritual he will destroy its effectiveness, and the community will suffer. So far, in living memory, no one has ever squealed.

Now the question is, "Can we say that the ritual that we observe in the cave is guided by a set of norms?" If so, these norms are known only by the high priest, for soon after the old priest tells them to the neophyte he dies, and his replacement is the only one who knows the secret. If norms are ideas about the kind of behavior that should take place, what its content should be, and how one act shall follow another in the progression of action, it must be argued that there are norms involved in his behavior. It does not matter how many people know the norms. What matters is the form and function of the ideas which constitute the norms.

Definition of Norms

A norm is a certain kind of idea. Specifically, it is an idea that takes the form of an obligation; it contains the notion of "ought" or "should" —in short, the notion of expectation. The norm is a thought which is prescriptive of behavior. We may illustrate by citing kinds of sentences. One kind of sentence is interrogative. "Does Mrs. Jones love her children?" A second kind of sentence is declarative, "Mrs. Jones loves her children." A third kind states a condition that should exist. "Mrs. Jones ought to love her children." This third kind of sentence is normative. A mother *should* love her children. A teacher *should* speak loudly and distinctly while lecturing. Harry *should* shave before going to work. Johnny *ought* to get his hair cut. All of these statements are statements in a normative form, and convey ideas of a normative sort. A normative idea conveys the notion that a certain act is right, proper, wise, intelligent, efficient, desirable, polite, or technically correct. It is not an idea about what exists as fact, but an idea about what should exist.

The amount of sharing of the idea is not a necessary component to normativeness. One person only may have the normative idea. That norm, therefore, is personal to him. On the other hand, everybody in society may have the idea. For example, "People should wear clothing in public." In other words, norms may vary in their prevalence within a human population. Some may be found with respect to a single individual in the society; others with respect to virtually everyone within the social system. Sharing is a question of the prevalence of norms, rather than a question of normativeness itself (4).

Transmission or Acquisition of Norms

Another idea which is commonly associated with normativeness is the notion that a norm is passed on from one person to another, from one generation to the next, or from one individual in the same generation to another individual in that generation; so that for an idea to be normative, it has to be transmitted through socialization (5). For example, our mythical priest passed the ceremony to his successor, so that the knowledge was shared at least at one time by two people.

But when does a norm become a norm? When norms are invented within or diffused into a society they represent ideas that are present there for the first time—that is, they represent innovation within the society. Is an idea a norm the minute it takes the form of an expectation? or does it have to be transmitted to and accepted by someone else in this form before it becomes a norm? For instance, ideas about how to produce weapons and how to use them are norms. They carry with them the notion that there is a technically correct way to go about putting together a certain object, for example, a bow and arrow. What we are asking now is, "When does an idea, such as the idea of how to produce a bow and arrow, become part of culture?"

Imagine, for a moment, that many, many years ago a sailing ship was anchored off the shore of an island inhabited by a primitive people. These primitive people had never seen or heard of a bow and arrow. Furthermore, the ship was anchored on the side of the island which was uninhabited. By chance, one lone native saw a boat put out from the ship carrying a man. The native hid in the bushes and observed the man as he stepped out of the boat carrying a bow and arrow in his hand. The native, of course, had never seen them before, and didn't know what their use was.

The man walked up and down the beach, looking into the bush. There were wild pigs on the island, and when one came out, the man took an arrow from his quiver, placed it on the bowstring, and cut loose at the pig, impaling him. Since the native had been chasing pigs through the bush all day without success, he was impressed, and as the bowman continued to hunt, the native kept careful watch. Soon the hunter had killed several wild pigs, and the native had been able to see that the object in his hand was made of wood with a string stretched tightly from end to end, and that the arrow was a shaft of wood tipped with a shiny substance. The stranger propped his bow and arrows against a tree and began to load his game into the boat. The native rushed down the beach screaming loudly and hurling rocks, snatched up the bow and arrows, and rushed back into the jungle.

The native, then, had a new hunting implement, and knew, basically, how to use it. The question is, "Had the bow and arrow become a part of the culture of his society?" Let us suppose that ten years later the same ship came again to the same island; but this time when men from the ship went ashore, they were met by a horde of natives armed with bows and arrows. Our lone native had been able to duplicate the original weapon, and had transmitted his knowledge to other members of his society.

We still have to decide when the bow and arrow became a part of the culture of his society. Was it at the moment when the native perceived how to put it together and how to use it? Or did he have to transmit his insight to one other member of his tribe? Did most of the members of his society have to become familiar with the idea before it became a part of the culture? Or did every member have to know and understand about bows and arrows, how they were made, and what they were used for?

Each of these four choices for defining norms in terms of prevalence and sharing with respect to the members of a society seem equally logical. At one extreme, we can insist that every member of the society understand bow-and-arrow making before it becomes truly normative within the society. At the other extreme, we can say one person is enough as long as the idea takes the form of a norm.

In between these two extremes lie two other choices. We can insist that a majority of the members of a society possess the idea, which means that 50 per cent plus one would be enough for an idea to take on the characteristics of a norm. Or, we can say it is enough for two people to share the idea, and that once our mythical native has passed his information on to one other person within his own society, it has truly become a part of the culture. We can also say that it is not necessary for the whole society to share the norms, but for only all of the members of a single group. But this merely reduces the problem to the group level, and leaves us with the same choices on a lower level of organization.

The best way to deal with invention and diffusion of cultural norms is to choose the lowest point on this continuum—namely, the point at which the norm first arises and becomes a norm through the form that it takes as an idea, rather than define it on the basis of its prevalence within the system. This is the point of one individual. Otherwise we cannot deal with the processes through which norms are spread throughout a system; nor can we deal with conflict within the system between and among norms. For example, within a group every individual may have a different normative concept of how a certain behavior should be carried out, so that each norm is common to only one person. It would be a mistake to say that norms do not exist within this group, because then we could not account for the conflict that arises precisely because individuals have different ideas about what ought to be the pattern of behavior.

If we choose to say that a norm exists as a behavior expectation in a single individual, what shall we say about how it must be acquired? Do we insist that norms always be acquired through socialization? or do we allow for other methods of transmission?

We think it is best to take a totally functional position with respect to this question, and to define a norm as any idea that functions as a behavior expectation, regardless of its prevalence and regardless of the method by which the actor possessing the expectation acquired it. If we insist on socialization as the sole method of transmission, it is true we will be able to explain the recurrence of the same behavior among many actors in the same society. But we will not necessarily be able to deal effectively with recurrence in the same individual. For a person may invent norms for himself that function as guides to his behavior, and account in part for the recurrence of a given pattern of acts in his behavior, despite the fact that he has not acquired them through socialization.

We do not mean to discount the importance of socialization with respect to norms. Instead, what our definition does is to make socialization a separate variable from norms—that is to say, socialization as a means of transmission is not a defining characteristic of norms, but a variable separate from them.

There are a number of advantages to this functional approach. It allows us to discuss a norm at its point of origin in both time and space. Obviously, norms must originate by some process. Existing norms have not always existed. If they must be transmitted by socialization to be norms, then they clearly must exist in some form before they are transmitted. So why insist on a certain kind of transmission before we call a behavior expectation a norm?

Secondly, it lets us discuss so-called deviant behavior, and perhaps even abnormal behavior, using the same concepts and theories that we do for conforming or normal behavior. Most sociologists now agree that most so-called deviants are really conforming to norms which are not shared with or approved by other people in their society. The last decade in our society should prove, if it did nothing else, that norms may be very personal and highly unstable entities.

Thirdly, by defining norms in terms of their form and function rather than their prevalence and method of transmission, we should be able to understand and explain the two phenomena that have given the structure-functionalists the most trouble—namely, conflict and change. An insistence on socialized sharing of norms is the major assumption of the so-called functionalist position (6). But much conflict arises out of an absence of sharing of norms; indeed, most of the conflict in American society in recent years involving civil rights, student or youth movements, and the women's liberation movement was due to a lack of shared norms. If we insist that sharing and socialization are the defining characteristics of norms, we cannot account for change, either; because by definition norms must exist as norms before they are transmitted.

A functional definition of norms permits us to regard them as dynamic, changing, fluctuating entities that arise in social systems and disappear, or are modified. From this point of view, prevalence and transmission become important issues affecting norms, rather than matters essential to their nature. A relativist position, incidentally, also clouds this issue. If we say, in Orwellian fashion, "All norms are shared and socially transmitted, but some are more so than others," then we will have to decide how much they are shared and how they must be transmitted socially.

The fourth advantage of this conception of norms is that it is compatible with learning-theory explanations of how people acquire behavior patterns through processes of conditioning. For it is true that the human animal may be conditioned to certain defined behaviors as expected or proper through social processes that do not necessarily correspond to the usual notion of socialization. In other words, a great deal of social conditioning may go on which is neither recognized nor intended (7). In a Mertonian sense a person may acquire norms as a latent function of his experiences in groups. These norms may be very individual in character, rather than conforming to a consistent social mold such as is implied by deliberate socialization processes.

Insofar as conditioned responses imply a stored pattern of behavior, and insofar as this pattern is complex enough to be described as consisting of a number of acts in sequence, then we can describe the elements in storage which act as guides for behavior (conditioned responses) as norms. It should be apparent that norms need not necessarily be verbalizable by the actors possessing them. Some will consist of elements of personality roughly corresponding to individual parts of a complex habit pattern. Smoking, for example, is a habitual behavior that involves a complex set of acts: opening cigarette packs, removing cigarettes, lighting them, smoking them, disposing of ashes and butts, and so on. It also involves ways to hold the cigarettes, and occasions with which smoking is associated. Each part of this pattern may be associated with a stored norm, which may have been acquired through operant conditioning, and may exist as nonverbalizable guides to the acts involved in smoking.

These problems will be covered in more detail in the chapter on personality, where the process of norm formation will be discussed as it is related to the processes of conditioning. It should be said here, however, that our conception of norms is compatible with Skinnerian operant conditioning (8).

Norms and the Division of Labor

If norms are defined as being characteristically shared or held in common by most of the members of the social system in which they exist, then we will not easily be able to deal with social organization and social structure. Cultural structure establishes a division of labor in society. It has the effect of dividing up the total normative content of the culture of that society, and allocating parts of it to different segments of the social order, where specialists learn the norms and perform the behavior prescribed by them. Social structure consists of the unequal distribution of norms among the population that makes up a society, in such a way as to divide the total behavior necessary to maintain that society.

Viewing social structure from this perspective, we see that certain norms must be shared in order for members of the society who specialize in various aspects of the total behavior to communicate with each other, and to exchange the functions that they produce. This means that we can expect some norms to approximate universals. Virtually every member of the society will be aware of their content and know how to perform the behavior that is related to them. At the other extreme, certain norms will be specialities which apply to the behavior of one person within the social system. The study of cultural structure, as opposed to the study of social organization, consists of the study of the distribution of norms within a theoretical human population.

The Operation of Norms

Now that we have defined norms in terms of their form and function, it is necessary to consider, for a moment, how they operate in the determination of human behavior, particularly in group situations.

Norms are stored conceptions about how to respond to a configuration of stimuli received by an actor from his situation, from social interaction with other actors, or from within his own organism. These are the elements in a behavioral program which specify for the actor how he should respond to various internal and external events. They are conceptions of how to act, rather than acts themselves, and exist prior to specific real acts they produce. For example, if an actor has a stored set of norms for cigarette smoking, a set that exists as a part of his personality system, then we can explain specific instances of smoking by saying that such stored norms are activated by certain events, which function as triggers to bring the norms into play as operating factors in behavior determination.

By conceiving of norms as stored behavioral rules or guides, we can account for the recurrence of the same behavior in a given actor on successive occasions merely by assuming that, between two or more instances of actual smoking behavior, the norms of smoking remained in storage as a "program for smoking" waiting to be triggered into a state of activity. We can explain successive occasions when a housewife cooks breakfast, or an executive dictates a letter, or a cashier rings up a sale on the same basis.

Once formed in the personality of an actor, whatever the source, norms exist constantly through time as stored potential action patterns which can be triggered into a state of active operation by a given set of internal or external stimuli. These stimuli may be in the form of actions performed by other actors, or in the form of perceptions of various objects in the situation. They may also arise internally; for instance, feelings of hunger or pain.

However acquired and however triggered out of latent storage, the norms of an actor *operate from within his own personality*. The norms which operate on ego as guides for his behavior are ego's norms, not the norms of other actors with whom he is associated. To put it another way, a norm operates as a norm when it functions from within the personality system of an actor as a rule for that actor's behavior, held by that actor himself.

Let us refer again to cigarette smoking. Ego has the smoking habit. As a habit, smoking consists, in its stored form, of a set of norms which specify how, when, and where to smoke. These norms are tied to internal and external triggering stimuli which bring them into a state of activity. These norms, stored in ego and triggered by ego's perception processes, are what produce the stylized form of behavior called "smoking" on ego's part. Each individual act of cigarette smoking on ego's part is a real act produced in part by these internalized norms.

Suppose ego is associated with another actor, let us say his wife, who also smokes. The wife's norms of smoking do not operate as norms for ego. They operate as norms for alter and alter alone. Now if the wife, following her own norms, lights a cigarette in ego's presence, this is perceived by ego as an event occurring in the environment. This event may trigger ego's smoking norms, but it would be incorrect to say that alter's smoking norms produced ego's behavior by operating as norms for him. Instead, alter's behavior was a trigger that activated ego's norms, which in turn produced ego's behavior. In other words, alter's norms affected ego's behavior only *indirectly*, by first shaping alter's behavior to which ego responded.

If we treat alter's norms as being norms for ego, we are placing norms external to the actor they affect, and it is our belief that norms operate entirely from within the actor. Since they affect the behavior of the actor, and when other actors perceive this behavior, it is true that the norms of ego may indirectly affect alter—not as a direct normative influence, though, but as a part of interaction.

Similarly, if alter has an antismoking norm, and, acting in response to it, expresses the idea to ego that he should not smoke, this verbal communication is received by ego as a perceived meaningful event expressing alter's norms. As such it acts upon ego not as a norm, but as a complex stimulus pattern which must be evaluated and responded to in terms of his own norms. Thus the norms of others may and do affect ego, not as norms but as perceived external behavior.

Smoking is a very simple example, however. We must keep in mind that norms, wherever located and however conceived, are but one among a number of factors or variables that influence the behavior of an actor. Ego's behavior is also and simultaneously affected by at least three other groups of complex variables: (1) The behavior of alter actors with whom he is interacting or anticipates interaction; (2) The objects and events occurring in the situation in which he is acting; and (3) Other parts of his own personality system, including other norms, organic events, and information and attitudes.

The concept of norm sharing or consensus as a defining characteristic of norms can and does lead to the notion that norms exist and operate external to the actors who possess them. Some sociologists talk about the norms of a group as though they exist in social space apart from the members of the group, and like so many bolts of lightning issuing from a cultural cloud, strike actors and start them performing behavior in response to the group's culture. But if this were true, then in Durkheimian fashion, norms must exist in some kind of collective mind. It seems to us, though, that this collective entity is an abstraction that cannot operate as an influence on human action. It makes more sense to regard a norm as a particular conditioned response pattern in a particular person, operating as part of that person to shape and mold his behavior.

Norms produce acts which are social in nature through interpersonal processes. These acts are the outputs of the actor as a behavior system; but since they are performed in social interaction, they may affect or be affected by the behavior of others. Thus ego's behavior in response to his norms act as stimuli to which alter responds in terms of alter's own norms. If ego and alter have compatible norms, their behaviors have a good chance of being compatible. If they do not, then stress and conflict may be expected to arise between them.

Through interaction, then, the effects of ego's norms are registered in alter's behavior. The mechanisms through which ego's norms affect his own behavior and alter's behavior are quite different, however. Ego's norms affect ego's behavior through internal psychological processes. They affect alter's behavior by first being translated into ego's acts, which are then perceived by alter and evaluated by him in terms of his own norms. In computer terminology, ego's norms function as a behavioral program from within his personality, through which he processes information received from the environment and responds to it. Ego receives data from alter in the form of perceived behavior which has issued in part from alter's normative program. But this data is received as information to be processed, and not as norms to be responded to as norms.

Given this point of view on norms, how do we deal with the traditional sociological perspectives about the normative order of society? Since the beginning of the discipline, sociologists have explained individual behavior in part by saying that the individual learns and then conforms to "group norms" (9). When he does not conform to group norms, then "social controls" are exercised on him by the group in an attempt to bring him into line. What do group norms mean to us?

We begin to answer that question by saying that a group consists of the behavior of several actors who interact with each other in an organized or patterned fashion. Each member of the group contains in his personality some norms which operate as guides to his own behavior with respect to other members of the group. Let us talk about a situation in which each actor not only possesses such norms for himself, but also possesses ideas in the normative form which specify for him how he expects alter actors to respond to his behavior. In addition, let us assume that his ideas concerning how he expects alter to act, and how alter expects alter to act, are either identical or extremely similar—that is, they agree; and that this situation exists among all combinations of ego and alter actors. Let us go one step further, and assume that through previous verbal and nonverbal behavior the actors are aware that there is agreement among them—that is, consensus exists.

Under these circumstances, where both agreement and consensus are present, we will concede the existence of group norms. But certainly this particular situation is relatively rare in real groups. Normally what prevails is *relative agreement* and *relative consensus;* and the conformity or deviance of group members will be relative to the actor perceiving the behavior. Ego may conform to his own norms and deviate from alter's; or he may conform to his own norms and to some of alter's norms, but not to others. Or, because of alter's sanctioning power, ego may deviate from his own norms and conform to those of alter.

We would prefer to talk about the norms of a group rather than group norms. The norms of a group consist of all of those norms held by group members relative to their relationship to one another, regardless of the amount of agreement or consensus. There is one set of norms for each group member; and the norms of the group consist of all of these sets taken together.

Certainly, it is of great importance how internally consistent this larger set of norms for the group is. If there is both agreement and consensus, it seems to follow that certain kinds of interpersonal conflict will be very low. It would be wrong, however, to assume that conflict would not exist, since the norms themselves may call for conflict. But at least there will be agreement and consensus on the rules of warfare, and conflict over the rules will be low.

This may be taken as proof that high consensus and agreement make for harmonious relations among group members, but any such idea is merely a hypothesis. Two disastrous conditions for the group can exist along with harmony. The peaceful behavior of group members might fail to produce the functions or products for which the group exists; and second, the group might fail to adapt and change in response to environmental conditions. In other words, it is a definite mistake to assume that high consensus and agreement are conditions which "should" exist in "healthy" well-functioning groups—and yet this biased assumption has always been part of the traditional sociological definition of the normative concept.

Dimensions of Norms

Once we have defined a norm as an idea that a given behavior is expected because it is right, proper, moral, wise, efficient, technically correct or otherwise defined as desirable, we can go on to identify a number of dimensions along which norms vary. The first and foremost is the dimension of *prevalence.*

Norms vary in the frequency with which they occur as ideas in a human population. The norm of adult males wearing pants under certain circumstances is extremely prevalent in American society. As a matter of fact, it is hard to believe that any adult member of the society can be unaware of this norm. Other norms which apply to bodily functions, such as dress, eating, sleeping, sex, toilet behavior, and so forth, also seem to approach universals. At the other extreme are the occupational norms, especially those that apply to esoteric occupations.

Norm Sharing, Consensus and Commonality

When we say that people have norms in common, we mean that upon examination it can be determined that they have the same idea about what behavior should take place under a given set of circumstances. When we say that people share norms, we mean that they agree upon the norms which apply in a given situation. Agreement implies knowledge of the other person's norms, and consensus on normative standards. Sharing thus implies some kind of like-mindedness which is mutually agreed upon. Commonality does not imply such consensus or sharing, but simply a recurrence of the same norm in a given population. Commonality thus implies like-mindedness without mutual agreement.

This is an important difference; for sharing, which implies interactive communication, is limited by the possibility of interaction among members of society. Any given person can interact only with a very small number of the people within the total population of a large complex society. Thus consensus is only possible within a relatively small circle. Commonality of norms, however, is limited only by the ability of a social system to implant through socialization the same norms in the personalities of the members of society. The mass media, through advertising and propaganda, can create common norms without creating consensus.

Rigidity and Flexibility of Norms

A second dimension along which norms vary is that of *rigidity*. This is the dimension identified by Sumner in *Folkways and Mores*. Norms vary in the degree to which they are regarded as matters of morals, ethics, or mere convenience. Some norms are mandatory; others are optional. The expectation that a certain behavior should occur may vary all the way from the notion that it is absolutely unforgivable not to perform the behavior, to the attitude that it is probably best to perform a certain kind of behavior under certain circumstances. This is perhaps the best known dimension of norms, and therefore need not be discussed in detail here.

Frequency of Activity in Norms

A third dimension of social norms is their *frequency of activity*. Some norms call for behavior that occurs with a high degree of frequency. The behavior is performed several times a day, every day in the year, by the person to whom the norm applies. Other norms call for behavior that occurs only under rare circumstances. Frequency of activity differs from prevalence; it refers to the number of times during a given span of time that the norm calls for an act on the part of the individual to whom it applies. A highly specialized norm can call for highly frequent or infrequent behavior. Similarly, a universal norm can call for highly frequent or very infrequent behavior. A woman is expected to dress every day in a certain way before she appears in public; however, once in a lifetime she is expected to dress in a particular fashion suitable for being a bride.

Directionality of Norms

The fourth dimension of norms is *directionality:* some norms are positive, and others are negative. That is to say, some take the form of specifying behavior which is expected, while others take the form of specifying behavior which is ruled out, or taboo. "One should not kill his neighbor" is a negative norm. "Harry should shave before going to work in the morning" is a positive norm.

Specificity-Diffuseness of Norms

A fifth dimension of norms is that of *specificity-diffuseness.* Some norms are highly specific and call for precise acts on the part of an actor; others are extremely vague and call for a general direction in behavior, rather than a specific act. The norm of stopping your car at a stoplight is highly specific, compared to the one that states a mother should love her children. The norms which make up the culture of a society vary between these two extremes. Some are highly precise, leaving no room for ambiguity or variation in behavior, while others are so vague that they allow for tremendous range of interpretation.

Object of Orientation for Norms

A sixth dimension of norms involves the object toward which they direct behavior. Some norms call for behavior directed toward the self; these are *reflexive norms.* Others call for norms directed toward other actors: these are *interactional norms.* A third class calls for behavior directed toward inanimate objects or natural environmental conditions; these are *material norms.* The norm that says that a man should shave before going to work calls for behavior performed upon the self, and is therefore a reflexive norm. The norm that says that a father should punish his children when they misbehave calls for behavior performed upon another individual, and is therefore an interactional norm. The norm which says that a cook should salt and pepper food while cooking it calls for behavior performed upon an object, and is therefore a material norm.

We must distinguish here between the object upon which behavior is performed, and the person or persons who expect the behavior, because these two do get confused. When a housewife is frying eggs for breakfast, she sprinkles salt and pepper over them—which is behavior performed on and toward an object or set of objects, and therefore a material norm. Some sociologists would say she is performing behavior toward her husband or for her husband. However, the husband need not be present and interacting with his wife for her to perform this behavior. She can deliver the eggs to him already seasoned; so what she does is not behavior performed in interaction, but in relation to objects.

A great deal of human behavior is performed with and upon objects, and not in interaction. The secretary who types a letter *for* her boss uses a set of objects toward which she acts in the process of typing the letter. While she is actually typing, she is not interacting *with* him. A young man preparing to go out on a date, who is shaving for the second time that day, is performing behavior upon himself, using certain objects in order to do it. It is true this behavior is in preparation for interaction with another human being, but it is not performed in the process of interaction with her. These examples illustrate that much behavior is normally performed in preparation for, or as the result of, previous social interaction; but to say that it is performed *in* interaction makes interaction an almost meaningless term. It makes much more sense to restrict the concept of interaction to those situations in which two or more actors are actually in each other's perceptual field, and in which stimuli are being received by every party to the interaction from other parties involved in the interaction.

Norms Classified by Type of Behavior

Norms also vary in terms of the type of behavior called for by the norm—a point that was made as part of our discussion of feeling, thought, and action. Some norms call for overt muscular activity; others for emotional behavior; still others for mental or cognitive behavior. Norms which call for feeling, thought, and action are all distributed unevenly within the social system, and vary with the specialization of actors in terms of the various roles that they perform within society.

Ego and Alter Norms

Still another important distinction needs to be noted: that between the person to whom the norm applies as a behavior expectation—the ego actor—and the person who expects the behavior or toward whom the behavior is performed—the alter actor. There is yet another category: those who stand external to the relationship between ego and alter, and hold the expectation toward ego—the tangential actors. For example, the norm of expecting a husband to provide shelter for his wife places the husband in the ego role and the wife in the alter role. Families and neighbors may also hold this expectation with respect to a husband; so that we see the idea of a norm may be held by a wider population than the persons to whom the norm actually applies in social interaction. The more universal a norm, the larger the number of tangential actors. The more specialized a norm, the smaller the number of tangential actors who will be familiar with it.

When we speak of specialization of behavior in society, we are referring to the distribution of norms among ego actors—that is, the way in which behavior expectations are divided up and assigned as responsibilities to various classes of individuals in society. This division of labor creates a system of interdependence—of reciprocity—between ego and alter actors. Ego performs behavior called for by a specified norm toward alter, and through performing the act supplies alter with some function that alter needs, or that the group in which ego and alter are both located needs.

Norms are also complementary; they specify a behavior expected of ego toward alter and a response to that behavior on the part of alter. Thus, individuals who are involved in social interaction are able to identify the proper response to virtually every act performed by another human being in their society.

And finally, norms are located at a particular place which is determined by where the norm exists with respect to social space. For example, the norms that govern breakfast cooking for Mrs. Jones may be identical in form, content, and function to Mrs. Smith's norm of breakfast cooking. But these two sets of norms will occupy different locations in social space, defined by the different locations of the two housewives in the structure of their societies.

CHAPTER 6 DEFINITION OF ROLES, STATUSES, AND POSITIONS

The norms that form culture, and the acts associated with them are not randomly distributed throughout the structure of society. Neither are they evenly or homogeneously distributed within that structure. Instead, both norms and acts form definite clusters or sets which occur at specific locations in time and space. Certain norms are associated with certain other norms, and together as a set they are tied to definite locations in the structure of the social system. It is only at this particular location that they operate as direct influences over the behavior of human beings. This clustering of norms and of the acts associated with them constitutes the social structure and social organization of the society (1).

In this chapter and in the following two, we will examine the clustering of norms to form the structure of small groups, and of acts to form the organization of group behavior. To do this we have to introduce three new concepts that are so intertwined in their relationships to one another that they cannot be defined independently. These are the concepts of *role, status,* and *position.* It is important to realize at the outset that each of these terms applies to progressively more complex sets of social norms, on the one hand, and of actions on the other.

The structure of roles consists of norms in the latent state, and of acts in the active state. Statuses are systems that are made up of roles as units of structure, and positions of statuses as units.

The mythical Jones Family can help us define role, status, and position. The Jones Family consists of Mary and Harry Jones, and their two children, Tom and Jane. Together, the four Joneses constitute a social group. We wish to describe the structure of this group. How can we do that best?

Remember that we distinguish between the cultural structure of a social system, and the social organization of that same system. The structure of the system is cultural and norms are its elements; while its organization is behavioral in nature and consists of acts. Remember also that groups such as families pass through periods of time during which no member is acting out behavior that may properly be considered family behavior—for instance, while they are dispersed and performing action in other groups. Nevertheless, during such intervals of time we must assume that the family remains a part of the structure of the society, but in a latent state.

When it is in a latent state, a family exists as a system of norms or behavior expectations. In contrast to acts, which occur one at a time, many norms may be stored and exist side by side simultaneously for a given actor. This fact makes a structural image of a whole group, which is essentially spatial in character, easier to construct using norms than using acts as particles. So we will first deal with the group in its latent state, and later examine how latent group structure is related to observable group behavior. In this way we will be able to deal with the whole group structure at one time.

To start with, let us assume that each group in society occupies a particular region of social space different from every other group. This region is located in space relative to others, in terms of the structural linkage among groups and the associated input-output relations that occur among them over that linkage system.

Like all groups, the Jones Family in our example occupies a particular region of social space. The norms which constitute the Jones Family structure are therefore located in this region.

There are norms within the culture of society that apply only to family behavior, and not to other groups in society. These norms are located within the structure of family groups, and apply to family actions. But of all the family norms in a society, only particular ones are related to the behavior of Jones Family members. That brings us to a subset of family norms that apply at a very specific location in social space, the region occupied by the Jones Family. Remember that norms are ideas which people hold about how they should act under certain circumstances, and that a particular norm is an idea of this sort held by a particular actor. Several actors may have the same idea; but if they do, then each person's idea will be a separate norm.

Accordingly, we may say there is a set of particular norms which exists as ideas concerning behavior held by particular real people called the Jones Family. These norms exist in a region of social space occupied by the Jones Family. Another set of norms exists for the Smith Family and the Brown Family and so forth. The sets may be similar in content and organization, or they may be different in certain respects. The thing that makes them norms is not their similarity, but their function as guides to behavior. Each set occupies a different region of social space, and as a consequence is regarded as a separate and distinct set.

Positions as Parts of Group Structure

To define the cultural structure of the Jones Family, we must define a set of relationships among norms and the functions they perform toward each other. Let us begin the task of defining relationships among norms by attempting to locate them in the region of social space occupied by the family (2). This can be done by identifying four social positions, one for each member of the family. One position is called the "father-husband" position; another the "wife-mother" position; another the "son-brother" position; and the last the "daughter-sister" position. Thus, the structure of the family can be diagramed as shown in Figure 6-1.

The particular norms that apply to the Jones Family are divided up and allocated to the various positions that make up its structure. There are norms that apply to the father and husband, and others that apply to other members of the family. In the position occupied by Mr. Jones, the father and husband in the Jones Family, a number of norms are located. These norms form a set, or cluster, located in a certain subregion of the social space occupied by the family. They are related to each other so that they form a set by virtue of being located in a common region in social space, and also by virtue of applying to the behavior of the

Figure 6–1 Positions Forming Family Group Structure

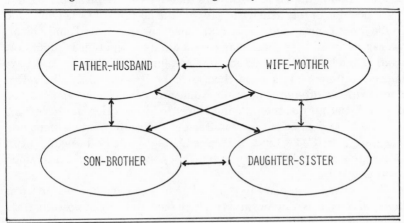

particular person who occupies the social position located in that region. Other sets of norms are located at each position in the group structure.

The cluster or set of norms that makes up the father-husband position for Harry Jones is a cultural blueprint for being a father and husband in the Jones Family. This set of norms consists of all the behavior expectations that apply to the behavior of Harry Jones as a husband to his wife and as a father of his children. Similarly the other positions in the group structure define the behavior expected of Mrs. Jones as a wife and mother, and to Tom and Jane Jones as son and daughter, brother and sister.

It is obvious that the normative structure of the Jones Family is spatially ordered. Particular norms occur at particular locations in social space. This, of course, is the same as saying that norms apply to the behavior of particular actors in the group, and not necessarily to all members of the group. The total culture is subdivided, so that part of it applies to one exact location in social space and other parts at other specific locations in that space. Within the structure of particular real groups, which themselves have particular spatial locations, culture is further subdivided, and norms are located at different positions within group structures.

When we say that there is a particular set of norms that defines the behavior expected of the father-husband in the Jones Family, we are referring to the norms held by the position occupant. These are the norms that define the position, and not the norms of other position occupants in the same group, or, for that matter, in other groups.

Sociologists have traditionally taken the view that norms are defined by consensus or agreement among group members (3). This position clouds the issue of how to identify the norms applying to a given position or role. Are we to say that the position of father-husband in the Jones Family contains only those norms that Jones Family members agree upon? Mrs. Jones may have a different set of ideas about how a father and husband should act from Mr. Jones. The children may have entirely different ideas from their parents. It is certainly likely that norms will be different concerning some areas of behavior and alike on others. What norms, then, define Harry Jones' position and roles?

We have defined norms as affecting the norm holder's behavior. They are stored as a kind of idea, and they must be brought out of storage to act upon the actor to produce action before they can act upon another actor.

It has been customary to think of an actor's behavior in a group as being affected by group norms (4). There seem to be three possible ways such an effect could occur. First, an actor may learn and accept norms, which when internalized, operate from within his personality as guides to behavior because they are accepted by him as legitimate and binding. Second, alter actors in a group may have normative expectations which lead them to expect certain behavior of ego. They may act on the basis of these norms, and apply social controls to ego's behavior to force him to conform to their expectations. This could happen even in a situation where ego's norms call for some other form of action, in which case the norms to which ego is conforming are external to his personality and internal to the personalities of alter actors. In such an instance, the norms operate as norms from within alter actors, they are translated into acts called social control behavior, and it is this behavior to which ego responds. His actions are not therefore guided by norms in the same sense that they are when he conforms to his own norms. He is directly affected by norms as norms when they are his own, but indirectly affected by norms when they have produced social control behavior in alter to which ego must respond.

Still a third possibility exists. Suppose ego, in this case Harry Jones, has a norm. For example, he believes that when one of the children disobeys, the child should be punished by being denied some privilege. His wife, on the other hand, believes the child should be spanked by his father. Harry is well aware of his wife's normative expectations with respect to his disciplinary behavior, so that Harry has norms with respect to discipline, and he also has information about his wife's norms with respect to the same subject. At times Harry may act on the basis of this information. He may, without holding the same norms as his wife, use the information he has about her norms and spank the children. In doing so, he deviates from his own norms and conforms to his wife's.

Although the information Harry has about his wife's norms acts from within him as a factor affecting his behavior, it does so as information, and not as a norm. To act from within as a norm, it has to be accepted by Harry as a legitimate guide to his action—not merely as the basis for a calculated decision. In fact, we can assume that Harry's norm against spanking also operated along with his information about his wife's norm, and that as a side effect, Harry felt some sense of guilt for acting expediently. Also, the spanking behavior itself might be affected by the conflict between Harry's own norms and his behavior. Certainly he would spank with a different attitude if he were acting according to his own norms, rather than according to someone else's.

We cannot assume that group norms operate as a force or factor outside of actors as organisms. That is, we cannot assume norms to exist in social space in a superorganic sense, from which as an influence, external to and separate from personality, they operate as determinants for action. They are not products of, or perhaps the manifestation of, consensus. Lack of correspondence in normative definitions exists as a result of normative variability among group members. For if norms required consensus, then obviously they could not exist and operate when people don't "agree." But it is apparent, as Harry's case illustrates, that norms, or something which operates like them in every respect, do exist and function in the presence of disagreement.

What, then, are the norms that define Harry Jones' position as father-husband in the Jones Family? The answer: Harry Jones' norms. They alone operate directly on his behavior. But Harry has two kinds of norms with respect to family behavior: those which he sees as applying to him as the actor, and those he sees as applying to others. How are these two categories of norms located in social space?

In the past sociologists and anthropologists have used the ideas of rights and duties to answer this (5). For a given position, say father-husband, the norms which specify how the actor occupying the position is supposed to act are called *duties,* and the responses are called the *rights* associated with that position. Thus the rights of a position occupant refer to norms which specify how other actors should react to behavior performed by the position occupant.

Harry Jones thus has two kinds of normative ideas which are associated with his position as father-husband in the Jones Family: (1) norms concerning his own behavior, his duties; and (2) norms for the behavior of alter actors, such as his wife and children, his rights. Harry, for example, thinks he should take out the garbage, but he expects his wife to put it in a bag so he can do it. It is his duty to take out the garbage, but it is his right to expect his wife to prepare it properly for disposal.

Some sociologists consider that the duties of one position in a relationship correspond to the rights of the other position (6). In the husband-wife relationship, the duties of the husband would correspond to the rights of the wife, and the rights of the husband to the duties of the wife. This mutual correspondence has been called reciprocity between the positions involved, and can be diagrammed as in Figure 6-2.

A hidden difficulty inherent in this conception is that it assumes a consensus; otherwise it is not valid. When a husband defines as his right some behavior which the wife does not define as her duty, then the two are not identical, and each actor has a different and somewhat independent definition of the rights and duties involved in their relationship. Harry Jones' definition of his rights and duties with respect to his wife are therefore one set of norms; and Mary Jones' definition of her rights and duties with respect to her husband are a different set of norms. Only when they are in complete agreement are rights and duties identical. And even then, the norms that act as duties for Harry are separate and distinct from the norms that act as rights for his wife.

What norms, then, comprise a given position in the structure of a group? Our answer is: The norms that comprise the units of cultural structure for a given position are the norms as defined by the position occupant at the time of observation. These norms take two basic forms: duties—that is, norms which apply to ego; and rights—that is, norms which ego *believes* apply to alters.

The reasonableness of this point of view is apparent when we shift our attention from latent behavior to active behavior. If we describe the group as consisting of behavior, then the acts which will comprise Harry Jones' position as father-husband will be Harry's acts. But then, latent acts which comprise the position as cultural structure should be Harry's own norms, which are Harry's acts in a latent state. Any other choice would mean we could not deal with groups in terms of their active and latent phases.

If the rights associated with the position are norms contained within that position, and specify expected behavior, then expecting is itself an action (7). When Harry actively expects his wife to put the garbage in a proper bag, his expectation is a behavior or an act. Anticipation is thus a mental behavior or action performed by an actor with respect to an alter actor. The rights of ego will result in thoughts or mental actions called expecting or anticipating behavior on the part of alter. Conformity to or deviance from ego's expectations by alter may create active feelings or emotions on the part of ego. These statements should not be interpreted to mean that all thoughts and feelings are derived from the type of norms called rights. Some feelings and thoughts may be the direct results of norms themselves, as when an actor is expected to think

Figure 6–2   Reciprocal Relationship Between Rights and Duties

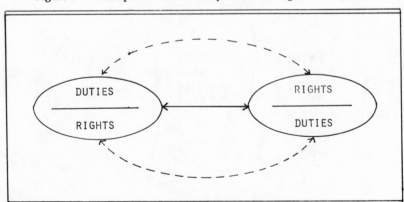

certain thoughts and feel certain emotions himself as part of his own role behavior. In addition, feelings, thoughts, and overt actions as real behavior must always be regarded as the outcome of the combination of culture, personality, situation, and interaction.

Statuses as Systems of Norms

Let us now examine the internal structure of the set of social norms located in one of the positions that make up the family structure. The father-husband position will serve quite well. Obviously the person who occupies the father-husband position expects to act differently toward his wife than toward his children. In other words, some norms in the set comprising the position call for behavior toward the wife, others for behavior toward the son or daughter. The norms that apply to the behavior of a husband toward his wife therefore form a subset of norms within the position of father-husband. Similarly, the norms that apply to a father's behavior toward a son are another subset, and those specifying his behavior toward a daughter a third subset.

The position of father-husband, which itself constitutes a subset of norms taken from the larger set of family norms, can be diagrammed as consisting of at least three subsets of norms. This is illustrated in Figure 6-3. The name *status* is given to this subset of norms which specifies behavior relative to a single alter actor (8).

Figure 6–3   Statuses Comprising the Father-Husband Position

FATHER OF SON STATUS   FATHER OF DAUGHTER STATUS   HUSBAND STATUS

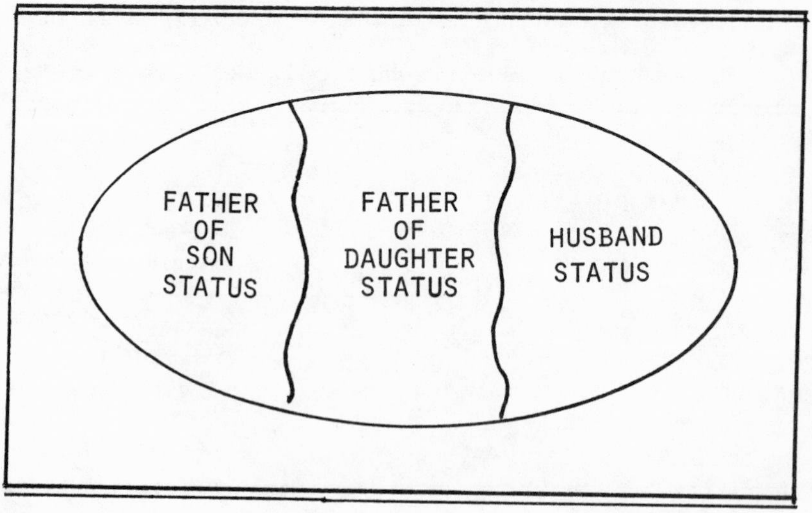

Position, then, refers to the total set of norms that are associated with the behavior of a single group member; *status* refers to all of the norms that specify behavior expectations toward a given alter actor or class of similar alter actors in a particular group. All of the norms that call for behavior toward a wife on the part of a husband make up the husband status. A different set of norms define the behavior appropriate for a father toward his son, and still a different set for the behavior appropriate toward a daughter. A social position, therefore, as shown in Figure 6-3 may consist of several statuses, each representing a distinct cluster of norms, and each located in a different part of the social position.

Roles as Sets of Norms

Can we discern subsets or clusters of norms within the set of norms which regulate husbandly behavior? or would it be best to visualize the husband status as an undifferentiated cluster? In our opinion, it is more accurate to think of the husband status as being differentiated or subdivided into a number of norm clusters. We will call these clusters, *roles.*

First of all, husbands perform a number of distinct functions toward wives, and complex sets of norms exist that define how, when, and where these functions will be fulfilled through the performance of complex sets of activities. For example, the three functions, sex partner, provider, and household member represent different and distinct husbandly functions that are associated with distinct complex clusters or systems of norms. The sex-partner function is defined by a set of norms that specify appropriate or expected sexual behavior between husband and wife. Another quite different set of norms defines the obligations of a husband with respect to providing for a wife, and calls for very different behavior. Still another set of norms specifies how a husband will act toward a wife in her capacity as housekeeper, calling for neither sexual nor providing behavior, but for behavior as a consumer of the wife's housekeeping services.

Each of these clusters of norms is so organized as to furnish a cultural design for performing a distinct function within the family group. On this basis, therefore, we can define roles as "clusters of norms organized around functions." Roles represent distinct substructures within social positions and statuses, and are situation-specific. The time, the place, and the surrounding set of objects related to the three roles listed above are quite different. Sexual behavior, providing behavior, and household-member behavior are situationally separated from each other. They take place at different times, in different places, and in the presence of different objects.

The norms that make up the structure of a family may therefore be defined in terms of five coordinates:

1. The function to which they are attached
2. The physical location or locations regarded as appropriate for the performance of the behavior
3. The temporal context within which the behavior is appropriate
4. The actor who is expected to perform the behavior
5. The actor or object toward whom or which the behavior is supposed to be performed

The norms that have similar coordinates on all of these variables simultaneously constitute a role. A role, therefore, consists of a set of norms organized around a given function that one exact actor performs toward another actor, within a single real group, in a given temporal-spatial context. Figure 6-4 diagrams these relationships.

We may also regard the norms that make up a role as a system of mutually interacting parts. The cultural structure of a society, or of any social system within it, is comprised of norms, which are clustered in terms of time, place, ego actor, alter actor, and function to form roles. Roles themselves are clustered together in terms of ego actor and alter actor to form statuses which constitute dyadic (two-person) relation-

Figure 6–4   Norm, Role, and Position

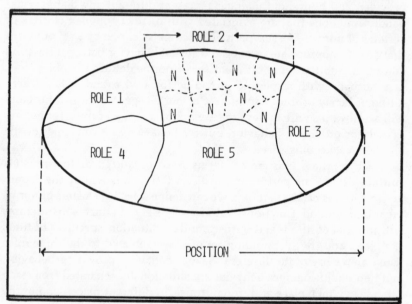

ships. Statuses cluster together in terms of ego actors to form positions; and finally, positions cluster together to form group structures. Thus, the concepts norm, role, status, position, and group structure are so defined that each of the units of structure, beginning at the level of role and extending through group structure, are regarded as systems. As systems, each is comprised of parts which stand in definite relationship to one another and are mutually responsive to one another (9).

There is a process called a *strain toward consistency*, to be discussed below, that operates on the content of roles, and subsequently on the content of statuses, positions, and group structures. This concept allows us to associate the parts of these systems with each other in definite structures and substructures.

CHAPTER 7

**DIMENSIONS OF ROLES,
STATUSES, AND POSITIONS**

Relationships Among Norms, Roles, Statuses, and Positions

Everyone who has written on the subject of social roles has noted that roles normally come in related pairs or in larger sets. For every role there is said to be a reciprocal or complementary role, which defines the appropriate response behavior (1) —like merchant and customer, teacher and student, supervisor and supervisee, provider and dependent, doctor and patient, lawyer and client.

Because the various positions that go into making up the structure of the group are linked together by role relationships, the idea of reciprocity or complementarity in roles is critical to understanding groups. For example, the father-husband position in the family is linked to the wife-mother, son-brother, and daughter-sister positions by a network of complementary roles. The father is assigned the role of provider. The other positions in the group structure contain complementary dependent roles. The relationship between the father's provider role, and the dependent role found in the other positions in the group structure supplies one system of linkage among the various positions in a system of relationships.

We will call the linkage between roles, such as that between provider and dependent complementary rather than reciprocal, and use reciprocal to describe a particular kind of complementarity. For the moment, let us explore what we mean by a complementary relationship between two roles, and by the statement that such relationships link units of structure, like social positions, together.

Complementarity in roles implies a relationship on the one hand between and among the norms that make up the structure of roles, and on the other, between the acts of persons who perform the roles in real behavioral situations. In the normative sense, complementarity refers to the fact that the norms contained within an ego role, such as that of provider, imply and require the existence of certain norms in an alter role, such as that of dependent (2). The norms of the father-husband position call for providing behavior on the part of the father toward his children and his wife. These norms specify the kinds of behavior expected and the person toward whom the behavior is directed, as well as the circumstances under which it is appropriate. This behavior is directed toward the wife and children; their positions contain a dependent role whose norms specify the kind of response expected of wives and children toward the father-husband who acts as provider.

In saying that one role implies and requires the other, we mean that one cannot provide when there is no one to provide for. That is, no one can engage in this sort of role behavior without directing that behavior toward someone who is expected to respond to it.

Rights and duties refer to the norms that make up the content of roles (3); duty applies to behavior required of the ego actor toward alter, rights to the behavior ego feels he can legitimately expect in return from alter. The rights of ego are, as far as ego is concerned, the duties of alter, and the duties of ego the rights of alter; the two roles are reciprocal or complementary. In the doctor-patient relationship, certain norms exist that define the behavior appropriate for a doctor toward a patient. A complementary set of roles exists that defines the behavior appropriate for a patient to perform in response to a doctor. Complementarity is built into the structure of the culture, since the norms that define the role expectations for the two positions imply complementary behavior.

Complementary role relationships call for interaction among individuals assigned the roles. When they put the norm into effect and perform the behavior called for by the roles, ego and alter must interact with each other. The provider, in order to provide for the dependent, must interact with him. The doctor, in order to treat the patient, must interact with the patient. As the norms function as guides to behavior, ego and alter act and react with respect to one another.

In the cultural structure of a group, therefore, the relationship among roles exists because norms are complementary to each other. In social organization, the role behavior of one actor is related to the role behavior of another actor through the medium of social interaction. Thus, roles, as parts of social structure, are linked to each other in both the normative structure and the social organization of the group.

But as we have previously said, both ego and alter have individual definitions of their own rights and duties. We may therefore speak of a continuum of agreement-disagreement between the norms of ego and the norms of alter. At one end of the continuum, ego's definition of his duties will be in agreement with alter's definition of his rights; and ego's definition of his rights will correspond to alter's definition of his duties. Consensus on norms will exist, and we may expect the actions generated by norms to be organized and relatively free of conflict over norms. At the other end of the continuum, ego's definition of his duties will be completely at variance with alter's interpretation of his rights; and ego's conception of his rights will be completely different from alter's notion of his duties. In such a case, we have a total lack of normative consensus on role definitions; and we may expect the interaction generated by the norms to be disorganized and conflicting.

Since most actors learn the norms associated with their roles in social interaction with actors playing the alter roles, the probability of complete disagreement is relatively low. But because learning is, at best, an imperfect process through which to transmit norms, the probability of complete consensus is also quite low. This means that in virtually every social relationship there will be a certain degree of disagreement between ego and alter, arising out of differences in the way they define their complementary roles.

How can we reconcile these two seemingly conflicting facts? That is, how reconcile the fact that social relationships are usually defined by norms learned from others who are members of an already functioning system, which means they are learned under conditions that lead to a degree of consensus with others; and the fact that conflict and disagreement exist among actors in most groups over the norms which define their relationships. We can do this by postulating degrees of complementarity. This way of looking at things does not rule out the idea of consensus on role definitions, nor does it rule out the idea of complementary or reciprocal roles. It merely makes it possible to use our concepts even under conditions of relatively low consensus and high conflict.

We must, however, distinguish between complementary roles and complementary functions if we are to think in terms of relative complementarity. Recall that a role, in the structural sense, consists of a system of norms organized around a function that one person performs in relation to another. We may therefore distinguish between the set of norms that comprise the role and the function they are associated with. That means we can say that the provider function is complementary to the dependent function, regardless of whether or not the norms that constitute the role are complementary. The norms may not be complementary, although the functions of the roles are. This conception of complementary functions makes it possible for us to state that two roles are complementary and lead to interaction, even when the norms are noncomplementary.

When we say functions are complementary, we mean that they are interdependent, and that the fulfillment of one function depends directly on the fulfillment of the other. That's why a person cannot perform the provider function unless there is someone performing the dependent function, and vice versa. The mode of performance and the patterned norms which specify that mode are not fixed and determined by the function. There are, even within the same group or society, functional alternatives for role definitions. The concept of complementarity functions allows us not only to compare variations in a given society, it also permits us to compare different societies with respect to the kinds of role content which are associated with the same function.

Range of Complementarity Among Roles

Every role in the structure of a given position is not in a complementary relationship to every other role in alter positions in that same group structure; instead, the connections between positions that make up the structure of the group are more complex than that.* For example, all the roles of the father-husband are not reciprocal to all the roles of the wife-mother. Instead, particular roles stand in a complementary relationship to one another. The provider role is in a complementary relationship to the dependent role in every position in the family group structure. The sex-partner role in the husband's status is in a complementary relationship to the sex-partner role in the wife's status. The disciplinarian role in the father-husband position is complementary to the subordinate role in the son and daughter positions. But the sex-partner role in the husband's position is not in a complementary relationship to the wife's housekeeper role or to her dependent role.

In Figure 6-1, several positions are shown linked to each other by a single line, which does represent relationships among the positions. In truth, however, many lines, representing complementary relationships, should be drawn between and among the positions which make up the group structure to show the fact that roles exhibit a range of complementarity (4).

Every role is not complementary to a role in every other position in the group structure. Compare the sex-partner role relationship between husband and wife to the provider-dependent relationship which exists within the family structure. The sex-partner role relationship exists

*Traditional definitions of role hold that there is one role for every position. Since roles are regarded as reciprocal to alter roles by implication, the entire content of one position is defined as being reciprocally related to the entire content of the other.

only between the husband and wife statuses in the father-husband and wife-mother positions. The father-husband does not have a sex-partner relationship with the children. On the other hand, the provider-dependent relationship system is such that the father-husband is expected to provide for the wife-mother, son-brother, and daughter-sister. This role therefore stands in a complementary relationship to a role in every other position in the group structure.

We may describe this variation in the range of complementarity among roles by calling them *unilateral, multilateral,* and *omnilateral* roles. A unilateral role is one which has a complementary or alter role contained in one and only one other position in the structure of the group in which it occurs, as the sex-partner role does. An omnilateral role is one which has a complementary or alter role in every other position within the structure of the group in which it occurs. The provider role is an example of this type. A multilateral role falls between these two extremes. It contains a complementary role in more than one, but less than all of

Figure 7–1   Range of Complementarity

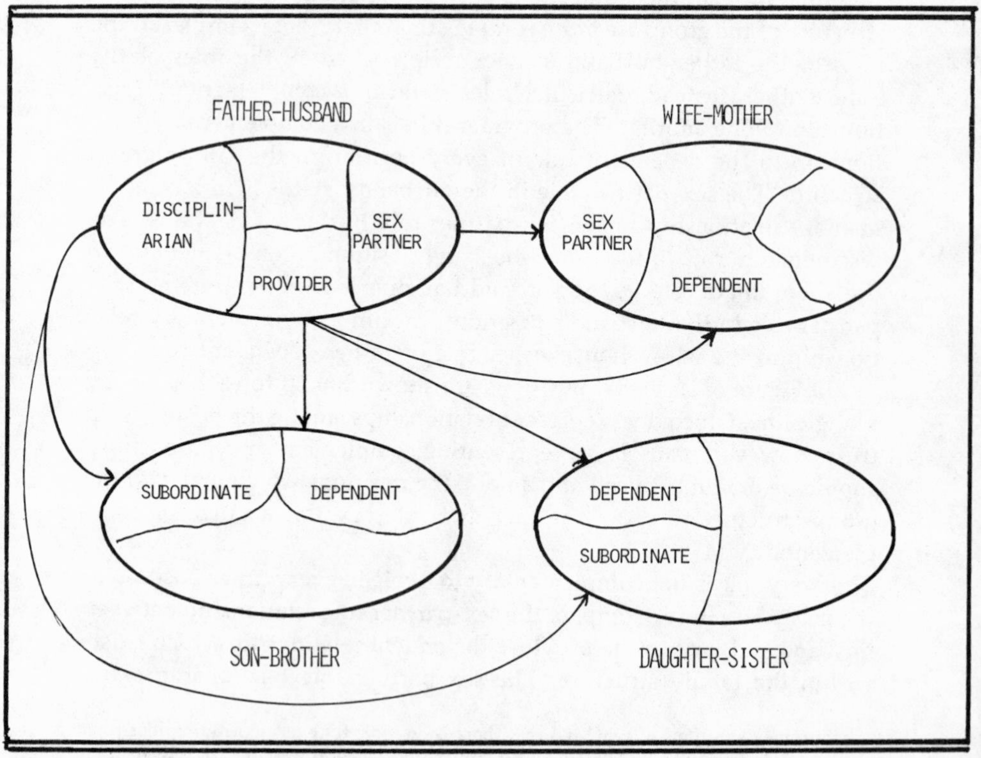

the positions that make up the group structure. The disciplinarian role that the father plays with respect to his children but not to his wife is an example of a multilateral role.

Figure 7-1 illustrates these three concepts. Here it will be seen that one line connects the sex-partner role in the father-husband position to the sex-partner role in the wife-mother position. This is a unilateral role. The provider role is connected by one line to each one of the other three positions making up the group structure, and is therefore an omnilateral role. The disciplinarian role within the father position is connected by two lines, one going to the son-brother position, the other to the daughter-sister position. No line connects it to the wife-mother position. This means that the father-husband does not perform the disciplinarian role with respect to the wife-mother. No complementary role is contained within that position.

Span of Activity of Roles

There are several other dimensions of role structure to be explored, but first we must have a new example of social position whose role content can be outlined in greater detail than can family members'. A secretary in an office group will serve our purposes for the moment. Let us analyze the position of a secretary who works in the office of Mr. Jones at the Ajax Black Box Factory. The group in which the position is located consists of two positions, the one occupied by the secretary, and the one occupied by her boss. The secretary's position in this group contains a number of roles—one for each of the different functions assigned to her in the structure of the group (5).

Let us assume that this particular secretary has been assigned the following functions: (1) typist; (2) stenographer; (3) file clerk; (4) book-keeper; (5) receptionist; (6) telephone operator; (7) supply clerk; (8) subordinate; and (9) employee. According to our definitions, each function has a number of norms organized around it that specify the types of behavior which, when performed, will produce the functions. Thus, the function of typist has a number of behavior expectations or norms clustered around it which are learned by the secretary, and which specify how she is expected to perform the functions of typing. The typist role, therefore, consists of a cluster of norms calling for a rather complex set of behaviors that require the use of machines and other paraphernalia. The role also specifies certain prescribed forms for putting things on paper, such as legal documents, letters, contracts, and so on. The stenographer role, in contrast, consists of behavior expectations organized around the function of taking shorthand notes for transcription.

It also involves a complex set of behaviors which utilize various physical objects and paraphernalia.

These same kinds of statements can be made about each of her functions. Each has a set of norms or behavior expectations clustered around it which define the kinds of actions appropriate to performing that function in the particular group under study. The norms consist of behavior expectations held by the secretary toward herself, in various degrees of agreement with norms held by her boss, and by other members of society who are familiar with the occupation of secretary.

A word needs to be said about two of her roles. The role of subordinate consists of behavior expected by the secretary with respect to the boss, in the process of giving and receiving instructions, orders, and directions. There are, in other words, norms that tell the secretary how to act as a subordinate to a supervisor. These norms call for behavior which is quite different from typing or filing or acting as receptionist, and consequently they form a role distinct from these other types of activities. The role of employee also contains a number of expectations distinct from those involved in other roles in the group. These expectations are organized around being employed by the organization or group in which the position is located. This role contains norms regulating leave time, hours of work, pay, sick benefits, and other employee types of behavioral expectations.

Figure 7-2 diagrams the position of the secretary, and represents all the behavior expected of the secretary in the group comprised of herself and her boss—in other words, all the norms that apply to her behavior in that particular context, included within the structure of that social position. Similarly, the diagram shows the entire repertoire of roles assigned to the secretary in that group. Obviously, the secretary in this group does not perform all her roles simultaneously, nor does she perform any single role during all her time. Sometimes she is typing and therefore responding to norms in the typist role. At another time she is engaged in filing, telephone answering, or taking shorthand from her boss.

Let us imagine that we go to her office to observe. When we enter, we see her sitting at her desk typing; in other words, in the midst of performing her typing role. The norms contained within her typist role are operating as influences over her behavior; and theoretically, these norms, interacting with her personality, the situation in which she is located, and with interactional components, determine the acts that she will perform. When we come in, she stops typing, looks up from her work, and says, "May I help you?" At this point she shifts from performing her role as typist to performing her role as receptionist. Norms that define receptionist behavior are now operating as factors influencing her behavior, and those that guide typist behavior are no longer operative. The norms of the receptionist role, combined with her personality and the situational interactional variables, are producing the acts which we observe.

Notice that she stopped performing one role at a given moment, and began to perform another role. We pointed out earlier that a person cannot perform all his roles all the time; instead, he performs one role for a while, then shifts to another one and perhaps still another, and then goes back to the first, so that there are sequences or series of role performances. We describe this activity in terms of active and latent roles.

An *active role* is one which is being performed at the moment of observation; a *latent role* is one which has been learned by an individual and is assigned to him in a particular group structure, but is not at the moment of observation being performed. Thus, while the secretary is performing her typist role, the other roles contained within her position are latent. This implies that the norms which make up other role definitions have been learned by the actor, but that they are not operative as direct influences over the actor's behavior.

Clearly, most of the roles assigned to a given person at any given

Figure 7–2   Secretary Position

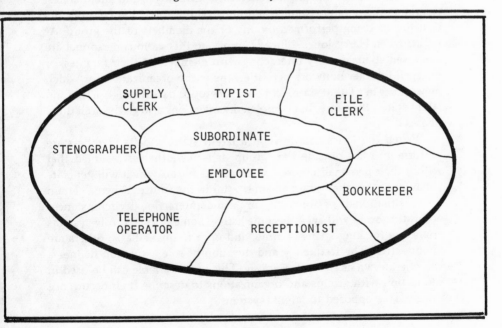

time during a day's activity are in a latent state. While the secretary is acting as receptionist, she is not acting as file clerk or stenographer or typist; or, for that matter, as daughter with respect to her parents, or wife with respect to her husband, or customer with respect to a merchant in a store, or in any other roles which might be latent in her various positions in society. In the morning Harry Jones performed roles in his father-husband position; later in the day, he occupied the position of boss in an office, and interacted with his secretary. At still other moments he performed other roles in the context of other positions.

We may, therefore, conceptualize latent and active positions, and also latent and active group structures. For example, while Harry Jones is at work interacting with his secretary, he is occupying a position in a work group. As he performs roles within the context of that position, his position as father-husband within the family is entirely latent, with not a single one of its roles active. Consider what the Jones Family is doing at 11:00 on a Monday morning. Mr. Jones is at his office, interacting with representatives of the home office, Mrs. Jones is at the grocery store shopping, and Tom and Jane Jones are at school, one in a geometry class, the other in a history class. Not one of the roles contained within the positions within the Jones Family structure is active, and the family as a social group is in a latent state.

Both positions and groups, therefore, have active and latent states. A group is in a latent state when none of the roles that comprise its structure is being performed by any of the members of the group. At night, when Harry Jones' office is empty and its various personnel are dispersed about the city interacting with members of their families, or engaged in other nonwork activities, the entire organization for which he works is in a latent state. Not only do groups pass through active and latent states, therefore, but complex organizations also go through these phases.

When the Jones Family is in a latent state, and its members are performing roles outside that group, it is nevertheless assumed that within their personalities are contained the norms which will generate behavior within that group at some point in the future. When a certain set of situational, personal, cultural, and interactional circumstances occur, the group will again become active. Some roles and role systems are active for long spans of time, and on a frequent basis; others are rarely active. The frequency and duration of role activation defines a variable known as the *span of activity*. This same variable can be used in connection with groups and organizations to describe their occurrence as active, as opposed to latent, systems.

Role Replication

The same role may be replicated—that is, recur many times—in the structure of society. Roles may be repeated as an aspect of the same position, which recurs in the structure of certain groups, which themselves recur in society. For example, the provider role may occur in the position of every father in every family group within the structure of the society. Since there are many family groups, each of which contains the same position, the same role will be found numerous times within the structure of society.

The second way in which roles may replicate is as aspects of different positions in different kinds of groups. For example, the disciplinarian role may occur as part of the father-husband position in the family. Here the role is performed toward children. The same role may occur in the structure of the schoolteacher's position in an elementary school class group, in the position of foreman in a factory, or a platoon sergeant in an infantry company. In this case, totally different kinds of groups contain a similar role within their structure.

The concept of function is involved here. What we are saying is that the same function is performed in several different kinds of groups within society, and that the culture of the society contains a set of norms which defines the way in which this function will be performed. This set of norms organized around a function forms a role.

Because we define roles in terms of function, we can speak of two roles as being the "same" role, even when they are not exactly alike in terms of norms, if the norms are organized around the performance of the same function for the groups in which they occur. That is why we can speak of Mr. Jones' provider role and Mr. Smith's provider role as the same, even though variations may occur in the norms that define the behavior appropriate to the two actors. On the same basis, we can compare the mother's role in the family as disciplinarian with the teacher's role in the classroom as disciplinarian, because they are performing the same function even though the normative definitions of appropriate role behavior may be different.

Structure and function, however, are not the same. The teacher's role as disciplinarian and the mother's role as disciplinarian, although they have the same function, do have different structures. The structure of the role, or the role itself, consists of a set of norms or, in behavior, of a set of acts, and thus is not identical to the function which it performs (6).

Theoretically, norms making up a role within each person tend to become consistent with each other through the operation of what is called a *strain toward consistency;* and two roles contained within the same position will also tend to become consistent in their structures. This means that we may expect two disciplinarian roles contained in different positions to be different from each other in content, because they must be consistent with different sets of roles in the two different positions. The mother's disciplinarian role with respect to her children is combined with a certain set of roles to make up the position of wife-mother in the family; the schoolteacher's disciplinarian role is combined with a totally different set of other roles to make up her position in the classroom group. As a consequence, we may expect the disciplinarian role to involve different norms in the two settings. The operation of the strain toward consistency in the two positions will inevitably result in differences in role definition.

Within a given culture, however, roles that recur in different groups will tend to maintain some similarity in content. This means that the disciplinarian role, no matter where it occurs within the structure of a given society, will tend to be defined pretty much in the same terms—insofar as similarity can be maintained, since the strain toward consistency is operating simultaneously to modify roles to fit different structures. Because there is this relative consistency of the disciplinarian role in different positions, people are able to move from one group to another, and respond as alter to a given role, without making major shifts in their orientation. A child can respond to a mother's discipline at home, then go to school and respond to the teacher as a disciplinarian without making major shifts in his alter behavior. If the two roles were completely different in their content, he would have to discriminate between the two situations in order to avoid errors in behavior. Errors in behavior are most likely to occur when the function of two roles is identical, but the roles are quite dissimilar in content.

Essentially, what we are saying is that the structure of society is built out of a limited store of roles. These roles tend to recur in different combinations to make up different positions and group structures within the society. As they occur in different combinations, the strain toward consistency operates to change their content to fit the new combinations. The nature of social behavior, however, is such as to constrain the variability of the ways in which a given function is performed within the society: the same person must act as alter and ego actor in many different group structures where the same functions occur over and over again. Were these functions to be performed in radically different ways every time the structure of the group changed, members of society would have to absorb a larger repertoire of norms, and learn to discriminate between a tremendously large number of situations to which those norms would apply. When some degree of consistency is maintained throughout the structure in the way a given function is performed, the process of learning a culture through socialization becomes more efficient, and the process through which roles are performed in behavior is also less subject to error and stress.

Ideal and Real Behavior Comparisons

The function concept in connection with the definition of roles allows us to compare ideal behavior with real behavior in a given group situation, and provides a basis for comparing the norms of the disciplinarian role, on the one hand, and disciplinarian behavior on the other. If we ask ourselves, "How is the disciplinarian function performed within the family?" we are led to observe behavior. If we ask, "How is the disciplinarian function supposed to be performed within that structure?" we are led to examine norms.

When comparing the normative definition of a role with the behavior of people in performing the role, we can use the concept of function to determine which behavior to compare with which norms. Without it, we could not be able to determine what part of the total behavior of the individual should be compared with what parts of his total repertoire of norms. For in order to define deviance from norms, or to identify variation in behavior from the role definition, it is necessary to have some way of deciding when one is dealing with behavior which is related to normative definitions. The concept of function does this for us. It enables us to compare the mother's definition of her disciplinarian role in its normative form with her behavior as a disciplinarian, because we can view the disciplinarian function as related, on the one hand, to the normative structure, and on the other, to behavior.

Incorporating the concept of function into the definition of the role also enables us to make cross-cultural comparisons. We can ask, "How is the disciplinarian function performed in the American family, and how is it performed within the Japanese family?" Of course we expect the role content in the form of norms and behavior to be quite different in the two cultures; and we can also expect the operation of the strain toward consistency within the total culture of the two societies to produce differences in the context of the roles.

Though roles do repeat themselves within the structure of society, they vary in the degree to which they recur in the social system. Certain roles are widely replicated, while others occur infrequently. Some are unique to a single group in the structure of the society. The replication of the same role in many different groups will, through the operation of the strain toward consistency, produce variability in the definitions of a given role. The provider role exists within a particular family structure in a particular position in that structure. But since each group structure varies slightly, as do the personalities of the individuals who perform the roles, the situations in which the family structure operates, and the interaction patterns within the particular family group, the definition of the provider role will be different for each of the families involved. In other words, while it is true that the provider role in American culture with respect to the family will contain certain more or less consistent sets of normative themes, the exact contents will vary from one family to another. There is no such thing as *"the* provider role" within the structure of society. There are only particular provider roles contained within particular family group structures. The provider role in American society is derived from a generalization about the similarities between contents of roles that exist in particular families.

It is important to realize that the provider role in American society does not operate as a guide to any behavior, and therefore, influences no action within society. Particular provider roles within particular families operate to produce the behavior of particular human beings in those exact groups. This means that the consequences of averaging or generalizing about particular roles in society to the level of the provider role has the effect of reifying society as an actor. If we refer to the provider role in society, the next logical step is to talk about the society which performs the provider role. This is obvious nonsense. It is comparable to talking about the heart of the American population, when we know that the heart of the American population pumps no blood within any organic body. It is only particular hearts that beat, and particular bodies that live, within society.

Society does not hold norms, nor does it define roles. Similarly, it does not have a culture. Only individual human beings perform roles and have a culture. For this reason, we stress that the norms that act as guides to behavior are located at particular points in the structure of society; it is why we define a role as a particular set of norms that is organized around a function and performed in a *particular group* in society, instead of defining it as a set of norms organized around a function performed in a certain *type* or *class of groups* in the social system.

This is not to underrate the importance of the similarities that exist within the contents of roles contained in different groups within society. It merely places society in a realistic perspective. People learn their roles from other particular individuals with whom they associate within society. A man learns to perform his provider role not from the entire society, but from a few individuals with whom he comes in contact. Similarities in role content in society are therefore evidence of an intricate network of social relationships in social systems; otherwise, similarities in the definition of a given role in one group to the definition of the same role in another group could not exist except by accident.

The Population of Role Definers and Consensus

When many people in society have the same role assigned to them, we can expect variation in both role definitions and role performances, since, among other things, they perform this role toward particular but different alter actors. For every role whose content we wish to describe, we have to consider the three classes of actors—ego actors, alter actors, tangential actors—whose normative definitions may be employed in defining role content. The ego actor is the person to whom the role is assigned for performance; the alter actor is the person toward whom the role is supposed to be performed; and tangential actors are all individuals surrounding the relationship between the ego and alter actors who have an interest in defining ego's role.

For example, in the husband-wife relationship, the husband's provider role may be defined by his wife and children (alter actors), or by his mother- and father-in-law (tangential actors). So, not only the parties involved in the provider-dependent relationship have conceptions of the norms governing the performance of the function; other actors outside of the relationship may also have definitions of the role. If we were to interview husbands, wives, and tangential actors, such as parents, children, and neighbors, about their relationships, we would find that each subject would have a conception of the norms governing the provider-dependent relationship. Given this fact, whose definition of the provider role should be used in defining the cultural structure of the family group?

Earlier we said that a norm, if learned by an actor and stored in his personality, results in an act on the part of that actor, given a certain configuration of personality, situational and interactional variables. Note that this formulation states that it is the norm of the actor who performs the act that affects his behavior, just as it is *his* personality, *his* situation, and the interaction in which *he* in involved that produce the act. It is not norms in general, nor personality in general, nor situation and interaction in general, but *particular* instances of each one of these that lead to action. Consequently, if the concept of role is used to explain the behavior of an actor, it must be *his* norms that are used in defining the role. And it also follows that the structure of a family group in terms of role definition is a matter of knowing each actor's definition of his own roles, rather than knowing how the actors define norms in common or in concert.

This does not mean that we can ignore the existence of role definers other than ego. Ego is a husband-father in a particular family. The provider role is assigned to his position in the group. He has learned and incorporated into his personality a definition of how this role is supposed to be performed. He acts on the basis of this definition in interaction with an alter actor, his wife, in a given situation. The wife, however, has absorbed a definition of her role as dependent. If the husband's behavior as provider does not conform to her definition of her rights as dependent, the interaction between ego and alter will be conflicting. Alter's definition of ego's role affects alter's behavior, but not ego's directly. Instead, it affects ego's behavior indirectly through interaction.

If we wanted to predict conflict between ego and alter, one way of making the prediction would be on the basis of knowledge of their role definitions. If ego and alter define their relationship differently, we may expect conflict or stress to arise in the relationship.

Alter's definition of ego's role affects ego's behavior through interaction. Ego's definition of his own role, however, affects his behavior through mental association processes which are keyed to interaction and to situational elements. At the same time, we have to consider the role definitions of tangential actors. A tangential actor, such as a mother-in-law, may affect ego's behavior with respect to his provider roles through either direct or indirect interaction with him. A tangential actor's role concepts can affect ego's behavior indirectly by affecting the behavior of his wife or other role definers with whom he interacts directly. It can affect him directly through interaction between ego and the tangential actor in some other context, where the tangential actor becomes an actor in an interactional relationship with ego.

Thus it becomes clear that ego's definition of his role must be the one upon which our concept of group structure is based, since effects of other role definers' ideas about the events within a group are part of interaction, rather than the cultural structure variable. This is not the same as saying that a given role may be defined in many different ways by different actors who have an interest in the performance of that role in a particular group. Instead, we are saying that a given role has but one definition, that of the ego actor. This definition may contain internal inconsistencies or ambiguities; but it is this role definition which is part of the structure of the social system, because it is this role definition which produces ego's behavior in relation to alter.

As a consequence of this point of view, we have to conclude that society has thousands upon thousands of provider roles contained within its structure, rather than a single one located in an abstract family. There is one such role for every group structure containing the provider function.

Conceiving of the structure of society in this way frees us to deal with the variables of similarity and differences among roles. We can treat the replication of a given norm within the structure of a social system in a given role as a variable, rather than a constant. We can ask ourselves such questions as, "Which role within society seems to have the highest degree of similarity in content across ego actors, and which seem to have the largest variability? Which roles in society seem to have the highest degree of agreement in definition among ego actors, alter actors, and tangential actors?" These questions, which relate to conflict and stress within the social system, cannot be answered by using a consensual approach to the definition of a role, since they do not deal with conflict and stress, or indeed with the causation of action in particular situations. Instead, they deal with action in general, and with stress and conflict in the abstract.

To sum up: the concepts of position, status, and role furnish valuable tools for analyzing the structure of social systems. They allow us to analyze and study the structure of culture and the structure of human behavior, from the level of the norm and the individual act up to the level of the group or social system, by furnishing a method of systematically classifying data on norms and on behavior. The concept of position provides us with a category for dealing with the participation of the individual actor in a single small group. It represents all the norms which apply to the behavior of an actor in one single group in the structure of society. It also furnishes, through the concept of active and latent positions, a way to classify all the behavior performed by a single actor in a single group. In other words, an active position consists of the behavior of an actor toward other actors in a single group, and all his behavior toward actors in that particular social system. This behavior is the product of interaction among the culture, the actor's personality, his situation, and his interaction with other actors. With respect to the cultural variable, the concept of position provides a category for containing all the norms which relate to that behavior.

If we took an individual's total behavior, and classified it according to group participation, we would arrive at a list of all of the social positions he occupies in society. There would be one position for every group he belongs to.

Status provides a category for classifying all the behavior expected of a given actor toward a single type of other actor in a single group. Conversely, in behavioral terms, it provides a way to categorize observations on the acts performed by one actor toward a single other actor, or class of similar other actors, within the structure of a single group. Role provides a category for classifying observations made about the behavior of actors in performing individual functions within the structure of a single group. In normative terms, it provides a way to deal with all the norms contained within the culture that call for behavior designed to produce these functions in that particular group.

These concepts are more than a classification scheme, however. Joined to a theory of behavior causation, they provide a way to explain actions at various levels of complexity. At the simplest level, they provide a way to explain individual acts of human beings. At the most complex level, they provide a theory to explain the behavior of persons in group situations in structural terms.

These concepts allow us to specify several structural dimensions which otherwise would be difficult to identify. These dimensions are: (1) the range of complementarity; (2) the span of activity; (3) the degree of replication; and (4) the population of role definers and consensus. As we develop more complex concepts based on these terms, we will be able to identify more structural dimensions.

CHAPTER 8   *THE STRUCTURE OF HUMAN GROUPS*

The group concept has been a part of sociological thought since the very beginning; nevertheless, it has been defined in many ways. There are two general classes of definitions, one generic and the other particularistic (1).

Generic definitions of groups focus on organized social interaction as the defining aspect of a group as an entity. Any social system which displays this quality, therefore, warrants the title of group; society, human communities, bureaucratic organizations, families, and dyadic relationships all may be called groups. Size and internal differentiation of structure are not part of the definition. The particularistic definition, in contrast, views the group as a building block for complex social systems. Thus, the group is by definition a small group, and organizations, communities, and societies are multigroup systems rather than groups themselves.

In this book, *social system* will be used generically to refer to organized pluralities of interacting individuals. Thus, societies, human communities, organizations, and groups are all types of social systems. The group, however, will be defined as one type of social system which is a unit in larger social systems like organizations, communities, and societies. By using this approach, we can discuss social systems in terms of their order of complexity. A group will be defined as a social system of the first order of complexity, and therefore, a first-order social system. Organizations will be defined as multigroup systems comprised of groups as units; they are therefore of second-order complexity. Human communities will be defined as third-order social systems, because they may contain organizations as parts. And finally, societies will be defined as social systems of the fourth order of complexity, since they may be comprised of a number of communities.

To do this we must define *group* in such a way that boundaries can be established, so that one group will be separable from another.

The Group as a Particular Kind of Social System

An adequate definition of the group has to do five things: state precisely the kinds of units which comprise the group; state clearly what kind or kinds of relationships exist between and among these units; include criteria for establishing the boundaries of the group as a social system; indicate how groups are linked to each other to form multigroup systems; and finally, define the effects of group structure on behavior.

A definition with two conditions meets these requirements. The first condition states the units of which groups are comprised and the relationship between them; the second condition establishes boundaries.

Condition 1: A group consists of the behavior of at least two actors who interact with each other as the occupants of two positions, each of which contains at least one role that stands in a complementary relationship to a role in the other position or positions.

This condition says that positions occupied by actors are the units that comprise the structure of a group (2). These positions are related to each other through complementary relationships, and the actors who perform the roles are related to each other through interaction. This condition, in other words, establishes the content of groups in terms of units and relationships, without establishing boundaries.

To illustrate: Mr. and Mrs. Smith occupy respectively the position of husband-father and wife-mother in a family. They have two children, Tom and Mary, who also occupy positions in that group structure. Each of these positions contains roles which stand in a complementary relationship to roles contained in the other positions. According to the first condition in our definition, it is therefore obvious that the Smiths belong to some group in common. If, however, we had no knowledge of the kinship system or previous information about family groups, we could discern eleven possible groups that are composed of these four individuals.

1. The husband-wife group
2. The brother-sister group
3. The father-son group
4. The father-daughter group
5. The mother-son group
6. The mother-daughter group

7. The father-mother-son group
8. The father-mother-daughter group
9. The father-son-daughter group
10. The mother-son-daughter group
11. The father-mother-son-daughter group

Let us say that Mr. Smith works at a machine shop where Mr. Brown is his supervisor. Thus, he interacts with Brown within the context of a system of complementary roles. Let us further consider two possible circumstances: that Mr. Brown and Mrs. Smith have never met or communicated with each other at any time; or, they see or communicate with each other frequently. Are Mr. Brown, Mr. Smith, and Mrs. Smith members of the same group? Could that group be some version of the Smith Family or of the machine shop in which the two men work?

In the case where no interaction has ever taken place between Mr. Brown and Mrs. Smith, our definition clearly furnishes the necessary criterion for stating that no group composed of these three individuals exists. Without interaction, complementary roles could never have been performed between Mr. Brown and Mrs. Smith. Therefore, we can conclude that Mr. Brown does not belong to the Smith Family, nor does Mrs. Smith belong to the machine shop.

In the second case, however, a different problem arises. Mr. Brown and Mrs. Smith interact frequently. Common sense, as well as the first condition of our definition, tells us to classify that situation as a group. Common sense also leads us to state that, even though Mr. Brown interacts with members of the Smith Family, he is not a member of that Family. Thus, we arrive at two conclusions: (1) Mr. Brown and Mr. and Mrs. Smith must be members of the same group; (2) that group cannot be the Smith Family.

But suppose we have the situation where Mr. Brown, as supervisor of the machine shop, interacts with Mr. Jones, supervisor of the welding shop in the same factory. Would Mr. Jones be a member of the machine shop because he interacts regularly with Mr. Brown, its supervisor?

Since we regard groups as real systems having precise, perceivable parts that are related in perceivable relations, we need a definition that will include the behavior of all group members within the boundaries of the group, but which will admit the behavior of no persons who cannot be classified as members. Can we exclude Mr. Brown's behavior from the Smith Family behavior system? How are we to exclude the behavior of persons who have contacts with individual members of the family in some capacity from inclusion within that group? This is not an academic problem. Every person in society has multiple group membership, and each of us is an actor who occupies positions in numerous groups within the structure of society (3), with direct associations in the context of complementary roles with a large number of people. Each actor who occupies a position in the family will occupy positions outside that family, and perform complementary roles within other groups. The kind of relationship that exists between Mr. Jones and Mr. Brown occurs daily in all our lives (4).

Condition 2: A group is composed of all individuals who occupy positions containing complementary roles to all other positions in the group structure, and includes the behavior of no individuals who do not meet this criterion.

Only   situation   eleven—father-mother-son-daughter—satisfies

Figure 8–1   The Determination of Group Boundaries

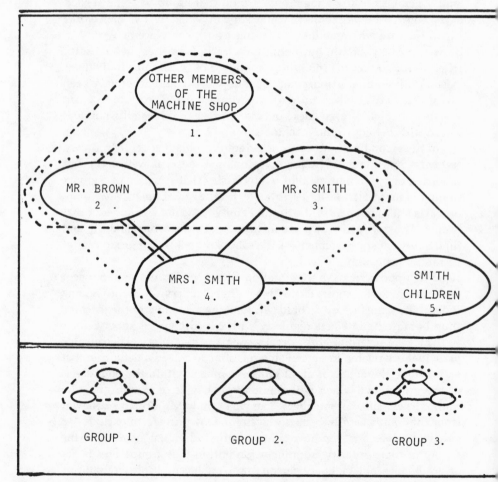

Condition 2 for the Smith Family, as well as Condition 1. Mr. and Mrs. Smith perform complementary roles toward each other and toward their children, and the children perform complementary roles toward each other, and their parents. Any other situation would exclude the behavior of at least one person and the position he occupies.

Condition 2 also lets us take care of Mr. Brown. Mr. Brown, Mr. Smith, and Mrs. Smith all occupy positions in which they are all reciprocally related, so they meet both conditions of our definition. Mr. Brown and Mr. Smith have positions through which they are reciprocally related to other members of the machine shop. Mrs. Smith, however, does not perform roles toward these actors, and therefore cannot be included in the shop group. Condition 2 states that she must perform roles toward *every other member* of the group in order to be included, and she performs roles toward only two members of the shop group, her husband and Mr. Brown.

On the other hand, Mr. and Mrs. Smith are both related reciprocally to a number of people to whom Mr. Brown has no relationship, namely, the Smith children. Thus Brown cannot be a member of the family group, since he does not stand in a direct relationship to all of the members of the group.

We must analyze the case of Mr. Brown and Mr. and Mrs. Smith further, because it is important to the study of social structure. A system of three groups exists here which is defined by three separate systems of complementary role relationships. The situation is illustrated in Figure 8-1. The first group is made up of Mr. Brown and Mr. Smith and other members of the machine shop. The second is composed of Mr. and Mrs. Smith and their children. The third is composed of Mr. and Mrs. Smith and Mr. Brown.

How do we justify positing the existence of this third group as a separate sociological entity? It is separable from the other two on the grounds of the criteria stated above; but it is also separable on an independent basis—that is, behavior performed within this group comprised of Mr. Brown and Mr. and Mrs. Smith is not entirely referable to the structure of this group and its functioning. Instead, its existence is dependent on the existence of two other different groups, and in a sense it represents an overlapping of the structures of these groups. In other words, the structure of this group depends largely on the existence of two other group structures; and the members of this third group interact in terms of their membership in those other structures. Mrs. Smith is related to Mr. Brown as the wife of Brown's co-worker, and were it not for Mr. Smith, no relationship would exist between Mrs. Smith and Mr. Brown.

Let us take another example of this type of group. Figure 8-2 shows two groups, each consisting of three persons occupying positions containing complementary roles. Suppose these two groups represent a machine shop and a welding shop in a heavy equipment factory. One of the pieces of equipment being manufactured requires both welding and machining, so that some work is done on an item by the welding shop, and then the item is turned over to the machine shop for finishing. In order for the production process to function smoothly, the supervisors of the two shops must communicate with each other, and discuss working schedules, work techniques, quality control, the flow of material, and plans to coordinate the work of the two shops. In order to accomplish these things, the two supervisors must play complementary roles toward each other.

In playing these roles, the machine shop supervisor, person 1, represents his shop and communicates for it with person 2, the supervisor of the welding shop, who acts in a similar fashion for his own work group. In other words, the machine shop supervisor's position requires him to coordinate the actions of his group with those of the welding shop group. He does this by interacting with the supervisor of that group in the context of the position he occupies outside of the shop, in an entirely different group consisting of himself and the welding shop supervisor.

Figure 8-2 indicates that persons 1 and 2 have complementary role relations. If we focus on person 1, the supervisor of the welding shop, we see that he occupies a position complementary to person 2, the supervisor of the machine shop; his position is not complementary to persons 5 and 6. Likewise, person 2 occupies a position complementary to person 1, but not to 3 and 4. Therefore, according to our definition of a group, person 1, the welding shop supervisor, cannot be a member of group 2, the machine shop. Nor can person 2, the machine shop supervisor, be a member of group 1, the welding shop. In other words, simply because the supervisor of the welding shop interacts regularly with the supervisor of the machine shop, that does not mean that he is a member of the machine shop group (5).

But since the two supervisors play complementary roles toward each other, they must occupy positions in the same group structure. The only way out of this dilemma is to conceive of a third group existing between groups 1 and 2.

A group that stands between two other groups and draws membership from each, we will call an *interstitial* group; and the groups from which its membership is drawn we will call *elemental* groups. In other words, elemental groups do not depend for their structure on the existence of a relationship to a particular other group; and interstitial groups do depend on the existence of particular other group structures for their own structure. The group comprised of Mr. and Mrs. Smith and Mr. Brown is an interstitial group that stands between the family and the work group, and draws its membership from these particular elemental groups. It exists in order to furnish a connection between these elemental groups. Similarly, the welding shop and machine shop is each an elemental group; and the interstitial group made up of the two supervisors exists in order to provide a linkage between them.

Interstitial groups thus exist to furnish structural connection between and among elemental groups. Their function in the social system is to accomplish some kind of transfer of the consequences of behavior from one group to another, or to furnish a channel through which information, orders, directions, instructions, and other inputs and outputs may flow from one group to another. Another way of putting it is to say that interstitial groups exist so that the function performed within one group can flow into another group within the social system; or, more properly, that functions performed within analytically separable groups can flow back and forth among them.

As Figure 8-3 shows, persons 1 and 2, the supervisors of the shops,

Figure 8–2   A Simple Multigroup System

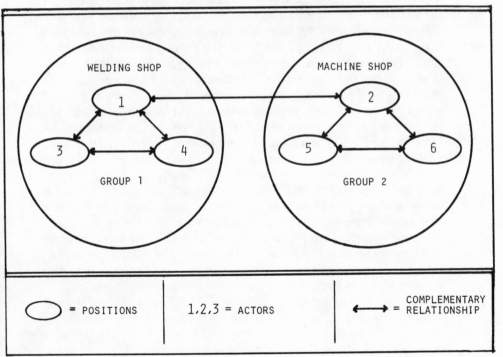

occupy positions containing complementary role relationships that are separate and distinct from those that they occupy in the welding shop and the machine shop respectively. In other words, these two actors occupy two positions each in the structure of a multigroup system: one in their shops; and the other in the group comprised of supervisors only.

Recall that we defined complementarity as a relationship between two roles, such that the performance of one implies and requires the performance of the other; and the two positions involved are occupied by different actors. Husband-wife, merchant-customer, parent-child or teacher-pupil relationships are all bilaterally complementary, or reciprocal. In each case, the two positions and the roles contained within them are occupied by different actors. Using these criteria, what can be said of the relationship shown in Figure 8-3 between positions A and B, both occupied by the welding shop supervisor in two different groups; and between C and D, both occupied by the machine shop supervisor?

These two sets of positions are related to each other; but they are each in different groups and occupied by the same actor, rather than by different actors. The existence of position A, welding shop supervisor, implies the existence of position B, a co-supervisor position outside of the welding shop; and a parallel situation exists for positions C and D. The position occupied by the welding shop supervisor in this shop thus requires behavior on the part of himself in a group outside the welding shop—that is to say, the performance of the behavior implied by position A implies the performance of behavior called for in position B. In other words, the quality of reciprocity or complementarity is present, except that in this case a single individual occupies both positions, and the positions are in the structure of two different groups. Instead of the ordinary bilateral type of complementarity or reciprocity, therefore, *reflexive complementarity* exists between the two positions (6).

We may now restate our definition of the group: *A group consists of the behavior of at least two individuals who interact with each other as occupants of two positions, each of which contains at least one role complementary to a role in every other position in the group.* By insisting that each member of the group occupy a position with a role directly related to a role in every other position in the group, we can identify group boundaries. "Directly" means that the members of a group interact with its other members without an intervening individual entering into the relationship.

In other words, groups are systems in which every person, at some time, is expected to interact directly with every other person in the group in the performance of an assigned role. He may do this in a face-to-face situation, through writing, or by electronic communication; however, the interaction is between the actors without a third person necessarily being involved. Figure 8-4 shows both direct and indirect interaction between ego and alter. Direct interaction is diagrammed in Case 1, where ego acts toward alter and alter toward ego. Indirect interaction is diagrammed in Case 2, where ego and alter both interact with a third party, X, which maintains the relationship between ego and alter. Indirect interaction is specifically excluded from the definition of a group.

Figure 8–3   A Multigroup Structure Including
Both Elemental and Interstitial Groups

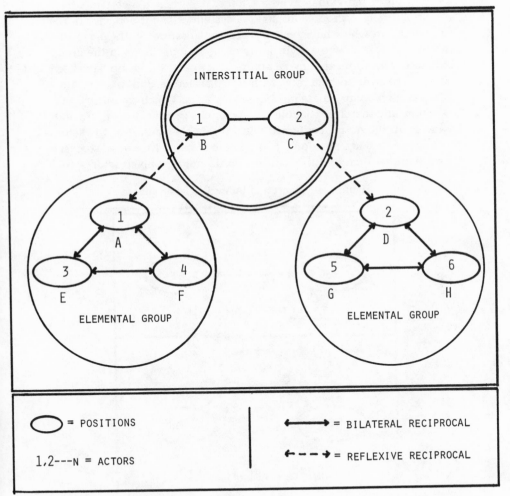

Group Structure and Group Membership

As a sociological entity, a group consists of the active or latent behavior of the actors who occupy positions in the group structure. That is to say, a group is defined by its social structure or social organization, rather than by its membership. The tendency to think of a social group as consisting of a number of specific people who are joined together by a system of social interaction is almost irresistible; but it makes more sense to conceive of a group as a system of human behavior, rather than a collection of individuals who are joined together in a certain way.

Structurally, a group consists of a system of latent behavior in the form of norms which have been learned and are stored in the personalities of individuals who are currently occupying positions in the group structure. The norms that make up the structure of the group have been allocated to positions and roles within that structure, and to the persons or actors who occupy these positions. The norms which comprise group structure, and therefore the roles and positions that make it up, are only some of all the norms contained within the personalities of the actors who are occupying positions in the group. This is true because every actor occupies many positions in many different group structures, and

Figure 8–4   Direct and Indirect Relationships

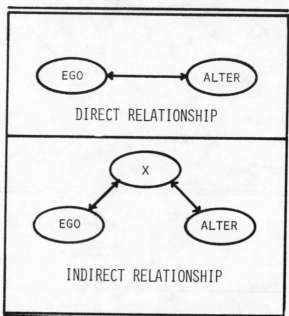

therefore has learned and incorporated into his personality many systems of norms that define roles in these different groups. Therefore, it is proper to say that the entire actor or the whole personality of the individual does not belong to the group. Instead, only a portion of the personality of the individual can be legitimately viewed in association with group structure: namely, that portion of the individual that contains the norms which define the roles assigned to the position that person occupies in that particular group.

When we speak of groups in terms of their structure, therefore, we must conclude that their structure is contained within the personalities of individuals. In this sense, a group is a latent structure or a latent behavior system. In the sense of real behavior, a group consists of a system of actions performed by actors toward each other in the context of a set of roles that they perform toward each other. Again, it must be said that the actions that make up a group form only a part of the total actions performed by any given individual in society, because other parts of each individual's actions are performed in other groups within the structure of the society to which they belong. A given group therefore consists of parts of the behavior of actors, rather than all of the behavior of the given actors; and a group consists of parts of individuals, rather than total individuals.

The part of the individual that belongs to the group as a behaving entity is the behavior performed by that individual in relation to other actors who occupy positions within that group structure. Here groups consist of part of the behavior of people; in a sense they consist of parts of people, rather than total individuals. In other words, the Jones Family, as a latent group, consists of the learned roles which have been incorporated into the personalities of Mr. and Mrs. Jones and their children, Tom and Jane. These roles define the kind of behavior assigned to each member of the group. When the membership of the group is dispersed, and no two individuals within assigned positions in the group are interacting with each other, the group is in a latent state: it consists of learned behavior patterns stored as expectations in the personalities of actors who occupy positions within the group structure. Mr. Jones' father-husband roles are stored within his personality when he is at the office interacting with his secretary. Since these roles comprise only part of the repertoire of roles which he has learned to perform in society, therefore only part of Mr. Jones as an actor, even in the latent state, can be said to belong to his family. Other parts of his personality contain other roles which have been learned, and which are, structurally, parts of totally different groups. These behaviors do not belong to the family group, but to other groups within the structure of society. If the family consists of only part of the behavior of actors, its membership consists of parts of actors rather than total actors. Other parts of individuals belong to other groups, both behaviorally and normatively.

Our point here is that groups are action systems, made up of action rather than people. Social action occurs in two phases: latent and active. In the latent phase, social action consists of norms stored in the personalities of the individual, and associated with certain stimuli which act as cues to activate the stored-up norms to influence behavior. In the active state, action consists of acts, or real observable behavior.

If we conceive of groups as action systems, we can say they exist when no members of the group are performing behavior toward each other, and instead are performing actions in other systems within the structure of society. Active and latent groups, or active and latent behavior or actions are necessary concepts, because no group within the structure of society is ever constantly in the state of activity, with its members performing behavior toward each other all the time. Although the family is a group whose individuals spend a large amount of their time interacting with other members, there are nevertheless periods of time during which no two members of the family are in interaction with each other. It is ridiculous to say that the Jones Family ceases to exist as a part of the structure of society when no two of its members are interacting with each other, or is recreated each time the members come back together.

Furthermore, if we define groups as systems of action, rather than as systems of individuals, we can deal both with continuity through time and with social change. Consider, for example, a sociology department at a state university. Let us say it was created in 1930, when four people were hired as professors. These four individuals assumed positions within the structure of a group called the Sociology Department, and in this group they had a system of roles which they performed toward each other. Other groups formed around this group—the various classes in sociology. As time went on, other teachers were added to the department, the first four members left, and by 1950 not one of the original professors in the department was still in it, all having either retired or taken jobs elsewhere. New members occupied positions in the structure of an expanded group of twelve individuals. The question arises: "Is the Sociology Department at State University in 1950 a continuation of the same group which was first formed in 1930, or is it a totally different group?" Or, to put it another way: "Is the Sociology Department of 1950 the same group which has undergone change and modification over a period of twenty years; or is it a different group from the one that existed before?"

If we were to define the group in terms of its membership, we would have to say that we are dealing with a totally different group—not one which has undergone change, but a different group from that which had existed before, since there are no individuals left in 1950 who occupied positions in that same group in 1930. As a matter of fact, if we define groups by their membership, we have to say that each time a member changes, another and different group exists. This is quite different from saying that the same group has undergone change: for if groups are defined by their members, and the membership changes, we are not seeing the same group change over time, but instead we are dealing with several different groups, and no concept of transition between periods is possible.

It seems obvious that, in order to deal with the facts of continuity of organizations and communities over time under conditions of change, we have to conceive of a group as growing or shrinking in size, and being elaborated or simplified in structure through processes of social change. Our point of view is that the Sociology Department in 1930 and the Sociology Department in 1950 at State University is the same group entity that has undergone a series of changes. For in order to be able to conceive of change, we have to conceive of an entity which exists through time, and upon which change is wrought. That is why we do not conceive of groups in terms of their membership. It is obvious that human beings as actors are perishable. They are born, reared, participate in society, and die—yet society goes on. The State University was founded a hundred years before the Sociology Department was added to its structure, and nobody who had been a member of the system when it was first founded was still alive when the Sociology Department came into existence. But the University was still there.

Action systems, therefore, persist through time, even though members change. The Sociology Department at State University remains the same group as long as it occupies the same place in the structure of the system that it occupied to begin with, and performs the same functions within that system. It is also the same group if an unbroken chain of action has persisted throughout its entire period of existence, from past to present. New members assume positions formerly occupied by old members, and engage in actions which perform the same functions in the system as those performed by the old actors. The system continues to function and operate, even though the same actions or actions performing the same functions are performed by a variety of individuals. Thus society persists past the lifetime of a given individual, and survives changes in personnel.

The definition of a group thus may be refined further. We have already said that a group consists of the behavior of at least two individuals who interact with each other as the occupants of two positions, each of which contains at least one role complementary to a role in every other position in the group structure. Now let us add: *In contrast to the group itself, the group structure consists of part of the norms learned by at least two individuals, which define the roles assigned to two positions that these individuals occupy in the structure of the group. Even though the position occupants may change, the group may remain as an entity of the particular social system.* That is to say, group structure is the latent group, and group behavior is the group itself. In other words, the structure of the group is the group in a latent state. The behavior of members toward each other, which we have defined as the organization of the group, is in effect what we observe as the group in the real world.

Three Common Fallacies in Identifying Groups

Three errors are often made in defining the boundaries of groups. The first may be called the *territorial error,* the second the *membership error,* and the third the *temporal error.*

The territorial error assumes that all behavior that takes place within the territory commonly occupied by a given group belongs to the structure of that group; for example, that all behavior that takes place within a given household is family behavior. This assumption is clearly wrong. Mr. and Mrs. Jones may invite Mr. and Mrs. Smith over for an evening of bridge. We may observe these four individuals playing—Mr. Jones has won the bid, Mrs. Jones is acting as dummy, and the Smiths are playing against them. Their behavior takes place within the Jones household, but we cannot assume that this foursome is a family group; nor is it a group comprised of two families. Instead, it is a game-playing group whose roles and positions are defined by the rules of bridge. These rules are not built into the family structure in the form of norms which define roles. Therefore, they do not belong to the structure of the family. It just happens that two husbands and wives are performing roles within the bridge game. Mr. Jones therefore occupies two positions with respect to his wife: one as husband, which is in a state of latency, and the other as bridge partner, in an active state. These positions exist in entirely different group structures.

For a second example of behavior that may occur within a household, but which is not family behavior, we may cite the situation in which Mrs. Jones is at home, and her neighbors, Mrs. Brown and Mrs. Smith, come over to visit her. They sit in the kitchen drinking coffee, and discussing various matters of interest in the community. This behavior takes place within the Jones household, but again cannot be classified as family behavior. Instead, it constitutes a different group—

a friendship clique, or neighborhood group in which the three women play a different set of roles from those they play in their own families.

The territorial error can be illustrated further using a factory setting. If we assume that all of the behavior that takes place within the confines of a given factory, for example, the Ajax Black Box Company, is part of the Black Box Company as an organization—that is, all the behavior performed by people who work in that factory while they are at work is part of the social organization of that particular plant—we are again making the territorial error. This mistake was made in the Hawthorne studies of the General Electric Plant, in which so-called informal organization was first pointed out (7). The assumption was made that any behavior performed by men or women working in the bank-wiring room was behavior which must somehow be a part of the social organization of the plant. The "recreational activities" on the part of the men or women working in the bank-wiring room were therefore necessarily considered to be a part of the social organization of the bank-wiring group. Since this activity did not conform to the expectations of either management or the observers, they called it "informal organization," and they assumed that informal and formal organization were combined to define the structure of a single group or system of groups that made up the organization.

But this same observation may be interpreted differently. Behavior may be related to a totally different system of action which, although it occurs inside a factory, has only coincidental relationship to its work activities. For example, a father and son who work in the same plant may eat lunch together, at which time they act toward each other as father and son—that is, as members of a family group whose headquarters are located in a given household many miles away. Their behavior is not part of the social organization of the factory. We may conclude, therefore, that the behavior which goes into making up a given group is not confined to a given territory. It takes place in social space in a given location; but in physical space it may be quite diffuse (8). Family behavior may occur at church, at work, in an automobile, at home, or elsewhere. To assume that all the behavior taking place within a given territory is related to the group which owns or dominates that territory is wrong.

The membership error is the one made when we assume that all behavior performed by two or more persons who are related to each other in a given group is necessarily a part of the structure of the same group. Thus, if we see Mr. and Mrs. Jones and their two children, Tom and Jane, interacting with each other, we tend to assume that their interaction must be a part of the family structure, since they all belong to the same family. But suppose the Jones family operates a grocery store. Mr. Jones acts as buyer and general manager; his wife and two children perform roles as cashier, delivery boy, and stock clerk. In the store we might see Mr. Jones sitting at his desk going over various papers, Mrs. Jones at the cash register checking out a customer, Tom Jones in the back of the store putting up cans of food on the shelves, and Jane Jones arranging a display in the front of the store. These behaviors constitute part of a group which we may call the grocery-store group. The individuals are performing roles within the structure of the grocery store that are quite distinct from those contained within the structure of a family. They are located in a different region in social space, and they perform functions in the larger system of social action different from the roles performed within the family.

Even though the same people belong to both groups, this group is entirely different from the family. The family group has a structure defined in terms of the positions they occupy, containing various family roles which perform certain functions in the over-all social system. In the grocery-store group, the same individuals occupy four different positions which contain a different system of roles. These roles perform entirely different functions in the social system from those contained within the family. It is possible, therefore, for the same individuals to belong to two different groups together.

Suppose one day we go into the Jones household and find Mr. and Mrs. Jones, and Tom and Jane playing bridge. They are performing roles within this game, and their positions are defined by the rules of that game. They do not constitute a family, therefore, but a bridge group, which contains a different set of roles organized into a different set of positions. As a matter of fact, it's an interesting group, in that individuals may change positions within the group while the behavior constituting the group continues. Different players act as dummy at different times, for instance; but the bridge-playing group itself persists even though persons change positions.

Suppose that during the bridge game Mr. Jones has to discipline one of his children, thereby ceasing to act out a bridge role and beginning to act out a disciplinarian role. A part of the family group temporarily becomes active, and a part of the bridge group becomes latent. Throughout an evening of bridge, we might observe a sequence of events during which family behavior is active, then latent, then active again—interspersed with active bridge behavior, latent bridge behavior, and active bridge behavior.

Similarly, in the grocery store during the course of the day, Mr. and Mrs. Jones may interact with each other not only as store manager and check-out clerk, but also as husband and wife. It is not necessary for individuals to change their location in physical space to change from occupying a position in one group to occupying a position in another. Sometimes a change in location does serve as a cue to an alter that a different role is to be enacted, but ego can go from acting as bridge partner to acting as a husband without moving from his seat at the bridge table. Ego may also move from performing behavior in one group to performing behavior in another group without changing the alter actor toward whom the behavior is being performed, as when Mr. Jones changes temporarily from being a store manager to being a husband.

So far as membership is concerned, then, several groups may be comprised of the same individuals, or two individuals may belong to several different groups together. What makes the groups different is their structure in terms of positions and roles, and their function within, and articulation with respect to, the larger system. Since we consider groups consist of action patterns rather than persons, we can conceive of the same persons performing different action patterns.

The temporal error amounts to assuming that two actions performed close to each other in time must belong to the same set of actions, or to the same group behavior. During an hour's time in the grocery store, Mr. and Mrs. Jones perform behavior in terms of their roles as store manager and checkout clerk toward each other. They also perform roles toward each other that are part of their husband-wife relationship. We cannot assume that because behaviors are performed within a short span of time, and are interspersed with each other, that they are all behavior within a single group. In actuality, the behavior of individuals as members of different groups does not take place in discrete blocks, with all actions contained within a given time span being part of a given group. Instead, a person acts for a few moments as a member of one group, then as a member of another group, and then back to the first and then to a third, and so on. During a day's time, an individual participates in many different groups, and we cannot define group behavior in terms of time span. The behavior that goes into making up a given group typically occurs in a sporadic fashion with respect to time, rather than in discrete sequential blocks of behavior (9).

The point is to think about groups in terms of behavior, rather than in terms of membership. Groups are behavior systems that are located at certain points in social space with respect to larger behavior systems. These behavior systems, called groups, perform functions within the larger system and for persons who participate in them as actors, through active and latent stages or phases. This has to be true because of the sporadic nature of the behavior that constitutes the groups as a social system. All groups have periods during which behavior is quiescent or absent, other periods during which behavior is actually occurring. We cannot account for continuity in the social system over time, given the fact that group behavior is sporadic, unless we conceive of groups passing through active and latent phases.

The location of a group in social space is a region within which group norms and behavior exist or take place; it is determined by the articulation of the group with the larger system of which it is a part. By *articulation* we mean the specific relationships that link the group to other groups in its environment. External role requirements that generate reflexive relationships, and interstitial groups define the mechanism through which a group is joined to other groups in social space; they specify the channels through which inputs and outputs are exchanged among groups.

The grocery-store group is articulated with other groups in society —food wholesalers, people who supply grocery-store equipment, banks that handle the store's money, the system of groups which constitute customers, and the system of family groups which supply employees. A particular grocery store is related to particular exact groups existing in particular exact communities, and its location in social space is determined by these relationships.

The Jones Family, on the other hand, which operates the grocery store, is located in social space according to its articulation as a family, not only with the store it operates, but also with other groups such as other families, the school, the church, the neighborhood, and so forth. It follows, therefore, that the family occupies a different region in social space than does the store, and the boundary between the family and the store is partly a function of this fact. This is a particularly useful criterion for drawing group boundaries in cases where the members of two groups are identical, for in such cases boundaries are identified not by the criterion that requires each person to perform a role toward another, but by the fact that the external relationships which join the groups to their social environment place them in different regions in social space.

CHAPTER 9

SOCIAL GROUPS AND
SOCIAL SPACE

By defining act and norm as active and latent aspects of behavior which, in combination, constitute roles, statuses, positions, and group structures, we have placed each particle of behavior at a particular location in social space. Each particle or bit of behavior may be located in one of the roles that constitute one of the positions, which in turn makes up one of the groups included in the structure of society. According to our conception, an actor can perform only one act at a time. This means that, at any given instant, an actor can be acting as a member of one, and only one, group.

Because movement in social space is independent of movement in physical space, an actor at one second may be acting as a member of one group, and at the next be acting as a member of an entirely different group located in a region of social space far removed from the first. Movement in social space only requires that the actor change the role he is performing. When he changes from performing a role in one position to performing a role in another position, he has, by definition, changed the group he is participating in, and has, as a consequence, moved from one location in social space to another.

Of course, what is true of one group member is true of all group members. This means that as two or more members of the same group interact in the context of their various complementary roles, they occupy a common region of social space. As they disperse, or cease to interact without dispersing, and when they begin to perform roles included as parts of other group structures, they have moved apart in social space; and their original group has gone into a latent state.

Each real group in society occupies a separate and distinct region of social space. No two real groups can occupy the same region of space at the same time. The location of the particular region occupied by a group is determined by the external linkage of that group to others in its structural environment. In the next chapter we will discuss multi-group systems, and locate one group in relation to another; meanwhile, there are some important questions about groups that still have to be discussed.

First, we must consider the question of whether all behavior taking place in society is group behavior, or whether there are other forms of action. So far we have built our model as if all behavior taking place in society at any given time takes place in a particular location, a specific social position, and is therefore a part of a given group. In other words, until now we have implied that all behavior is group behavior. We must examine this viewpoint carefully, and determine whether or not we need to qualify our assumptions.

Social Behavior and Social Interaction

The first point that needs to be clarified concerns the distinction between social behavior and social interaction. For the moment, let us assume that *social behavior* refers to any behavior which constitutes actions performed by a member of a group in performing one of his roles within that group. If we define social behavior this way, it becomes apparent that much of the behavior performed by actors in groups is performed in social interaction with other group members. It seems equally apparent that other behavior performed by group members is performed outside of social interaction, or in solitude by individual group members.

Insofar as an actor is performing actions that can be classified as part of his role in his position in the group, he is performing behavior in the group. We need not require that all this behavior be performed in actual social interaction with other group members.

For example, Mrs. Jones occupies the position of wife-mother in the Jones Family, and one of her roles is that of housekeeper. After her husband leaves for the office, taking the children to school on the way, Mrs. Jones is at home alone. She engages in a number of housewifely chores. She washes the breakfast dishes, makes the beds, vacuums the floors, does the laundry, and so on. All these activities are performed alone and not in interaction with other members of the family. But they are clearly part of the system of action called the Jones Family. It is true that they are performed in response to activities occurring earlier on the part of other family members, who dirtied the dishes and slept in the beds. The results of her activities will also affect the behavior of other group members at a later time. For these reasons alone we are justified in classifying them as a part of the same group action system.

It would be unwise, however, to broaden the concept of social interaction so as to include under its rubric all instances where an activity performed by one actor eventually affects the behavior of another, just as it is unwise to exclude solitary behavior performed by group members as a part of their roles. If we defined all group behavior as interaction, since we are using the system frame of reference, every actor in the same society could be regarded as interacting with every other one due to the mutual responsiveness among the parts of a system. This assumption would be valid, in the sense that interaction presumes mutual cause-effect relationships; but then we could not easily deal with stimulus-response relations among actors, and separate their direct intercommunications from the indirect effects that any kind of behavior can have on members of the social system.

In groups, actors sometimes engage in behavior toward each other in actual interaction, and at other times they perform behavior alone. This solitary behavior may perform some function in the group. For this reason it can be said that individuals who engage in solitary behavior as members of groups are performing functions for each other, even though they are not engaged in interaction. When we say people are performing behavior toward each other, or in interaction, we refer to occasions in which ego and alter are simultaneously receiving stimuli from each other and responding to them. In other words, they must actually be receiving immediate feedback in the form of responses from the alter actor to be interacting.

We must nonetheless allow for the possibility that communication occurs without interaction. For example, when people exchange letters or messages, ego cannot observe alter's response to the actual receipt of the message: the two actors have communicated, but they have not interacted. In such an instance, immediate feedback does not occur. It would not even be proper to say they *are* communicating, since while ego is preparing his message, alter may be engaged in any activity located at any point in the structure of the social system. When alter receives the message, ego may be located almost anywhere in social space. The messages cover social space; but the path the actors take through social space is another matter.

Communication, as a concept, covers more types of behavior than does social interaction. Interaction may involve communication, but some communication does not involve social interaction. This point of view is helpful in dealing with a number of troublesome matters—for instance, the flow of paper in bureaucratic organizations through which communication is carried on without interaction. We can also discuss communications inputs and outputs from groups—for example, the

daily flood of advertisements, bills, magazines, and personal mail—
without having to create a fiction that interaction is taking place even
though the persons interacting are separated and not perceiving any part
of each other's behavior.

Sociologists have customarily equated social behavior and social
interaction, and have usually said that behavior not performed in social
interaction is not essentially social in character, and therefore not a
proper concern for sociologists. This assumption has been honored more
in theoretical discussions than in substantive practice. After all, sociologists do study occupations, virtually all of which involve some behavior
performed by practitioners outside of social interaction. Plumbers work
on pipes alone, automobile mechanics tinker with engines alone, professors read and write in their offices alone. If these occupations are to be
studied by sociologists, then they will have to deal with social behavior
which is not performed in social interaction.

It begs the question to say that such behavior is really social interaction since it takes place in response to the behavior of others, and
produces future responses in others. This dodge merely weakens the
notion of social interaction. Why not simply say that sociologists study
social behavior, and are especially interested in how social interaction
affects that behavior?

Communication in Contrast to Interaction

Communication refers to behavior in which an actor, through one of
a number of means, conveys a message or a bit of information to another
actor. There may be a considerable time lapse between the sending and
receiving of the message, or, as in live television, the message may be
received immediately. The receiver of the message may or may not
respond by sending a countermessage directed toward the message
sender.

As a matter of fact, we can classify communications relationships
according to the identity and relationship between the sender and receiver of the message. For example, one form of communication is
two-way: the message sender expects and receives a response from the
person with whom he is communicating. Exchanges of letters and
memoranda, or of bills and payments, are examples of this form. In
bureaucratic organizations, one level of organization may carry on a part
of its business with another on this basis. Similarly, members of families
who are separated by physical distance may use two-way communication to keep a relationship alive. There are, of course, thousands of other
examples possible. The difference between two-way communication

and social interaction is the delay between the sending of the message, and the response of the receiver of the message in the form of a countermessage.

A second form of communication is one-way communication. A message is sent, but no response or countermessage is sought or received. Most so-called mass communication—advertising, television and radio broadcasting, newspaper and book publishing—falls into this category. In such cases, information, messages of various sorts, or stimuli in other forms are transmitted from some source to a public. In two-way communication there is always a specific alter actor toward whom the message is directed. In one-way communication there is usually a category of actors, the public, toward whom the message is directed. Through such mass communication, information input of some sort may be conveyed simultaneously to many different points in the social system; or inputs may be made into various groups, without there ever being a specific structural linkage between the communicator and the person receiving the communication.

What is the social structure of mass communications? Can we conceive of the sender and receiver of mass communication as occupying positions and playing roles while they are engaged in such communication? What groups are the positions and roles located in? Do the positions and roles bear any sort of relationship to one another that is in any way complementary?

The sender of a mass communications message can certainly be said to occupy a position, and play some role which is a part of that position, while he is engaged in various aspects of the behavior necessary for sending the message. Television announcers and performers work as part of organizations, and within organizations as parts of work groups, as they prepare and send their messages. Teams of technicians and professionals, whose jobs are defined by the positions they occupy in groups and the roles they play, are responsible for sending the signal which reaches the public. So, at the sending end, we can analyze the structure of the groups and organizations whose output the message represents, using concepts already defined. Of course the structure of the sending system will be quite complex, and we will have to take that complexity into account, rather than speak of a single person occupying a single position called message sender.

As far as the receiving end in mass communications is concerned, though, it is much more difficult to form a conception. For example, we might observe several men reading The Wall Street Journal. One is sitting on a commuter train headed for his office, another is at home in his living room, and a third is behind his desk at the office. Where are they located in social space? What position in the structure of what group are they acting within? Suppose we observe a housewife watching an afternoon soap opera. Where will we locate her in social space?

Even if we postulated an amorphous position and role called "television viewer" or "newspaper reader," we would still be unable to locate this position in social space relative to the other groups and organizations that are parts of society. A better solution is to locate each reader or each viewer in an exact location with respect to the social system. We said above that when an actor, ego, receives a stimulus from his environment, this stimulus tends to take on meaning, and in so doing activate certain specific norms that ego has stored in his personality. These norms, along with other personality elements and elements of his situation, act as guides to his behavior. It is possible to view stimuli received from mass communication in the same way. That is, given stimuli received from reading newspapers, or viewing television, will activate certain parts of the actor's normative system. These norms will be located as parts of one or another of the roles he plays by virtue of occupying one of his positions. The person thus moves to whatever that location is in social space, and will occupy it so long as no new stimulus is received which will move him to another location.

From this point of view, mass communications may produce movement of an actor from one location in social space to another by playing upon the actor's stored, latent positions and roles and activating them.

If the reading of *The Wall Street Journal* activates norms, and, as we shall see later, calls to mind information and attitudes associated with the reader's job, it will be received by him as the occupant of that position; and the information or message will be fed into the group structure of which this position is a part. It is therefore more likely to produce future behavior in that position than in any other he occupies. If an advertisement is so structured as to activate a family role on the part of a housewife, it is received by her as the occupant of that position. An advertisement for a dishwashing detergent will move the viewer in social space into the region occupied by the set of norms associated with dishwashing. If the ad then says it will make her sexy, it moves her to the region occupied by sex-partner norms. And it may then point out a real or fictitious role conflict between the roles, and promise a resolution through the simple act of changing soaps.

To our way of thinking, then, the actor as a receiver of mass communication is located in a region of social space represented by the roles that are activated by the communication. This point of view leads us to say that the effectiveness of mass communication in eliciting a given sort of behavior is a function of the roles it activates in the public, and of the structure and content of those roles with respect to the rest of the system of which they are a part.

Audience behavior is both similar to and different from the behavior of individuals in a public. The individuals making up an audience may interact with other members of the audience, and also receive communications from a performer on the stage.

Audiences are typically comprised of a large number of small groups which become active and latent off and on during the performance. A husband and wife may attend the theater together. As they enter the theater, and before the performance begins, they act out husband-wife roles. When the performance begins they become members of an audience. They are shifted in their location in social space here and there by the stimuli they receive from the stage, and the associations they make between the stimuli and the roles they have already learned to play. They may shift back to husband-wife roles at any time. They may also be prompted to applaud or laugh or react in other ways by hearing others do the same.

This last fact demands that we conceive of a position and a set of roles which amount to a theater-patron position. This position and those roles contain the norms specifying the behavior expected toward other people in the audience—persons like ushers, ticket sellers and takers, and performers. It is therefore necessary to say that there is a large group, called an audience, in which people occupy positions and play roles. In addition to theater audiences, we also include, of course, audiences at sporting events, political rallies, banquets, professional meetings, church congregations, funerals, and weddings.

Since a group is such that all the members of a group need not be performing roles toward each other at any given moment, the fact that a person in the back of the theater does not see or interact with a person in the front is not of critical importance. The point is, that were these two people to encounter each other directly, they would know how to act, since they occupy complementary positions. In other words, in an audience situation all members of the audience occupy positions which contain complementary roles toward each other, even though, on a given occasion, they may not be called upon to play the roles toward every other member of the group.

Audiences, then, are groups in which the position occupants change so rapidly that each occupant may never have occasion to perform all of his roles toward all of the members of the group. The contents of the positions and roles will vary, depending on the type of audience, but the general form of the group will be relatively similar. In audience situations, during the time that the audience event is occurring, people may act as members of small groups, such as families or friendship cliques, and also act as members of a complicated group called a theater audience or a football crowd. Depending on the stimuli they receive, they may be moved from one location in social space to another.

Our interpretation of the location of the receivers of mass media communications is based on our conviction that thought and feeling, as well as overt action, are behavior associated with the positions people occupy. Since mass communication can produce both thought and feeling, associated with a given position and role, it seems logical to assume that it moves people to the locations in social space where such thought and feeling are relevant to overt action.

Solitary Positions

Are there any social positions or roles that are detached from groups, and in effect represent one-person groups?

Let us consider a husband and wife, Mr. and Mrs. Smith, who have no children. The structure of this family group consists of two positions which contain husband-wife complementary roles, and it seems beyond question that the Smith Family is a two-person group. Now let us suppose that Mrs. Smith dies, and her husband for a time stays in the same place, keeping house for himself. Can we say that he occupies a position in the structure of society which is no longer a part of any group? Obviously the roles of husband can no longer be active, since to be active they must be performed toward an alter actor called a wife. It must follow therefore that the husband position is in a latent state, at best; and since the wife position, which was formerly a part of the family group structure, is no longer occupied by a living actor, the group itself is latent.

When Mr. Smith keeps house for himself, he does some things which are similar to his behaviors before he was widowed. But he also cooks his own food, cleans the house, and shops, which his wife used to do. He has, in other words, taken up some of the roles formerly performed for him by his wife and is now performing them himself.

His behavior may be seen as a set of roles. This set of roles depends upon inputs from outside, such as groceries from the store, and produces outputs for groups outside, so it can be viewed as a social position that contains only roles performed toward the self and toward objects. This cannot be called a one-person group, however, because groups consist of two or more positions. We have to conclude, therefore, that some social positions are not parts of groups at all; otherwise we could not locate all of the behavior of actors in social space.

Physical Locomotion

People occupy multiple positions in society, and, as we have said, move about in social space, activating first one and then another of these positions. Physical space frequently bears a rough relationship to social space, for a person may have to cover physical distance to move in social space. Mr. Jones must leave home and go to his office to perform some of the behavior associated with his job. The question is, how shall we treat the physical transfer? What position or positions in social space does Mr. Jones occupy while he is driving his automobile to his office?

As we follow him on to the highway, we can observe men driving trucks with the names of various business firms. These men are most likely playing one of the roles associated with their occupations, and therefore acting as members of a work group or organization as they drive—that is to say, their behavior takes place within the position they occupy in that group.

We can also see buses loaded with passengers. What are the spatial locations of driver and passengers with respect to the social system? The answer would be similar to the one for an audience. There is a group which is comprised of the driver and his passengers, and this group involves a set of positions and roles that defines the relationship of the persons in the bus to each other. However, each person on the bus occupies a number of positions in society other than the one he occupies in that group. A husband and wife, or a mother and child, may be traveling together; and at any given moment their family roles may be active and their roles as passengers latent. Or a student may be on the bus who is reading his textbook and studying for an examination. One of his student roles is active, and his roles as passenger are latent. The bus driver may be playing a role toward the passengers. But at any given moment, he may change to behavior involving the bus, and thereby be located in a position as an employee of the bus company, in a work group to which the passengers do not belong.

In other words, movement in physical space may be accompanied by somewhat independent movements in social space. We would commit the territorial fallacy if we assumed that all of the behavior taking place in the bus is part of the behavior system of one, and only one, group. There is a position called passenger; but passengers may perform other behavior while in transit.

Deciding how to deal with Harry Jones, who is driving along the highway alone but headed for his office, is more difficult. Shall we include his behavior as part of that belonging to his work group; or shall we posit the existence of a separate position called motorist? There is a good deal to be said for both points of view. There are norms which regulate driving a car, which specify how drivers will act toward other drivers, the police, hitchhikers, ambulances, school buses, and so on. It can be argued, therefore, that there are roles which define the position of driver with respect to others who occupy, at least temporarily, alter positions.

But while driving, Harry may be planning his day's office activities. This would place him in a work group position, and not in that of motorist. He might also be driving a car with other people in it; if these other people work with him, he is therefore performing work group behavior. Actually, while traveling along the highway, he may shift the position he is actively performing any number of times.

In order to decide how to treat Harry's behavior, we have to examine fully the content of the behavior, and allocate that part of it which belongs to each of several positions to those positions. At the same time, we must try to avoid assuming that all acts performed while in movement are a part of that movement behavior, or that all acts performed within the confines of a conveyance like an airplane, bus, automobile, elevator, and so forth all belong to the same behavior system.

The reader will recall that we have said that acts occur one at a time. But then, how can we say a man is driving a car and at the same time talking to his work associates or thinking about his job? Our answer is that we do not think that he actually does these things simultaneously. Instead, for a second or perhaps microsecond, he attends to his driving; then that part of his behavior shuts off and he performs behavior associated with work for a few seconds or microseconds; and then he goes back to driving the car. It may look as if the two actions are going on simultaneously, but they are not. It is our failure to allocate the parts of the behavior, acts, to their exact time location that leads us to see them as simultaneous. All of this amounts to saying that various positions and roles may turn on and off rapidly during an interval of time during which some behavior belonging in one group and some behavior belonging in another group take place.

One more question about human behavior: How shall we treat behavior performed upon the self, like grooming behavior, bathroom behavior, or dressing and undressing? Is there a position in the social structure called the "self-care" position that contains those actions a person performs on the self? The answer is that virtually all grooming behavior is a part of the groups which expect that action. That is, shaving and toothbrushing are expectations or norms for behavior in specific groups, and the behavior belongs in the structure of these groups. If a man shaves so that he can go to work looking the way he thinks he should, then that particular instance of shaving is a part of his work-group behavior. If he shaves in order to be properly groomed for a date, the shaving is part of the dating group. Thus, two acts exactly similar in content may be performed in response to norms which are parts of entirely different role definitions. The behavior in each case belongs in social space where the norms that call for it are located.

Any grooming or other self-oriented behavior which is not referable to norms in particular groups may be considered as a mere physiological function, and as such does not concern a sociologist.

Summary of Group Concept

At this point, when we have discussed in detail a number of the issues surrounding the group concept, we can summarize how our ideas differ from more traditional sociological views. The following statements outline what we think is true about groups, and also what we think is not true.

1. Groups are open social systems.
2. As systems, groups are made up of the behavior of their members.
3. The behavior of group members, which constitutes the group, constitutes only part of the total behavior of persons counted as belonging to the group.
4. The group as a behavior system exists as a part of the structure of society, even when no behavior is actually occurring within its boundaries.
5. When the group is in the latent state, and no real behavior is occurring, it exists as a set of behavior expectations that define the roles that members expect to perform toward each other. In other words, it exists as a relationship system.
6. The actors who play the roles in a group may change, and the group nevertheless persists through time.
7. Some of the behavior which makes up a part of most groups may be behavior performed by solitary individual members.
8. Some of the behavior which makes up part of a given group may occur at virtually any location in physical space, and at virtually any time—depending on the social situation present at those times and places.
9. Groups are bounded entities whose structure requires direct role relationships among all members.
10. Groups are usually parts of larger systems upon which they depend for inputs and to which they send outputs.
11. The mechanisms through which groups as open systems carry on input-output relations with their environments are extramural roles

and the reflexive relationships they create with external systems.

12. Nothing comes into a group or passes out of it except over one or more of these specific linkages.

13. The location of a group in social space is determined by examining its specific relationships to other systems in its environment.

There are certain things that we rule out as requirements for regarding a social system as a group.

1. A group does not consist of a specific set of real actors.

2. For a social system to be called a group the members need not have positive feelings toward one another; they do not have to share a set of common goals; they do not have to agree on norms; and they do not have to display any specific degree of solidarity. All of these traits are variables; they do not define essential characteristics of groups.

3. Groups cannot contain any part which is only indirectly related to any other part. Indirect relationships may exist in groups, but they are always accompanied by direct relationships.

4. An actor does not have to be aware of being a member of the group to be included within it. On the other hand, a person may act as a group member when others in the group think of him as an outsider. The boundaries of a group are established on technical grounds, not on the basis of the members' perceptions or definitions, or on the basis of cultural traditions.

5. Groups do not necessarily cease to exist when their members all change, or when they are not currently active.

6. Groups are not necessarily systems for promoting cooperation; they can be systems for carrying on controlled conflict.

We have thus defined the group concept in such a way as to permit us to use group for the smallest or simplest form of social system. In future chapters, we will treat groups as units in larger systems.

PART III
MACRO STRUCTURE OF SOCIAL SYSTEMS

CHAPTER 10   *COMPLEX ORGANIZATION*

In Chapter 8, we defined *social group* as a bounded system of interaction; and the boundaries of groups were carefully delineated, so that we could view larger systems as made up of groups. We shall call these multigroup systems, *complex systems.* Complex systems are made up of a number of groups bound together into a common structure by a network of social relationships. Such entities as universities, automobile companies, hospitals, armies, and transportation companies are examples, as are also human communities and whole societies. In other words, organizations, communities, and societies are all complex systems—structures comprised of more than a single group.

This approach raises two important problems. The first is to determine what links the groups into complex structures—that is, what structural mechanisms join individual groups, as bounded sociological entities, into larger structures which themselves have boundaries. The second problem is how to establish criteria for determining the boundaries of complex systems.

Among the many complex systems that sociologists are concerned with are: (1) organizations; (2) associations; (3) kinship systems; (4) neighborhoods; (5) communities; (6) societies; and (7) civilizations or multisocietal blocks. Each one of these sociological entities is a complex social system, but they are seldom compared with one another to see how they differ from each other structurally, or in what ways their parts are similar. As a consequence, the concepts of community, organization, and society are usually treated as separate entities, and no one tries to link them together in a consistent and systematic way.

At first glance it may look simple to differentiate among these entities. One possible way is on the basis of scale. It seems reasonable to say that social systems range in size: the small group; the organization; the community; the society; the civilization or multisocietal block. Another apparently logical way to differentiate is on the basis of content. That is, each successively larger system contains the next smaller one as a unit: organizations are comprised of groups; communities of organizations; societies of communities; and civilizations of societies.

For several reasons, the problem of differentiating between forms of complex systems is much more difficult than it appears on the surface. The first is that organizations sometimes exceed in scale the size of communities or even whole societies. Measured by the number of human beings involved, and the amount of man-hours that go into maintaining it, the amount of property it owns, or the territory it occupies, The American Telephone and Telegraph Company is much larger than many sociological entities classified as communities. For example, Bugscuffle, Georgia, Cripple Creek, Colorado, Tonopah, Nevada, or even Las Vegas are smaller, measured in these terms, than AT and T. And organizations like the Metropolitan Life Insurance Company have offices (small groups) in many communities, which means that parts of the same organization are to be found as parts of many different communities. As a consequence, it is impossible to say the entire organization is included within the boundaries of one single community. Certain organizations, such as the United States Army or Navy, even maintain communities as parts within the boundaries of an organization. This blurring of boundaries between communities and organizations also applies on the societal level. That is, some organizations are bigger than some societies. Furthermore, some communities, such as Metropolitan New York, are larger than some societies, for example, Jamaica.

Because social systems refuse to conform in either scale or content to any neat pattern, we cannot use either of these two bases to differentiate types of structures. And folk beliefs and definitions—political categories, geographic boundaries, or psychological loyalties—are also of no value, since they are over-simplified and also tend to incorporate notions of scale.

What we must do to differentiate between complex systems is to examine their structures, and see how their parts, relationships, and functions differ from each other in form or type.

Organizations and Communities as Different Types of Social Structures

Both organizations and communities are multigroup systems. Each contains a set of groups that are linked together to form the larger structural entity. What functions do organizations and communities perform as structures within the larger system called society?

The Functions of Organizations

Organizations exist for the purpose of producing particular products, or for performing particular functions within larger social systems. They are a means of accumulating, through an articulated structure, the efforts of a large number of people in the pursuit of some defined set of objectives. At one extreme these objectives may be quite concrete, and the product produced by the organization may be tangible; at the other extreme, the objectives may be quite diffuse and ill-defined, and the product intangible. Nevertheless, organizations perform the general function of accumulating, through an articulated structure, the efforts of multiple individuals in the production of some function or product (1).

As a consequence, organizations can be characterized as unifunctional systems. If we cannot see them as having only a single objective, purpose, or function to perform within society, we can think of them as being limited in the number of products or functions that they export to the larger social systems of which they are a part. Because they are limited in the functions that they perform and the products that they produce, organizations must depend on other parts of a larger social system for things that they need in order to operate. They do not, in other words, produce all of the functions necessary for their own operation, but must exist in a larger social system where other organizations and groups produce other products and functions consumed by members of the system in question.

We have already noted that some organizations are larger than some communities, and may have parts located within several communities in several societies. When we refer to the larger social systems of which organizations are a part, what the "larger social system" will be will therefore depend on what organization we are referring to. The larger social system for some organizations will be one comprised of several societies linked together to form an international social system. For small organizations, the larger system may be a relatively small community. As social systems, organizations are mechanisms through which many individuals may co-operate in producing a common output. Co-operate, here, does not imply a conscious, willing, or even deliberate effort by a set of human beings to pursue a known and well-defined common objective. Instead, it implies that the behavior performed by the various persons participating in the system is so oriented by the structure of the system, that it contributes to the production of some larger product or function being produced by the individual members. We mean, in other words, structural co-operation, rather than social psychological co-operation.

It can be said that organizations exist in order to: (1) make it possible to combine the efforts of a larger number of people in the production of a function than would be possible under the limitations of group structure; (2) or to allow the efforts of a number of people to be spread over a larger territory than would be possible, given the limitations of group structure; (3) or to combine a larger number of roles that require a greater variety of skills on the part of actors than would be possible within the limits of group structure; (4) or to accumulate the physical resources or property necessary to produce some complex function or product, which would be beyond the capabilities of a small group; (5) or to produce a product or function whose scale is larger than could be dealt with utilizing a single small group of individuals.

Groups are limited in size by the requirement that all members must act in direct relationship to all other members. According to our definition, direct social interaction must take place among all of the members of a system before they can be called a group. Indirect relationships are not enough. This means that there is a theoretical limit to the size of a group. This limitation is a function of the available time and energy, and also of geographical space. It is easy to see that a group of 100,000 individuals would be impossible, since no single human being could interact even during a whole lifetime with 100,000 other individuals. Even if it were possible, the group could not produce any function other than interaction.

If, however, indirect relationships may link the behavior of one person with another, the size of the social unit may be quite large; and these large units are organizations. They are social systems which, through indirect relationships, link together a large number of individuals into a common social system; they produce a limited number of products and functions that they exchange with other organizations and groups within the larger social system. Examples are hospitals, industrial concerns, educational organizations, military establishments, and so forth.

The Functions of Communities

In contrast to organizations, communities are structures that exist to serve the function of exchange between groups and organizations producing specialized products or functions. Organizations exist to accumulate the efforts of a large number of individuals in the production of some common function or product; communities exist to disperse or allocate the products of groups and organizations through the mechanism of exchange. Communities, therefore, are multifunctional systems, in the sense that within their boundaries many diverse functions are performed. A variety of products, services, or functions are produced within groups and organizations, and are exchanged among them through various structural linkages that constitute the structure of the community.

The cultural structure of organizations in the form of norms and role definitions has been evolved to perform the function of inducing structural co-operation among the various members of the system, so that their efforts may be added together or multiplied to produce some common output. Thus, the norms are designed, though not always consciously, to induce co-operation. In contrast to this, the norms which are characteristic of community structure are designed to facilitate exchange. The norms that define roles within the structure of the community are oriented toward controlling and mediating any conflict or competition that may arise in the process of exchange between groups and organizations that have different interests and perform different functions within the system, rather than toward inducing co-operation between them. Communities, as structures, do not function to produce a co-operative effort between or among groups and organizations in pursuit of some defined set of common objectives. Instead, they function to allow groups and organizations, that depend upon each other for things that they need for their own operation, to exist side by side in relative peace, and to obtain from each other products and functions they need.

Although structurally articulated to form a social system, communities are not systems that have objectives or produce products. It is true that some organizations within communities, such as the Chamber of Commerce, city governments, the Rotary or Kiwanis Clubs, may insist that the community set objectives for itself, and pursue certain goals. But this sort of behavior is merely an example of those organizations pursuing goals and objectives, and does not, in any way, affect the fact that communities as social systems cannot, by their nature, be regarded as systems in which members participate in order to pursue common objectives. Within communities, certain organizations may pursue objectives in the name of an entity labelled "the community"; but that does not mean that the entire community, as individuals, directs its efforts toward accomplishing some common goal. The norms of community life which define roles that people perform in relationship to each other in community settings, do not require individuals to have a set of common objectives—nor do they require wholehearted or even grudging co-operation between individuals. Communities, as structures, facilitate exchange among organizations and groups that specialize in the production of particular products. These norms are designed to allow exchange to take place, rather than to require the co-operation of individuals in the form of exchange.

Indeed, confusion between the ideas of community and organization has led to the disillusionment of many people within our society with respect to the communities they live in. They expect communities to operate as if they were organizations; and they make the mistake of thinking of the city as if it were an organization in which each person has some set of roles articulated in a structure designed to produce some kind of common output. They therefore have the notion that city government or the power structure is a kind of board of directors or executive committee for the community as a whole, and that it should somehow articulate the efforts of all the organizations and groups in the community toward some common objective.

As a matter of fact, a number of political philosophies have the objective of converting communities into organizations, or, more properly, whole societies into organizations. Both Nazism and Communism conceive of society as a giant organization in which every person has a set of roles to perform, in pursuit of some set of objectives defined by an organizational structure. In such a system, communities are not seen as being comprised of groups and organizations that exchange the products of their efforts; they are viewed as comprised of groups and organizations that are allocated functions through an organizational system, and required to furnish each other the things they need by a common organizational hierarchy. But communities, unlike organizations, have no hierarchy. There is no board of directors, chain of command, or particular articulation of roles, so that one person reports to another, or is required by the structure of the system to interact with particular other groups or individuals within the system. Communities are not even loose confederations of organizations, bound by agreements into fixed relations. Instead, they are systems comprised of autonomous organizations that negotiate an exchange in a sociological arena, where interaction is the medium through which the structure is maintained as a system. Any city with a definite hierarchy directing all of the actions that go on within the system is, by definition, an organization rather than a community.

Forms of Social Relationships

Let us now examine the structural characteristics of these two kinds of multigroup systems. Groups form parts in each system; but since organizations may transcend the boundaries of a single community, we cannot say that a community, as a system, always includes as its parts whole organizations as units. Instead, we must seek for structural differences in the relationships that exist between and among groups that form the structure.

Let us return, for a moment, to the idea of complementary roles—relationships in which the behavior required by one role is performed toward a person who responds in terms of behavior required by the other role. In this interaction, an exchange of behavior takes place such that the individuals performing the roles perform complementary functions for each other. We will use *complementary relationship* to refer to all cases in which two roles stand in such a relationship to each other. There are two types of complementarity: reciprocal relationships and conjunctive relationships. Let us see now how each relates to the concepts of community and organization.

Reciprocal Relationships

Take, for example, the Ajax Black Box Company, a small factory that manufactures black metal boxes. These boxes are containers for electrical instruments manufactured by entirely different organizations, and are sold to them for a number of different uses. Our factory consists of several work groups. On the production line the work is organized in terms of two shops, the Box Shop and the Paint Shop. The Box Shop, through the use of various tools and machinery, converts sheet metal into box-shaped objects of the proper dimensions. The Paint Shop takes the boxes after they have been fabricated by the Box Shop, and paints them black. Each shop is organized in terms of a supervisor and several workers. The workers are specialists in various parts of the process of either box-making or painting. A purchasing and supply office supports these two production groups; it buys the raw materials, tools, and equipment, and supplies whatever else is necessary to keep the organization operating. Another group exists, called the sales force, made up of salesmen who are responsible for disposing of the products of the factory in the market place. This particular organization is wholly owned by a single individual, the company president. He operates an executive or managerial office which consists of himself, his secretary, and his accountant.

As can be seen, the organization consists of five distinct groups. Each has a specialized set of functions to perform within the organization. Figure 10-1 diagrams these five groups. Within each group every

Figure 10–1   The Five Elemental Groups
Comprising the Ajax Black Box Company

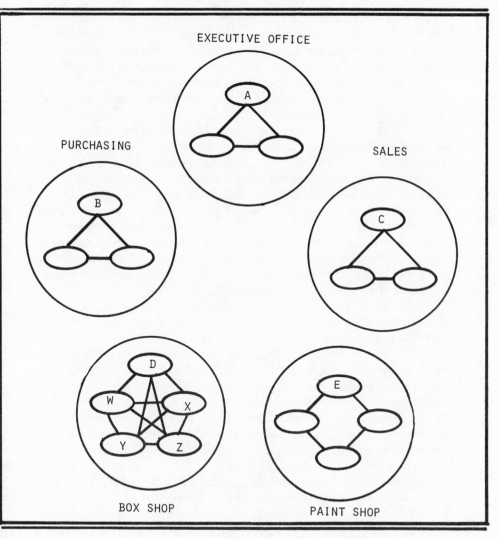

person stands in a complementary relationship to every other one through the medium of complementary roles. In each case, the normative structure of the organization calls for the persons occupying different positions within the same group to work together in producing some common product or function.

If we were to examine the relationship between positions one and two in the Box Shop, for instance, we would find that the specialized functions performed by each of these individuals are so related to each other through the structure of the group that they contribute to the accomplishment or performance of some common function—that is, directing their behavior toward producing a metal box, as yet unpainted and unsold. Members of this group are not responsible for painting the boxes, selling them, purchasing the supplies for the organization, or performing other functions assigned to other groups. Their specialized roles are designed normatively, at least, in such a way that if the actors perform the behavior expected of them, their behavior will add up to the production of a metal box.

We may say, therefore, that the various positions contain roles oriented toward producing a common function. This is shown in Figure 10-2, where two individuals occupy positions one and two. The two positions contain roles oriented toward a common function, production of metal boxes. Let us call this form of relationship *reciprocal*—meaning that the roles and the positions are oriented toward the production of a common product, or the accomplishment of a common function for the same group or organization. There are three elements that enter into this definition: the existence of positions in relationship to each other; the actors who occupy the positions; and the function involved in the relationship between the positions.

In Figure 10-2 there are two different positions containing different roles, occupied by two different actors with a single common function between them—that is, they are bilateral relationships (see Chapter 8). The behaviors of these two actors are merely specialized parts of the larger process of social action. Given sufficient time and skill, one individual could perform both sets of roles; but within the group in question, responsibilities have been allocated and a division of labor has taken place so that two different individuals are performing specialized aspects of the larger process. A single man, that is, could produce a metal box; but in this particular group, individuals perform specialized roles in the process of producing a metal box.

In order for the five groups shown in Figure 10-1 to form an organization, a relationship system must be built between and among the groups making up the system. If, in this relationship system, every position in the organization has a reciprocal role in relation to every other position in the system, then the system would constitute a single group. But in this particular factory, every person does not perform reciprocal roles toward every other person in a direct interaction. Instead, it is structured in terms of separate groups that are then linked together to form a larger structure through interstitial groups (see Chapter 8).

The five groups shown in Figure 10-1 are the elemental groups. The system of interstitial groups that joins them is diagrammed in Figure 10-3. Interstitial group Number 1, which appears at the center of the diagram, is the Management Committee. This group consists of the supervisors of each of the elemental groups which make up the factory as a system. The requirements of the Box-Shop supervisor's roles oblige him periodically to interact with the supervisors of the other groups within the organization, in order to co-ordinate the operation of his particular work group with the others; so that his position within the group contains extramural roles.

The behavior required by extramural roles cannot be performed within the elemental group in whose structure they are located, without the individual's first performing roles in other groups as a precondition to internal performance. As we pointed out earlier, extramural roles thus create a reflexive relationship between two or more positions occupied by the same actor. This is illustrated by the positions occupied by the supervisor of the Box Shop, Mr. D, in that shop and in the Management Committee—two positions occupied by the same actor in different groups. The relationship between these two positions is reflexive, since they are occupied by the same actor. Is the relationship between these

Figure 10–2   A Reciprocal Relationship

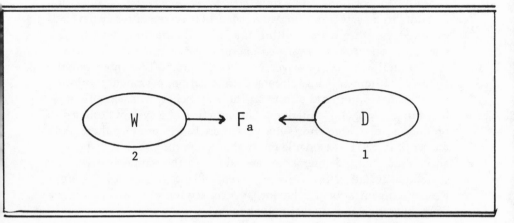

two positions, one in the Box Shop and the other in the Management Committee, reciprocal as well as reflexive?

As Mr. D changes from playing roles in the Box Shop to playing roles in the Management Committee, he changes from performing one specialized function that contributes to the production of a larger product or function, to the performance of another specialized function that contributes to the performance of the same larger function. In other words, included within the relationship system shown in Figure 10-3, there are two forms of reciprocal relationships. Within the groups, both elemental and interstitial, there are bilateral relationships. Between and among the groups, there are reflexive relationships. All these relationships, however, are reciprocal, because all of the roles contained within the structure of the system represent specialized activities designed to produce the same product. In other words, the system of roles is articulated to produce structural co-operation among the members of the system.

The larger function performed by the organization—producing black boxes for sale, so as to make a profit—is accomplished through the mechanism of specialized activities which have been allocated to group structures, and within group structures allocated to individual actors for performance. It is important to note that in actual behavior within a real Black Box Factory, real co-operation among members of the system may not exist. The structure of the system is so formed as to define roles normatively in terms of expected co-operative effort. But when real personalities engage in real interaction in real situations, actual behavior may take the form of conflict or competition; and real co-operation may not occur. The structure of the system, however, refers to its normative order in terms of the way roles are defined and allocated to positions and group structures. Structural co-operation amounts to a system of allocation, such that co-operative behavior is expected. In other words, within the cultural structure there exists a normative orientation toward co-operative effort.

Cultural structure, however, is only one variable that enters into the behavior of human beings. Interaction, situation, personality, or other variables have profound effects on the way behavior is actually organized in live, ongoing situations. The structure of a system designed to produce co-operative efforts may therefore fail to produce them. As a matter of fact, it is reasonable to say that when the variables of personality, situation, and interaction are added to the variable of cultural structure, deviation from the expected will occur most of the time. Real-life organizational behavior, as a consequence, is always a blend of co-operative and conflicting behavior.

As Figure 10-3 shows, a system of interstitial groups exists

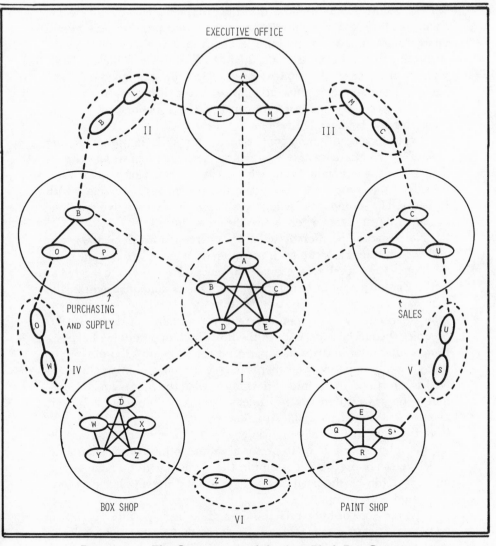

Figure 10–3 The Organization of the Ajax Black Box Company

within this single organization. There is an interstitial group between the Box Shop and the Paint Shop, for example. This interstitial group consists of a position occupied by a man from the Box Shop, Mr. Z, whose job is to take the finished metal boxes, and deliver them to Mr. S, a man in the Paint Shop, whose position puts him in charge of storing and handling the boxes on their way through the painting process. In order to do this, Mr. Z and Mr. S must interact with each other in the context of a set of roles assigned to them. This interstitial group thus accomplishes the exchange or transfer which is necessary in order to perform the functions of the two shops for the larger organizations.

Typically, organizations contain many interstitial groups, which are created by the existence of two structural mechanisms of social systems. The first is the extramural role, which requires behavior of some actor outside of the group toward members of other groups supplying it with its needs. The second is the reflexive relationship between two positions occupied by the same actor in two different groups.

Note that the position occupied by a person in his elemental group and the position he occupies in the interstitial group are two different positions. They are different in several senses. First, they are located at two different points in structural space. One is contained within the boundaries of one group, the other within the boundaries of a different group. Secondly, they contain different roles required of the actor who occupies them. The supervisor in the Box Shop, in occupying his position as supervisor in that Shop, performs roles toward subordinates. In that group, he supervises his men. He gives orders and instructions, as well as directions. In the interstitial group called the Management Committee, he has a different set of roles. Here he is the subordinate, and takes orders, directions, and instructions from other people. He does not have the right or the obligation to engage in supervisory activities, to use disciplinary action, or to perform various other functions around which roles are organized for him in the elemental group from which he came. Thirdly, the positions have entirely different alter positions connected with them.

The presence of interstitial groups and multiple positions occupied by the same actors means that we cannot say that a person who belongs to an organization always occupies one, and only one, position within that structure. He will of necessity occupy several positions in different groups within the same organization. It is possible for a man to belong to several elemental groups and several interstitial groups in the same organization, and to perform roles within each. For example, take a college professor. Each class in a given subject, such as Introductory

Sociology, constitutes a different group. It contains a professor and students who occupy positions that contain a number of roles that they perform toward each other. They are elemental groups, because they form a part of the division of labor in the structure of the university. A given professor may occupy positions in several of these groups, by teaching several classes of the same subject. He may also belong to several research teams, to committees, and to various other groups within the structure of the system, all of them elemental groups. In addition, he may occupy a series of positions in interstitial groups whose function is to join together various elemental groups in a common structure.

We need some way to refer to this situation, where the same actor occupies many positions in a single organization. We shall call it a *situs* (2). A person's situs consists of all the positions that he occupies in all the groups contained within a single organization to which he belongs. Mr. D's situs, as shown in Figure 10-3, would consist of the position he occupies in the Box Shop, and the position he occupies in the Management Committee.

Figure 10-4 is a diagram of situs structure. Some of the positions may be in elemental groups, and others in interstitial groups; but all are included within the boundaries of a single organization (3).

Conjunctive Relationships

A second form of complementary relationship is conjunctive—two positions oriented toward the performance of different classes of functions for different systems. To see what this means, let us turn our attention to the Sales Department of the Ajax Factory.

The positions occupied by salesmen contain certain extramural roles which require them to leave the confines of the factory as a social system, and to associate themselves with members of other groups or organizations who are potential customers for the product of the factory. Figure 10-5 diagrams the Sales Department of the Ajax Black Box Company and its relationship to representatives of the Acme Instrument Company, a potential customer for black boxes. It shows the Purchasing Department in the instrument company, and the Sales Department in the box company. Each of these groups is regarded as an elemental group within its respective organization. In between the two organizations an interstitial group exists, within which the salesman, Mr. C, performs his role as salesman for the Black Box Company, and tries to sell black boxes to Mr. X, a purchasing agent for the instrument company. This interstitial group belongs within the boundaries of neither company. It is comprised of representatives of each.

In performing his role as salesman, in the interstitial group, Mr. C is still performing a function for the Ajax Black Box Company. This is shown by the arrow which points back to Function 1. Similarly, Mr. X, in acting as purchasing agent for the Acme Instrument Company in the interstitial group, is still performing a function for the company he represents. This is shown by the arrow pointing back to the function he performs within the original organization. Mr. C performs his function best when he sells the largest number of black boxes at the most advan-

Figure 10–4 The Situs Concept

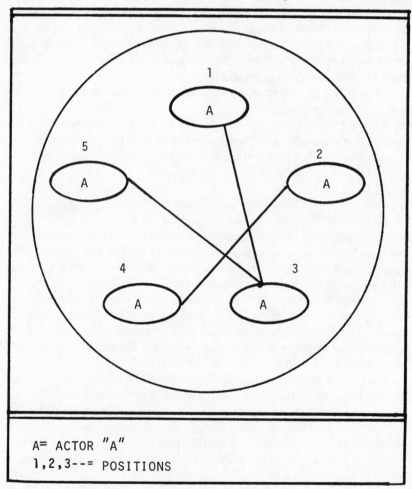

A= ACTOR "A"
1,2,3--= POSITIONS

tageous price, and under the most advantageous conditions for the Ajax Black Box Company. The Ajax Company prospers in proportion to the degree of effectiveness that Mr. C achieves in performing his role within the interstitial groups. In contrast, Mr. X performs his role best when he is able to purchase black boxes for his company at the most advantageous prices, and under the most favorable conditions for his company. What is advantageous for one company is not so for the other. Thus, the performance of Function 1 and the performance of Function 2 are not directly dependent upon each other, for if we increase the performance of Function 1, we do not also increase the performance of Function 2. Therefore, we cannot say the relationship between C and X is reciprocal, because in reciprocal relationships, the two positions serve the same function.

Also, in reciprocal relationships within organizations, there is usually a specific and precise alter for each position. That is, the supervisor of the box shop performs his role as co-supervisor toward Mr. E, the supervisor of the paint shop. It is not any old paintshop supervisor toward whom he is permitted to perform his role by the nature of the structure, but a specific one within the specific organization of which he is a part. This is not true of the relationship between a salesman and a purchasing agent. Mr. C, as salesman, may relate to a whole class of alters who act as purchasing agents or potential buyers for the product of the company. He is not structurally tied to a specific alter, but to a class of alters. Similarly, Mr. X, as purchasing agent for his company, is not structurally tied to a specific salesman for a given product. If there were only one Black Box Company making black boxes, and only one instrument company to which they could be sold, and the instrument company had to have black boxes in order to produce instruments, then structurally the two companies would exist as one organization. The performances of Functions 1 and 2 would be entirely dependent upon each other, and the relationship between C and X would be reciprocal.

The type of relationship shown in Figure 10–5 between C and X is *conjunctive*. A conjunctive relationship exists when two positions, and the actors who perform the roles contained within them, interact with each other in order to perform functions for two entirely separate organizations, and when these functions are structurally independent of each other—one position performs Function 1, and the other position performs Function 2. Such relationships are potential sources of conflict and competition within society. The actors who occupy the positions and perform the roles are oriented toward separate and distinct functions, which may be in conflict; for sometimes one function may be accomplished best when the accomplishment of the other is lowered, rather than increased. The salesman performs best when he receives the highest price for his product, while the purchasing agent performs best

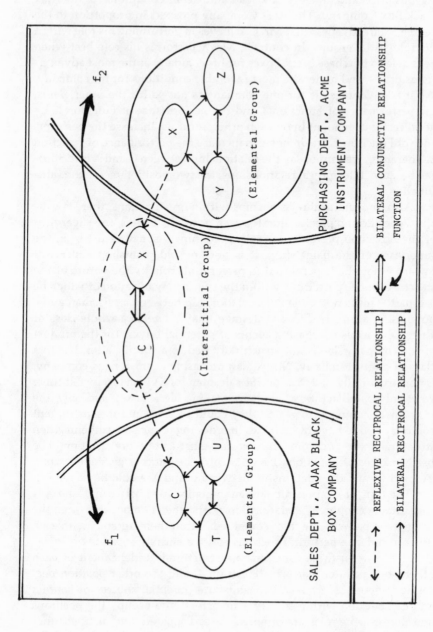

Figure 10–5 The Relationship Between Organizations

when he can buy the product for the lowest price.

In other words, a conjunctive relationship exists when the role performance of one actor contributes to the maintenance and operation of one system, whose functions are separate from those performed by the representatives of another system with whom the actor interacts. Figure 10-6 contrasts conjunctive and reciprocal relationships for different actors. In reciprocal relationships, actors A and B occupy two positions, 1 and 2, whose roles are oriented toward the performance of a common function. Such relationships exist within the boundaries of organizations inside both elemental and interstitial groups. Conjunctive relationships exist when two actors, A and B, occupy two positions, 1 and 2, but the two positions perform functions for different systems— position one performing function 1, and position two performing function 2. Both the relationships shown in Figure 10-6 are bilateral relationships, since two different actors are involved.

Reflexive conjunctive relationships are also possible. Consider Mr. A, the president of the Black Box Company, in his position in the company, and in his position as husband and father within his family. At the Ajax Box Company, Mr. A serves as president. His roles are oriented toward performing functions for the box company. The requirements of these roles in terms of norms are oriented toward the operation and welfare of the Black Box Company as a social system. The behavior requirements fit into a system of action which maintains the Black Box Company as a functioning organization.

Figure 10–6 Bilateral Reciprocal
and Conjunctive Relationships

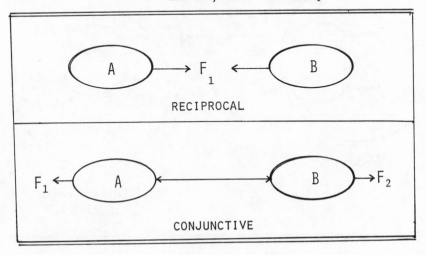

In contrast to this, the norms that define roles within the family to which Mr. A belongs are oriented toward maintaining this family unit as a functioning system through the performance of behavior within that system. Within the family, the roles are oriented toward one set of functions, of class one; in the Ajax Black Box Company, they are oriented toward a different set of functions, class two. This is illustrated in Figure 10-7.

Furthermore, what is functional for the welfare of the Black Box Company may be dysfunctional for the family and vice versa; so that an actor occupies two positions in two different groups, but the two positions contain roles oriented toward different sets of functions. When Mr. A leaves his family and enters the Black Box Company, he changes the set of functions toward which his behavior is oriented, and these two sets conflict. The roles contained within his position in the company may require him to spend large amounts of time away from home, so he neglects his family roles. Such time away may be functional for the operation of the Ajax Black Box Company, but dysfunctional for the family.

Figure 10–7   A Reflexive Conjunctive Relationship

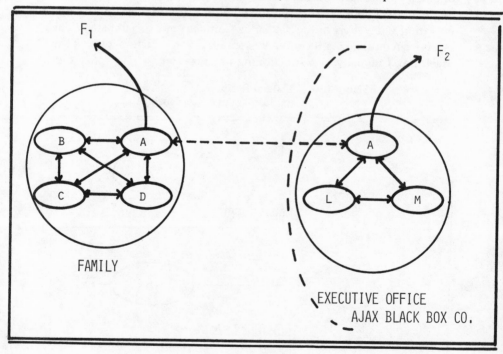

Summary of Conjunctive and Reciprocal Relationships

To recapitulate: Complementary relationships exist directly between two positions, and therefore do not require an intermediate position and actor to join them. There are two major forms of complementary relationships—reciprocal and conjunctive. A reciprocal relationship exists when the two positions are oriented toward the performance of the same class of functions for the same system. A conjunctive relationship exists when the two positions are oriented toward the performance of different classes of functions for different systems. Either of these two major forms of relationships may be bilateral or reflexive. Bilateral relationships exist when two *different* actors occupy the positions that are related to each other. Reflexive relationships exist when the *same* actor occupies both positions. All these forms of relationship are shown in Figure 10-8.

Bilateral reciprocal relationships exist within the boundaries of organizations, and necessarily, therefore, within the boundaries of groups contained in organizations. In contrast, bilateral conjunctive

Figure 10–8   Conjunctive and Reciprocal Relationships:
Bilateral and Reflexive

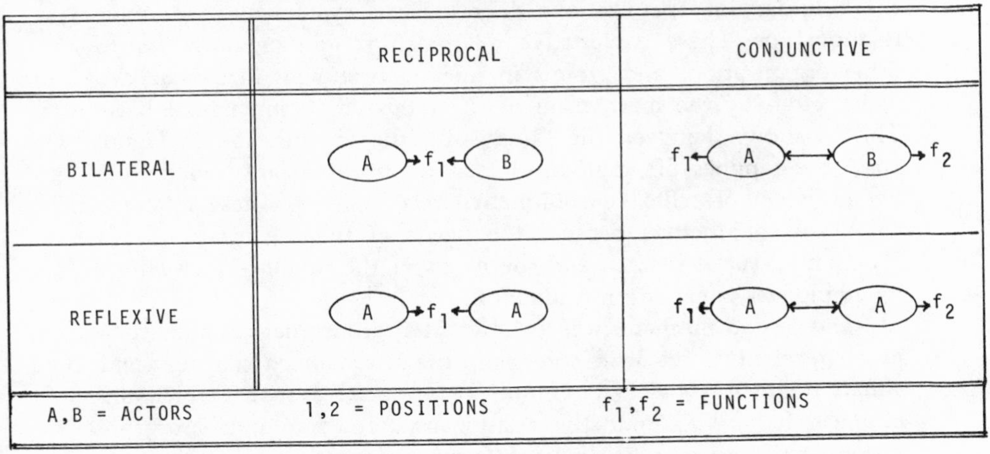

	RECIPROCAL	CONJUNCTIVE
BILATERAL	(A) →f$_1$← (B)	f$_1$← (A) ← → (B) →f$_2$
REFLEXIVE	(A) →f$_1$← (A)	f$_1$← (A) ← → (A) →f$_2$

A,B = ACTORS   1,2 = POSITIONS   f$_1$,f$_2$ = FUNCTIONS relationships exist only in interstitial groups which stand between the boundaries of organizations. Reflexive relationships always join two groups to each other through sharing a common position occupant. Bilateral relationships always exist within the boundaries of a group. Bilateral relationships obviously imply interaction between two different actors. Reflexive relationships imply the movement of an actor in social space from performing roles within one group to performing roles within a different group. Reflexive reciprocal relationships exist between positions within the same organization. Reflexive conjunctive relationships exist between positions in different organizations.

Communities and Organizations in Contrast

We can now discern the difference between communities and organizations as social structures. Organizations are systems that contain only reciprocal relationships within their boundaries. They contain, by definition, both interstitial groups and elemental groups. Interstitial and elemental groups are joined to each other by reflexive relationships, but the reflexive relationships are always reciprocal. At the boundary of organizations there exists a system of conjunctive relationships. These conjunctive relationships join organizations to other organizations and groups in their environment in one of two ways. First, by the mechanism of the reflexive conjunctive linkage. This is shown between the family and the organization in Figure 10-7: the families of employees of an organization are bound to it by a system of reflexive conjunctive relationships. These relationships are conjunctive, because the needs of the organization as a functioning social system, and the needs of the families from which its employees come, are not identical.

The second mechanism is an interstitial group that contains conjunctive relationships at its core, as in the salesman-purchasing agent situation given above. Communities are social systems which are bound together by conjunctive relationships. In communities, organizations and groups, which have different functional interests, are required by the nature of the division of labor within society to depend upon each other. They are forced to associate structurally through interaction between and among their members. Within the structure of communities, a variety of conjunctive interstitial groups exist whose functional justification is that they permit exchange of some sort to take place among the units involved. The marketplace, and the system of structured groups that exist within it, is one such system designed to facilitate exchange; others also exist within the structure of communities. In the next two chapters, we will examine organizations and their structure in the context of reciprocal relationships; then, in Chapter 13, we will examine community structure in some detail, focusing upon conjunctive relationships as the key to community structure.

CHAPTER 11   *ORGANIZATIONS AND ASSOCIATIONS*

The Functions of Organizations and Communities

Organizations and communities differ not only in the form of the linkages among their parts, but also in the functions they perform in the larger system called society. If we examine the general functions of the two types of systems, the significance of the structural differences we have already noted will become clear.

Organizations are systems for the promotion of co-operation among small groups in the production of a common product or function. Within an organization, the division of labor amounts to the assignment of specialized functions to particular groups to be performed in a common effort to accomplish some joint mission. In organizations, therefore, the constituent groups perform specialized aspects of the same production process (1).

The internal division of labor in organizations implies obligations to co-operate for groups and for the members of groups. Members are expected to share role obligations with each other. These obligations are arranged within the organization's division of labor to accomplish some mission. This mission may be ill-defined and diffuse in character—education, public welfare, or advertising; or it may be quite concrete—the production of automobiles or rockets. Whatever the mission of an organization, and however ill-defined and diffused, group members are expected to contribute their role behavior toward its accomplishment. In contrast, the division of labor in communities implies no such obligation to co-operate in the pursuit of specific and known objectives. Instead, units in the community (most typically, organizations or parts of organizations) exchange specialized outputs with each other in the form of products, services, or functions. The exchange is expected to take place by each party on terms favorable to itself.

Obviously, in distinguishing between organizations and communities, we are making a distinction between exchange and co-operation. In this we differ from exchange theory, as developed by Homans, Blau and, Gouldner, which treats all relationships among actors as exchange (2).

Co-operation designates the function of reciprocal relationships, which is to combine individual efforts in pursuit of some common goal. *Exchange* designates the function of conjunctive relationships. Co-operation is a game in which two or more actors compete, not with each other, but as players on a team which wins or loses absolutely or relatively as a team. The game is so structured that individual players cannot play the game alone, but must combine their efforts in order to play at all. It is possible that individual players may achieve different rewards for their performance, and that within the team or organization, members may compete with one another for positions or for credit; but winning or losing is done as a team.

The conjunctive relationship between organizations produces exchange among organizations. Exchange is the game played by two or more organizations with one another. Each organization represents a team, and the teams are playing a game or series of games with each other. In all the games played between organizations, each one must obtain something from the other organization that it needs in order to stay in the competition; but the other organization or team is not obligated by the rules of the game to supply it, and must be induced to do so by receiving something it needs in exchange. The game amounts to one in which teams or organizations attempt to benefit more by the exchange than they lose in it; or, in some cases, to minimize the losses from some exchanges so that they do not offset the gains obtained from others.

An organization's employees or members stand in the same relationship to the organization as the organizations do to each other. That is, an employee, or team member, acts as a member of the team only so long as he receives in exchange for his participation something he needs for performing behavior in other parts of the society. We call this a reflexive conjunctive relationship.

As an example of a reflexive conjunctive relationship, let us take the one between the role of provider in the Jones Family and the role of employee in the Ajax Black Box Factory. The role of provider requires resources for its performance, but these resources are not produced in the family and must be obtained elsewhere. These resources, in a money economy, amount to an income. The Ajax Black Box Factory has money at its disposal, obtained from other exchanges; it therefore exchanges money for something it needs, namely, role performance within its system. Both parties to the exchange act within the exchange itself to obtain something they need from the other for something they can afford to trade.

This particular exchange takes place at the border between the family and the organization. Recall, however, that the actor, Mr. Jones, occupies a system of positions within the organization that places him in work groups with others with whom he does not actually exchange money for services. These positions in these groups involve him in reciprocal relationships as a member of a team, and he is expected to act out roles as a team member so long as he accepts membership in the groups.

Exchanges, then, occur all around the boundaries of the organization. But within the organization, the relationships among members are structured so as to produce some output for exchange. Under conditions of complete conformity to the norms, each player on the team would perform according to his role obligations within work groups, rather than making performance contingent upon how well other persons in the group performed their roles. The exchange between an employee and the organization would take place within the context of the relationship between his position as a family member and his position as an employee, not between his position in a work group and that of alter actors within his work group.

Exchange theory takes a different view. Essentially, it addresses itself not to the problems of how organizations and communities are put together as systems, nor how they function in producing outputs, but how individuals interact in small groups regardless of their structure or place in the social system (3). Exchange theory views social relationships as a common game in which the players accumulate credit, and exchange it for compliance to their expectations. It is an interpersonal game which involves more than the structure of the system; and interaction itself is an exchange.

But exchange theory does not take into account the fact that exchanges of the sort discussed by Blau take place in the context of different structural relationships (4). Exchange-theory type exchanges may take place within both reciprocal and conjunctive relationships. When they take place within reciprocal relationships, the strategies employed will necessarily be different from those taking place in conjunctive relationships. Specifically, Blau-type exchanges in reciprocal relationships will be influenced by the structure of the role system in which they take place, and will ultimately be limited by the fact that they must produce some level of co-operation to persist. To order conjunctive relationships, the exchanges of the Blau sort must, in the long run, produce the function of obtaining some benefit for the organizations represented by the parties to the interactional exchange, not only for the actors involved in the interaction, but also for the systems they represent. Not only must something pass back and forth among actors in interpersonal exchanges in order to sustain conjunctive type social interaction; something must also pass back and forth through the medium of the actors' relationships between the systems they represent. Thus the type of interactional transaction called exchange by the exchange theorists may operate to sustain both co-operative effort in groups and conjunctive exchanges among them.

Reciprocal and Conjunctive Relationships and Categories of Actors

There is another difference between reciprocal and conjunctive relationships. In reciprocal relationships, there is always a particular, exact actor who fills a particular, exact position, toward whom the role is supposed to be performed. In conjunctive relationships no such condition exists. Instead, an actor representing an organization must establish a relationship with some one of a number of possible alter actors, from whom a resource needed by the organization can be obtained. Instead of exact alter actors being required by the relationship, there is a class of potential alter actors with whom an interstitial group may be formed. This interstitial group may exist as a group for a short or long period of time, depending upon the circumstances of the exchanges that take place.

In conjunctive relationships, therefore, the interstitial groups are not permanently a part of the structure of the community system. Instead, they form and disappear, to be replaced by others containing other members, depending on circumstances. The Ajax Black Box Factory, for example, needs black paint. To get it, a conjunctive relationship must be established, at least temporarily, with a representative of a group or organization that is willing to exchange paint for something the Ajax Black Box Factory has to offer. Any number of suppliers may exist who could potentially serve the purpose. There is no built-in organizational specification that a certain group or organization must supply the paint. If this specification did exist, the Ajax Black Box Factory would, by definition, be a suborganization in a larger organization that also contains the paint manufacturing subsystem.

Reciprocal relationships are therefore specific, and conjunctive relationships are classificatory. It is the specific as opposed to the classificatory nature of the relationships that underlies the difference between co-operation and exchange, or between co-operation and the potential conflict of reciprocal and conjunctive relationships. By their structure, organizations fix the relationship system in a definite form, so that each actor owes his role performance to specific alter actors. In contrast, community structure allows for continually changing patterns of relationship among actors who represent different units within it.

In organizations, therefore, members play roles toward each other; but no fixed link between one individual and another is implied by the structure. As members of communities, people may or may not feel obligations toward abstract entities such as society, or mankind, or the community. In organizations, obligations toward specific human beings under specific sets of circumstances are implicit. Quite definite role requirements go along with membership in an organization. In communities, role obligations are contingent upon the interests of the parties involved. Co-operation among all the members of the same community is in no sense an obligation, but instead is a function of the interests of the parties to the exchange.

Organizations, in sum, are systems whose structure orients and directs the behavior of members in rather specific ways in relation to each other for the purpose of producing some common output. Any system having this characteristic is an organization, regardless of what it is called by members of society. Communities are multigroup systems or multiorganizational systems that exist to facilitate exchanges among functionally differentiated parts, each of which depends on the others, not for aid in the production of a common product or function but to supply some needed input.

Structural Co-operation

When we speak of reciprocity in organizations, and of co-operation between role players, remember that we are referring to the normative structure, rather than to the organization of real behavior in such systems. In the ideal or normative sense, structure consists of norms, role definitions, and ultimately of group structure and organizational structure. In structural co-operation, the norms of organizations imply and require co-operative effort. Actions, however, may not correspond to normative structure.

In the first place, actors almost never spend all of their time performing roles in one and only one organization. Typically, they belong to several. This means that roles within any given organization will be active only part of the time. Consequently, actors are often involved in reflexive conjunctive relationships where their loyalties are divided. For example, let us regard the kinship system for a moment as a multigroup system, or, in other words, an organization. A man may belong to a kinship system and owe certain role performances to it in pursuit of its rather diffuse and ill-defined mission. At the same time he may belong to a bureaucratic structure—for example, a factory—where certain other role obligations are owed. Since he is a member of two distinct organizations, it may be necessary for him to deviate from the expectations of one in order to fulfill the expectations of the other. Such deviance may result in a lack of co-operation or conformity to the norms of one or the other system. The behavior of the individual may deviate from what is expected, and his actions in one or the other system may produce conflict where the structure calls for co-operation.

Deviance from structural role expectations is not sufficient reason to reclassify a social system from organization to community. If all of the members of the system act as if they stand in conflicting relationships to each other, but at the same time hold norms which require co-operation, the system is still an organization. It will, however, be a system whose social organization deviates considerably from its cultural structure.

In organizations, compliance, conformity, loyalty, and obligation are characteristically part of the role expectations assigned people. In communities, in contrast, the obligations to negotiate, maneuver, bargain, and trade are characteristic. Although organizations exist within communities, behavior occurring within them is regarded as organizational behavior, and only behavior between and among organizations and independent groups is properly community behavior.

Organizational Structure

Organizations that form discrete subsystems within the total society must have identifiable boundaries, and we must be able to distinguish where one organization ends and another begins. We prefer to define organizational boundaries in functional terms, and say they are reached when we encounter a conjunctive relationship—that is, a point in the relationship chain where the behavior performed in the relationship between actors is oriented toward entirely different organizational missions or functions. Remember that organizations are systems of behavior; their structure consists of latent roles, while their organization consists of organizational behavior. Only that part of an actor's behavior which takes place in relationship to the behavior of other actors in the system belongs to the organization of that system. Similarly, only those role definitions contained within actors which define behavior appropriate to a given system belong to the structure of that system.

Organizations, then, are behavior systems that include part of the behavior of actors, in both the active and latent sense. Any behavior performed by actors within the context of the organizations's structure belongs to that organization, regardless of formal definitions and memberships, and regardless of the physical location at which it occurs. A professor of botany collecting specimens on a field trip high in the Rocky Mountains is performing a role contained within one of the positions located within the organizational structure of his university. He is acting as a member of that organization, and his behavior belongs to it, regardless of where he is in physical space. The same professor at home, writing or grading examinations, is also performing roles located within the social space of the organization, and is therefore acting as a part of it at that moment.

Boundaries, then, are not defined by physical locations which are identified with other groups, but by where the behavior which contributes to an organization in terms of roles ceases, and behavior contributing to other systems begins. Behavior taking place within the home that contributes to the university as an organization is university behavior, rather than family behavior; and it belongs to that organization rather than to a kinship organization. Similarly, behavior may occur within the territory identified with the university which is nonuniversity behavior, and belongs to a different group entirely. A professor's wife may call on him at his office, for instance; family behavior then occurs within the university's physical space. In a word, all behavior that takes place within a given territory is not necessarily identified with the group that is said to own that territory.

It is also true that persons ordinarily not defined as members of an organization by its formal rules of membership may be regarded sociologically as members of that system—the wives of faculty members, for example. A gathering at the home of Professor X, let us say, involves Professors A, B, and C, their wives, and a visitor who is being considered for a position in the organization. The party amounts to a recruiting group, performing roles for the university as a system. In these circumstances, the wives are members of the recruiting group, and their behavior is part of the organization.

Organizations frequently define groups as being outside their boundaries which sociologically are within them. Excellent examples are the independent dealership arrangements that exist between large corporations and their wholesale and retail outlets—for instance, the independent gasoline station. Uniform Oil Refining and Distribution Co., let us say, has an arrangement with various independent gasoline stations owned by independent dealers to distribute their gasoline. The idea that these gasoline stations represent independent businesses that are entirely separate from the parent organization, the refining company, is a fiction. Using our functional criteria, we can see that the managers or owners of these stations and their employees perform roles that are reciprocally related through a chain of indirect relationships to the parent company. They do not stand in a conjunctive relationship to the refinery, but in a reciprocal relationship to the company; therefore, they are within its boundaries. Sociologically, the oil refinery, and the retail distributors at the corner gas station all belong to the same complex organization within which all relationships are defined in reciprocal terms.

Types of Organizations

Two major types of organizations may be discerned in the structure of various societies: primary or folk organizations; and secondary or formal organizations. Primary organizations are "folk" organizations because they are multigroup systems that have arisen through structural evolution and social change, rather than through deliberate, rational planning. Their structures are beyond the control of members of society, in the sense that they are not easily subjected to rationalization and manipulation. There are three forms of folk organizations—kinship systems, neighborhoods, and friendship circles. Secondary organizations are rationally planned or formally organized multigroup systems that serve particular limited functions within society—bureaucracies and associations.

Even primitive societies consist of many groups that are combined into the larger system; bureaucratic organizations, however, are relatively recent social creations (5). Bureaucratically-formed social systems do not exist in the preliterate societies still extant, and presumably were absent from all earlier societies, also. Since all societies appear not to have evolved bureaucratic structures, should we therefore regard primitive societies as organizations rather than forms of community? How were such societies put together structurally? Was their structure communal, with conjunctive relationships among the constituent units; or were they systems in which reciprocity among groups produced complex systems which warrant being called organizations?

Primary Folk Organizations

Primitive societies typically contain a number of folk organizations, which are joined by systems of interrelationships into the larger system called primitive society. Kinship systems represent the most important forms of human organizations in such societies. Kinship systems are organizations that consist of a number of nuclear conjugal or consanguineal family groups bound together to form an extended kinship organization. Depending on the type of kinship system, the elemental groups which form the organization can be regarded as nuclear conjugal families, kin-based households, or consanguineal bands. It is easiest to perceive kinship systems as organizations by taking conjugal family systems as an example (6).

The elemental groups that make up conjugal family systems are nuclear conjugal families, which consist of a husband-father, wife-mother, and their offspring, whether biologically related or adopted. These nuclear families share members through a system of reflexive reciprocal relationships. For example, the father-husband in one family occupies the position of son-brother in another. The norms of kinship are such that role expectations require him to act in a reciprocal fashion, as if his family of origin and his family of procreation have a set of common interests, objectives, purposes, and so forth. He owes specific obligations to specific people in each one of these groups. Unlike conjunctive relationships, in which a person is bound not to a specific other, but to a class of alters, a person is always bound in kinship to specific people. That is to say, the father-husband in one group is son and brother to specific alters in other specific groups.

Kinship systems contain various interstitial groups that provide for exchanges among nuclear family units. The family visit in which a married son and brother takes his wife and children to visit his parents triggers the activation of an interstitial group, in which the wife acts as daughter-in-law—sister-in-law, the children as grandchildren, and the father-husband as head of that particular unit. In this interstitial group there are recognized positions that people occupy, and roles that they perform. Similar interstitial groups join the families of grown brothers and sisters to each other. In such interstitial groups, the roles of uncle, aunt, niece, and nephew form part of the structure of the group. In other words, the kinship system provides a system of interstitial relationships to join all the various elemental groups, or nuclear conjugal families, into a larger functioning social system. Within this system, people are expected to treat each other as if they stand in reciprocal relationships. They are expected to perform their roles because the roles are assigned to them along with their membership in the system. The norms do not call for negotiation and maneuver, but for co-operation, mutual aid, and assistance.

The roles which make up the structure of such a system are not defined by a set of formalized rules, rationally planned and defined; instead, they have evolved out of the long history of social relations in kin groups. Kinship structure is traditional, rather than bureaucratic. The systems can be described in terms of elemental and interstitial groups, and of reciprocal relationships. In the elemental groups, the relationships are all of the husband-wife, father-mother, son-daughters, brother-sister type (7). In interstitial groups, the relationships are implied by in-law terminology; by nephew-niece, uncle-aunt, cousin terminology; or by the *great* or *grand* prefix, as in grandfather, and great-aunt. Any group in which people perform roles other than those implied by the positions of father-husband, wife-mother, son-brother, or daughter-sister is an interstitial group.

In consanguineal systems, blood kinship rather than marriage and direct descent form the bonds; classificatory kinship titles again permit us to distinguish elemental and interstitial groups. In a matrilineal, consanguineal kinship unit, those persons called mother and aunt in a conjugal family system occupy similar positions. These positions contain similar roles with respect to alters. The elemental group that forms the basic family unit is comprised of the descendants of the women; they are all classified as brothers or sisters, and occupy similar positions. In this elemental group, husbands are outsiders. Relationships between husbands and wives occur as interstitial, rather than elemental groups. Other interstitial groups exist among consanguineal family units headed by women who are called "sisters" in conjugal family systems.

These analyses are not definitive; they merely show that kinship systems are organizations. The point is that extended families may be viewed as complex systems made up of many elemental groups joined by a system of interstitial groups—that is, that the structure of primitive as well as modern societies contain folk organizations. Furthermore, if extended families are regarded as organizations, then relationships among families are conjunctive; and the larger system, which contains many extended families joined into a network of exchange through conjunctive relationships, is a community.

Neighborhoods

Neighborhoods have been regarded, more by default than by deliberate intent, as miniature communities. We believe that neighborhoods are social systems of the organizational form. Like other organizations, they may be regarded as parts or units within the larger system called the community. As organizations, neighborhoods must stand in conjunctive relationships to other organizations in the community, and conjunctive relationships exist between individual neighborhoods. To the sociologist, neighborhoods are not geographical areas, nor pieces of physical real estate; instead, they are action systems. The units that comprise this action system are elemental groups joined by a system of interstitial groups.

In neighborhoods, the elemental groups consist of households, or nuclear family units which may correspond to households. These households or nuclear families are joined in terms of neighbor relations. Rudolf Heberle, in "The Neighborhood as a Social System," points out that the essential ingredient of neighborhood organization is a set of mutual obligations that neighbors hold with respect to each other (8). It is this set of neighborly roles that comprises the essence of neighborhood, and not commonality of residence within a given territory.

The set of obligations that defines neighbor roles to be performed between members of different households or family units are reciprocal rather than conjunctive relationships. One owes his neighbor certain role performances, and can expect from him certain role performances in return.

We have to keep in mind, though, that as far as neighborhoods are concerned, ideal structure and real behavior are not always the same. In the modern, urban American environment, persons who live next door to each other may not occupy the positions and perform the roles of neighbors with respect to each other. The residents of an apartment building may not assume the position of neighbor; as a matter of fact, they may have no social relationship whatsoever with other dwellers in the same building. This example shows clearly that the essence of neighborhood is not territoriality, but instead, the occupancy of positions that contain neighbor roles.

Though neighborhood organizations and kinship organizations have both declined in modern American society, to be replaced by other forms of social structure, our language still retains earlier usages. *Neighbor* still refers to someone who lives close by, even when he does not assume the role obligations that once were characteristic of the position. Similarly, although people describe their biological and marital relationships in the conventional terms, they often do not assume the positions and perform the roles implied by kinship terminology.

If we regard nuclear families or households as the elemental groups out of which neighborhood organizations are built, what are the interstitial groups that join them together? In real neighborhoods, children's play groups; wives who visit each other to play bridge, drink coffee, and discuss family matters; groups that entertain each other; and ceremonial groups that are involved in such occasions as marriage, birth, and death (as suggested by Heberle) are some of the interstitial groups, within which behavior solidifies nuclear families and households into a larger social system. Formalized groups, such as Neighborhood Protective or Development Associations are also interstitial groups; so are garden clubs and bridge clubs. These latter groups utilize formalized role structures in interstitial relations, rather than the folk role structures that are characteristic of children's play groups.

Americans tend to formalize folk organizations, and even kinship groups are not immune. Some kin units elect presidents and family treasurers, and hold meetings conducted according to parliamentary procedure. Such family associations are interstitial groups designed to hold together the larger system of nuclear families as an organization under urban industrial conditions.

Neighborhoods in modern American communities frequently stand in conjunctive relationships to one another. When it comes to voting behavior, bond issues, the location of schools, the issue of racial integration, busing, and zoning, the interests of various neighborhoods may diverge, and as folk organizations, they conflict. On most issues—the construction of a freeway, for instance—neighborhoods benefit or are disadvantaged differentially; so it cannot be said that what is good for the community as a whole is good for each and every constituent part of it. What benefits one neighborhood may harm another in the view of the people who live there. As a consequence, neighborhoods tend to stand in conjunctive relationships to each other rather than reciprocal ones, and the community is a system through which their various interests are mediated.

Friendship Circles

Friendship circles are folk organizations in which the essence of the roles performed is reciprocity.

The friend-relationship is distinct from neighbor or kin, although these three—plus another, the colleague or co-worker relationship—are all also based on reciprocity. As a consequence, the norms that regulate the interaction between friends, colleagues, neighbors, and kinsmen are in many respects similar, although the roles performed may differ widely. Typically, colleague relationships involve highly specialized role performances that depend on the particular work group involved, whereas the positions occupied by neighbors, kinsmen, and friends (in our society at least) share many roles. This circumstance perhaps reflects the fact that friendship relations have acquired many of the functions of kinship and neighborhood, and also that certain kinship obligations have been assumed by neighbors and friends. It is also a function of the fact that friendships are highly related to residential patterns for children and housewives, while for men, they are related to work patterns.

Friendship circles, in contrast to neighborhoods and kinship units, consist of a number of elemental friendship groups or cliques joined to each other by shared members, or by interstitial groups containing representatives from the elemental units. Elemental groups in friendship circles are often based on the occupation of the husband, and on colleague relationships at work. For example, in a given town the doctors and dentists may form a friendship circle. Various small cliques of especially congenial doctors and their families are the elemental groups out of which this larger system is comprised. Parties, country club gatherings, visits among wives, and associational patterns among children form the interstitial relations that cement a friendship circle into the larger multigroup organization. In such a system, the County Medical Society might be a group that actually functions as an interstitial link within the larger friendship circle (9).

It is likely that the upper social class, as a social organization, is in reality a system of friendship circles and kin organizations, interlocked to form a larger system. It may also prove to be true that the power structure or the establishment exists as a real functioning social system only in the form of a friendship circle. Like everything in modern urban industrial society, however, formal groups may be organized within such friendship systems to preserve them as functioning entities. Fraternities, sororities, fraternal orders, and clubs are examples.

Religious Groups

Religious cults or various occult groupings may also form folk organizations in some societies. For example, the Hopi had many secret societies of Kachina dancers and Kachina priests. Each of them formed an elemental group in the larger folk organization making up the religious life of the Hopi. Within the structure of the Hopi community a system of interstitial groups linked the various societies together. Other

American Indian societies, for example, the Cheyenne and the Sioux, had warrior societies or cults. These groups formed elemental units in a larger system which, in a sense, constituted the army of the tribe. The warrior societies were the elemental groups, and their headmen or chiefs, together in council, constituted an interstitial group which bound them all together into a folk organization.

The concept of folk organization—a traditionally organized multigroup system—thus applies equally well to both urban-industrial and preliterate societies, and is a useful tool for making crosscultural comparisons of social structure.

Bureaucracies and Associations

Bureaucracies and formal associations are multigroup systems based on the production of some limited and specialized product or service. or on the representation of some specialized interest in society. Associations and bureaucracies share the characteristic of formalized structure, in contrast to folk organizations whose structure is traditional and informal. Folk organizations may have difficulty in identifying their missions. Bureaucratic structures and associations have recognized, though sometimes ill-defined, missions to perform, normally limited and specialized in nature. It is at least partly accurate to say that bureaucratic organizations and formal associations are specialized in their functional contributions to the society as social systems, while folk organizations are usually more generalized.

A bureaucracy is defined as a functionally-differentiated organization that exists in order to produce some product, service, or function to be exchanged with other organizations or groups for things that the bureaucracy needs in order to continue to function. Associations are defined as formalized organizations whose output is primarily for their members rather than for exchange with other organizations in their environment. Archetypes of the bureaucratic organization in our society are industrial concerns—such as an automobile company—or government agencies like the Department of Agriculture. Archetypes of the association are labor unions—the AFL-CIO; or professional societies—the American Sociological Association; or political associations—the Democratic party.

Bureaucracies orient the role behavior of a number of members through a more or less well-defined structure toward the production of some product or service. This product is not necessarily utilized by the members of the system, but is exchanged with the environment for money, other goods, services, or functions. These are then either consumed by members of the system in the production of the product, or exported from the system in the form of income or property to be consumed in other organizations or groups. Bureaucratic organizations exist, in other words, to produce things that nonmembers need, which are exchanged for things that members need.

The association produces things which members themselves need or desire directly. To do this, it normally acts upon the environment and upon members in their own interests. Professional societies exist to produce something for the professional, and labor unions for the worker; but the automobile factory exists to produce automobiles meant to be utilized by other social systems.

Both associations and bureaucracies are formalized—that is, they usually have stated and written rules that are enforced through recognized structures; and they permit and utilize rationalized planning with respect to organizational procedures and structure. Within their structure, roles tend to be codified, and people are trained deliberately and formally in their requirements. The descriptions of bureaucracy given by Weber and modified by Blau present excellent descriptions of the climate of bureaucracies, and summarize the character of the norms which characterize their structures (10). We will concentrate here on the way that bureaucratic organizations structure and combine groups into the network of relationships that constitutes the organization.

CHAPTER 12

BUREAUCRATIC ORGANIZATIONS AS INPUT-OUTPUT SYSTEMS

Bureaucratic organizations are specialized in the production of some product or service that is exchanged with other social systems in their environment, and so they may be regarded as input-output systems. They assemble resources and raw materials from their environment, and employ a technology to convert these raw materials and resources into a product or service. This product or service is then exchanged for further resources and raw materials.

Technology

The technology of an organization is a system of behavior patterns that employs various tools, machines, and physical devices to convert resources and raw materials into a finished product or usable service. Technology is a man-machine system, which defines roles in terms of the use of material culture in a human relationship system. The relationship system involves the specialization of people in the performance of various roles in a process of production (1).

Technology is not simply the machine aspect of social organizations such as bureaucracies. Machines and tools are only used in relationships among human beings where they are employed in the performance of some role in a complex system of behavior. From one point of view, the so-called organizational structure of a bureaucracy is its technology. Since the organizational structures define roles in terms of the utilization of various technical devices, these physical objects or machines are part and parcel of the role definition. For example, the roles of the secretary in an office involve behavior performed on typewriters, file cabinets, telephones, recording machines, and so forth. As a consequence, social organization and technology are two different words that refer to the same thing.

Input-Output Relationships

As an input-output system, the structure of a bureaucratic organization can best be understood by separating the system of relationships that connect the organization to its environment, from the system of role relationships employed in relations within the organization. Relationships that exist at the boundaries of the organization, and connect it with its environment, perform two functions: they assemble the raw materials and resources from that environment which are necessary for internal organizational behavior; and they export its product or service to that environment in exchange. Internal relationships are organized in terms of the production of the system's product and the maintenance of the system as an operating entity.

External Organizational Relationship Systems

Figure 12-1 shows an expanded diagram of the Ajax Black Box Company, illustrating its external connections to organizations and groups in the environment, from which it receives raw materials and resources, and to which it exports its products or service. The organization's boundaries are indicated by a double line, as are the borders of other organizations or groups with which the members of the Box Company have some form of external relationship.

Exchange interstitial groups: The diagram shows that two structural devices connect the organization of the Ajax Black Box Company to groups and other organizations in its environment. The first kind of link is the interstitial group, where members of the Ajax Black Box Company interact with representatives of other groups or organizations upon which the Black Box Company depends for raw materials and resources, and with which it exchanges its output. One typical interstitial group, marked *1* in the diagram, connects the Box Company and the Bank, where Mr. A, the president of the Ajax Black Box Company interacts with a representative of the Bank. In order for Mr. A to fulfill his function as president of the Ajax Black Box Company, he is required by extramural roles to perform a number of functions external to the Box Company in relationship to the Bank—for example, to borrow money for new equipment and plant expansion. He must therefore establish a relationship with some representative of a lending agency,

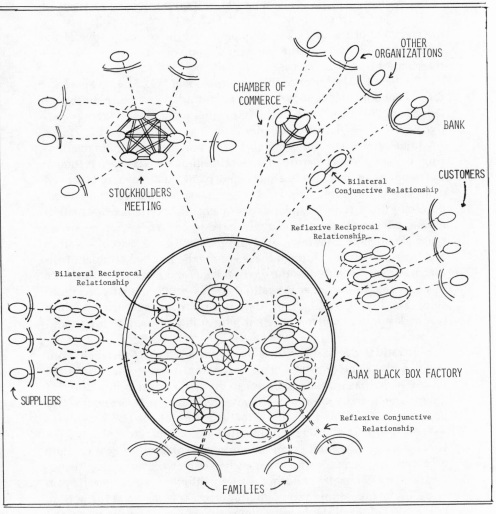

Figure 12–1 The Relationship of an Organization
to its Environment

forming with him an interstitial group. In this group, his roles require him to further the interests of the Ajax Black Box Company, and his behavior is oriented toward performing a function for it. In contrast, the representative of the bank is obligated to look out for the interests of the bank, and perform a function for it. Hence, the relationship between the president of the Black Box Company and the representative of the Bank is conjunctive, and the interstitial group created by the conjunctive relationship is an *exchange interstitial group.*

By definition, all relationships internal to an organization are reciprocal. Therefore, the boundary of the organization is drawn between the representative of the bank in the interstitial group and the representative of the Ajax Black Box factory.

Interstitial group Number 2 portrays a purchasing agent in relationship to a supplier. The structural mechanism is the same, even though the resource—which may be sheet metal, paint, equipment, or other raw material—is different. This kind of exchange relationship may occur dozens of times at the boundaries of any organization, since raw materials, supplies, and equipment might have to be obtained from a wide range of suppliers. Four interstitial groups, labeled 3, consist of salesmen and their customers. Through these groups the finished product of the organization is exported to the environment, and money is returned to it. These are also exchange interstitial groups with conjunctive relationships; and like all such groups, they furnish a channel through which feedback information from its environment flows back into the organization.

Interstitial groups all connect an organization to its social environment in the same way. A set of extramural roles exists within the organization that requires the actor to occupy a position in a different group, and thereby creates a reflexive relationship between the two positions occupied by the same actor. This second position constitutes a set of roles defined inside an interstitial group structure which has the effect, through the interaction among representatives of two or more organizations, of producing some exchange between or among them.

Direct member sharing: Another, entirely different type of mechanism also joins an organization to its environment, as is shown at the bottom of Figure 12–1. Each employee occupies two positions, one in one of the various shops, and the other in his family. In this case, no interstitial group stands between the family and the organization; instead, one person occupies a position in both. The exchange that is involved between family and organization exports income, in the form of salary or wages, from the organization into the families, in return for which the employees perform organizational functions.

Since the functions required of the individual in his roles within the organization are quite different from those required of him within the family, the relationship between the work group position and the family position is classified as conjunctive; and the boundaries of the organization are drawn between these two positions. Families are separate from the organization and are considered to be in their environments.

A kind of exchange does take place between families and organization, however. When a man comes to work in the morning, he is importing into the organization the results of his behavior when he was at home. He may be rested or tired, emotionally upset, or tranquil; he may be motivated or satiated. Organizational norms expect certain behavior of him as part of the role he plays inside their structure. Employees are expected to arrive ready to perform their roles; and the organization expects that income paid to the worker in return for his services within the organization will be spent in such a way that he is ready to work. In this sense, an exchange does take place between organizations and families, or other groups that help to support the employee's capacity to work.

In sum, two devices connect organizations with their environment. One is the interstitial group, comprised of a mixture of members from different organizations, in which some type of exchange takes place. The other device is the direct sharing of members. A person who belongs to different groups or organizations, and occupies two positions, imports into the one group things obtained from the other. Both these mechanisms depend upon extramural role relationships in the structure of an elemental group. Such extramural roles, through requiring external behavior, create a connection between a sending group—the sales department, the interstitial group of salesman and customer, or the family of the worker's; and a receiving group—the paint shop whose workers labor to fulfill some of their extramural family roles.

Coordinative interstitial groups: Two other interstitial groups are shown in Figure 12-1—the stockholders, and the Chamber of Commerce. These groups are slightly different from the others. The stockholder group consists of persons who own stock in the company, and who therefore occupy positions with certain roles that are related to those of the executive officers of the company. In the diagram, Mr. A, the president of the company, is one member of this group, along with stockholders. Stockholders own stock as individual investors, or as representatives of families, other companies, associations like professional societies, or other organizations like universities or foundations.

The interstitial group is shown on the occasion of a stockholders' meeting. The stockholders represent the group from which they come and for which they hold stock; Mr. A represents the company bureaucracy. If he also holds stock in the company his position may be both president and stockholder.

The relationships between stockholders and the president are conjunctive, on the basis of the fact that the interests of families and of different groups or organizations that hold stock in the company are structurally and functionally separate. As a consequence, the stockholders' group is an interstitial group that contains conjunctive relationships among its parts. While its members may have some over-all common interests, such as higher profits, the variety of their external interests generates disagreements and conflict. People maneuver for control, and barter for the advantage of the organizations and groups that they represent.

The Chamber of Commerce is an interstitial group comprised of representatives of various companies and interests. This group is also based on conjunctive relationships. Each organization represented by membership in the Chamber of Commerce has a different set of functional and structural interests in the community the Chamber of Commerce is supposedly promoting. The group itself is a structural device for mediating these interests, so that participating members can get things they need in exchange for things they are willing to give to others. They are expected by their organizations to represent the interests of that organization.

Both the stockholders' meetings and the Chamber of Commerce are *co-ordinative interstitial groups.* Co-ordinative interstitial groups are devoted to decision-making on issues that affect the interests of the parties involved. They co-ordinate these decisions in the interests of these groups, within which interests may vary widely. They are structures designed to control conflict in the process of pursuing such varied interests. Ordinarily, the rules that control the behavior of people in such groups specify a method for making decisions that allows the various diverse interests to express themselves. Usually the procedures take the form of voting, and specify controlled debate and discussion by means of constitutions, by-laws, and the use of Roberts Rules of Order.

Exchange interstitial groups do not exist in order to make decisions, but to accomplish a transfer of goods, services, money, information, or other valued inputs and outputs with the environment. An organization obtains its power to bargain and to influence decision-making from exchange interstitial groups. That is to say, the Black Box Factory has the power to influence decisions in the Chamber of Commerce through its president insofar as, through the exchange network of interstitial groups, it achieves a favorable balance between inputs and outputs. Similarly, it has a powerful voice in determining policies in the Chamber of Commerce if many other organizations depend on it in an exchange network for things that they need.

Organizations, then, achieve power over their environment through exchange; but their power is exercised over the environment through co-ordinative interstitial groups (2). The bank's power to induce the Black Box Factory to co-operate in Chamber of Commerce affairs comes from the exchanges within the exchange interstitial groups that the bank shares with the Box Factory. In those exchange interstitial groups, the bank can only comply with its request for funds or deny them. But this power can be translated into pressure in the Chamber of Commerce to induce the Box Factory to co-operate, let us say, in floating a municipal bond issue that the bank underwrites and benefits from. The larger the number of organizations and groups in the environment that depend upon an organization for things that they need, the greater the amount of power that organization will have in co-ordinative interstitial groups. The place of an organization or group in exchange networks will therefore determine the positions occupied by members who represent the organization in the community power structure. This statement extends to the organizational level the reasoning used by Blau in his *Exchange in Power in Social Life* (3), and by Homans in his *Elementary Forms of Social Behavior* (4).

The behavior that takes place in interstitial groups, like all social behavior, is a function of the cultural structure of the group, the personalities of individuals involved, the interaction, and situational elements. The structure of such groups, in terms of role definitions, is one among several independent variables acting upon behavior within them. This structure, like all group structures, consists of positions that contain systems of roles defined in terms of internalized norms. In conjunctive interstitial groups, these roles and norms call for the occupant of the position to represent the interests of the company or group from which he came. His membership in such groups is generated by the existence of extramural roles in positions contained within groups inside his organization. These extramural roles are also defined in terms of norms that require the role player to pursue the interest of that group.

The complementary nature of the roles between positions within such interstitial groups is structured so that interaction will take place between representatives of different functional interests, and, through the mediation of role definitions and norms, conflict will be managed. The management of conflict is necessary so that individual interests may be served in the exchange. In other words, the structure of such interstitial groups is designed to control conflict to a level that will permit exchange to take place. If extreme conflict is permitted, the exchange relationship will be destroyed; and the parties to the exchange will fail to obtain resources they need.

The structure of co-ordinative interstitial groups also consists of positions that contain various roles that people perform toward each other in complementary relationships of the conjunctive form. Such groups are structured to maintain interaction in a situation where conflict threatens to disrupt the relationship among organizations that are interdependent.

Co-ordinative interstitial group structure is not designed to induce co-operation between varying interests, but to permit varying interests to maneuver in relationship to one another without breaking off the relationship, or disrupting it through open conflict. For this reason, such groups as the Chamber of Commerce or the stockholders' meeting normally operate under a system such as the Roberts Rules of Order. These rules represent formalized ways of controlling interaction in a situation where differing interests are attempting to maneuver for advantage. An exchange interstitial group, such as that between the salesman and customer, operates under a system of contract, price, or barter; the norms of exchange are understood by the parties involved, and certain rituals are observed to avoid breaking off the relationship before the functions that it is designed to perform have been accomplished.

Another interstitial group that might have been drawn into Figure 12–1 is that between labor unions and management representatives. The bargaining session, like the board of trustees or stockholders' meeting, represents an interstitial group where the relationships between sides are conjunctive. Similar relationships also exist with employment agencies, insurance companies, management consulting firms, and so forth.

In a complex society such as ours, a bureaucratic organization is normally surrounded by an intricate system of exchange interstitial groups, co-ordinative interstitial groups, and by groups with which it directly shares membership. Thompson, in his *Organizations in Action* (5), discusses the kind of things that organizations pursue in some of these interstitial groups at their boundaries. He suggests that in exchange interstitial groups, organizations attempt to obtain control over the supply of raw materials and other factors of production, so that internal organizational functioning can be made rational and predictable. Insofar as the exchanges which occur with the environment in conjunctive interstitial groups yield predictable results, the organization will be satisfied with maintaining this relationship to its environment. When, however, in such exchanges, the organization loses predictability, it will attempt to incorporate organizations in its environment into its own structure to render its operation more predictable. For example, as long as the organization can obtain supplies from its environment through conjunctive interstitial relations in a predictable fashion which satisfies the needs of internal functioning, it will probably not extend its boundaries in that direction. When, however, the source of supply becomes unpredictable, and disrupts the internal functioning of the organization due to the maneuvering of the supplier to gain advantage, the organization will reach out into its environment and attempt to incorporate the supplier into the organization in a system of reciprocal relationships.

Only if the entire society were made into a single organization, could there be no exchanges between organizations and other social systems in their environment. Extending organizational boundaries to include suppliers merely means pushing the need to relate to an environment one step back; for a new set of conjunctive relationships is encountered at the new boundary of the organization. Unless the entire society is encompassed, there will always be a system of conjunctive relationships at the boundary of each organization. This means that organizations are always subject to some degree of nonpredictability, and internal structure must always be so designed as to take this into account.

External co-ordinative interstitial groups are mechanisms through which organizations attempt to make conditions in the environment favorable to its internal functioning, and to its exchange with that environment. In Thompson's terms, external co-ordinative interstitial groups are avenues through which organizations obtain a measure of control over their environment. They are frequently used to manipulate the external situation—for example, by influencing highway construction, the production of water systems, and so forth. They are also used to gain control over the normative structure of other organizations, particularly government, by influencing laws, taxation, elections, and the selection of candidates. In other words, organizations attempt to influence politics and government, if and when the actions of government make the internal functioning of the organization unpredictable, and reduce the possibility of rationality within it. To achieve this influence, organizations participate through representatives in co-ordinative interstitial groups in the communities to which they belong.

Organizations and Communities as Systems of Small Groups

All behavior within organizations and between organizations takes place in small groups. These groups are either elemental or interstitial groups, and are either internal to the organization, or external and located in the interstices between two organizations. There is no such thing as organizational behavior which is not at the same time small group behavior. If, then, we understand the functioning of small groups, and can systematically relate it to organizational structure, we can deal with the problem of organizational behavior more effectively.

According to our point of view, all behavior in small groups is a function of four variables interacting with each other—the cultural structural variable, the situational variable, the social interaction variable, and the personality variable. The cultural structure variable consists of the role definitions that are assigned to positions in the structure of the group, and internalized by members of that group. They influence the behavior of individuals through being converted from latent roles, which have been learned, to active roles which are enacted through the process of interaction between specific personalities in a situation. In other words, social interaction, in a situation between real actors with real personalities, triggers role definitions in the form of normative expectations, and along with these other elements produces the behavior that takes place within these small groups.

It stands to reason, that to change the behavior in any one small group, one must manipulate one or the other of the four variables—for example, change the personalities of individuals and maintain the same role definitions, situations, and interaction patterns; or change role definitions, and maintain the same personality, situation, and interactional characteristics.

The personality variable, which will be discussed in some detail in Chapter 16, imports into one group the influences of behavior which occurs in other groups. This was illustrated above in relation to the family that shares a member with a work group. Its output—the results of behavior within the family—is registered in the personality of the individual; and when he goes to his work group, he brings it with him. Therefore, behavior taking place within the family has an indirect effect on behavior taking place within the work group. Individuals who occupy positions in different organizations, and therefore occupy positions that stand in a conjunctive relationship with each other, are subject to various kinds of role conflicts which stem from the divergence of structural and functional interests between the two separate groups or organizations to which they belong. The effects of these conflicts are also felt in small groups within the organization. In summary, it can be said that all behavior taking place within different, somehow related small groups may indirectly affect each other.

Internal Relations in Bureaucratic Organizations

The groups constituting parts of the internal structure of organizations are also joined together by a network of interstitial group relations. This was illustrated in Figure 12-1, where the elemental groups of the

Black Box Factory are shown as the executive office, purchasing department, sales department, box shop, and paint shop. Between each of these groups there is at least one interstitial group which joins it to other groups in the structure of the system. It is important to realize that this single interstitial group is meant to represent a potential network of relations which might exist between two elemental groups. In other words, several such interstitial groups in empirical organizations may function to accomplish various exchanges between these groups. Furthermore, the group structure consists of positions that contain various roles.

These positions may be occupied by different actors at different times. As an example, take the relationship between the purchasing department and the box shop. Purchasing is responsible for obtaining raw materials for the organization; in this group, people play specialized roles oriented toward importing into the organization the materials necessary for producing its products. Once these materials are obtained, they must first be stored, and later transferred to members of the box shop who use them in the production process. A structure, therefore, must be created to accomplish the transfer. To do this, an interstitial group structure is established; a clerk in the purchasing department acts as supply clerk in an interstitial group. Let us assume that he is the only one who occupies this position.

Another position is set up in the structure of the organization which is comparable to a customer position; in the diagram, it is being occupied by Mr. W from the box shop. This position defines the roles to be performed by a person who goes to the supply section of the purchasing department to obtain supplies. The position is structured so that it can be occupied by successive individuals—that is, the same individual does not necessarily occupy this position all of the time. Instead, different representatives of the box shop, members of the paint shop, sales department, or executive office may occupy this position at different times.

We can describe the situation in figurative terms by saying that the position is open part of the time. People step into the supply office, temporarily occupy the position, and perform its roles. They leave; others come in and occupy it temporarily, in turn to be replaced. Some positions in the structure of organizations, therefore, have permanent occupants—the supply clerk position in this particular interstitial group. Other positions have only temporary occupants, and their roles are performed by a variety of people, depending on time and circumstances. The interstitial groups shown in Figure 12-1 between the purchasing department and the box shop; the box shop and the paint shop; and perhaps also between the paint shop and the sales department may have this nature—that is, different people occupy the positions and perform the roles at different times. These groups are exchange interstitial groups, but they are different from those outside the boundaries of the organization. These are reciprocal exchange interstitial groups, while those at the boundaries of the organization are conjunctive.

The case of the interstitial group called the management committee, shown in the middle of the diagram of the Black Box Company given in Figure 10-3 has a different nature. The positions of this interstitial group are occupied by particular members all of the time. It is the management committee for the organization, and is structured so that its occupants are the supervisors, foremen, or executives who head the other groups in the organization.

No group in the organization is completely active all the time. That is to say, groups that comprise organizations usually do not involve interaction between all of the members in the performance of roles all the time. Instead, it is more typical at any given moment for subgroups to be active, and for some groups to be totally in a latent state. For example, take the situation where all the members of the organization are interacting with members of their respective elemental groups. Under these conditions, all the interstitial groups in the organization would be in a latent state. What this means is that the structure of an organization is larger and more complex than any activity that can be observed at any given moment. Organizational behavior is thus an ebb and flow of behavior between various groups, where different roles are active at one time, then inactive at others, and where different subgroups are more active at one stage than another.

The activation of relationships in an organizational system is a function of the variables of interaction, personality, and situation. The activation of the interstitial group between the purchasing department and the box shop, for example, depends on events that occur in the interaction within the two elemental groups. People in the box shop interact with each other in a situation; an event occurs which produces the activation of one of the extramural roles within the group which requires behavior outside that group in relation to the purchasing department. Supplies run low, let us say, and a decision is made to get certain raw materials immediately in order to continue the work of the shop. Similarly, events occurring in the interstitial group may activate roles within elemental groups. Mr. W, who occupies a position as client of the supply clerk, returns to his work group with a new piece of equipment to be installed in the shop. This triggers the activation of roles within the positions of the supervisors and other workers within the elemental groups. Interaction takes place within the context of reciprocal roles related to installing and maintaining the equipment of that shop.

In other words, the ebb and flow of role behavior within an organization amounts to the activation of certain roles within certain groups, while others are returned to a latent state. During the process of activating roles and returning others to a state of latency, people move about the organization in physical space as well as social space; and interaction shifts from the context of one group to another. Within a group, action shifts from one subgroup to another, or from one role relationship to another. Never at any given time is the whole repertoire of roles contained within the positions that comprise the structure of an organization active.

This means, of course, that the entire structure of an organization is never active within a given small space of time. In order to see the entire repertoire of roles that comprise the structure of an organization actually performed, it is necessary to observe the organization over a span of time long enough to allow each possible event to which the structure addresses itself to occur.

Remember, a member occupies more than a single position in an organization. He participates in a multigroup system as a member of several groups. In each one of these groups he has a different repertoire of roles assigned, and involves himself in a different relationship system. Also, an organization is a completely articulated system, in the sense that every part of the organization is joined either directly or indirectly to every other part. Every role performed within the system through a chain of reciprocal relationships, both bilateral and reflexive, is linked by either direct or indirect relationships to every other one within the system. This means that, to some degree, performances in one part of the system have effects on all other parts of the system.

The closer together any two roles are in the system of linkage, the more immediate and stronger the effect of role performance will be. Two roles that are directly linked to each other will have the most immediate and the strongest effects on each other, and the behavior of one actor will at once affect the behavior of the other. Since the roles are complementary, the behavior of one actor will be directly dependent upon the behavior of another, and the effect will, therefore, be rather strong—that is, a change in one role performance will almost certainly produce a complementary change in the other role performance.

In the case of indirect relationships—let us say, the performance of a role by a worker in the box shop as the operator of a sheet-metal bending machine, and the role of the president of the company as corresponding secretary for the organization—the effect of behavior in one role will not immediately and strongly affect the other. When the man in the box shop changes the way in which he bends metal, his behavior may immediately and strongly affect his co-worker who performs the next part of the production process in interaction with him; but it is unlikely that the behavior of the president of the company as corresponding secretary will be immediately or strongly affected. He will most probably go right on dictating letters. Eventually, through a chain of events which produces indirect effects, the technological change may affect his behavior. If some of the boxes sold to a customer prove defective, for instance, he may receive a letter of complaint which he has to answer.

Although the strongest and most immediate effects occur in proportion to the closeness of the actors' behavior to each other structurally, other variables may modify this fact. If an angry worker in the box shop sets fire to the shop, the president's behavior is apt to be almost immediately affected, and strongly. So, in generalizing about structural distance in an organization, and the effects of behavior throughout the system, we are assuming that the import of the behavior for the survival of the system is held constant.

Power and Authority in Organizations

Much attention has been given, in the literature on complex organizations, to the subjects of power, authority, and decision-making. In our terms, the power structure of the organization consists of a system of authority roles assigned to positions within the organization and performed by actors. Within positions, in other words, roles exist which define the rights and duties of people with respect to such matters as giving orders, directions, and instructions; allocating rewards and punishments; maintaining order; and creating rules or norms for the system.

In the box shop, Mr. D is foreman. His position contains the role of supervisor, and the other positions within the group contain roles of supervisee. These roles are defined in terms of norms which call for behavior on the part of the supervisor and the supervisee in relation to each other. Mr. D also occupies a position in the management committee. Here he also has an authority role, but in this case his authority role is supervisee; and Mr. A, the president of the company, has the role of supervisor assigned to his position. These roles define rights and duties in making decisions, giving and taking orders, allocating rewards and punishments, and formulating new norms for the system.

In complex groups, specialized aspects of these roles of supervisor and supervisee may be allocated to different individuals within the same group. One person may have a role with respect to directing the minute-by-minute operations of the group as a kind of overseer. Another person within the group may occupy a position that contains the decision-making aspects of supervisory behavior. And still another may act as judge and policeman for the group. In other words, the authority structure of a system may be differentiated in terms of various specialized authority roles, and these may be organized into an intricate system of relationships whereby, through a system of interstitial group relations, a chain of command is created with respect to the power function within the organization.

In dealing with power it is necessary to differentiate between real power, which is practiced in real behavior and is therefore a part of the social organization of the system, and structural power. Structural power consists of authority roles that are defined by the normative system of the organization in terms of an organized network of role definitions. In this sense, they may consist of latent roles. Structural power is called "authority," since it stems from the positions that people occupy, and the role definitions contained within these positions (6). Real power, on the other hand, is a function of the behavior that takes place within the system, and is produced by cultural structure, personality, situation, and interaction in combination. A person in the Black Box Shop, other than the person who occupies the position of foreman, may actually wield the power in the organization, because cultural structure, which contains the authority role definitions, is only one among a system of variables that produce behavior. If the foreman, let us say, abdicates his authority for reasons of personality and relationships, it may be assumed by others within the work group who have personal ascendancy over him. For, when real people occupy positions, and interact with each other in live situations, behavior often deviates from structure.

A worker in the Box Shop knows that his role calls for him to take orders, directions, and instructions from the foreman. The foreman of the organization also knows that it is his responsibility to direct the activities of the workers. If the workers resent the authority of the foreman, however, they may resist complying with the role definition. In other words, in order to understand authority behavior within organizations, it is necessary not only to understand the way in which roles are defined, but also how individual personalities, when combined with authority roles, produce behavior. Some personality types may not be able to accept a subordinate role; others may be incapable of accepting a superordinate role in social relationships.

Decision-making must be regarded as a social process that occurs within organizations. It consists of the behavior of actors within the system in relation to each other as they make choices between alternatives for action. In this process of decision-making, various individuals perform different roles, so that a variety of decision-making roles are incorporated into the structure of social organizations. Organizational theory differentiates between staff and line roles with respect to this process. Staff roles are those devoted to assembling information, and advising, on the basis of expertise, someone who is responsible for making the choices. Line roles consist of making the choices, and converting them into the form of action within the system. Decision-making roles, therefore, vary all the way from the choice-maker role to that of the opinion-expresser and adviser. Such roles are incorporated into the positions that people occupy in various groups within the organization; and through their performance, parts of decision-making are carried out within the organization. To view the entire process of decision-making with respect to a given decision, it is usually necessary to study the role behavior of a large number of people in relation to each other. In a sense, decision-making can be translated into the effects that one person's behavior has on another's within the system; so that it is perhaps best not to consider decision-making a rational process of choice-making, but a special process of behavior determination.

The same variables and processes operate in all groups, regardless of their type. Elemental and insterstitial groups both involve the interplay of the four sets of variables, and behavior is the output of this system of interacting influences. Groups differ in their form and content, but not in the nature of the social processes that occur within them; and the same group processes occur in executive groups high in the hierarchy of an organization, as occur in production line groups at the bottom.

The difference between groups lies in how they are organized, what roles go into making up their positions, and how they are linked to the larger system internally and externally. They are alike in that all involve a structure, defined in terms of role relationships, which orders internal and external relations. They are also alike in that real people, with their own personal characteristics, interact in the context of social situations. It is a mistake to assume that there are special processes or distinct groups of variables that operate to produce the behavior in one group in an organization, as opposed to another. This is not to deny that real differences in content are important as far as explaining differences in the behavior of executive as opposed to production-line groups. The point is, rather, that sociologists should not spend time accounting for variations in content among various groups. Instead, they should try to learn how systematic variations in internal form or external linkage relate to the operation of the four factors which enter into the determination of behavior in all group situations.

The study of organizations, as opposed to groups as groups, ought to emphasize the linkage system that binds the elemental groups in the organization into a larger system—that is, it should focus attention on interstitial groups, and on the structures and processes that surround them. It is these mechanisms that give the complex organization its special character as a social system. The study of the internal operation of elemental groups misses the major point of the structural distinction of an organization as a social system.

CHAPTER 13   THE STRUCTURE OF HUMAN COMMUNITIES

Human communities are social systems of a particular sort, and differ from organizations, associations, and small groups in specific respects. The principal difference lies in the way in which the constituent units making up the system are bound together in a system of relationships, for communities are social systems whose parts are held together by conjunctive, rather than by reciprocal, relationships.

In 1955, George Hillery examined the literature for definitions of *community*, and found that social scientists use the term to refer to a variety of social, economic, and political phenomena (1). There were almost as many definitions of the word as there were people who used it, and the situation still remains as confused as it was when Hillery wrote. The problem is that "community" is a folk-concept, and as such is the province of politicians, social and political action groups, booster organizations, and romantics who comment upon society in the context of public debate.

Every culture contains a conception of the society and of the community that explains their form and nature to the members of these social systems, and gives meaning to their functioning. Just as folk cultures contain ideas about the nature of man as both an organism, and as a behaving being, so they contain notions about the nature of community and society. These concepts perform functions within the belief system of the society; but they are not necessarily accurate representations of the nature of things within that social system. In many respects, these folk conceptions state ideals for what communities ought to be like, rather than describing what they actually are. In this sense, folk concepts of both community and society are value orientations, as well as beliefs about the nature of the community as a social system.

The folk conception of community that is current in American society says that persons living in the same community share a common set of interests; therefore, they should develop common goals and objectives, and co-operate with one another to accomplish them. Furthermore, people living in the same community should develop "a sense of community," and along with it community loyalty and identification. These are all value statements about the ideal characteristics of social relations among neighbors living in the same community. They are in no sense statements about the actual state of affairs in any real social system. Upon occasion, however, these values have been used to define characteristics for systems called communities. The result has been that any social system which deviates from the ideal characteristics is somehow regarded as less of a community, or, at best, malfunctioning.

So strong is the belief that people should feel some sense of community, that some have founded utopian societies or communes in an effort to recapture, or to create anew, the social conditions deemed healthy and desirable among neighbors. Others, engaged in community development work, have attempted to infuse the proper sense of loyalty and identification in people within the community, and to develop formal mechanisms to encourage their co-operation in pursuit of common goals. Furthermore, many people feel that something is wrong with our society, because people no longer live in true communities.

In addition to value judgments about proper relationships among neighbors, the folk conception of community incorporates ideas about property—that is, *community* is also defined in terms of land and other physical facilities and property. In the popular mind, therefore, the community is not only a system of relationships among people, but also a geographic area in which the people live and have various property rights. This physical view of community is so strong that our language designates communities primarily as places, and has no colloquial way to describe them as systems of social relationships.

In many respects the folk concept of community is embodied in Toennies' concept of a *Gemeinschaft* (2). In noting the emergence of the *Gesellschaft* type of social system, Toennies pointed out the appearance of a new form of relationship system. It is not correct to say, however, that as the transition from *Gemeinschaft* to *Gesellschaft* occurs, communities cease to exist; but their forms do change.

The folk concept of community has been transmitted through generations. In the second half of the twentieth century, however, society is organized in a way that is inconsistent with folk belief, since folk belief no longer corresponds to the new forms of social organization produced by technological change. A scientific sociology demands a precise concept of community that must correspond to observable behavior and reality, which folk belief is not required to do. As a matter of fact, folk beliefs are necessarily diffuse and imprecise. They need not correspond to anything that exists in the real world. Very often, when one examines real behavior, and determines the way in which norms, values, and beliefs are put together, one finds only a few instances in which the folk belief about community is true. Let us examine some of its fallacies.

The Territorial Fallacy and its Theoretical Consequences

Many definitions of community in the sociological literature begin with the phrase: "A community is an area . . .", and then proceed to add such phrases as "within which a group of people share common interests, values, and beliefs, and pursue common objectives and goals" (3). But it is wrong to say that a community is an area, even in ecological terms. It is an ecosystem, the web of life that exists within the area (4, 5), that depends on and is related to the physical area within which it exists. The community is the system that exists within the area, and not the area itself.

Translated into sociological terms, this means that the human community consists of the behavior system that exists within a given locality, which acts upon that locality and responds to it in terms of action. Thus, the community must be viewed as both an independent and dependent variable with respect to territory or area.

The territorial fallacy with respect to community becomes obvious if we analyze a slogan like, "Keep our community clean." This slogan clearly refers to trash, refuse, and other forms of pollution in the territory occupied by a human social system, and not to the morals expressed in the behavior of people. Streets, buildings, utilities, parks, playgrounds, and other physical objects cannot be regarded as part of human communities. They are the stage upon which the human community as an unfolding system of behavior occurs, or they are the products or outputs of human behavior systems at previous points in time. They are not, however, part of the system called community.

One reason we have to separate the notion of community from the notion of territory is that two different social systems may occupy the same territory at different times. Mexico City, for example, was once the home of the Aztec, as Manhattan Island was the habitat of an Indian tribe. In both places, one social system supplanted another. Since two different human communities can, therefore, occupy the same area at different times—that is, an area is not always the same community— we must separate the idea of area from the idea of community.

There is another, perhaps more important, reason to separate the social system called community from the idea of territory, and that is, that the daily actions of human beings spill over the boundaries of any area established for them. Let us consider a few illustrations. The Ajax Black Box Factory, in which Mr. Jones acts as a salesman, is located in Boxtown, a city of 100,000 people. Mr. Jones, however, does not stay in that city; instead, he travels around the country playing his roles as a salesman in relation to potential buyers scattered over a wide territory.

One day Mr. Jones is in the offices of the Acme Instrument Company, in a city five hundred miles away from his home office, taking an order from Mr. Brown, the purchasing agent for the instrument company, for two thousand black boxes to be delivered within the next three weeks. After observing the amenities of business etiquette, he leaves the Acme Instrument Company offices, returns to his hotel room, and places a long-distance call to the shipping department in his plant. In his conversation with the shipping agent, what community social system is he participating in? And while he was interacting with the purchasing agent of the Acme Instrument Company, what community social system was his behavior a part of?

This type of incident may be happening a hundred times over while Mr. Jones is telephoning. As a matter of fact, Mayor Black of Boxtown is at that very same moment in the state capitol, dictating a letter to his secretary at his home office over the telephone. Mrs. Smith, an elementary school teacher, is riding in a school bus with her children toward the state capitol, taking them to visit places of historical interest as part of her duties as teacher of the sixth grade. Many other people who make their homes in Boxtown are in transit to and from the city, located somewhere outside its political boundaries, performing roles in various groups and organizations.

Let us return to Mr. Jones, talking on the phone with the shipping agent of the Black Box Factory. We may say that the Black Box Factory is a constituent unit in the structure of Boxtown as a community, since the factory building is located within the territory of Boxtown. Mr. Jones is now outside that territory, *but* is performing a role within the Black Box Factory as an organization. At the same time, he is physically located within the boundaries of Capitol City, where the Acme Instrument Company is located. At the moment however, he is not performing a role within the Acme Instrument Company, and is not interacting with any of its members.

If the Ajax Black Box Factory is indeed within the community of Boxtown, then at the moment that Mr. Jones is on the telephone with the purchasing agent of that company, his behavior is a part of Boxtown as a community—despite the fact that he is located in a territory far distant from it. In other words, the boundaries of the community social system are located in social space, not physical space. This space is defined by the performance of roles by persons as members of social systems. These roles may be performed in various territorial locations. What determines membership of behavior in a social system is therefore not its physical location, but its social location. A territorial rather than a sociological boundary for the community will not suffice to account for all of the behavior that takes place within organizations which, on a territorial basis, are part of the community social system.

Endless problems stem from trying to identify the boundaries of social systems on the basis of geographical space. For example, suppose Mr. and Mrs. Jones, and their children Tom and Mary are driving down a highway a couple of thousand miles from their home in Boxtown. While driving, they are planning a neighborhood get-together to be held when they get home. They are making out the guest list, deciding on the menu, and planning the time and course of events they expect to occur on this occasion. In other words, they are interacting with each other as a family, planning an event that will activate roles in positions they occupy in a neighborhood social system that exists in Boxtown. Is their behavior a part of the social system called Boxtown? To locate it within any other social system would be ridiculous; nevertheless, it occurs outside the confines of the community as a physical area.

Sociologically, we must assume that behavior belongs within a social system when it performs functions within that system, and when it is articulated through time and space with other events that occur within that system. Similarly, role definitions, and therefore behavior in the latent sense, belong within the structure of a system when they are articulated through reciprocal or conjunctive relationships to other behavior expectations that belong within the same system.

Social behavior is affected by the physical properties of the situation within which it takes place. Situation, along with interaction, personality, and cultural structure all contribute to the action which actually occurs. When the Jones Family is riding along the highway in their car, they are positioned at certain physical locations. Within the automobile certain stimuli occur around them. The conversation may be interrupted by events occurring in that particular situation. They may have to speak louder because of wind noise. They may not be able to judge each other's attitudes well, because they cannot easily see the facial expressions that accompany words. They may not be able to gather certain information pertinent to the neighborhood get-together. They may not know, for instance, that the next-door neighbors, the Whites, will not come back from their vacation in time to attend. The situation, by influencing the amount of information available, has an important impact upon the behavior which actually takes place. The determining criterion for inclusion of the behavior in a given community social system, however, is not the physical situation within which the behavior takes place. It is, instead, the articulation of that behavior with other behaviors in a larger system which exists in social space.

To get back to Mr. Jones and the purchasing agent from the instrument company: while they are interacting, one performing his roles as salesman and the other as purchasing agent, they are located within the structure of an interstitial group that exists between the instrument company and the box factory, and their relationship is conjunctive, since they represent different structural interests in the interaction. In what community shall we locate this interstitial group? Does it belong to Boxtown as a community, or to Capitol City as a community? In it, Mr. Jones is performing behavior oriented toward the Ajax Black Box Company, located within Boxtown as a community; and the purchasing agent, Mr. Brown, is performing behavior for the Acme Instrument Company, located within Capitol City. The interstitial group, therefore, seems to stand between two communities, and constitute a point of exchange between them.

As we noted in Chapter 5, the units of communities are joined by conjunctive relationships. The interstitial group in question here is one of the links in a network that joins Capitol City as a subcommunity to Boxtown, thus forming a larger community social system. Boxtown and Capitol City have a lower order of complexity as communities than the larger system in which each constitutes a part. It is apparent, therefore, that we cannot speak of communities as being of only a single order of complexity or size. Instead, we must think in terms of orders of communities.

A first-order community consists of a system of organizations, associations, and independent groups, joined to each other by a system of interstitial groups that contain conjunctive relationships at their cores. On this level, only one interstitial group relationship is necessary to join one organization to the other. This means that the box factory, and the suppliers that furnish it with raw materials through a system of interstitial groups in which each has a representative, are by definition in the same first-order community.

Second-order relationships exist between organizations that are connected by two systems of interstitial groups. Suppose that we are dealing with a relationship between the box factory and a paint company from which it purchases paint. A single interstitial group exists between the box factory and the paint company. If we move back a step further in the chain, we will discover that the paint company obtains its raw materials from another set of suppliers, for example, suppliers of pigments. Between the pigment companies and the paint company, another interstitial group exists that connects those two organizations. Thus, the box factory is connected to the pigment company through a two-link chain of interstitial groups. This puts the box factory and the pigment company in the same second-order community with each other. By the same method, we can generate a system of indirect relationships that forms different orders of community relationships. A third-order community is connected by a chain of interstitial groups having three links in it, and so forth. An nth-order community consists of the entire society, and contains the entire system of organizations and groups that are either directly or indirectly related to each other through extended chains of interstitial groups that form exchange networks.

The boundaries of various orders of community depend on where we start. If we start with the box factory, the first-order community within which it exists is defined by those organizations and groups to which it is linked by a single-step chain of interstitial groups. If we start with a given family, the first-order community consists of those groups and organizations to which it is linked by a single-step chain of interstitial groups. Although the two first-order communities generated by these methods will not correspond with each other, they may have common elements that place the two systems in the same second-order community. Only societies, which are defined as nth-order communities, will have identical boundaries, no matter what organization or group one starts with.

Earlier, the point was made that a given organization may have parts located within various communities. This statement now needs to be reinterpreted in terms of our definition of community. Let us take a nationwide insurance company located in Capitol City with branch offices located throughout the country. These branch offices are part of the organization of the insurance company. If we used the folk definition, we would say they were located in different communities. When we use the definition of community given here, we must say that all the parts of the organization are parts of the same first-order community, as are all of the groups and organizations to which they are linked by a single set of interstitial groups. The community that they are a part of is not confined to one piece of geographical space; instead, it is diffused over a wide territory within which various groups are linked to each other in social space. Two organizations or groups are parts of the same community when they stand in a conjunctive relationship to each other, and are linked by at least one interstitial group.

The Humanistic Fallacy

Folk definitions also say that real biological people are the units out of which the structure of community and society are made (6), as though a person belonged to one and only one community within the structure of society. We shall call this the "humanistic fallacy."

Political and social practice limit the community membership of an individual to one political unit for tax and voting purposes, the effect of which is to define the community as a political entity. Usually each person is regarded as being a member of the community in which his household or his residence is maintained. The notion of citizenship in a political unit thereby gets mixed up with the sociological notion of membership in a community. Individuals in our society tend to think of themselves as members of a given community even when they are away from it, and performing behavior within the context of another. An American in Paris, performing roles, acts within the context of the Parisian community; yet if we asked him what community he belonged to, he would most likely answer with the name of the community where he resides. Shall we regard a person—an American in Paris—who is performing roles in relation to Parisians as a member of the social system which he left at home? or shall we include his behavior within the Parisian social system? If we must allocate him as a unit or as a total individual to one, and only one, community, then we have to choose between Paris and his place of residence.

To answer this question, let us define the total individual as a real functioning behaving entity, consisting of all the behavior he performs during a given span of time. To define the limits of the total individual behaviorally, we must say that the total individual consists of all of the behavior performed by that person between birth and death. It is more convenient if we think of the total individual as being the whole repertoire of behavior that he performs within a more limited span of time —let us say, one year. During a year, an individual may perform behavior at various physical locations that are widely separated from each other—for instance, Boxtown and Paris. We will resolve our problem about his community if we allocate to community A the behavior that takes place there, and to community B the behavior that takes place there. Thus, the individual as a behavior system belongs to more than a single social system.

This is what we did with small groups and organizations. Mr. Jones at home, performing roles toward his wife as husband, preparing to go to work, is part of the family as a social system. When he arrives at the office, and interacts with his secretary, his behavior is a part of that social system. All of Mr. Jones's behavior does not belong to any one of these systems; only part of him as a behavior system belongs to any one of them. This same solution can be used with respect to the community.

Let us say that Mr. Jones takes his family to Paris, and they are in a restaurant. He is interacting with the waiter to order a meal. The effects of his behavior are registered in the behavior of the waiter who transmits this effect to the chef, and through a chain of relationships his actions are registered within the social system of Paris. In order to explain the behavior of others within that system, we have to regard the behavior of Mr. Jones and his family as being part of the same social system.

Consequently, we must view communities as systems of behavior, and not as systems of actors. It is incorrect to say that a community is an area within which certain things hold true. It is equally incorrect to say that the community consists of a number of people who stand in a given relationship to each other. Instead, we must think of communities as systems of behavior that are put together in a certain way.

There are other reasons to regard communities as behavior systems, rather than systems consisting of persons. Foremost is the idea that communities outlast their members, and persist for many generations. People are born, grow up, act out their roles within the system, die, and are replaced by others; but the community social system persists. The thing that persists is the system of behavior. It persists even though actors come and go. Whole families move into and out of communities, yet the system of behavior persists.

So, folk practice misleads us on this point. Many values in our society reinforce the ideas that the individual—not society or the community—is most important, that communities exist to serve individuals, and that they offer a setting within which the individual realizes his various ambitions and satisfies his various needs. The American value and belief system thus leads us to think of society as made up of a number of persons who, as total systems, relate to each other to form the larger thing called society. It is against American values to think of individuals as if they were so many cogs in a giant machine. It is even more against our belief system to think of the individual, not as a single cog in a large machine, but as a series of cogs that fit into a machine at various points in space.

Nonetheless, it is a useful exercise to think of society as a large clocklike mechanism, whose various subassemblies correspond to communities. Within communities there are still smaller subassemblies, corresponding to organizations and groups. The individual as an entity does not correspond to one and only one single cog in the machine, having one and only one place in one subassembly within it. Instead, the individual performs various coglike roles located in different subassemblies within the machine, at one moment performing a function within one of the subassemblies, at another, performing a function in a different one. At one time he is located within one community performing roles, and at another time he is located within a different community performing roles. Within the same community, he shifts from one group to another and from one organization to another. As a consequence, if we were to remove the individual from the whole social system, not a single part, but many parts of the system would be affected; and these parts would be widely separated from each other.

Because this view of the individual runs counter to the value system of American society, sociology has clung to the folk conception of community and society, and scientific thought on community has had to conform to the notion of the individual as the central unit of concern and importance.

Another factor that leads us to define social systems in terms of real people is that each individual perceives his own behavior as if it were a unified system. Each actor is the only observer of his own behavior as a total system, of course; ego's behavior is perceived by alter in a different way, since alter only sees that part of ego's behavior which takes place in interaction with him. As a consequence, no single alter ever experiences ego as a total system. Since ego perceives himself as a total system, it seems reasonable for him to think of groups, organizations, and communities as being made up of total human beings like himself. Therefore, the folk belief that society is made up of total persons as parts or units seems reasonable to each one of us. If, however, we shift our perception away from self to others, it is easy to perceive that groups, organizations, and communities are made up of fragments of people rather than total individuals.

The humanistic fallacy, therefore, makes the error of utilizing a social-psychological concept of the individual as a total system in formulating concepts of social structure. It stems from humanistic concerns over the value and worth of the individual. But the total individual at any given moment consists of two forms of action, latent behavior and active behavior. Latent behavior is a set of role definitions that have been learned, and we perceive these role definitions as fitted into the social structure at different points in social space. Some roles fit into the structure of one group, and other roles into the structure of another group. Similarly, some roles belong to the structure of one community and other roles to the structure of another.

Let us go back to Mr. Jones. He lives in Boxtown with his wife and two children, where he performs the roles of father and husband in a kinship organization that is part of the structure of Boxtown community. His parents, brothers, and sisters live in Capitol City. His father occupies a position of father-husband in the structure of a family in which Mr. Jones occupies the position of son and brother. This family is located within the structure of Capitol City. As a social group, it is articulated with that structure. At a given moment, Mr. Jones is in his home in Boxtown actively interacting with his wife and children, while his roles in the other family are latent. In the latent state, they consist of a set of norms that have been learned by him and internalized into his personality. Sociologically, these role definitions are located within the structure of a group that is part of a community some distance from where Mr. Jones is momentarily behaving. When he activates these roles in terms of behavior—for example, when he visits his parents— his behavior must be regarded as taking place within the structure of the community to which his parents' family belongs.

If we defined all of Mr. Jones's latent and active behavior as belonging only to the community of Boxtown, certain of his behavior that has consequences or functions within the social system of Capitol City would be excluded from that system, and it would be incomplete. Or, if we used this approach with the entire society, much of the behavior essential for keeping communities operating would be misplaced in the wrong social system.

There are more groups in a structure of society than there are members. This is a function of the fact that there are more permutations and combinations of a number of individuals than the number of individuals who contribute to these permutations and combinations. Furthermore, the same combination of individuals may be assigned different roles in different positions, and form several different groups. Just as we cannot think of a person belonging to one and only one group in society, if we want to generate an image of the structure of society, so too we cannot think of each individual as belonging to one and only one organization or community, and still generate an image of society.

This is most easily illustrated with respect to the group. If all of Mr. Jones's behavior belongs to the family that consists of himself, his wife, and his children, then there would be nothing left of him to belong to any other group within the system. If we interpret "all of him" to mean all of his latent and active behavior, then if all of Mr. Jones' behavior, both latent and active, is performed within the family, then none of his behavior can be performed within other groups. If this were true of every individual in the society, the only groups that would exist would be families; and there would be nothing left in the way of behavior to form work groups, school groups, play groups, or any other kind of group.

We must not be misled by humanistic concern over the individual into thinking of him as belonging totally to every situation in which he involves himself. If we do, we will not be able to construct an image of the social system within which the individual participates. Society fragments the individual, and allocates his behavior to various social systems, as a necessary and natural consequence of social differentiation. Our values with respect to the worth of the individual, and the integrity of the person as a psychological entity, should not mislead us into distorting our image of the social system so we can maintain that value position. Regardless of whether we are for or against social differentiation, we must not fail to recognize it when it is encountered in the real world.

The Personification Fallacy

A third fallacy involves the personification of the community—that is, attributing to the community and other social systems characteristics peculiar to the person as an organism. This fallacy is a consequence of making an analogy between an organism and society, either consciously or unconsciously. Sociological literature is filled with references to social systems "seeking ends," such as "boundary maintenance" or "equilibrium" or "integration." It is also filled with references to communities having goals, objectives, and motives for behavior with respect to common goals (7).

All of these notions imply directly or indirectly that social systems behave, when, in fact, social systems are systems of behavior. The idea that social systems behave implies, at least tacitly, that they perceive, think, and act in their own interests. Sometimes personification takes a statistical guise, and the claim is made that members of the community have common values, beliefs, and interests. This, in turn, implies that statistical distributions of these traits differentiate one community from another. From the statistical commonality of social-psychological traits, it is only a short step to the notion that, as a consequence of these common beliefs, values, and interests, people in communities pursue goals or objectives that are generated by them.

From this point of view, community associations, such as the Chamber of Commerce, the city government, or the power structure of the community, are like a board of directors or a leadership structure for the community. They make decisions for the community, and, guided by a set of common beliefs and values, direct activities of community members toward the accomplishment of common goals and objectives. A variation on this theme is the notion that the power structure misdirects the activities of the community, and instead of pursuing the true common goals, conforming to the true values and beliefs of the people, it pursues selfish interests in the attempt to manipulate the community for private gain. Both a conspiratorial view of the power structure, and the view of the power structure as an expression of the common will, imply that the community is one gigantic organization or organism functioning in pursuit of some definable, if as yet undefined, objectives.

The booster spirit of civic organization assumes certain value positions, illustrated by such a slogan as "We should all pull together for the common good." But communities, unlike organizations, do not have objectives that they can pursue as organized systems of behavior. They do not have a structure oriented toward the output of a definable product. They are different kinds of systems entirely, and must be viewed from a different perspective. Someone who says that a community is a system pursuing certain objectives is saying that a system of behavior exists which is oriented toward the accomplishment of some goal. But the community is not so oriented; instead, it is a behavior system within which various groups and organizations are oriented toward the accomplishment of sometimes conflicting, and sometimes symbiotic, but always distinct goals or objectives.

Community Interstitial Groups

As we said in Chapter 12, the function of community structure is to provide a system of structural linkage among differentiated parts that permits these parts to exchange the inputs and outputs necessary to their own operation. It is this linkage system that constitutes an added structural element beyond those elements already included within groups and within organizations. We think, therefore, that the study of community structure should focus upon the study of interstitial groups and conjunctive relationships, as the critical structures that constitute the unique ingredients of the community as a social system.

Since this view departs widely from the usual one in a number of respects, we must specify the critical interstitial groups that constitute the linkage system in contemporary American communities. Also, we must clarify what we think are organizations and independent elemental groups.

There is a tendency to think of government as if it were the directorate for the community organization. Local, state, and national governments, and associated political groups and organizations are regarded as though they function as progressively higher-order community systems. That is, local government operates in a community system that has a lower order of complexity than state and national government. In our view, governments can realistically be viewed as consisting of three types of units: executive, legislative, and judicial. In addition to the political subsystem of a community, or the so-called community power structure, there are other quasi-governmental or political groupings— political parties, pressure groups, civic organizations, patriotic associations, and temporary commissions or boards.

How can we account for these various divisions and units in the governmental subsystems as parts of a community? We regard all executive groups, organizations, or bureaus as organizations which, like all organizations, specialize in producing some product or function to be exchanged with other organizations and independent groups for inputs. From this viewpoint, the mayor's office, the police department, the school superintendent's office, the city sanitation department, and so forth, are, like all organizations, merely a specialized part of a larger system called the community. Within this system they stand in a conjunctive relationship to other specialized organizations, and they must establish and maintain a system of interstitial group linkage with them in order to obtain inputs or to produce outputs for the system. Thus, executive governmental agencies are not seen as ruling or presiding over the total life of the community, but as producing certain specialized outputs within it in exchange for inputs.

We consider the legislative branch of government to be a system of formalized co-ordinative interstitial groups that join various independent units of the community for purposes of controlling conflict that arises as these units pursue their diverse interests. County commissioners, state legislatures, the Congress of the United States, therefore, are regarded as interstitial groups within which members stand in a conjunctive relationship with one another, and through parliamentary procedures carry out a controlled conflict in pursuit of divergent objectives and interests. Other bodies of a legislative sort may exist for special purposes in communities, and perform the same sort of mediating function—for example, school boards.

The courts and other judicial bodies are also, from our standpoint, interstitial groups designed to control the conditions under which conflict between representatives of various interests can be carried out and resolved, without destroying the conditions necessary to maintaining the exchange system of the larger community. In the court, judges, juries, lawyers, defendants, prosecutors, and plaintiffs operate together as an interstitial group standing between various groups and organizations in the community. They carry out a controlled conflict in order to resolve some issue which stands between or among them.

It may prove useful to regard some parts of legislative bodies and of the courts as either elemental groups or organizations, and other parts as interstitial groups. For example, the judge's office, consisting of himself, his clerk, the bailiff, and other court officials, may best be regarded as an elemental group, while the actual court session involving a trial is best called an interstitial group. The individual offices and office staffs of United States Congressmen are elemental groups, but a session of the Congress is an interstitial group. The way in which groups are actually classified must depend on empirical observation. In general, however, we may say that the courts and Congress exist to perform interstitial group functions, while the executive branch of government exists to execute certain operations that produce some output other than exchange or the mediation of conflict for the community.

Businesses, hospitals, schools, churches, neighborhood social systems, extended families, and executive government agencies constitute the organizations which are parts of community structure. They are joined by many different interstitial groups. In addition to those interstitial groups already discussed, we can identify many others: Civic organizations, such as the Chamber of Commerce, the Lions, Rotary, and Kiwanis Clubs; Parent-Teachers Association; county or state or national political parties or clubs; citizen advisory groups, such as human relations councils, the county ACSC committee, the Red Cross disaster committee; the stock exchange and other exchanges, such as livestock and commodity markets; salesman-customer groups, professional-client groups; temporary or permanent coalitions of citizens who form political cliques or power structures; neighborhood associations and clubs; and local boards and regulating bodies.

Each of these groups exists either to produce an exchange among parts of the community, or to regulate the conditions under which such exchanges take place. They are therefore interstitial groups, and as such, they represent the connective tissue that joins the parts of the community into a larger social system.

CHAPTER 14

SYSTEM-CENTERED ANALYSIS

In the past several chapters, concepts designed for analyzing the structure of social systems have been defined. The focus has been on systems of human behavior in which more than a single actor participates, and we have been only incidentally concerned with the actor as a system. In dealing with social systems, our concern has been to create a set of concepts that will permit sociologists ultimately to deal with societies, the largest and most complex social system encountered by man.

Societies are real objects. They exist as surely as individuals exist. As behavior systems they are as real as the behavior of persons who contribute to their make-up. They increase and decrease in size; they grow in complexity or are simplified. They change; they persist through time; we can locate them at particular points in space. But although society as an object is real, in the same sense that a tree, an animal, or a solar system is real, we must not mistake our conceptions about society, which are synthetically constructed, for the object itself.

Thus far we have built a model of society starting at the microscopic level and progressing through various levels of complexity. Figure 14–1 depicts this progression and illustrates graphically how the structure of real social systems of varying scale can be described, using a common frame of reference for all levels of complexity. We started constructing the model at the microscopic level by identifying and defining small particles of behavior called acts and norms, and progressed to the macroscopic level by combining these concepts, introducing ideas concerning relationships as we increased the level of scale. Acts and norms were defined in relationship to each other. Because we conceive of a norm as an act in storage, it is possible for us to deal with cultural structure and social organization by using a single set of structural units. Figure 14-1

STRUCTURAL UNIT	LEVEL OF SCALE
NORM	I
ROLE	II
STATUS	III
POSITION	IV
GROUP	V
ORGANIZATION	VI
COMMUNITY	VII

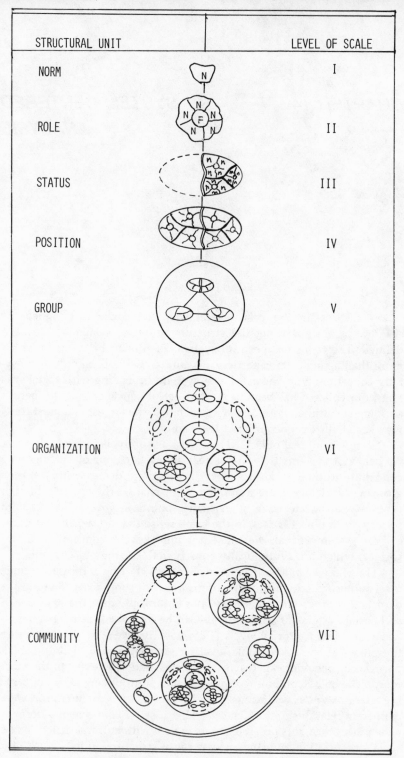

Figure 14–1 System-centered Structural Units
at Various Levels of Scale

shows only the cultural structure of social systems at various levels of scale. However, each concept depicted can be used either in discussing real behavior or normative structure.

The strategy employed in building our concepts of structural units has generally been to regard each larger unit of structure as being comprised of the next smaller unit as a part. For example, roles are defined as systems comprised of norms or acts as parts, and statuses are defined with roles as parts. Positions, in turn, are comprised of statuses, groups of positions, and organizations of groups. At the level of the community it is necessary to modify this approach to allow for the fact that communities sometimes contain only fragments of organizations instead of whole ones, and therefore must be regarded as systems of a different sort than we might anticipate on the basis of studying organizations or groups. Societies, the largest systems to which the behaviors of individual human actors belong, are regarded as complex, nth-order communities, which can be comprised of several communities and can contain whole organizations as parts, depending on the real society being studied.

In order to conceive of each higher level concept in terms of the next lower level one, it is necessary to refer to the relationships that exist among the smaller parts as they form the larger whole. Figure 14-1 shows only the concepts referring to progressively more complex social units, arranged in order of scale. If these concepts can be related to sociological theory, the model presented can do more than merely offer a means of describing the structure of social systems. They can furnish a foundation for explaining their operation. To assist us in moving in this direction, we have suggested that human behavior in the form of real action is a product of four groups of variables—cultural structure, personality, situation, and interaction. This theoretical position allows us to deal with the anatomy of social systems by defining cultural structure in normative terms, and social behavior or social organization in terms of acts. Let us now examine some propositions relating to system theory, and join them also to the model in Figure 14-1.

The first may be called a *chain reaction* assumption. System theory maintains that all parts of a social system are joined to each other, so that events occurring in one part of the system, through the structure of the system, will affect events occurring in other parts. As a matter of fact, in its purest form system theory contends that all parts of a system are so articulated with each other that each affects the other, no matter how much structural distance separates them. It further maintains that such effects are not felt equally throughout the entire system by all the parts, but are diminished as they proceed through chains of relationships from their point of origin to the most distant points in the system.

An event occurring in one part of the system has its strongest and most immediate effects upon the other parts of the system closest to the point of origin; but eventually some minute effect will be felt in the part of the system most distant from the point of origin.

The second assumption in system theory is the idea that there is a tendency toward achieving equilibrium, balance, consistency, quiescence, satiation, or integration within the system. Which of these particular concepts is employed depends on the type of system. In all cases, however, equilibrium implies that systems move toward a state in which stress and strain are reduced, and the energy necessary to maintain the system is minimized. System theorists do not say that systems attempt to maintain themselves, since that attributes motivation as well as rationality to systems; instead, they describe equilibrium in terms of systems moving inexorably toward a point at which any input introduced into them from the outside is absorbed as part of the routine operation of the system. The system thus achieves a regular pattern of functioning which minimizes both the amount of stress in the system, and the amount of energy expended by it. Given this assumption, it follows that if new energy is not introduced, the system will eventually disintegrate into a state of entropy.

Systems thus have a built-in tendency to seek the lowest point of energy expenditure. As they inexorably move toward their dissolution, they conserve energy through reducing strain and stress. Strain and stress take energy, and so the maintenance of a system in a state of strain and stress takes more energy than when stress and strain are reduced. Stress and strain are minimal when the parts that form the structure of the system are related to one another in such a way that they are structurally consistent. Two cog wheels in a machine, for example, produce the least stress and strain when their teeth mesh perfectly.

When we speak of society as a social system, we assume two things. First, that various parts of society are so articulated with each other that an event occurring in one part will have repercussions in other parts of society. Second, that social systems operate in such a way as to eliminate stress and strain. They seek to adjust their parts so that the amount of energy expended in maintaining the system is minimal. These statements about whole societies apply equally to subparts of society, such as communities, organizations, and groups. Below the group level, these statements also apply to positions, statuses, and roles as systems of behavior. How can we apply these two assumptions to social systems?

The Chain Reaction Assumption and Social Systems

In discussing the structure of social groups and larger systems such as organizations, communities, and societies, we pointed out that intricate networks of social relationships join all parts of the system, either directly or indirectly. For two parts to be included within the same system, they must be joined to each other by social relationships.

There are two kinds of social relationships through which events in one part of the system can affect events in other parts. First is the reflexive relationship, where a single actor belongs to two groups. An event occurs in the first group that affects him as an action system. When he moves to the other group, his behavior transmits the effect from one group to another.

The second kind of social relationship is the bilateral relationship. Here social interaction is the medium by which the effects of events occurring in one group are transmitted to another. A and B meet and interact in an interstitial group situation. A has been affected by events occurring in elemental group Number 1. As he interacts with B, the effects of these events condition or influence his behavior. His behavior affects B, who then returns to elemental group Number 2, and carries with him effects of events occurring in Group 1.

Chains of relationships of this nature make it possible for an event occurring in any part of a social system to have an effect on all other parts of the system. It seems reasonable that, as the chains become longer and longer, the effect will be diminished. At some point it will become so small as to be unmeasurable, and therefore insignificant. We cannot assume that it ever disappears entirely until it reaches the boundaries in the system.

An event occurring in one part of the system thus has its strongest and most immediate effects on those parts of the system closest to it. At work, Actor A interacts with Actor B in a way that irritates B immediately and strongly. B later interacts with his wife in a different group altogether, and transmits the effect in the form of irritable behavior; the wife is affected and transmits it to the children. By this time the original event has been combined with so many other variables that it is difficult to discern and measure the effect which has been transmitted across the relationship system to the children. Nonetheless, we are still warranted in using the system notion of chain reaction with respect to social behavior.

The Strain Toward Consistency in the Structure of Social Systems

Social systems, like other systems, tend to maintain themselves in a state of operation by eliminating inconsistent or strain-producing elements or influences which threaten to impede or impair their functioning. The processes through which stress and inconsistency are eliminated are regarded as automatic. They are neither deliberate, nor are they necessarily directed by human intelligence. They occur as part of the nature of systems.

What in social systems justifies the notion of a strain toward consistency? Are there social processes that automatically operate within social systems to reduce stress, and bring about a state of consistency among the parts, so that the structure and the operation of the system tend to remain intact?

There are two sources of stress within social systems: (1) intrapersonal conflict and stress; and (2) interpersonal conflict and stress. Intrapersonal conflict or stress refers to events occurring within the person as a system of action; it is tension that arises out of a psychological conflict experienced by the individual. Interpersonal stress or conflict occurs in the interaction between two or more persons, and amounts to the opposition of one individual or group of individuals by another in activities performed in interaction.

Both these forms of stress have punishing or damaging effects on the social system and its members. Both intrapersonal and interpersonal stress and conflict are punishing, because they produce unpleasant, distasteful, damaging, and debilitating effects on the individual and on the system in which he takes part as an actor. They reduce the effectiveness of the actor in performing behavior, by making him expend time and energy on managing the conflict that he might otherwise have spent on productive activities either for himself or for the system. As a consequence of the punishing nature of stress and conflict, actors attempt to avoid them or reduce them in favor of some more rewarding experience. In seeking some more rewarding experiences, the actor sets processes in motion that tend to eliminate the source of stress in the social system.

Stress may also arise from lack of rewards. That is to say, an actor as a system, as well as groups or larger systems, require inputs to support his behavior. These inputs are the basis of a reward system which reinforces patterns of behavior. When expected and needed inputs are received, they act as rewards; when they are withheld or changed in some way, the system is punished. When expected inputs are not received, a stress is established between the system and its environment. The result is that the system reacts by seeking a new source of inputs; changing so that the input is no longer required; or becoming disorganized and ceasing to function.

The morphogenesis of social systems may be said to be a product of stress-elimination processes through which systems learn new, less stressful forms of adaptation to their environments. New norms—individually-defined behavior expectations which may or may not be shared—may be introduced into social systems through the learning behavior of individual actors in reacting to stressful situations.

We can use role conflict to illustrate this point. Role conflict arises when an actor faces a situation in which the definition of his roles calls for behavior which is inconsistent or in conflict. In other words, two or more norms which define his roles call for behaviors which are mutually exclusive, or morally or logically inconsistent.

Mr. Brown, for example, the salesman for the Ajax Black Box Factory, is required by his job to travel and therefore to spend a great deal of time away from home. He is married, and has a teenaged son who is due to graduate from high school. He realizes that he has made an appointment with Mr. Green, the president of the Acme Instrument Company, to discuss his company's bid on a large contract for black boxes on the day his son graduates. He knows that his competitors are working hard to get the contract, and that he does not have much time left if he is going to make this sale. He also knows that his commission on the sale will pay a good part of the tuition for his son's first year in college. His dilemma is over which role requirements he will satisfy. Will he miss his son's graduation and make the trip as scheduled? or will he cancel the trip and take a chance on losing the sale in order to attend graduation? He thinks, "Will I really miss the sale if I don't go? Maybe the decision has already been made. But if not, I might miss the sale just to do something that's really not that important."

Mr. Brown realizes that whichever choice he makes, he will have done something other people are not going to approve. He also realizes that whichever he does, he will feel guilty and uneasy. In short, Mr. Brown is experiencing a very unpleasant set of mental stimuli in the form of anxiety, guilt, and anticipation of future punishment from social disapproval. His conflict involves two norms which cannot be satisfied at the same time. If one is followed, the other one is ruled out. Mr. Brown cannot be at two places in social and physical space at the same time.

The second sort of role conflict is illustrated by the case of the physician who has a patient suffering from a terminal illness who is in great pain. The norms of his profession, on the one hand, say that he is obligated to preserve life at all costs. Other norms say that he is supposed to reduce human suffering and treat his patients humanely. He is practically certain that his patient can live only a short time, and that nothing can be done to save him. He sees the anguish of the patient, and of his family who want to preserve the life of the patient as long as possible, since he is someone they love. Even they, however, agonize over the patient's physical pain. Shall the doctor follow the norms that call for preserving life as long as possible? or shall he end the pain by ending the life? Either action will be defined as wrong in terms of the other norm. So again, the conflicted individual feels anxiety, guilt, fear of social disapproval, and fear of sanctions that may be brought to bear on him, no matter what he does.

Both these examples illustrate that role conflict is experienced as a punishing set of internal stimuli affecting the actor involved. It is something to be avoided, if possible, and eliminated with dispatch, if feasible. Actors therefore search for ways to redefine the norms, so that the stress will be eliminated. Or, they withdraw from one or more of the roles that involve the norms. Role conflicts are no longer experienced if and when either of these attempts to eliminate stress is successful, so that the structure of the system will have been changed to become more internally consistent. Mr. Brown, for instance, could withdraw from one or the other of the relationship systems; that is, either divorce or separate from his family, or leave his company.

If many individuals tried to resolve the same situation in these ways, the selective processes would operate so that unmarried individuals survive to become the most effective salesmen, or high divorce rates occur among salesmen. The doctor's role conflict may be resolved by developing sets of private norms, either within the medical community or by the individual physician, that formulate expectations that define when one norm takes precedence over the other. Professional secrecy may be developed to shelter the individual physician from public sanction when the choice that he has made runs counter to the norms of alter actors outside the profession.

The point of this discussion is that the strain toward consistency in the structure of social system has its source in stresses experienced by the individual as role conflict, in the punishing effects of inconsistencies experienced by the individual, and in the reinforcing effects of reward received when a solution to a conflict or stress problem is found.

Interpersonal conflicts also work to eliminate stress. When individuals undergoing some intrapersonal stress from role conflict choose the norms they will follow, they automatically deviate from the expectations of some alter actors in the situation, and come into interpersonal conflict with them. The anticipation of interpersonal conflict and its punishing effects is a source of anxiety for the individual, for individuals in interpersonal conflict use various forms of sanctions to modify the behavior of the other person to conform with their own expectations. These negative sanctions are punishing, and are therefore to be avoided. Both inter- and intrapersonal conflict waste energy, time, and effort on activities that do not satisfy the normative requirements of any particular role. They therefore impair the functioning of the individual as a member of the social system, and consequently the functioning of the system itself.

When actors interact, they also exchange rewards; and these rewards tend to reinforce the pattern of interaction among them. When one actor deviates from the established pattern, the deviation has the effect of withholding rewards from the other actors dependent on him —that is, assuming, as we do, that actors interact with one another in order to exchange some things that each needs out of the interaction, and that all behavior is potentially rewarding or punishing to the parties who are interacting. We also assume, along with the learning theorists, that the parties to interaction learn new forms of behavior and maintain old ones through being rewarded or reinforced; and that they engage in exploratory or avoidance behavior to eliminate punishment, or to reestablish a satisfactory set of rewards. We contend that the strain toward consistency in social systems operates to establish a structure through which rewards will reinforce behavior, and punishing stresses, which interfere with reward and reinforcement, will be reduced for actors who participate in it. Since actors are interdependent in each social situation, the resolution to these problems must in the long run be social rather than individual.

In Figure 14-1, the role, status, position, group, organization, community, and society are all regarded as system concepts. Consequently, the strain toward consistency must operate in each one of these systems. Roles are systems of norms organized around a function performed by one actor toward another in a group. The strain toward consistency operates among the norms to produce an internal adjustment among the various parts of the role. In statuses and positions, a strain toward consistency operates among roles; at the group level it operates among positions; and at the level of multigroup organizations among the structures of groups. The strain toward consistency in social systems operates with greatest force among parts which are structurally close to each other. This means that two norms that are part of the same role are more apt to become consistent with each other than norms which are a part of different roles in widely separated parts of the social system. We will discuss this more fully below.

The reactions of human beings to stress orient social systems in a direction of internal consistency. It would be wrong to say, however, that a state of internal consistency is ever achieved. Changes are constantly being introduced into the structure of social systems and these changes simultaneously introduce inconsistencies. When a change occurs, processes are set in motion that tend to incorporate it into the system as a consistent part of its structure; but before such internal consistency is ever achieved, new waves of change occur. So, although the system is always oriented in the direction of achieving internal consistency, it may move toward or away from a state of perfect consistency as changes are introduced into it, and these are incorporated into a system as a regularized part of its structure. It is also possible that successive waves of change may combine to produce such a large amount of inconsistency and stress that the system is unable to contend with it. As a consequence the processes set in motion may never function to produce morphogenic adaptation, but instead may lead to the breakdown and dissolution of the system.

PART IV

THE ACTOR
AS A PARTICIPANT
IN SOCIAL SYSTEMS

CHAPTER 15

PERSON-CENTERED ANALYSIS

The last several chapters have been devoted to analyzing the structure of social systems. Such analysis focuses attention on the system as an organiz entity having its own internal structure. The system being studied is a social system—either a group, an organization, a community, or a society. Despite the fact that all social systems involve the participation of individual actors, system analysis focuses on the structure and functioning of groups and multigroup systems. The individual human being is not the center of attention.

In person-centered analysis, the opposite is true: the individual is the center of attention, and the focus is placed on understanding the structure and functioning of the actor as a system of behavior. The difference between person-centered and system-centered analysis lies in the way in which observations of human behavior are classified, and the use to which they are put in testing hypotheses, constructing descriptions, or building models. Both forms of analysis rest on the same data—observations of human behavior; but structural models for person-centered analysis involve slightly different concepts from those used in system-centered analysis.

Person-centered Structural Units

We can speak of the structure and organization of social systems. We can also discuss individual human beings in these terms. The individual, as an actor, is both a system of latent action and a system of real behavior. In terms of latent action, the individual may be viewed as a personality system whose structure at any given moment predisposes the individual to respond in certain ways to stimuli received from the environment. Let us explore first that part of the personality that corresponds to an individual's internalized cultural structure.

The individual as personality is, in a sense, comparable to a computer that has been programmed. The personality's program, its circuitry, and its current state of repair predispose it to react to data fed into it in certain ways. The personality of the individual, therefore, can be regarded as a set of predispositions, the result of a complex combination of factors that have acted upon the individual in the past and are acting upon him at the present. One subset of predisposing factors is the collection of norms stored as ideas about what kind of behavior is expected or appropriate under given circumstances—that is, the internalized cultural structure of social systems within which the individual participates or anticipates being part of. Other factors exist within the personality of the individual which interact with cultural structure to form the set of predispositions to act; they will be discussed later.

Beside seeing the person as a set of predispositions to act, or as a personality, we can regard him as a series of acts actually performed in real time and in real space. Therefore, some of the concepts of system-centered analysis can be applied to analysis of the actor as a behavior system. Position, for one, will allow us to talk about the normative structure that applies to the person's participation in one group, as well as to the acts he performs. Status will allow us to talk about his action in relation to a single class of alters. And role, to speak of his actions in relation to a given function.

Figure 15-1 compares person-centered and system-centered concepts. Norm, role, status, and position, apply to the behavior of one person, either in the cultural structure or the social organization form. Acts and norms combine around functions to form roles. Roles are learned by individuals in the form of norms stored within their personalities, and are enacted by individuals in groups. Repertoires of roles are learned by persons to be performed toward specific alters, and are referred to as status. Finally, individuals perform behavior in groups, and the collection of roles performed in one group is referred to as position.

The concepts necessary for person-centered analysis diverge from those necessary for system analysis at the multigroup level. In organizations, communities, and societies, individuals occupy many different positions. By definition, each position is in the structure of a different group. These positions, all occupied by the same actor, but in different groups within multigroup systems, form sets of positions by virtue of the fact that the same person occupies them (1). In other words, there are reflexive relationships among the positions in these sets. Figure 15-1

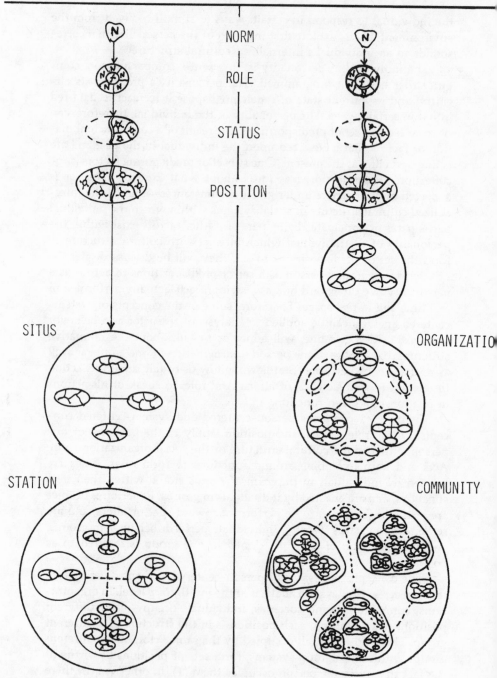

Figure 15–1   Forms of Structural Analysis

shows two types of position sets of this sort. One type is called a *social situs* and the other a *social station*.

Situs refers to the set of positions occupied by one actor in an organization or association (2). Mr. Brown occupies several positions within the multigroup system of the Ajax Black Box Factory. These positions form a set called his situs in that organization. Another example of a situs is the collection of positions occupied by one person in the many kin groups to which he belongs.

Station refers to all the positions occupied by the person in society (3). It is comprised of a collection of situses. Station thus refers to the total individual, and therefore, to the individual's total participation in society. This total participation can be subdivided into his participation in organizations, so that situses represent parts of stations. Each situs, in turn, can be subdivided into the positions the individual occupies in various groups that are part of an organization. Thus, in the station structure of an individual, there is one position for each group to which he belongs, and these positions are collected into situses according to the organizations in which the positions are located.

Beyond the level of the group, we have to use different concepts for person-centered and system-centered analysis. Social systems consist of combinations or sets of groups that are articulated with each other to form a larger structure. Groups are sets of positions in which each position in the structure of the group is occupied by a different actor. In contrast, situses are sets of positions, each of which is occupied by the same actor, as are stations. As a consequence, we cannot construct sets of situses, maintaining the integrity of the situs-set as a bounded entity, and at the same time construct sets of groups which form multigroup systems, maintaining the integrity of group boundaries, organizational boundaries, and other system boundaries.

Social systems form sets of positions which are put together to form group structures and multigroup structures in a geometric form different from the positions which form situses and stations. Consequently, it cannot be said that the structure of an organization consists of a set of situses. If we treat situses as bounded systems of positions, and relate one situs to another, we cannot at the same time construct an accurate image of the group structure involved in an organization. Situses and stations dissolve social systems, because they separate out all the behavior or all the norms which apply to a single actor, and put them into one set of categories. In contrast, social systems, which by their nature involve multiple actors, dissolve the individual by allocating those portions of his behavior that belong to different groups to different points in social space. This is why person-centered and system-centered analyses diverge at the multigroup system level.

Figure 15-2 contrasts groups and situses. It illustrates the fact that person-centered analysis places positions together, classifying them according to structural units. Group analysis is part of the system-centered approach; it classifies positions according to patterns of interaction which take place among actors, and derives a set of positions, each of which is occupied by a different person. Situs structure, as a part of person-centered analysis, takes all of the positions of a given actor related to a certain organization, and puts them together. And finally,

Figure 15–2   The Relationship Between
Station Structure and Group Structure

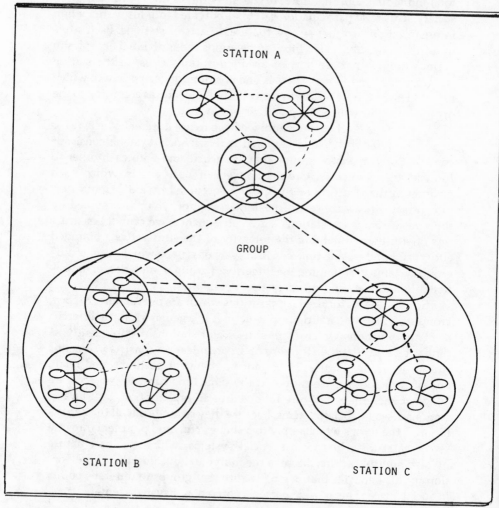

as Figure 15-1 shows, situs corresponds in size to an organization as a social system and its boundaries; station corresponds to society as a social system and its boundaries.

Let us now examine situs and station structure, and illustrate their nature as general analytical tools.

Kinship Situs

An example of a hypothetical kinship situs is shown in Figure 15-3. It will be recalled that extended families were classified above as organizations, since they consist of a number of distinct groups—nuclear families—joined together in a system of relationships to form a multigroup structure. Within this structure, a person occupies multiple positions. In Figure 15-3, ego is shown occupying the position of father-husband in his nuclear conjugal family group, comprised of himself, his wife, and their children. He is shown occupying another position of son and brother in his family of origin. These two nuclear families are two distinct elemental groups. He also occupies positions in certain interstitial groups that stand between the two nuclear families; for example, the position of uncle in an interstitial group that stands between his family of origin and the nuclear families of his married brothers and sisters. Ego here has only one sibling and one child. If he had several siblings, there would be several positions of uncle, with identical role contents, but in different interstitial groups joining ego's family of origin to the nuclear families of his siblings. The position of grandson exists in the structure of a group which stands between his father's family of origin and his family of origin. Similar interstitial group positions are occupied with respect to his wife's family, and to the families of his children's spouses. Taken together, all of the positions occupied within kinship groups form a set of interrelated positions that is classified as the kinship situs.

This set of positions forming the situs is a system of positions which are interrelated by virtue of having a common actor performing all of the roles contained within them. In Figure 15-3, the lines that connect the various positions are meant to indicate extramural role relationships between positions in elemental groups, and positions in interstitial groups. Every position that forms the situs is not directly related to every other one. Instead, there are definite connections, generated by extramural role requirements, that dictate specific connections between various positions occupied by the same actor in the kinship structure.

Situses therefore have a definite internal structure. This structure, like all structures, consists of certain parts that stand in a certain relationship to each other in space. Situses are not simply a collection of positions, each of which is equally related to every other one by virtue of being members of the same set. Instead, each position in a set fits into a specific network of interrelationships at a particular point. It is also true that a situs is a particular collection of positions in which each position exists in a particular group. The kinship situs of two different persons, therefore, may have quite different structures. The case shown in Figure 15-3 represents a male who has a child old enough to be married, and whose paternal grandparents are still living, but whose maternal grandparents are not. He is also a person who has at least one married brother, with children; and whose father has one brother or sister who is alive, with children. Some kinship situses are much more complex than this; others much simpler.

However simple or complex, though, a situs is a real unit existing in the real structure of society. It is not a model for an abstract, fully-developed kinship organization that applies to no particular case, but to all potential cases in a given society. If we drew a map of the group structure of a kinship unit to show the groups that exist within it; and also drew the connections between groups, both elemental and interstitial; and then lifted out of this map all the positions occupied by the same actor, we would have the structure of the kinship situs of that particular individual. If we did this with each set of positions occupied

Figure 15–3   Kinship Situs

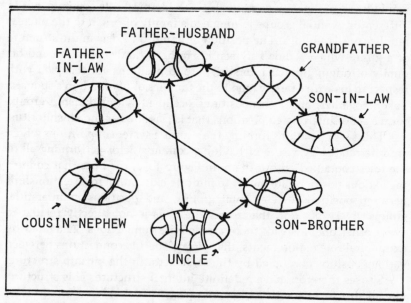

FATHER-HUSBAND

GRANDFATHER

FATHER-
IN-LAW

SON-IN-LAW

COUSIN-NEPHEW

SON-BROTHER

UNCLE

by the same individual, we would eventually remove every position from the map of the kinship organization. It is clear that the situses of two individuals removed from this system separately would be related to each other by complementary relationships only at certain specific points. These points would correspond to those groups within which each individual occupies a position, and in which they perform complementary roles toward each other.

All relationships within the situs structure are of the reciprocal, reflexive form. They are reciprocal because they are drawn from the structure of an organization, rather than a community; and they are reflexive because all positions are occupied by the same actor. As we remove a situs from the structure of a social system, we also remove some of the connective tissue that joins groups together into the larger system. From this perspective, situses structurally represent mechanisms through which parts of social systems are joined to each other through the device of multiple group membership by the same actor.

This phenomenon is illustrated in Figure 15-4, which shows a situs at the center; the various groups, in which the individual positions are located, surround it. The groups at the border are all connected to one another through the situs structure. This structure consists of positions occupied by the same actor connected by reflexive-reciprocal role relationships.

Reflexive-conjunctive relationships exist among positions contained in different situses in the same station. This is the result of the fact that each situs is drawn from a different organization or multigroup system. In system-centered analysis, each organization stands in a conjunctive relationship to all organizations in its environment. It follows, therefore, that positions lifted from the structure of one organization to form one situs will stand in a conjunctive relationship to positions lifted from another organization structure. However, this will only be true when an extramural role exists within one situs that generates a reflexive relationship to a role contained in another situs. When this occurs, a reflexive-conjunctive relationship is generated. All the positions contained within a situs do not necessarily have a direct relationship to every other position in the situs. Nor need every position in one situs be related to every one in all the others in the same station. Connections exist only where extramural roles and reflexive relationships are found.

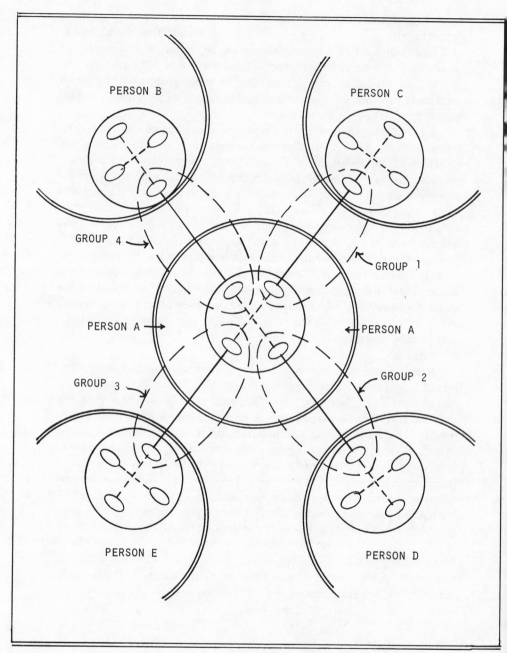

Figure 15–4   The Station of a Single Actor
Joining Several Groups

Occupational Situs

Figure 15-5 shows a hypothetical occupational situs that consists of all the positions that an elementary school teacher occupies in a particular elementary school, Public School Number 21. In the school, she occupies the position of fourth-grade homeroom teacher in a group that consists of herself and a number of elementary school students. In this particular group, she performs various roles with respect to students. She also occupies another position in a different group that consists of the faculty members and staff of Public School 21, shown as the "faculty-member position." Here she performs a set of roles toward other faculty members and the administration of the school. In this group she does not teach, nor does she discipline or examine. Instead, she performs administrative-colleague roles. She also occupies other positions in other systems of relationships that form groups within the elementary school. For example, the fourth-grade students in this school are divided according to their level of achievement in reading, and assigned to special reading groups. She occupies a position of instructor in the low reading group. In this group she has certain roles to perform which are

Figure 15–5 Occupational Situs Structure

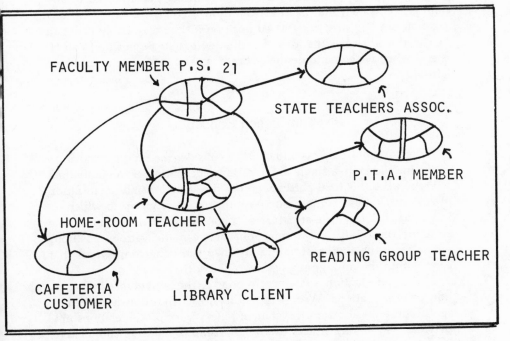

FACULTY MEMBER P.S. 21

STATE TEACHERS ASSOC.

P.T.A. MEMBER

HOME-ROOM TEACHER

READING GROUP TEACHER

CAFETERIA
CUSTOMER   LIBRARY CLIENT

almost, but not quite, identical to those she performs in the homeroom. She also occupies the position once a week of playground monitor during recess periods, and at other times interacts with the librarian as a client of the library. Once a month she can be observed performing the roles of P-T.A. member in a P-T.A. meeting, and at other times she can be seen as occupying the position and performing the roles of secretary of the State Teachers Association.

Each of the positions shown in Figure 15-5 is part of the structure of different social groups. All are joined by virtue of being part of the same organizational structure, or because they exist within interstitial groups where the teacher represents that organizational structure to persons from other organizations and groups in the environment. As in the case of the kinship situs, the structure of the occupational situs can be lifted analytically out of the structure of an organization. Within it, all relationships are reflexive-reciprocal and are specific in terms of extramural role requirements, so that the occupational situs has a definite internal structure.

A person has a situs for every organization to which he or she belongs, and that situs varies in the number of positions contained within its structure. Some contain only one position: that would be a situs for a group within the structure of society not attached to any multigroup system that is an organization. Actually, a situs with one position can be called an isolated position just as reasonably as it can be called a situs; but the idea of a situs with a single position will be useful when we come to define a station as a collection of interrelated situses.

The Station Concept

The concept of a situs allows us to consider the total participation of the individual in a single organization. The station of the individual corresponds to his total participation in the structure and organization of society. Stations contain one position for every group to which an individual belongs. The structure of a station can be lifted out of the structure of society; the connections between the various positions which form the station structure are then the same connections that exist within the multigroup system called society.

Within the station, situses correspond to the individual's participation in organizations. Within the situses, each position is related to specific other positions by a system of reflexive reciprocal relationships. Between and among situses, the relationship is reflexive conjunctive. For example, let us suppose that the public school teacher of Figure 15-4 is the same individual whose kinship situs is shown in Figure 15-3. The father-husband position of Figure 15-3 includes a provider role, which is an extramural role requiring the individual to have a job in an organization. In this case, a definite extramural connection would exist between this position and the position in Figure 15-4, employee of the county. This link would be a reflexive conjunctive link rather than a reciprocal one, because the function and structural orientation of the

Figure 15–6   Station Structure for a Mature
Middle-Class Male Showing Situses

Figure 15-6 shows the relationship between the situs

and station concepts. In this figure the solid lines

represent reflexive reciprocal relationships and the dotted

lines, reflexive conjunctive ones.

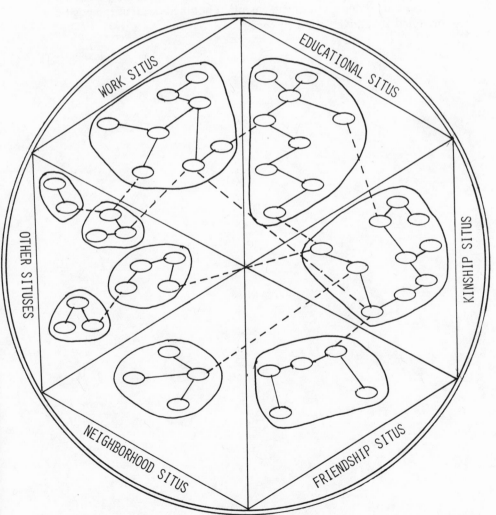

kinship system is different from the functional and structural orientation of the public school system. Therefore, the behavior performed within the context of the occupational position is oriented toward performing different functions in society. This means that the relationship is conjunctive. Thus, within stations, situses are joined by conjunctive relationships. These relationships are generated by particular extramural role requirements derived from a division of labor in society, and from the interdependence among groups and organizations created by this division of labor.

Figure 15-6 shows the relationship between the situs and station concepts. In this figure the solid lines represent reflexive reciprocal relationships and the dotted lines, reflexive conjunctive ones.

It should be noted that *society,* here, refers to the unit out of which the station has been lifted, rather than the community. In other words, the station refers to the nth-order community. If we use anything lower than an nth-order community, we might not include all of the positions occupied by a given actor in society.

CHAPTER 16

PERSONALITY AND SOCIAL STRUCTURE

The study of personality is not a central concern to the sociologist, or to the student of social structure and social organization; nonetheless, in order for us to understand the processes of interaction in groups, we must understand the actor as a system. Our theory of behavior is that four factors influence the determination of human action in real situations: cultural structure, personality, situation, and interaction. Until now, we have been concerned with defining the nature and form of the cultural structure variable, and with outlining a scheme for dealing structurally with real human behavior in large complex systems. Now we must consider the actor as a system, and see how the personality factor relates to sociocultural structure, on the one hand, and to the organization of human behavior on the other.

Conceptions of human personality have, for the most part, been formulated without particular reference to the details of the structure and organization of society. The study of personality has been properly directed, instead, toward understanding the actor as a system of behavior, and toward comprehending those psychological or social-psychological processes which occur in the individual or between the individual and his immediate social environment (1). As a consequence, we need a conception of the person and personality that is particularly designed to fit into the context of the structure of society.

Actors, Persons, and Personalities

In dealing with the individual, we face the same problem as we did in dealing with social systems, namely, the problem of latent versus active behavior. Since individual human beings perform all of the actions that constitute the group in an active state, and since they are the carriers of the role definitions that constitute the group in a latent state, it will be fruitful for us to begin formulating our concept of personality with the concept of the individual in terms of activity and latency.

Individuals may be viewed as a set of real actions that occur in real time and space. During any given short span of time, only a finite number out of the large repertoire of actions ever performed by the individual are actually occurring; in other words, only one part of the individual's repertoire of behavior is active. The repertoire, in the sense of the actions the individual is prepared to perform by virtue of a configuration of factors existing within him as a living system, constitutes latent behavior. Henceforth, we will use *personality* to refer to the individual as latent behavior, and *actor* to refer to him as active, real behavior. *Person* refers to both the active and latent behavior systems of the individual. These distinctions between the person as active behavior and latent behavior, and between the actor and the personality, will become clear once we define the contents of the personality and how they are structured to form a system.

Personality Structures

It is commonplace to say that human beings learn or internalize the culture of their society through the process of socialization. No individual in complex societies ever learns the entire culture; instead, individuals learn specialized aspects of the total culture. In particular, they learn those aspects of the culture that impinge upon the groups, organizations, and communities in which they participate as actors.

The culture of a society has a particular structure. It consists of norms which are organized to define roles, that are in turn combined into positions, group structures, and organizational structures. When people learn the culture of the society as it applies to them, they learn the roles that apply to the positions they occupy in society. They also learn their organizations as positions, and combinations of positions into other more complex structures. The culture, therefore, has a definite structure when it is internalized by the individual.

It seems reasonable for us to assume that for a given person, the internalized social structure that applies to him has the structure of a station. At any given time, the internalized station structure that applies to the person as an actor in society is contained within his personality. The station structure of Mr. Jones, the president of the Black Box Factory, exists within the personality system of Mr. Jones, the actor, who participates in the Black Box Factory and other parts of society. Ralph Linton remarked that culture exists in the minds of men (2), and our statements about the latent sociocultural structure of society are actually a refinement of Linton's point of view. But cultural structure does not exist in a collective mind; instead, parts of the total sociocultural structure exist in particular real minds of real men. Mr. Jones' station, as a latent structure, is a set of role definitions organized in certain ways to form a configuration of positions, which themselves are interconnected in intricate patterns and exist as internalized latent behavior stored in the personality of Mr. Jones.

Figure 16-1 diagrams personality as a large circle; inside it a smaller circle represents the structure of the actor's station. The larger circle represents the organism—all the organic attributes and processes which constitute the individual as an animal. This circle contains the biological apparatus of perception, thought, memory, association, muscular movement and control, motivation, and emotion that make up the person as a biological system. Figure 16-1 therefore depicts the person as an organic system imprinted with those aspects of the culture to which the individual has been exposed. It further depicts these aspects of culture as organized within the system in such a way that particular parts of the cultural structure are associated with each other to form the normative definitions of roles, positions, situses, and finally, station structure.

In psychological terms, the norms making up a particular role learned by the individual are internalized as part of his personality, and have been learned as a set. As a consequence, mental associational processes operate in such a way that one member of the set, a particular norm, is associated with other members of the set in a psychophysical storage system of the organism. The norms, in other words, are stored in configurations that correspond to the structure of the station of the individual at the particular time they were learned.

Cultural Structure: The Normative Subsystem

The cultural structure cell within the personality depicted in Figure 16-1 contains the station structure of the individual. It is apparent that the personality of an individual must contain more of the sociocultural structure than that which corresponds to his own individual station, since the person's station consists only of those role definitions that apply to him as the ego actor. In order for the individual to function in a social system, he has to know not only his own roles, but something about the roles of other people with whom he interacts. Ego must therefore have not only a conception of his own roles, but he must have some conception of the roles performed toward him by alters in the groups within which he participates.

Figure 16-2 expands the picture of the sociocultural structure component or cell contained within the personality of an individual, to show the station structure as the central element and organizing principle. Around the station are normative conceptions of the roles and positions of alters with whom ego interacts in society. This entire structure consists of a cognitive map comprised of norms defining the cultural structure of society from the perspective of ego.

Since ego occupies a particular region, or, more properly, set of

Figure 16–1   Station Structure as a Part of Personality

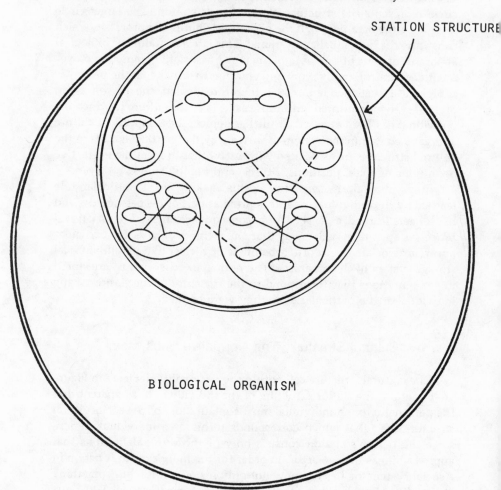

STATION STRUCTURE

BIOLOGICAL ORGANISM

regions, in the structure of his society, and he participates in it only in specific and limited ways, his conception of the structure of society in the form of role definitions and norms is limited. In other words, his cognitive map of the cultural structure of society is incomplete, and turns hazy and spotty in structurally distant aspects of the culture. The individual learns and internalizes only those aspects of the culture to which he is exposed either directly or indirectly, and these aspects of culture have a definite ordering as they are stored within the individual. Ego learns roles assigned to him by interacting with people in group situations. As he does, he also learns some of the norms which apply

Figure 16–2   The Cultural Structure Portion of Personality

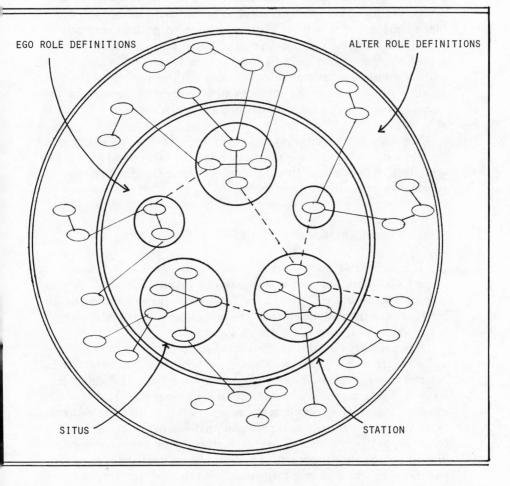

to the behavior of alters with whom he must interact.

A third category of norms that ego learns are norms that apply to positions and roles with which he has had no direct experience, but which are the subject of communications in group situations or in mass media. For example, ego may learn norms that apply to the behavior of the president of the United States, without ever having any direct contact with the situations in which presidential norms apply. He may learn such norms by hearing them expressed by others in group situations, by observing the president on television, by reading about him in books, or from a number of other sources.

The important point is that the normative map stored within ego's personality contains norms that define roles for (a) himself; (b) alter actors; and (c) certain nonalter actors who occupy positions known to him in the social structure. These norms are organized into sets or clusters, defining in varying degrees of detail positions and roles occupied by ego, and by persons to whom he relates either directly or indirectly in the social structure. We shall call this portion of the personality system containing the normative content of personality the *normative subsystem.* The normative definition of ego's station structure is at its core.

There are two other subsystems within the personality of ego that must be explored. These are: (1) the information subsystem; and (2) the attitudinal subsystem. Figure 16-3 shows these three subsystems of personality in relation to one another.

Informational and Attitudinal Subsystems

The normative subsystem contains ideas about how the world ought to be. Norms specify how ego thinks that he, alters, and certain other actors should feel, think, and act in relation to various stimuli received from their environments. The normative subsystem, therefore, is ego's ideal blueprint for action in society.

A personality contains another set of ideas gained from experience in the environment. These are ideas about what is or has been real, in contrast to what should be or should have been true. This subsystem consists of information, assumed to be factual, about the world in which ego lives. Ego receives certain sense impressions that are recorded in his psychobiological system as representations of what exists or what is occurring, both within ego as an organism and in the world surrounding him. In contrast to the normative system, the information system contains what ego takes to be information about the real world, rather than the ideal world.

For example, Harry Jones' normative system contains the idea that secretaries, when performing their role as typists, are not supposed to present letters for his signature that have strikeovers. This is a normative idea. One day, Harry is given a letter by his secretary for his signature that does have strikeovers. This situation is recorded in his personality as a bit of information, is regarded as a fact, and stored in his information system. When it is evaluated against norms, a third kind of idea—an attitude—is formed.

Figure 16–3   Personality as a System of Latent Action

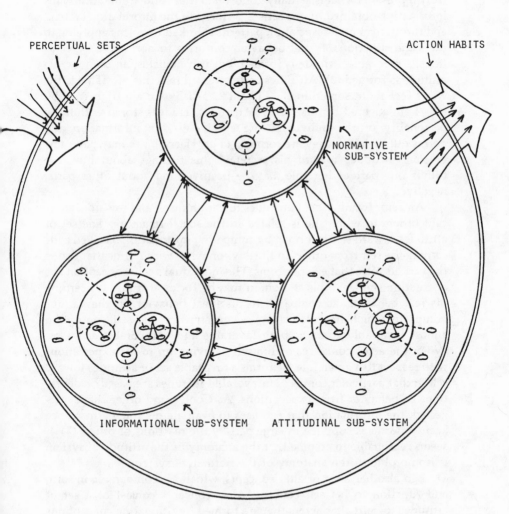

Ego forms attitudes toward himself, the world he lives in, and the people he deals with on the basis of a comparison between norms and perceived facts. Harry Jones has certain ideas about how his secretary ought to act in performing her various roles within the office, which amounts to a normative map of the way things should or ought to be, drawn from his perspective. Day by day, in his associations with his secretary, he receives bits and pieces of sense data in the form of information about the way she actually does fulfill her various roles. He considers this information as factual, regardless of whether or not it truly represents what is actually going on in the world around him. This information obtained by the senses is stored in the information system, and through mental-association patterns is linked to norms applying to the same situations. If real behavior conforms to normative expectations, a favorable attitude is formed; but if it deviates, an unfavorable attitude is formed (3). Attitudes are expressed in terms of, "This is the way I feel about something." "I like it." "I dislike or am frightened by it." "I am angered because of it." Attitudes, as ideas stored within the personality of the individual, are specific to the information and norms out of which they are formed. Thus, Harry Jones may have ambivalent attitudes toward his secretary: his feelings about how she fulfills one part of her role may be positive, and about other parts, negative.

An actor forms a set of attitudes toward himself and toward significant others to whom he is related in the social structure. The set of attitudes toward self is formed by comparing information received concerning the self from others in the environment, with norms that define the various roles that ego performs. The individual's self-conception has a structure similar to his station, in that he forms attitudes concerning his real behavior, as compared to his ideal behavior, in the various groups to which he belongs. As a consequence, his self-conception almost invariably contains both favorable and unfavorable attitudes. When the actor conceives of himself as living up to his expectations with respect to a given role, he forms a favorable set of attitudes toward self in that particular context. Unfavorable attitudes are based on deviations of behavior from expectations. As Cooley and others have suggested, the information that ego uses to evaluate his role performance against norms is supplied in large part by the reactions of others (4). It seems reasonable to assume that the anatomy of the attitudinal system is isomorphic to the anatomy of the normative system.

Ego also has a set of alter concepts, which are comparable in form and function to his self-concept. Alter concepts consist of a set of attitudes toward alter actors that are formed by comparing conceptions of alter's behavior with ego's normative expectations of alter. Furthermore, attitudes are also formed toward physical objects and phenomena of various sorts with which ego comes in contact as an actor—for instance, foods, automobiles, sunsets, or music. Since these objects and phenomena are encountered by ego in the process of occupying one of his various positions in performing one of his various roles, the attitudes toward them are formed in this context, and stored along with self- and alter attitudes appropriate to the same context.

Attitudes, like norms, must be defined in terms of active and latent states. An attitude is only activated within the proper temporal and spatial context. That context always contains some of the elements that were present during the formation of the attitude itself, and these elements trigger the attitudes. It is therefore incorrect to conceive of a person, who has a certain attitude stored in him, as feeling this attitude all of the time. Attitudes, like norms, are latent most of the time, and only activated at specific times. It is while they are in an active state that they operate as influences on behavior.

Structure of the Three Subsystems

Each of the three subsystems, then, contains a different kind of idea. A norm is an idea about how things ought to be. A bit of information is an idea about how things are. Attitudes are ideas about how ego feels about the way things are. Norms are filed in the memory of the individual according to the positions and roles to which they apply; therefore, the structure of the filing system is given by the structure of the station of the individual, and its articulation with alter positions and roles within the larger society. Things are stored in this way because they are learned this way. Norms that apply to a given role are learned in the same situation, with a limited number of alters acting as socializers. The norms are therefore encountered in close proximity to each other in time and space, associated with each other mentally, and stored in sets. These sets take the form of role definitions, positional definitions, situs structures, and station structure. The storage system for both information and attitude is similar in structure. As a matter of fact, these three systems are structurally isomorphic. The structure of the three subsystems is a consequence of the way human beings learn, and then recall or remember things that they have learned.

Socialization and the Formation of Norms and Attitudes

At birth, a human individual may be characterized as a biological or organic system possessing the capacity to assemble and process information obtained through the senses. At the moment of birth, this system is relatively, if not completely, free of information. At present the exact processes through which human beings, using their senses, convert stimuli received from the environment into information stored in the organism is not completely understood, although learning theory does offer a workable way to imagine what those processes must be like (5). It is enough here to say that, after birth, individual human beings do begin to register sense impressions in their minds as information.

Let us assume that this information comes in pieces or units called *bits*. We can imagine bits of information being received by the organism through its senses, in various sequences, and in various spatial combinations that form sets of information. Since the human infant is relatively helpless and dependent upon others, the flow of information from the environment to the infant is controlled and mediated by others. This means that the sequence with which information is received, and the combination of bits of information into spatial sets, are controlled—sometimes deliberately, sometimes unconsciously—by other persons in the environment.

Bits of information received close to each other in time and space, and joined to each other by some common qualitative element in the form of stimulus, are classified or stored together in the information storage system of the infant (6). As the same sequence occurs over and over again, with the same set of information encountered each time, expectations are built up in his mind. Let us say that three bits of information have occurred together over and over again—A, B, and C. The infant comes to expect that when he perceives A and B, C will follow. The infant's mother appears in his sensory field (A). She has a baby bottle in her hand (B). He expects that she will place the bottle in his mouth (C). In Pavlovian terms, when the infant sees the mother, bottle in hand, we can predict that he salivates, since he anticipates the third stimulus on the basis of the first two (7).

When a set of information is built up in the memory of the organism in such a way that some members of the set lead it to expect that other members of the set will occur, the basis of a norm has been laid; or, perhaps more properly, the basis for a set of norms has been laid. Norms consist of the idea that certain behavior is appropriate or expected, given a certain set of stimuli as perceived by the actor. It is a short step from the idea that, "When mother appears with bottle in hand, she will feed me," to the idea that mother *should* feed me.

When this generalization—that mother should feed me—is made on the basis of associating bits of information in sequences and sets, a norm has been formed, and stored. In other words, norms are ideas originally based on predictions that certain events will occur if other events have; or, when certain events occur, other events should also. Norms may be regarded as generalizations made about sets and sequences of information obtained through the senses. Once a human being has amassed enough experience, and assembled information on the basis of it, he forms at least a rudimentary set of norms. Later on, the process of norm formation becomes quite sophisticated. The individual may learn, for example, that "When my mother or father says a person should do a certain thing, and I do what they say I should, I am rewarded with approval and other rewards. When they say I should do a certain thing and I do not do it, rewards are withdrawn and punishments follow. Therefore, if I accept what they say as a norm, I will increase the probability of being rewarded" (8).

The individual may eventually learn norms directly by accepting the normative statements that other people make as part of his own normative structure. Ego observes through his senses a statement of norms made by another person, for example, a significant alter such as his mother or father. The statement of a mother's norms is registered in ego as information. Ego knows mother expects so and so. His information system already contains information to the effect that if she expects a given thing, and her wishes are not taken into account, then a certain set of consequences will follow. Ego is then faced with the problem of whether to accept the norm stated by his mother as a guide for his behavior, or to treat it as information which must be taken into account in his behavior. It is only when ego translates normative statements of a significant alter into an operative expectation for himself that it becomes a norm for him. Until this occurs, the norms or expectations of others with respect to ego are merely information that ego has obtained from his environment. In order for a norm to be accepted by ego as a guide to his behavior, it is probably true that he must practice it. He must expect, on the basis of certain signals or stimuli received from the environment, that certain events will follow that are right, proper, intelligent, correct, moral, just, or efficient.

Let us consider a situation that illustrates norms and information. Mr. Jones, president of the Ajax Black Box Factory, is sitting in his office reading the morning mail. Someone knocks on the door. Mr. Jones looks up from the letter he is reading, and says, "Come in." His secretary enters, followed by a middleaged man in a business suit. The secretary says, "Mr. Jones, this is Tom Green, who represents the Acme Instrument Company." Mr. Jones rises from his seat, walks around his desk, extends his right hand to Mr. Green, and they shake hands. Mr. Jones says that he is pleased to meet him and asks him to sit down. What has happened in terms of information and norms? When the door opens and the secretary steps in, followed by Mr. Green, Jones is bombarded by bits of information. He sees immediately that Green is a stranger, and also that he is dressed as he ought to be if he is on business. His secretary introduces the stranger as a representative of the Acme Instrument Company. Jones' problem, which admittedly is simple, is to decide what this information means in terms of how he should respond to Mr. Green's behavior.

The information received by Jones is being recorded in his memory, and stored away for later use. On future occasions, he will recognize Green; and since he has a good memory, he will associate him with the Acme Instrument Company. An image of Green's face, appearance, the way he stands, the sound of his voice, and so forth will become a part of his permanent information storage. A second aspect of the information received by Jones is related to information he already has as a functioning personality system. He has many similar memories of his secretary leading visitors into his office and introducing them. These memories are associated with complex, highly differentiated sets of similar information. The new bits of information about Mr. Green set off associated patterns within Mr. Jones that are tied into particular norms formed in the past. The norm which is triggered in this case is the handshaking norm. In response to the bits of information being received from the environment, Mr. Jones stands, walks around his desk, shakes the visitor's hand, and asks him to be seated. These norms define the behavior expected of him, or, more properly, that he expects of himself.

Stimuli obtained from the environment are thus registered first in the information system, and then, through associational patterns, trigger norms into activity. The structure of the information and the normative system are isomorphic, and furthermore, they take the form given by the individual's station structure in society. To understand why we say this, let us go back to the human infant, and see how he learns information and norms.

Let us assume this infant is cared for in a family where maids or other relatives do not have much to do with raising him. The infant is a member of a group, the nuclear family, and he occupies a position within that group. To begin with, the content of this position, in terms of norms, is nonexistent as far as the infant is concerned. All the information he receives in the beginning is in the context of the position he occupies within that group. His sense impressions are of the surrounding situation, and of the actors and their behavior with regard to him in that situation. The behavior that he performs is a product of the variables of personality, culture, situation, and interaction; but in his case, the culture does not exist. His personality is defined by his organic predispositions, and by the information he is receiving from the environment. He is contained within a situation, and interacts with individuals who control the flow of information he receives, and by controlling the flow, guide him in the process of making normative generalizations about it. This information and the norms based on it are classified together in his mental storage system of the individual. Categories into which the information is stored are given by the position, and, ultimately, by the roles.

As the infant grows sociologically as well as biologically, he is exposed to new positions and group structures. He is exposed to new information, and forms new norms on the basis of these new points. Bits of information that occur close to each other in time and space are classified together, and stored in configuration with certain common objects that recur in those time and space locations. The individual's filing system, then, is built up according to his exposure to the social system. That is why the information and the normative system have a common structure, and why this structure corresponds, in its various dimensions, to the individual's involvement in the structure of the society.

Personality as an Open System

The personality of a human being may be characterized as an open system, rather than a closed one. What makes it an open system is that it is continually being built, revised, or restructured as the individual receives new information from the environment through his senses. The information that the individual continually receives throughout his life from the environment falls into two categories: (a) feed-in information; and (b) feedback information. Feed-in information furnishes data to the individual about the characteristics of the situation in which he is operating. It defines for him the objects that exist within the environment, their configuration into sets, and the patterns of the events that are occurring within the situation. These data act as stimuli for action or response on the part of the actor.

The second kind of information, feedback information, furnishes data to the individual about the appropriateness of his behavior with respect to the situation in which he is operating. Feedback information, in effect, measures the effectiveness of the actor's response to feed-in information; in a sense, it tells him whether he has selected from his normative, information, and attitudinal storage systems the correct response pattern, and also whether the selected response pattern is achieving the anticipated results. Mr. Jones, for instance, sees Green enter the room, hears certain words spoken, and judges the situation to be one in which the norms of handshaking apply. He walks around his desk, and extends his hand to Green. Then he begins to scan his situation for feedback information. Was this the correct response? When Green extends his hand and begins the shaking ritual, feedback information confirms that his treatment of the feed-in information received earlier is appropriate. He then makes a new search of the situation for more feed-in information on the basis of which to pattern his next response.

Interaction between actors thus involves not only a stimulus-response chain, whereby the action of one person acts as a stimulus for the response of another and so forth, but it also involves a continual feedback of information into the information system of the actors involved in interaction. In interaction, two types of information play significant functions. The first type, feed-in information, furnishes a basis for selecting, among a repertoire of possible responses stored in the form of latent behavior, the exact response to use in a situation. The second type, feedback information, is designed to evaluate the appropriateness of the first decision.

Human actors are continually gathering both sorts of information. Feed-in information provides a fund of accumulated knowledge against which the individual can compare new information. Feedback information reinforces or undermines the association patterns between sets of feed-in information and the norms and attitudes stored in the individual's memory. If feedback is favorable in a given instance when a bit of information has triggered a certain norm, then the association is reinforced and is more likely to occur in future situations. If feedback information is unfavorable, that particular normative response to given bits of information is less likely to occur under similar conditions in the future. The feedback process continually tests the utility of the association between given sets of information, on one hand, and the norms which are triggered on the other. Due to feedback, also, norms are continually being changed and revised, as the individual redefines norms in response to more accurate information from the environment.

When a given set of information is tied to a given set of norms so that in response to the information the norms are activated, and when feedback has confirmed over and over again the appropriateness of the response, then a habit is formed. Once this has happened, future feedback is likely to have little effect in revising the normative structure.

Harry Jones has shaken hands so many times in response to information received from the environment, and the feedback has been favorable so many times, that his response has become automatic. He doesn't have to think, What shall I do? in response to this particular set of information. He automatically gets up, walks around his desk, and extends his hand, saying certain almost invariable words. In such a situation, although the actor is receiving feedback, it has little effect on his normative structure, other than simply to reconfirm a particular aspect of it.

The important point is that personality is not a closed system, but open in two ways. New feed-in information is continually being added to the information system of the actor, and he is continually revising it. Information is continually being reclassified and reshuffled, and new combinations of information are being formed. Secondly, the normative system of the actor is never complete, but is always being built, altered, revised, and reshuffled in terms of the feedback information the actor is receiving from his environment.

Whether or not changes in the personality system of the actor are significant depends largely upon the individual's exposure to new information in new situations. A routine life, and repetitive information are unlikely to change behavior patterns. Once the individual has gathered all the information available from repetitive situations, and built upon it a repertoire of norms and roles, it is unlikely that significant changes will take place within his personality. This kind of condition occurs in simple societies where, by the time a person has reached adulthood, he has encountered virtually the entire range of information he will ever be exposed to, and on the basis of it has formed the entire range of norms he will encounter during a lifetime. Most individuals do exist within highly repetitive life situations which yield highly limited stimulation and restricted ranges of information. Consequently, their personality systems tend to become stable and remain relatively fixed after some point in their lives. This does not happen because the personality system is closed, but because, as an open system, it receives continually reinforcing feedbacks from the environment that work to solidify its structure and to hold it constant. Even the most prosaic personality structure, in the most repetitive situation, must, by definition, be subject to change if exposed to new information of sufficient range and impact.

Traumatic experiences and crisis situations are those that produce a sudden flow of new information quite contradictory to what is already in the personality (9). The personality system has two alternative ways to adjust to this situation. One involves restructuring itself to accommodate the new information and fit it into already existing structures. The other is to ignore the new information by withdrawing from the stressful situation. Freud called these defensive maneuvers *sublimation* and *repression*. Perhaps we can say that functional mental illness—hysteria and other neuroses—arises when the individual cannot satisfactorily restructure his personality to accommodate radically new information. The research on consonance and dissonance is also relevant here, since it helps explain how the information system of the personality maintains internal consistency and external consistency with the normative and attitudinal systems also contained within it (10).

Norms and Feedback

In earlier chapters, instead of defining norms as commonly held behavior expectations, we defined them as a certain kind of idea that an individual has concerning his behavior in relation to the environment. We also said that if a single person has a norm with which no one else in the entire world agrees, nonetheless that idea is normative for him. Now we see that norms are formed on the basis of information received by an individual actor from his environment. They are personal ideas that he has about what he has a right to expect, given the information he has received from the environment in the past. For norms to function as guides to the behavior of an individual and furnish him with a response pattern, they must obviously be contained within his own personality. The fact that thousands of others have the same norms is only significant to the individual as information that he has about the expectations of others.

The existence of a feedback relationship between information and norms explains why so many individuals who exist within the same society have the same norms. Feedback, as an information process, tests the validity or appropriateness of a given normative response to information received from the environment. Feedback told Harry Jones, when he selected handshaking as a response to Mr. Green's appearance in his office, that he had made the correct choice, since the other actor responded as he expected. Feedback which tests the matching of norms with feed-in information, is most likely to be affirmative or favorable when the two actors involved in interaction have a common set of complementary norms.

Since feedback either reinforces the connection between norms and information, or undermines it, there is a built-in tendency for feedback processes to lead individuals who are interacting with each other to match appropriate bits of information with the same normative definitions. If two individuals try to interact on the basis of different norms for the same information, feedback will be unfavorable, inconclusive, or irrelevant for one or both. The connection between the information and the norms it triggered will be undermined. Both individuals will seek for responses that furnish favorable feedback to both, and in so doing, they will be forced into common definitions of the situation in terms of norms. Thus, in the long run, feedback itself tends to produce consensus among actors who habitually interact in common situations.

The feedback effect is stored in the personality system of the individual in the form of associational links between norms and information. In Figure 16-3, the three systems within personality are connected by a number of lines, which represent mental associational patterns. These patterns imply that certain bits of information are associated with certain norms, and act as triggers for them. A bit of information that has been previously acquired, and that has an association with a norm, triggers the norm into a state of activity when it is perceived again. In other words, the norm is drawn out of latent storage into a state in which it acts as a guide to behavior.

The strength of the associational link between sets of information stored in the information system, and norms stored in the normative system, is a function of feedback. Links are strengthened and reinforced by favorable feedback, and undermined and torn down by unfavorable feedback. In effect, memory of previous feedbacks takes the form of mental association patterns. The more favorable the feedback that has occurred, the stronger the associational patterns will be. A given bit of information is therefore more likely to trigger a given norm that is a determinant for behavior when previous feedbacks have been favorable and frequent. Repeated favorable feedback processes create a well-worn path in the mind between certain bits of information and certain norms. These well-worn paths or associational patterns are the relationships that exist between the parts of personality. They are, in effect, as much a part of the personality structure as the content of the information, normative, and attitudinal systems.

The human actor is in some respects like a self-programming computer. But whereas electronic computers are programmed by being fed a set of instructions for their operations, human beings build their own programs as they process sense impressions and learn from them. It would, of course, be wrong to say that the human actor actually programs himself by conscious or deliberate processes that he controls through his own will. Human beings learn by means of a dynamic relationship between themselves and their environment. This natural process produces the personality of the individual, and thereby determines its normative, information, and attitudinal content.

At birth, the human organism already has a system for processing the information that it receives through its senses from the environment. This information-processing system arises out of the way the infant's senses, nervous system, brain, and organic drives are structured and operate as organic systems. Together these systems furnish the organism with the capacity to learn—a capacity that is present at birth in normal individuals, and must be regarded as a characteristic of organic structure.

The capacity to learn may be viewed as a rudimentary set of rules that constitute a built-in program for processing, storing, and retrieving information. These rules are the principles by which learning takes place, and are therefore the basis for the formation of norms and attitudes, as well as for the acquisition of information. The existence of these rules may be inferred from examining the kinds of general behavioral problems an animal faces in adjusting his actions to the environment as he seeks to maintain life, and also from the results of research done on human and animal behavior. Human beings, like all other animals, use behavior as their primary means of adapting to their environment in order to acquire the things necessary to their survival. This action not only supplies the means of immediate survival to the individual animal, but supplies the means through which the species is perpetuated.

The use of behavior as an adaptive mechanism requires that an animal possess some way to acquire and use information about the environment. It also requires that, at least at some rudimentary level, the animal be able to store and retrieve information. This storage and retrieval amounts to learning.

There are a number of things an animal must be able to do in order to utilize behavior as an adaptive mechanism. First and foremost, he must be able to receive sensory stimuli from his environment, for actually, as far as the animal's behavior is concerned, the environment consists of the sense data he receives from it. Second, he must be able to recognize differences and similarities among objects and events on the basis of sense data. Third, he must be able to select, among possible responses, those responses that fit the sense data in some way. Fourth, as behavior progresses, he must be able to receive feedback from his environment and adjust his behavior to the changing sensory input. Fifth, he must be able to recall previous inputs of sense data, and make comparisons between past and present experience.

Consider, for a moment, a robin engaged in nest building. We will assume that she is born with a "nest building instinct": an innate set of instructions about what acts to perform, in what sequence, and with respect to which kinds of objects, in order to build a nest.

For our robin to build a real nest on the basis of her innate program, she also has to be able to receive and process real information. A robin usually builds her nest in the fork of a tree branch, using bits of grass, straw, and twigs; that means she has to recognize tree branches, straw, grass, and twigs in order to utilize these objects. Once she has selected a nest site, and has begun to build a nest, she must fly away from the tree branch to search for building materials. That means she has a problem with respect to her real environment. She may have been genetically prepared to recognize a proper nesting site and potential building materials, but now she has to recognize a particular, real nesting site, and when she is finished building, she must be able to recognize her own real nest. Furthermore, when she flies away from it, she must be able to return; and this too requires some special form of memory for real objects. To be able to recognize her own nest and return to it time and again, she must be able to remember certain learned information. This particular information cannot possibly be supplied genetically, but must be acquired through the senses. In addition, if the robin is ever to stop nest building, and consider the job done, she must be able to sense the effects of her own behavior output on the environment. Otherwise, without some sort of feedback on her own behavior, she would simply keep on building.

Rules of Information Processing

It seems apparent from this example that even animals whose behavior is largely controlled by so-called instincts must be able to process information and to learn from it. Even with in-born behavior patterns, they must be able to recognize objects and remember sequences of events in order to carry out real behavior in a real environment. For them to accomplish these things, certain specific rules must exist for the operation of information processing systems in animals that engage in relatively complex behavior patterns. These instructions must be part of an innate biological program for all higher animals. They can be stated like a set of instructions in a computer program:

1. *The Temporal Rule:* When bits of information are received in a temporal sequence, such as A, B, C, store this information in such a way that the order of the sequence can be recalled.

If such a rule were not present in the organism, then our robin could not return to her nest. In order to return, she has to have some way to recognize a set of stimuli that identify a path or route back to the nest. These stimuli are received during the movement away from the nest, and they are received in a temporal progression. Such a rule is also required for operant conditioning; that is, the animal in the Skinner Box must be able to record the pressing of the lever and then the receiving of the food as a sequence for conditioning to occur. If information were not stored in temporal sequences, animals could not learn sequential behavior patterns; nor could they orient themselves in space as they move from one place to another.

2. *The Configuration Rule:* When bits of information are received simultaneously as existing side by side in space to form a configuration such as A, B, C, store them in such a way that the configuration can be recalled as a definite spatial set.

If such a rule did not exist, then an animal would not be able to recognize particular objects or particular locations. How could a robin recognize her own nest or her own offspring, if she had not stored information concerning the configuration of sense stimuli that she received from them in a definite configuration? The gestaltist point of view is based on this rule. Furthermore, classical conditioning in the Pavlovian sense could not occur unless this rule operates. If ringing a bell simultaneously with presenting food results in the animal associating the bell-sound with the food, so that he salivates in response to the bell alone, then the two sets of stimuli—from the bell and from the food—must be stored in a spatial configuration.

The process of learning symbols—for instance, the words in a language—also depends on this rule. In order for a child to learn a word that stands for an object, he must be able to store information on a sound pattern side by side with information on sensory impressions of the object the sound stands for. It seems reasonable to assume, therefore, that learning vocabulary depends on this rule, because vocabulary depends on association between symbol and object without reference to order. Learning grammar and syntax probably depends on the temporal rule, because grammar depends on word order and therefore requires temporal ordering of information in the memory. The learning of language is therefore a function of the simultaneous operation of these two rules. Configuration is required for a human being to remember what his home is like, how the rooms are arranged, and where the kitchen is. And it is also required for people to be able to recognize each other, and perceive similarities and differences in objects.

3. *Comparison Rule:* When a bit of information is received which appears to be like a bit of information previously received, store the new information alongside the old information or in association with it, so that they can be compared and recalled together.

When two objects are the same shape, color, or taste, or are similar in any sense dimension or configuration of sense dimensions, they are stored together or cross-referenced in the memory. For instance, red objects are associated with other red objects. Without association, recognition would be impossible. That is, the animal must be able to compare present information with already stored information to recognize objects. For the robin to recognize her own nest, she must compare what she perceives at present with her memory of what has been perceived in the past. It is also possible to compare sequences or configurations in storage, and thus to recognize both objects and the behavior of objects.

4. *Attention Rule:* Search the environment for information related to (a) internal stimuli that are occurring, such as hunger, pain, sexual excitement, fear, and so on; and (b) the behaviors which are being performed (11).

Animals do not attend to all possible stimulations that are present. Instead, they select from among them at any given time. This means that only certain bits of information are permitted to enter the information processing system. Attention is a function of the motivation or goal orientation of the animal as he engages in behavior. When the robin engages in nest building, her attention is focused on finding and identifying nest building materials, and she ignores possible food objects. When she is feeding her young, she attends to potential food stimuli.

It is undoubtedly true that the information already present in the system also focuses the attention of the animal. Approaching her nest, the bird searches the environment for information which allows her to recognize her destination when it is reached. Recognition depends on the existence in storage of previously acquired information, and she is therefore looking for something like what has been stored.

This rule is required for feedback to operate. That is, the animal must search for certain specific stimuli, or attend only to certain ones, if it is to receive feedback from its behavior, and therefore learn when its behavior has attained its goal. In other words, feedback is patterned by the behavioral orientation of the actor, and selects information related to that orientation.

5. *The Probability or Expectation Rule:* If a sequence or configuration of stimuli is perceived and stored, raise your estimation of the probability of again observing the same elements in the sequence or configuration above the probability of seeing a totally different sequence and configuration of information bits.

This rule posits the existence within the organism of a tendency to expect or anticipate the future on the basis of the past. It says that if an animal perceives the sequence A-B-C once, when he perceives the beginning of the sequence, A, at some future date, there will be more of a tendency to expect or to anticipate seeing B next, than to expect any other event.

Rule 1 states that A-B-C should be stored in that order. Rule 3 says that when A is observed again later, it should be stored alongside the original A. A second occurrence of A will result in a recall of the original A, and since it is stored in sequence with B and C, then the whole sequence is likely to be recalled. This recall produces the expectancy of B, once A has occurred. Actually, the probability or expectancy rule is merely a function of the way the other rules operate. The rule might say that if one member of a stored set of information such as A-B-C is recalled, recall the other members of the set also. In other words, a rule of association operates so that bits of information are recalled in association with the other bits they are stored with, in accordance with rules 1, 2, and 3.

It must be assumed that the storage of bits of information such as A-B-C requires some sort of electrochemical change in some part of the biological storage system. The electrochemical storage charge, which amounts to the memory of A, B, and C, seems to be strengthened by repetition, so that with each repetition, the expectancy of B on the basis of the occurrence of A becomes stronger. Expectation or anticipation is therefore a function of the rules of information processing, and of the biological mechanisms through which information is stored. The rules themselves are probably a consequence of the structure by which the senses are tied to the nervous system and brain, and of the physical-chemical mechanisms through which information is stored and retrieved.

Together these five rules furnish the organism with a program for learning, and for the use of learned information in the process of behavioral adaptation. Without such a system of rules, or some set of similar rules, learning could not take place. Furthermore, it is necessary to assume that the rules exist prior to learning, as a part of the organism. An animal could not learn the rules by which he learns; there would be no biological way to learn the rules to begin with. Such rules must therefore be inherent in organic structure. It would be incorrect to say, however, that the organism is aware of the rules or of following them. They are automatic, and a function of the very process by which the senses, the nervous system, and the brain operate.

Human capacity to learn obviously exceeds that of other animals. The basis of this superior learning capacity is not yet well understood. When we acquired language, however, we did become able to amass information indirectly; and furthermore, humans can be trained to attend to a great variety of manmade and man-defined sense qualities. Despite these accomplishments, however, human beings probably begin by processing information much the same way as the rest of the animals, and therefore learn according to the same basic rules.

The Structure of Memory

The five rules stated above imply that the normative, information, and attitudinal systems of human personalities have isomorphic structures, and that the structure of these systems corresponds to the structure of the person's history of participation in the social system. For example, let us consider the storage of information, norms, and attitudes of a child in a family. Our rules lead us to conclude that information obtained from interaction with his parents and siblings would be stored according to rules 1, 2, and 3, in sets and sequences distinguishable from other sets and sequences. In contrast, information, norms, and attitudes derived from participating in school activities would fall into other sets and sequences. The information obtained by a person as a member of a family thus forms a set of sets that exists in a region of his memory corresponding to his position in the family group. Since norms are defined as a function of the probability rule, which is based on information, and attitudes are a function of comparing norms with information, then norms and attitudes should form sets corresponding to positions, also.

Thus the station structure of the person, through his life span, is the organizing principle for the storage of information, norms, and attitudes. It is also the organizing principle around which new information acts as a trigger for behavior, and feedback operates as a mechanism to guide action. In other words, the combination of the rules of learning, and the fact that learning in humans takes place in the context of a social system which already has a definite structure, results in the ultimate structuring of the personality system of the actor. His personality can therefore legitimately be viewed as consisting of parts corresponding to his participation in society.

This argument can only be a crude representation of the biologically inherited, information-processing program that operates in human beings. Based on this innate program, information processing enables the individual to create a new program, the internalized cultural structure of his station in society. This new program amounts to the normative system, and represents a set of instructions, built on the basis of information, that allows the person to respond to the environment in ways that are predictable to others, and through which, as an actor, he achieves his own goals and objectives. The feedback process, built in as selective perception, allows the human actor to program himself, and to continually revise his program in light of new information received from the environment as feedback and feedin.

Figure 16-4 diagrams an individual who already has a normative structure, and has built up a store of information. It shows an action

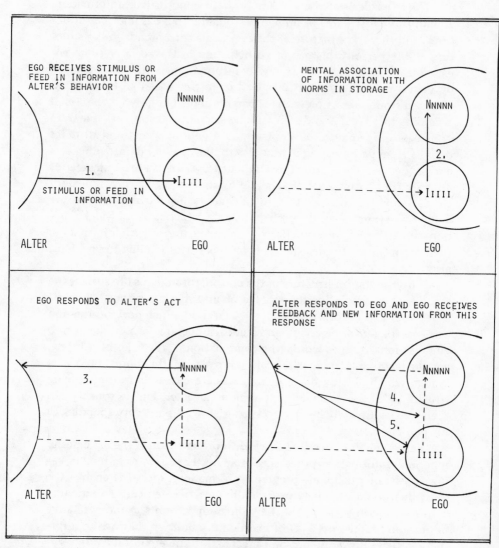

Figure 16–4 The Relationship Among Norms,
Information, and Actions

sequence for a personality system. The first step is the stimulus step—information being fed into the information system. The new bit of information, *I*, enters an information system that already contains other bits of information, *is*. Within the information system, it is associated with these previous bits of information, which in turn, triggers an associational process with norms. This association has been built up in the past between the same type of bits of old information, and the pattern of response which is normative to the individual.

In step two, a norm is triggered out of latency into activity. Through an associational pattern, the norm is the basis for a response that amounts to the feedout of information to the environment which includes another actor. This feedout is an action with an informational meaning to an alter actor who, incidentally, is going through the same process as shown for ego. The alter actor reacts. The reaction is fed into the personality of ego as a feedback. The next step either affirms or denies the validity of the association between the bit of information and the activated norm. If the feedback is affirmative, then another norm in the sequence or set which contains the original norm will be activated. If it is not, the feedback acts as a new stimulus, leading to another associational pattern with a different norm and a different feedback, until eventually the behavior of ego and alter become congruent.

The Attitudinal Subsystem

We said above that an attitude is an idea that stems from a comparison between norms and information. Norms define the world in which ego is involved in ideal, rather than real, terms; information, on the other hand, consists of ideas about the way things really are. The information system of an individual includes a cognitive map of what the individual perceives as being reality; the normative system includes a cognitive map that represents the way things ought to be. The structures of these two maps are isomorphic. They are like two maps of the United States, one topographical, the other a road map. They have similar structures, are shaped alike, and show things in relatively the same positions; but they differ from each other in their content.

Things in reality are rarely perceived to be as they are ideally supposed to be. In one of the processes of personality, ideal conceptions are continually compared with the real conception of things, and an evaluation made of the state of the world as perceived by ego. The result of this evaluation process is an attitude. Ego has an attitude stored in his attitudinal system for every associational pairing between norms and information. This attitude defines ego's emotional reaction to the state of reality as perceived by him in light of his normative expectations. The attitudinal system has a structure that corresponds in broad outline to the structure of a normative and information systems. We can illustrate this idea by examining the concept of the self.

The Self or the Self-Conception

The complex system of norms that defines the various positions that ego occupies in society, and the roles that they contain, furnishes an ideal cognitive map for the way ego is supposed to be as an actor. The set of norms that defines ego's station defines the qualities and actions that he accepts as appropriate for himself. By carrying out these norms in response to information from the environment, and from feedback as perceptions of the responses made by others, ego obtains information concerning the degree to which he is fulfilling the roles assigned to him in groups. By comparing this information with his normative definitions of roles, he is able to evaluate himself with respect to that particular role.

Charlie Brown, let us say, learns the norms that govern the role of a batter in a baseball game, and that define the way in which the role is ideally supposed to be performed. He may then attempt to perform the role in actual game play, at which time he perceives himself as failing to fulfill the various role expectations contained within his own personality. He strikes out every time he comes to bat. Unless he is deceived by the behavior of others, he will inevitably take the information about his role performance, evaluate it against his ideal conception of the role, and form an unfavorable attitude toward self about it.

The same process occurs with each role an individual learns, as he compares normative definitions with actual behavior in real groups. The person's self-conception therefore consists of a set of attitudes which represents evaluations of self role-fulfillment. An individual's self-conception can be favorable with respect to certain parts of his participation in the social system, and unfavorable with respect to other parts of it. The individual often has ambivalent attitudes toward self, attitudes that are tied to particular roles and norms, and to particular bits of information.

Attitudes, like norms, are not active all the time. They become active when they are triggered by associational patterns with norms that define role performance and the behavior that fulfills it. Once formed, attitudes become active factors in determining the behavior performed by ego in fulfilling his roles. When Charlie Brown comes to bat, he receives information from his environment that makes him think, "This is the kind of norm that applies in this particular situation, and I am supposed to respond in a particular way." At the same time he also triggers within his personality system the attitudes toward self with respect to this particular role. Since he has struck out every time in the past, his unfavorable self-conception in this role becomes a factor in his behavior. He does not approach the plate confidently and with self-assurance, but with considerable embarrassment and a low expectation of performing well.

His output in the form of behavior thus reflects not only the information he is receiving from the environment, and the norms he has learned that apply to this situation, but also the attitude toward self which is triggered in the process. In other words, an internal feedback exists within his personality system that feeds back the effect of attitude on information and norms.

These three systems of personality thus interact to produce the output of the system in the form of behavior. This process of behavior determination, of decision-making within the individual, involves the interaction among norms, information, attitudes, and motivation, and it orients the behavior of the actor. Interaction among these factors is determined by associational mental patterns formed on the basis of past experience. Feedback processes again perform the function of reinforcing the associational patterns or undermining them, depending on whether the individual succeeds or fails in achieving his objective, and on whether his response fits into the system of behavior as he had expected it to.

Alter Conceptions

Just as ego forms a set of attitudes toward self, he also forms a set of attitudes toward alters and tangential actors whose behavior directly or indirectly is a source of information or stimulation for him. The normative system of the individual contains not only his particular station, but a set of positions and role definitions that apply to alter actors with whom ego associates in groups and organizations. Ego evaluates alters just as he does himself. That is, ego has a conception of the way alter actors should behave. He also receives information from the environment concerning how they do behave. He compares his ideal and reality, and forms attitudes. These attitudes, too, may be ambivalent, and contain both favorable and unfavorable components.

Take a child, say, who forms a normative conception of what a father ought to be like with respect to a son. He builds up in his normative system a set of norms that specify a kind of behavior the father ought to perform. The child obtains information from observing his father in real situations. This information is compared with the normative definitions, and the father is evaluated. If the father's real behavior does not conform to the normative expectations, the son forms a set of negative attitudes toward the father.

Deviations from norms occur in response to attitudinal variations. The child also has a set of norms that defines what behavior he should perform with respect to his father. These norms are part of his station structure. Let us say that a situation arises in which stimulation from the environment feeds information into his system that activates a certain norm: his father tells him to pick up his room. The child's normative definition of his own roles are such that he believes that ideally he should do what his father tells him to do. He has a negative attitude toward his father, however, based on his evaluation of the way his father fails to conform to normative role expectations. This negative attitude becomes an active ingredient in the process of determining his behavior, and on this basis the child decides to ignore the norm which applies to the behavior. He does not perform the behavior because his attitudes toward his father are negative. Thus, people may deviate from their own norms because of attitudes, for they do influence the way people behave.

Ego has a set of attitudes toward every significant alter in his environment, and toward the positions occupied by tangential actors with whom he is not directly related, but about whom he has norms and obtains information. It depends on the situation which one of this large collection of attitudes is active at any given moment. Generally, the activation of attitudes depends on the perception processes of the individual, the association patterns built up between information perceived, and the norms and attitudes based on this information.

CHAPTER 17

LIFE CYCLE ANALYSIS

The individual's place in the structure of society has been analyzed, in previous chapters, in terms of his station—that is, in terms of all the positions that he occupies in the various groups and organizations in society in which he participates. Obviously, the individual's station changes, depending on the stages of his life and career. In this chapter, we will discuss life-cycle phenomena from a structural point of view, and examine how a person participates in society through time.

There are two ways to analyze the life cycle. The first focuses on personality growth and development, and is concerned with personality changes through time. The second focuses on the involvement of the actor in the social system, and on the growth and development of the individual's station structure as he progresses through life. It is concerned with how new positions and roles are added to the individual's repertoire of behavior, and how old positions and roles are dropped. In other words, it centers on the problems of the person's engagement and disengagement from society. We will use this second method rather than the first.

Structural Engagement and Disengagement

The life history of an individual may be described in structural terms as follows: during the first part, the station structure of the individual is developed, and new positions and roles are added to it. This process is called *engagement*. During the latter part of his life history, the individual gradually withdraws from various positions occupied in social systems, and his participation is reduced. This process is called *disengagement*.

Station Structure Through Time

It is obvious that a person's station at birth has a simple structure compared to his station in midlife. The unborn infant has no station in society. At birth, a position is ascribed to the individual in the kinship structure. In the case of a male child, it is the position of son and brother. At first, the number of positions is small and the roles contained in these positions are simple and few in number. Gradually, as the infant grows into childhood, the child into adolescence, and the adolescent into adulthood, new positions, containing new and more complex roles, are added to his station repertoire until maximum participation is reached with respect to the social system. As old age approaches, certain positions and roles drop out of the individual's station or become latent, and his participation in society is reduced. Death represents the final dissolution of the station's structure, and the ultimate disengagement of the individual from society. Figure 17-1 diagrams the station building process.

The members of the nuclear family into which the child is born have existing role expectations with respect to, let us say, the position of son and brother. These are the child's potential roles; he learns and enacts them as he grows into childhood. In other words, a child is born into a group in which he occupies a position that contains certain potential roles; through the process of socialization, these are converted into latent roles for him as an actor. In the same way, he has certain potential positions within his kinship organization. If his father and mother have living parents and other siblings, for instance, he is ascribed the positions of grandson, nephew-cousin, and perhaps other positions in the kinship system. As far as the infant is concerned, these positions at first exist only as locations in the social structure, and as a set of expectations that other people in other groups have. As the infant comes into contact with alters who have these expectations with respect to his behavior, he begins to learn these expectations, and latent roles emerge for him as learned behavior in his own personality. The infant, therefore, comes to occupy positions in the kinship system which have been ascribed to him at birth by learning the roles and performing behavior in interaction with persons or groups in the kinship structure.

At birth, and through the period of infancy, the child's station consists of positions either in the potential state, since they have been ascribed to him, or, after they have been learned, in the latent or active state. After a certain age, he associates with nonkinsmen in group situations where he occupies a different set of positions. The first of his nonkinship positions are apt to be in neighborhood organizations or

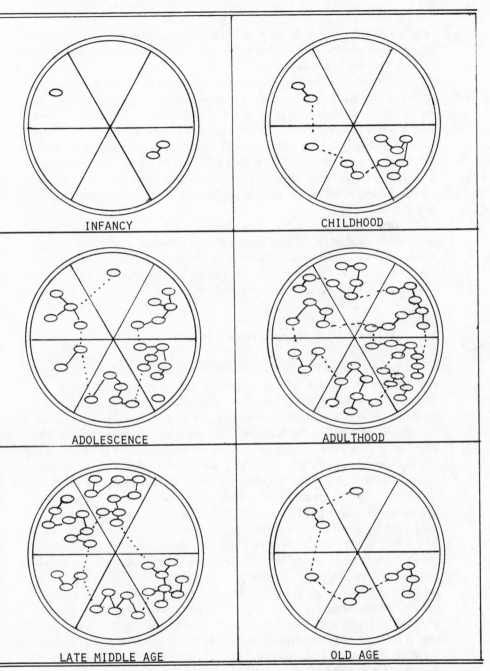

Figure 17-1   Station Growth and Change
Throughout the Life Cycle

childhood play groups. As he participates more widely in neighborhood groups, new positions are added to his station structure, and new situses outside the kinship area are built.

In our society, therefore, station structure of the individual begins with the kinship situs. Since kinship relations are largely ascribed, this means converting potential or ascribed positions into positions that have been learned, and that oscillate between latency and activity. The next situs structure that is developed is centered in neighborhood organizations and friendships. When the child goes to school, new positions are added to his station, and an educational situs develops. Here again, he begins by occupying a position, and then learns the roles that are associated with it.

In order to analyze a life cycle, we need a new concept of latency, designed to deal with a lifelong span of time, instead of a brief moment in an individual's particular stream of behavior. That is, we need to deal with his past participation and his future participation in the social structure, as well as his participation now.

Future Role Latency

A potential role is a kind of future role latency. An individual fits into society in such a way that certain positions will inevitably be occupied by him at some future time. This fact is recognized by members of the social system of which he is a part, and may even be recognized by ego. At the moment, however, he does not occupy the position or perform the roles. A classic example would be the Prince of Wales, who is born to the potential position and roles of King of England. Potential positions and roles for the individual are important to understanding the processes of socialization that precede his actually becoming an active position occupant in a social system. Long before they actually occupy the positions or are expected to perform the roles, actors may learn part or all of the behavior expected of them through socialization that is designed to ready them for this destiny. Potential positions are thus a form of latency, in that they affect the individual's behavior, and become a part of his functioning personality system before they are actually activated in any real social situations. Unlike the kind of latency that applies to roles already learned, however, potential roles do not have an active state. In order to become active, they must be learned and transformed into a state of latency. When they become latent, the person is actually occupying the position and expected to perform the roles which are appropriate when the situations arise.

Past Latency

Once a person has been the incumbent of a position, and has learned and performed the roles in relation to other people, the roles exist as learned behavior in the normative, informational, and attitudinal systems of the actor. In other words, they are latent and will become active, given the proper stimuli and configuration of situational elements. What about the case in which a person is no longer an incumbent of a position whose roles are known from past experience? An example would be a woman who has learned the various roles associated with the position of wife-mother, but whose husband dies, so that she has no alter actor toward whom the roles of wife may be performed.

Her case, in which a set of roles, or a given role within a set, is forced into a state of latency due to the absence of an alter actor or of situations necessary to the performance of the roles, is quite different from that of the housewife whose husband is at work for the day and will be home. A similar instance, in which the whole repertoire of occupational roles once performed by an actor and known to him becomes constantly latent, arises when a worker retires. In post-activity latency, a set of roles exists without a position located within a group structure. The position and role have been separated or detached from any structure in which they can be activated, and they are better described as deactivated positions or roles, rather than latent positions or roles. A retired college professor, for example, no longer occupies the position of teacher in a classroom. He knows the roles appropriate to such a position, but no longer has access to a location in the social structure where the position fits. Consequently, the roles cannot be activated, and exist only as memory stored in the personality system of the actor. Given the proper circumstances, of course—access to the proper situations and alter actors—these roles can be activated.

In the station-building process, therefore, positions and roles are present first as potential positions and roles. Then, the positions are occupied by the person as a real incumbent. Once learned and attached to a location in the social structure, these positions and roles vary between active and latent states, as the person performs behavior in the functioning social system. Later, positions and roles are deactivated as the individual disengages from various parts of the social system. Potential, latent, and deactivated roles all, however, exist in a state in which they can influence the behavior of the actor.

The Development of Station Structure

In infancy, the station contains positions only in the kinship structure. Later, neighborhood and friendship positions are added, followed by educational positions and roles. A typical educational history illustrates how potential, latent, and deactivated positions and roles apply to station building.

Once a child enters the educational system of our society, a whole system of potential positions begins to exist for him. The first-grade pupil occupies a position in a particular group in a school system. This position contains a number of roles which he learns by participation, and is included as a part of his station structure at that moment. Ahead of him lie potential positions in other groups in the second, third, fourth, fifth, and sixth grades; as he moves up, the first-grade position becomes deactivated as he occupies a position in the second grade, and so on. For a period of time, each position, though contained in a different group structure, involves the same set of roles. But when he leaves the elementary school system, and enters junior high school and high school, not only do the positions he occupies change, but the repertoires of roles contained within each position also change. This movement through the educational system represents a process through which the potential positions that exist for the individual are first converted into active positions occupied by him, and are then deactivated as new potential positions are occupied.

At any given moment, the person's station structure is made up of those positions he actually occupies in the social structure. These positions are located in actual groups at particular points in the structure of the social system. The first grader occupies a position of pupil in Mrs. Smith's first-grade class in Public School Number 95. It is this particular exact position that is contained within his station at that moment. If a child moves from one town to another, and changes from Public School 95 in Boxtown to Public School 23 in Capitol City, he has changed the positions that are contained within his social station. The position in Public School 95 is deactivated and the new position in Public School 23 is activated. When a child moves, the positions of friend and neighbor contained within his station will also change. It may be true that when he moves from one school to another, so that positions change, the roles contained within the positions remain the same; but even with the same role content, we are dealing with two different positions in the structure of society. Furthermore, as the position changes from one system to another, the exact definition of roles will also probably change, despite a certain amount of similarity. That is, the position of pupil in the first grade in Public School 95 will contain role definitions that are slightly different from the position of first grade pupil in Public School 23, and the individual will have to relearn his roles in the context of the new position.

The next stage of development in the life cycle involves adding work positions, and positions which involve the individual in the kinship system as a husband or wife, mother or father. Maximum participation in our social system is probably achieved somewhere in midlife. At this age, the occupational situs of the individual is developed to the fullest, and his participation in the kinship system reaches its peak. His parents, brothers, sisters, and their offspring are still alive and active, and he also has offspring of his own. Past middle age, as his parents, brothers, sisters, and other kinsmen die, participation in the kinship system is reduced and positions become permanently deactivated. Similar movement also occurs in other areas of his life as he retires from active participation in work, and as death claims alter actors who are neighbors and friends. By old age, participation in the social system is drastically reduced, and the structure of the station is simplified so that it contains only a few remaining active positions and roles.

Categorical Differences in Station Structure

The characteristics of station structure differ for men and women. Male and female station structures contain different positions and roles, achieve different levels of complexity, and change at different times during the life cycle. A man's occupational situs area will generally be more elaborate than a woman's; on the other hand, her neighborhood, kinship, and friendship areas are apt to be more complex than his. The sexes also differ in the amount of time spent playing roles in different areas of their station.

The station structures of persons from different socioeconomic statuses are also apt to be quite different. The lower socioeconomic groups have simpler station structures; that is, they contain fewer positions, especially in the occupational area, and these positions contain fewer and simpler roles. Data from studies of social class in the United States seem to indicate that the upper-middle class, as in Elmtown (1) and Yankee City (2), occupies more complex stations in society. Hollingshead, for example, found that the middle class are the great participators in voluntary organizations, neighborhood cliques, and groups. It may be true that maximum complexity in the structure of occupational situses is reached at about the managerial level of large-scale organizations. As a consequence, people who occupy positions in the upper ranges of the occupational hierarchy, probably below the absolute top, have the most complex occupational situses. Because of these differences between social classes, the processes of engagement with and disengagement from the social system are probably quite different for the upper, middle, and lower socioeconomic categories.

The Concept of Life Crisis and its Application

During the lifetime of the individual, at certain critical points on the age scale, his relationship to society is drastically altered, and the structure of his station in society undergoes a major change. Such changes create crises for the individual because they are accompanied by major shifts in the behavior he performs in the social system. In terms of station structure, this means that, at a life crisis, a sudden increase or decrease in the number of positions and roles contained within the person's station occurs. A significant number of new potential positions are activated; a significant number of currently occupied, regularly activated positions are kept in a constant state of latency; or a significant number of positions are deactivated on a permanent basis. Some life crises involve all three conditions.

Life crises affect the individual as a functioning behavior system. And they also affect the social system in which the individual experiencing the crisis operates as a member. Emotionally, his life crisis puts him more or less under stress and strain. It also changes, in a significant way, his behavior patterns, by changing the quality and extent of his participation in the social system. As the quality and extent of his participation in the social system changes, the behavior of others within the social system is affected through interaction. As a consequence, the functioning of the social group is affected. In life-crisis situations, roles that have normally been in a state of activity suddenly become latent or deactivated. Or just as suddenly, roles that have not previously been active are introduced, and become active parts of the individual's behavior.

The Classification of Life Crises

The life history of an individual, as conceived by sociologists, falls into a number of developmental stages. The point has often been made that how many stages exactly depends on the society, and is highly related to its particular social organization. Situations that would represent a crisis in one society do not do so in another; stages of maturation

that are reasonable representatives of an American life are not necessarily present in other societies.

Figure 17-2 diagrams an indeal life cycle for an American middle-
class male. It has six stages: infancy, childhood, adolescence, adulthood,
middle age, and old age. As each stage ends and the next begins, a major
alteration in the person's participation in society takes place. At the top
and bottom of the diagram are the events that mark the borders between
the stages.

Infancy is that period of the individual's life before he is able to
walk and talk. When he begins to communicate and move around under
his own power, his involvement in the social life of the group undergoes
a major change. People begin to treat him as a child rather than as an
infant, and his participation in groups expands.

Childhood, extending roughly from about one to 14, is divided into
two subperiods: preschool and pupilhood. A major alteration in the
person's status in society occurs when he enters formal schooling, and
it can be argued that in our society the period of childhood ends with
the entrance into school, and a new period of formal cultural apprenticeship begins. During pupilhood, the individual's major social involvement is at school, rather than the home; his positions and roles prolifer-
ate there, rather than in the kinship system.

Pupilhood ends with the onset of adolescence, when studenthood
—that is, participation in high school and college—begins. The relationship between the individual and the school changes at this time. The
pupil has one teacher and is associated with a relatively stable group of
other pupils. The student deals with many teachers in a variety of
classroom situations, and he becomes involved in a range of extracur-
ricular groups surrounding the school. The major events that separate
childhood from adolescence, and pupilhood from studenthood, are the
entrance into high school, the beginning of the dating pattern, and the
acquisition of a driver's license.

The end of adolescence and the beginning of adulthood correspond
to the beginning of a work career, marriage, the birth of children, and
parenthood status. Adulthood extends from approximately the ages of
21 or 22 to the age of 45 or 50. During this period, the adult male is
progressing through an occupational career toward the highest point he
achieves in occupational status. Somewhere in middle age he reaches the
zenith of his occupational career, and spends a period occupying this
highest position, making only relatively small advancements and
changes.

Middle age is separated from adulthood by two events—the
achievement of the career zenith, and the marriage and parenthood of
the individual's own children. Note that engagement within the struc-

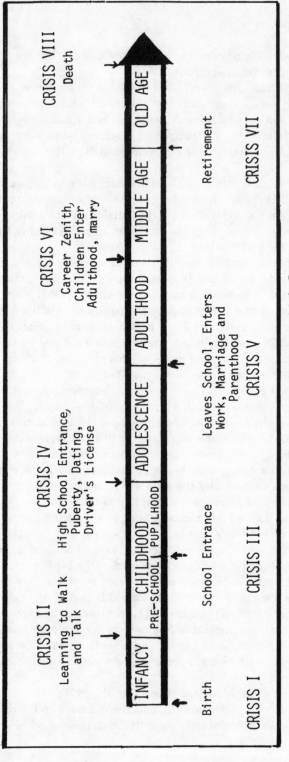

Figure 17-2 Life Cycle Stages and Life Crises

ture of society begins at birth and extends to the beginning of middle age. Middle age is the period of full engagement; the individual is fully involved in his career and in other activities associated with society. With the onset of old age, at retirement, disengagement begins and continues until death.

Figure 17-2 is merely an abstract ideal pattern, an average view, of what happens to a certain class of individuals within our society. The diagram for any particular person will differ according to his actual experiences. Furthermore, both sex and social class affect the timing of the significant events that separate one phase from the next.

Birth as a Life Crisis

At birth, the individual occupies the first position in the social system, and the first roles are learned and added to his station. Birth is considered a life crisis mainly because of its implications for the group in which it occurs, not because of its implication for the newborn infant. The birth of the first child into a family brings into activity a set of roles related to parenthood. As a consequence, within family structure, a real alteration of behavior must take place. Before the birth of a child, a married couple perform only husband and wife roles, and all the time within the group is devoted to husband-wife role behavior. With the addition of a child to the family, new roles become active, a reallocation of time to various new roles occurs, and a number of extramural relationships must be established. The behavior which occurs outside the family and within the community structure also must change. Thus, a change in the station structure of the parents occurs with the presence of their first child. The births of later children do not change station structure as much, since parental roles have already been activated, and external relationships established around parenthood.

School Entrance as a Life Crisis

Before the child goes to school, his individual station is largely comprised of kinship, neighborhood, friendship clique positions, and occasional positions which relate him to the economic and health care systems of the society. With his entrance into school, a major new set of positions and roles are activated. He must learn to adjust his behavior to an entirely different system of action from that which he has experienced in the past. School participation involves the activation of an entire situs structure, which ultimately contains a number of positions with relatively complex roles. It also involves a change in the activity latency patterns of roles performed in other groups. For example, the child is away from home, performing behavior within the school, at hours when roles within the family used to be active. The entire pattern of the activity latency of roles within his station structure becomes keyed to, and dependent upon, the cycle of activity latency within the school system.

Since this is true for the child, it is also true for those alter actors who perform roles toward him in other groups. The activity latency patterns of paternal roles become tied to the school calendar and the daily cycle of school activities. In addition to this, new positions and roles designed to relate the parents and the family to the educational system must be added to the station structure of the parents. In other words, interstitial group relationships must be established between the school and the home, and parents must occupy positions in these interstitial groups and perform roles within them. Without question, there are considerable class differences with respect to this phenomena. A larger change takes place in the station structure of middle-class parents after their first child enters school than is true of either lower-or upper-class parents. School entrance brings a major change in the station structure of the child and his parents, and creates for all of them a crisis in social participation.

For the child, entering school requires that he learn a new set of roles and how to perform them in a new set of groups. Considerable anticipatory socialization may occur before he actually enrolls. The child may gather from his peer group and his family what to expect, and he may learn some, if not all, the role requirements. Part of his crisis involves testing of the accuracy of his preschool socialization against actual participation. He learns within active group situations whether his conception of being a pupil reacting to teachers and other students is accurate and adaptive for him.

Another aspect of the crisis is that he has to learn to discriminate between different definitions of the same role within the structures of two different groups. Prior to school, his parents disciplined him. In addition, they also taught and socialized him. In school, the teacher performs the roles of disciplinarian and teacher. The child thus has to discriminate between the role of disciplinarian as performed by a teacher, and the role of disciplinarian as performed by a parent. Since children mostly tend to transfer whole roles from the family situation to the school situation—in effect, they expect teachers to act as if they were parents—a child is likely to expect the teacher to perform the role of disciplinarian the same way as his parents. Under these circumstances, he inevitably makes errors in perception and judgment. He thereupon experiences stress, as social controls are exerted against him to make him conform to a new model of behavior.

When any major change in social participation occurs, such as entering school, the individual's cognitive map—normative expectations regarding behavior of self and others—has to be faulty, and yield only partially accurate predictions of behavior. Without a normative map, the child can neither predict the behavior of others, nor adjust his own behavior properly in response to the behavior of others. Consequently, he will experience anxiety in anticipation of positive and negative social controls, and will also, of course, experience the real effects of these controls when they occur.

Adolescence, Graduation and Employment as Life Crises

Different cultures structure life cycles differently, and in many societies, adolescence does not represent a distinct phase in development. In ours, however, it does. We have to distinguish between childhood and adolescence because the participation of the individual in the structure of society is radically different in the two periods. Adolescence, as a sociological phenomenon, begins when the individual is permitted to date, drive an automobile or accompany peers who drive, or make decisions about personal grooming, clothing, and social activities. Essentially, adolescence begins with a relaxation of parental control over the child's activities. Dating and driving lead to new social relationships. Both these activities require the individual to occupy new positions, and to perform different roles within the social system of society. They also represent changes in the allocation of the individual's time in performing roles within family, neighborhood, and school, compared to activities outside these arenas. With adolescence, therefore, a major change in the structure of the individual's station in our society occurs, and a whole new repertoire of roles is added.

For the male, graduation from, or dropping out of, school, and entrance into the employment market mark the largest change that ever occurs in the structure of his station. As a pupil in the school system, he occupies various positions and performs various roles, both of which tie him to specific actors in familiar situations. When he either drops out of school or graduates, these earlier positions and roles fall into a latent state, and are permanently deactivated. The individual is apt to experience a period of disorientation as a consequence. He may miss performing these roles, and try to continue certain aspects of his relationships by hanging around the school. He may, in other words, attempt to keep in a state of activity certain parts of his station structure that are related to the school system beyond the point at which they are expected to be deactivated. The old grads who attend alumni gatherings, and the aging fraternity and sorority members, are trying to keep positions and roles in a state of activity long after they would normally have separated from the organizations and groups within which the positions and roles are located.

The crisis of graduation and the entrance into the world of work is ordinarily shortly followed by marriage and parenthood. Each of these phenomena alone represents a major change in the person's station structure. Because in our society they follow close on each other's heels, the individual at the end of adolescence is faced with a major reorientation of his participation in society.

Marriage and Parenthood as Life Crises

Marriage is critical in the sense that a new set of kinship obligations is introduced into the individual's life-participation pattern. Marriage usually comes at a time when the individual is recovering from or experiencing the shock of simultaneously withdrawing from the educational system and entering the employment market. The concurrence of these three life crises, followed by the birth of the first child, places the early stages of the husband-wife relationship under great stress.

For the most part, graduation or dropping out of school is a more or less irreversible change in participation. Entrance into the employment market by males is also more or less irreversible. The male may change jobs from one firm to another, or from one occupation to another, but once he has entered the world of work, withdrawal is difficult. Marriage, on the other hand, is not regarded in our society as an irreversible commitment to social participation.

Marriage and parenthood, as crises, may be resolved by reverting to an earlier stage of participation in the social system. Desertion of the family by the male, in particular, reverses the station-building process. It forces positions and roles associated with both parenthood and marriage into a state of latency, and considerably simplifies the station structure of the deserter. On the other hand, it makes the station structure more complex for the deserted wife and children, who must assume the positions and play the roles vacated by the absent father-husband.

Retirement as a Crisis

Retirement is a life crisis because it represents a deactivation of the occupational or work situs contained within the individual's station structure. Since the entire station structure of adult males, and by dependency the station structure of married females, is organized around the occupational situs, retirement drastically changes a worker's participation in society. Retirement is more of a problem with respect to some occupations than others. Farmers, for example, tend to withdraw gradually from the world of work. They do not reach a set point where their participation is drastically changed overnight. On the other hand, the industrial worker or the salaried white-collar worker experiences overnight changes in his participation in the world of work.

If a major portion of the station's structure is devoted to the area of work in the form of an occupational or work situs, and this situs is deactivated, then a reallocation of the individual's participation in society must occur. Other positions and roles contained within the already existing station structure must absorb the time, energy, and effort previously expended on occupational behavior; or new positions and roles must be added to the station structure to absorb the now-vacant areas of social time and space.

Retirement usually comes when the kinship area of station structure has already undergone simplification—when, for instance, children are grown and separated from the nuclear family. In this society, it is quite likely that they will be living far away from their parents; therefore, the possibility of expending time in playing parental roles is limited. The individual's participation in neighborhood groups is also likely to have been curtailed. As a consequence, sudden withdrawal from the world of work leaves the individual with few possibilities for easily expanding his participation into other areas.

The participation patterns of the alter actors are also affected by the retirement of ego. The wife of a retired husband suddenly faces the prospect of having him around the house all day. The children of a retired person, accustomed to a given level of participation in family contacts, may suddenly discover their aging parent activating roles toward them which had previously dropped into a state of almost constant latency. It is probably true that in our society, as its structure is now constituted, withdrawal from the world of work represents the most difficult of the routine life crises. And as more people live to be older, this particular crisis will become more of a problem. In the long run, we can expect that a new kind of station structure will be elaborated for older people that will amount to a culturally acceptable way of adjusting to an extended period of retirement. At present, however, the crisis of retirement, unlike other life crises which are usually resolved in a relatively short time, extends over a number of years. For some, it is never resolved except by death.

Death as a Life Crisis

Death represents the ultimate separation of the individual from the social system, and a complete deactivation of the individual's station in society. At least part of the worry that individuals feel with respect to their own deaths stems from the effects of this deactivation on the remaining members of the social units of which they are a part. Indeed, the life insurance industry is based on this concern. Structurally, insurance organizations may be regarded as systems designed to provide a continuation of the performance of various critical roles within family and other groups when a critical member of the system dies.

The anticipation of death from serious illness by ego, and by alters closely associated with him, is a crisis not only because of its emotional significance, but also its sociological significance. When a person is dying, it is known in advance that certain role and positional latencies are imminent. Provision must be made to continue the functioning of the groups and their members in the face of impending and inevitable deactivation of certain role performances. The death of a husband-father in a family leaves vacant the positions and roles which he has performed. As a consequence, alter roles that are reciprocally related to those of the deceased are forced into a state of latency. If the father-husband performs the provider role, and the wife and children the dependent roles, the dependent role will be forced into a state of latency along with the provider role. Insofar as providing behavior is essential to the group, provisions must be made in the behavior of others for the performance of this role.

Grief and mourning are in large measure a consequence of forced role latency. Ego is dead. Alter has learned, and been accustomed to performing, certain roles in response to ego's behavior. These role expectations are stored in a latent state in alter's personality. They are tied to specific cues or stimuli in various situations in which ego and alter have acted toward each other. As alter experiences the stimuli that normally trigger those roles into a state of activity which are now in forced latency, she is reminded of ego and his death. Alter role performance is frustrated by the absence of an actor toward whom to perform behavior. Until the alter actor can reorganize her behavior and tie her response patterns to roles performed toward others and to new stimuli, she will continue to feel grief. Insofar as the alter actor's relationship to the dead ego actor was sociologically and emotionally dependent upon ego, the life crisis for the alter actor will be relatively serious and cause a restructuring of alter's station.

Role Latency and Life Crisis

Once a set of roles is learned and becomes a part of a person's personality in the form of role expectation, it remains as a part of that personality system even after the person vacates the position in which the roles are contained. For example, the child learns to perform the roles required of him as an elementary school student, and practices his performance daily for six years. These role expectations are firmly imprinted in his personality system and do not disappear once he leaves elementary school. Later in life, after he has left the educational system and become a parent, and his child starts to go to school, the latent role of pupil is still present within his personality. Consequently, he transmits expectations about the pupil role to his child. Insofar as the structure of the school system has changed, these role definitions will be outdated.

Parents of school-aged children learn that roles in a state of latency can be triggered into activity, given the right set of circumstances. If the parents go to school to attend a meeting, and the teacher asks them to sit in the childrens' seats, they are apt to feel as though they are elementary school students again. They may experience some confusion as to which of their roles applies to the particular situation. This kind of role confusion is a result of the tendency of stored roles to be triggered into a state of activity by cues in the environment that have habitually brought them into a state of activity in the past. It is the same phenomenon that triggers grief for a dead spouse.

Role confusion is also significant for parent-child relations, particularly in the later life when the offspring have grown up and have their own children. Deactivated positions and roles are present as memory in the individual, and so they are available to act as models for socializing other people into the performance of these roles, and for judging their performance. Also, ego sometimes experiences difficulty in keeping these remembered roles from becoming active; and even as a grown child he may act toward his parents as if he were still very young.

Catastrophic or Idiosyncratic Life Crises

The life crises we have been discussing are routine and predictable, part of every individual's history. There is another kind of life crisis, however—specific catastrophes that are not scheduled by the structure of society or life. Routine life crises generally adhere to a sociocultural schedule. People enter school at a given time, and they graduate, marry, become parents, and retire according to a cultural blueprint that permits some variation, but which is, for the most part, predetermined. Catastrophic life crises are unpredictable. They drastically change, temporarily or permanently, the individual's participation in society, and hence represent temporary or permanent changes in his station structure. Illness, accident, injury, and hospitalization head the list, because any event that incapacitates the individual for the performance of his normal roles in society is a crisis both for him and for the groups in which he participates.

Institutionalization

Hospitalization, especially for a long period of time, represents a major life crisis in our society. Hospitalization, by its very nature, restricts the role performance of the individual to a narrow set of roles prescribed by the structure of hospitals as organizations. The individual's hospitalization must be regarded in terms of his regular participation in society. While hospitalized, he cannot perform his normal roles. Insofar as these roles are important in the structure of groups to which he belongs, other members of these groups are affected by his role latency. To the extent that the hospitalized person is concerned about performing his roles in these groups, hospitalization will present a crisis.

Hospitalization means that the groups within which the sick person plays his roles are left to operate without him, and they must find ways to fill the positions he normally holds. If his hospitalization is prolonged, the group may regard the positions as vacant, and make permanent adjustments in their structure. When the individual is released, therefore, he may find that his roles have been assumed by others, and that his station structure has undergone an irreversible restructuring. The positions that he formerly occupied are now occupied by others, and the roles that he formerly performed are being performed in other ways by other people. The place he thought he occupied within society is no longer available to him. This same phenomenon occurs with imprisonment or protracted military service, and is the major reason why an individual who has been institutionalized has difficulty when he tries to re-enter society.

Unemployment

Like retirement, unemployment represents a life crisis to the individual. The man who loses his job also loses his attachment to a significant part of the social structure. His occupational situs, and consequently his occupational roles, are kept in a state of latency. Furthermore, the unemployed person, lacking money, finds it impossible to perform other roles in other groups outside the occupational situs—for instance, the provider role. Unemployment insurance and social security benefits are structural attempts to keep these nonoccupational roles in a state of activity by providing a source of income. Through these benefits, the provider role, which is extramural, becomes attached to a union, a benefit system, insurance company, social security, or public welfare agency. Unemployment, here, means any situation in which the individual suddenly loses his means of livelihood, and includes bankruptcy for businessmen, and all other forms of financial catastrophe.

Social Mobility

Sudden social mobility, in the form of unusual occupational success or failure, may catapult the individual into new levels and types of participation in society, and represent a crisis for him and persons associated with him. Success is a catastrophe as well as failure, because promotion to a higher level of occupational status often results in the complete reorganization of a person's station. The newly rich who must fit into the strange social systems of the affluent communities into which they move may find this as traumatic as those newly-poor people who suddenly lose the basis of their prestige, fall to lower status levels, and move to lower-class neighborhoods.

Migration

Residential mobility, particularly long-distance migration, brings about significant changes in the station structures of individuals. When a family moves from one city to another, each member of the family must recreate a set of relationships in a new structural setting. The children must enter different neighborhood relationships. Similarly, the wife-mother and father-husband must build a new station structure at an entirely different point in the social system.

A migrant vacates a set of positions in one community to occupy a different set of similar positions in a different community. If the roles learned in the first community are similar in content to the roles performed in the new community, the crisis will be relatively easy. If, however, a person moves from one subculture to another, the definitions of familiar roles will change, and the individual will have to be resocialized to function effectively in the new system. Obviously, if he moves from one culture to an entirely different one, the problem is compounded. Cultural shock largely stems from the necessity to dismantle a learned station structure, and put together a new station structure that fits into a different community. Ethnic areas are often established in cities by migrants trying to soften the crisis of residential mobility by associating themselves in their new community with people who define the various roles that make up their station in a way that is close to their own.

A person's station structure, at any given time, consists of an exact set of positions and roles that exist in the structures of particular real groups. Thus, when a person moves from one community to another, the positions occupied in Community A are vacated and deactivated as far as the migrant is concerned, and an entirely new set of positions is activated in the new community. Insofar as people move as families, family positions and roles move with them; and to the extent that migrants maintain relationships in the old community, they continue to occupy positions there, and may still be regarded as members. This is certainly true in the case of kinship relations. If a nuclear conjugal family, whose entire kin system is located within Community A, moves to Community B, they do not cease to occupy the positions located in Community A with respect to other kinsmen, even though the activity-latency cycles of roles contained within these positions are profoundly affected by the physical separation. A person's station may therefore contain as parts or elements whole positions and situses that are located within the structures of two or more communities, and the communication between one community and the other may be influenced by his station structure. Migration, then, increases the complexity of the linkages between communities. Also, attempts to maintain the individual's station structure, particularly the kinship aspects, in a state of activity may result in the successive migration of different units of the same kinship system to the same new community.

Other Life Crises

Divorce, separation, and desertion are catastrophic for those individuals involved as either ego or alter actors, because certain roles and positions must be deactivated, and new structures activated to accommodate the change in relationships. Natural disasters, wars, and revolution also profoundly affect the individual's freedom or ability to perform roles contained within his station structure. Natural disasters, for example, may destroy the work situations in which people normally act out their occupational roles. Or they may destroy other aspects of the individual's situation, so that the normal activity-latency patterns contained within his station structure are disrupted and altered, and the individual suddenly cannot perform the roles to which he has been accustomed, sometimes for an extended period. War and revolution affect individuals in much the same way, by causing sometimes temporary, sometimes extensive and permanent changes in the contents of an individual's station.

PART V

DIMENSIONAL ANALYSIS AND CHANGE

CHAPTER 18   *SYNTHETIC FORMS OF*
                    STRUCTURAL ANALYSIS:
                    SOCIAL INSTITUTIONS

System-centered analysis focuses on whole social systems of various degrees of scale and complexity, and relates these systems to the next larger or more complex systems of which they are parts. Thus, it is concerned with entire groups, whole organizations, complete communities of various orders of complexity, or entire societies. These whole systems contain all of the parts necessary to their continued functioning or operation, given the assumption that exchanges exist between them and other systems of varying orders of complexity in their structural environment. A group, for example, is a whole system capable of functioning continuously if it receives from its environment the things it needs for its internal functioning. Similarly, organizations are systems capable of continued functioning, assuming exchanges with the environment.

Whole structurally-complete systems may be analyzed into functional subsystems that cannot exist alone without linkage to parallel subsystems that are a part of the same group, organization, community, or society. A group structure, for example, may be dissected into the structural components that produce various functions within the group. These structural components and the linkages among them form a functional subsystem within the whole system which is the group. Analysis made on a functional basis gives us a structural subsystem that closely resembles what sociologists have classically called a social institution.

The Institutional Concept in Sociology

Institution, as the term is used in sociology and anthropology, was originally a folk concept, and as such it has a number of quite different meanings, most of which have also been adopted by social scientists. An institution is defined as any strongly sanctioned and relatively complex social practice—for example, the institutions of marriage and private property (1). It also means any complex organization of considerable size—a university, museum, prison, mental hospital. Thirdly, it is defined as a complex system of action that produces some function for society—the economic institution, the educational institution. Talcott Parsons also uses *institutionalization* to refer to the process through which a practice becomes customary and normative, and thereby becomes an institution (2). And of course, *institutionalize* also means the induction of individuals into organizations, so that when someone is sent to a mental hospital, he is said to be institutionalized.

The third definition of *institution*—a complex system of action that produces some function for society—is the most important for the study of social structure. This concept is based on the analogy between society and a biological organism. The organism has a number of subsystems that serve various vital functions—the respiratory system, circulatory system, nervous system, gastrointestinal system, and so forth. Society, like an organism, can only survive if certain of its functions remain vital (3). What are these functions? and what social behavior produces these functions for the social system?

Bronislaw Malinowski (4) reasoned that society's requisite functions stem from various sources—some from the nature of the human organism itself, others from the nature of culture, and still others from the nature of group life. Societies must have people. People have certain requirements for life. Therefore, society must furnish a means of providing for the needs of human beings, including systems for providing food, shelter, and protection from enemies. Since people are perishable, there must be a system for procreation. Domestic and economic institutions thus arise to serve vital biological functions for the individual and the population of the society.

Malinowski further argues that human beings, lacking instinctive adaptive behavior, require culture, and culture requires a process of training or socialization to teach the individual how to secure food, shelter, and protection. As a consequence, the society must contain institutional arrangements for training the young in its culture.

Both the nature of the human organism, especially in the infancy and childhood years, and the nature of culture and the socialization process require life in groups. Group life in turn requires the maintenance of a degree of order, and hence the exercise of some kind of leadership and control. These requirements for order are met by the society's political institution. In short, inherent in the nature of human beings, their culture, and their society are certain prerequisite functions for any social system. Around these functions, in every society, complex systems of behavior arise which constitute social institutions.

The most commonly recognized social institutions are economic, political, educational, religious, and familial or domestic. Some sociologists would add recreation, others would include science, health, and military institutions. In some respects, any list of social institutions represents an attempt to match the biologically-based idea of functional requisites with those large structures that are said to exist according to cultural tradition. We are in the position to recognize that society does contain large, complex substructures that are devoted to producing different kinds of functions for society, such as the economic subsystem and the political subsystem; but we are not yet able to define fully the structure of these systems, or to understand how they fill prerequisite functions.

Problems of Defining Institutional Structure

The idea of a social institution has mostly been used in macroanalysis—sweeping statements about the broad outlines of the structure of society. As a macro concept, it allows us to talk about such phenomena as social change and social disorganization, and how they are related; and to formulate such ideas as Ogburn's hypothesis that differential rates of institutional change result in cultural lag (5).

In macroanalysis, we need not define precisely the internal structure of social institutions. But before we can use the concept of social institution here, we must understand what an institution is at the level of the acting individual in the ongoing social situation. It is not enough to say that there is a large complex system within society called the economic institution. We also have to be able to describe behavior at the level of the small group or subgroup that is a part of that larger structure. In other words, we have to be able to see the social institution at the level at which observation takes place and data are collected.

In structural terms, an adequate concept of *social institution* must specify what parts comprise the institution; how these parts are related to form a larger system; and how the larger system called the institution relates to other institutions in the complex system called society. Furthermore, the concepts of parts and relationships should be such that we can recognize the difference between two institutions at any level of scale or complexity in the structure of society. If we are dealing with a small group, we should be able to recognize what parts of the group relate to which institutions. If we are dealing with organizations or communities, we should be able to specify which aspects of community behavior or organizational behavior form parts of what social institution.

Institutions constitute subparts of society. Societies are comprised of groups, which are in turn organized into complex structures such as organizations and communities, which are in turn related to each other through matrices of relationships to form the thing called society. Institutions, therefore, as another way to categorize these same phenomena, must be comprised of the same ingredients as groups, organizations, and communities. If the concept of a social institution is to be truly useful in analyzing the structure of society, we must know what these ingredients are.

The Parts of Social Institutions

Are institutions comprised of whole groups and whole organizations? or are they comprised of certain parts of these types of systems? Take, for example, the economic institution. Are its parts all of those groups and organizations devoted to the production, distribution, and, perhaps, consumption of goods and services in society? With this approach, the Ajax Black Box Factory would be a part of the economic institution, and *all* of its structure, including *all* of its activity patterns and its constituent groups and subgroups, would be included within the structure of the economic institution. As part of the economic institution it would, therefore, be analytically separated in the structure of society from other groups that are parts of other institutions.

If this definition is followed faithfully, no part of an industrial plant could be regarded as a part of the political, religious, educational, or domestic institutions. If we classified groups such as a political party, the Congress of the United States, or the Department of Agriculture as part of the political institution, then all of their structure would be included within this institution, and *none* would be left over to be regarded as a part of other institutions. We would then be defining institutions as structures comprised of whole groups and organizations devoted to the production of some specialized aspect of the function around which the institution is organized.

An alternative approach toward defining the parts of institutions is to use segments or parts of groups and organizations as the units out of which institutional structure is built. From this point of view, institutions are structures comprised of all of the behavior that serves a given function in society, and includes only that behavior which is directly related to the function of the institution. This way, only economic behaviors, and, therefore, economic roles, are regarded as parts of the economic institution; and only that behavior that takes place in the factory and is actually economic behavior is classified as a part of the economic institution. Behavior taking place within the factory that is political in nature is classified as a part of a different institution, the political institution. In these terms, the factory as a whole social system contains parts of several social institutions, and therefore is not included entirely within the boundaries of one or another institution.

Some sociologists prefer to think of institutions as being comprised of all those groups and organizations whose primary function or reason for being is related to the function of that institution. Thus, factories, farms and other economic groups are seen as being the units out of which the economic system or economic institution is comprised.

Other sociologists prefer to think of institutions as systems of behavior devoted to the production of a given function in society. They consider institutions as comprised of parts of groups and organizations. There are many strong arguments to be made in favor of this behavioral approach to defining social institutions. A church, for example, is an organization that certainly appears to belong entirely to the religious institution of society. Obviously, churches as organizations are specialized social systems devoted to a religious function in society. In our society, however, churches own property, pay salaries to ministers and other functionaries, collect money, keep books, and engage in various types of economic exchanges. A good deal of the behavior that takes place within the church as an organization is economic behavior, similar to economic behavior in a business establishment; and this behavior should probably be regarded as being a part of the economic institution. Churches also contain power structures. They have hierarchies of authority, bodies that make decisions, procedures for enforcing rules, means of filling offices, and ways of exercising social control and leadership. These functions are all political in nature, and should be regarded as parts of the political institution. Churches as organizations socialize their members, and have complex subsystems devoted to formalized education. It seems apparent that this aspect of the organization is related to the educational institutions of society, and not to religion at all.

Churches, therefore, as whole organizations contain behavior which contributes to the political institution, the economic institution, and the educational institution of society. Only a portion of the behavior that goes on within church organizations is related to religion. It is apparent, then, that if we included the entire church organization as a part of the religious institution, we would leave incomplete the structures of other institutions within which churches perform specialized functions. Part of the economic institution of the community, and part of the educational and political institutions as well would be lacking if we ascribed the entire behavior of church members to one and only one institution.

This multiple-function phenomenon has been most readily recognized with respect to the family, which sociologists have traditionally regarded as a social institution (6). Students of family sociology however, have noted that families as social groups perform political, economic, educational, religious, and other types of functions, and that the behavior of family members appears to be a part of several different social institutions. But if parts of the behavior of people in families belong to different institutions, how then can the family itself be called a social institution?

As organic systems most, if not all, groups and organizations have the same multiple-function characteristic as the family. As we have seen, churches as organizations contain a range of behavior related to various institutions. A factory, which may appear at first glance to be a totally economic organization, contains political, educational, and religious behavior within its boundaries. And schools and banks, armies and hospitals, stores and transportation companies also share this characteristic.

The assumption that institutions include entire organizations and groups as parts of their internal structure simply fails the test of empirical observation. If we classify factories as economic organizations, churches as religious organizations, schools as educational organizations, and legislative bodies as political organizations, we will overgeneralize. We cannot classify these organizations by their primary functions only, and ignore the fact that they contain behaviors which are only indirectly related to these functions. Social institutions rarely, if ever, contain entire groups and organizations as parts of their structure. Instead, they contain aspects of the behavior that takes place within these entities as parts of that structure.

Another reason to reject the view that institutions contain entire organizations and groups is that it makes it exceedingly difficult to state how one institution relates to another to form the structure of society. Only if we take the point of view that organizations like factories, churches, and legislative bodies contain within their structure parts of the various social institutions, can we understand how the relationship between various institutions becomes a function of the structure of groups and organizations themselves. That is, organizations and groups as organic systems relate the functional subsystems that make up the various social institutions to each other, through group structure and process. In a shop in a factory, for example, the system of supervision and control exercised by the foreman over the worker is part of the political institution of the society. Therefore, the interaction between foreman and workers with reference to work relates partially to the political institution in that group. Its economic, educational, and perhaps even religious and domestic activities are directed and controlled through political behavior.

This point of view also makes it possible to see that every social institution extends into every functioning group that exists within society. Take the political institution, for example. Shops within factories have a power structure. Families as social groups have a power structure. Classes in the school room, and congregations at church have power structures. All these power structures are related in a network that makes up the political institution of the society. The political institution, therefore, does not consist simply of government in the classical sense; it consists of government in every group and every organization within society. Groups that specialize in other functions, such as religion or education or economic production, therefore have governmental structures which belong to all other governmental structures within the society. Thus, government or politics extends from the classical political groups, such as city government or federal agencies, into nongovernmental groups like families, churches, and schools. This approach shows clearly how one institution is related to another. And of course, the parts of the larger structure of the total institution are linked together through extramural roles, interstitial groups, and by the conjunctive and reciprocal relationships that form chains of relationships.

A Practical View of Social Institutions

The basic problem with using Malinowski's idea of requisite functions lies in identifying those that can be demonstrated to be truly prerequisite to all societies.

This problem will not be completely solved until we have enough detailed data on the anatomy or social organization of a large number of societies to establish empirically what structural arrangements actually exist. Unfortunately, at the moment we possess very little empirical information indeed. So, it will be wisest for us to remain conservative in postulating the existence of specific functional subsystems within the organization of society.

Let us, therefore, stick to the list of five social institutions offered earlier—that is, economic, political, educational, religious, and familial or domestic—and hypothesize about what functional subsystems organized to produce these functions in society. Let us assume, also, that every organization or detached elemental group within the structure of society contains at least one role that calls for behavior which constitutes a part of each of these social institutions. This means that each institution reaches into and contains a part of each organization in society, and that therefore no organization can be considered to be completely within any one institution.

In other words, each organization and each detached elemental group in society has a structural linkage which joins it to the economic, political, educational, religious, and domestic institutions. Through this linkage the specialized functions performed by the various specialized social systems in society flow from one to another. Through it the organizations obtain the inputs they need to keep them functioning, and that allow them to produce the outputs needed in other parts of society.

Inputs and outputs are the functions and around which institutions are organized. For example, all organizations and detached groups receive political inputs from their social environment, and produce political outputs for that environment. By a political input we mean some form of power-oriented behavior that transmits decisions, directives, orders, instructions, commands, or injunctions to the organization from outside; or that creates and enforces rules or norms which are transmitted into the organization, and become factors to which the behavior of members of organizations must adapt. Thus the consequences, or output, of political behavior performed external to an organization flows into it through its external linkage system, and then is reacted to in terms of internal political activity. The same kind of thing happens for each institutional function.

Institutions, then, act as sociological pipelines. They consist of networks of interconnected social relationships that transmit functions produced in one part of a complex social system through the behavior of actors to other parts of the system. Institutions are also to be regarded as structures through which these functions are produced. The division of labor structurally separates the groups and organizations in society; in the process, a division of labor occurs not only between institutions, but within them. That is to say, the division of labor separates groups and organizations primarily specialized to produce political functions (government agencies) from those primarily set up to produce economic functions (factories). But it also separates those groups and organizations that produce part of the political function from other groups and organizations producing other parts of the political function. For example, the courts are separated from the legislative, which is also separated from the executive branch of government. The exercise of power and control within a bureaucratically-organized industrial company, a political activity, is separated from the exercise of power and control over public works or taxation or military affairs, which are other political activities. The division of labor that causes specialization of groups and organizations in society does not, however, change the fact that those functions vital to the operation of society and its various component parts must of necessity be performed. It merely subdivides the performance of these functions, and allocates various parts of them to specific differentiated locations in the social system.

Politics, religion, economics, socialization, and domesticity are found everywhere in the social system. Members of society may believe religion is a function of the church, the mosque, the synagogue, the temple; but that does not mean that religious activities are restricted to these locations. Similarly, the fact that our culture sees political activity as a part of government does not mean that private enterprise is free of politics, or that government is free of religious or economic activity. These beliefs reflect folk views of our social organizations, and are actually expressions of values, rather than accurate representations of the way our society is structured. People may say there ought to be a separation of church and state, or that free enterprise demands a separation of government from economic affairs, or that a man's home is his castle and the government ought not to interfere with it. All these ideas are values and aspirations. They may say that the power structure of an industrial bureaucracy is economic rather than political, but this does not change the reality of the way the power and control function in society actually works. The industrial bureaucracy governs that part of social behavior which takes place within its boundaries just as surely as the Department of Agriculture governs the production of cotton or corn.

Our theory thus far amounts, then, to the following argument:

1. There are certain vital functions necessary to establishing and maintaining a society as an operating social system.
2. These functions must be performed with respect to every differentiated or semiautonomous social system which forms a part of society.
3. The following five are vital institutional functions in our society: (1) economic, (2) political, (3) educational, (4) religious, (5) domestic.

The list of five institutional functions is probably not complete, and future research may produce a different set.

An important property of role relationships does exist that ultimately may allow us to identify social institutions on an inductive basis. This property can be stated as follows: Whenever two or more roles are linked to one another by either bilateral or reflexive relationships, whether reciprocal or conjunctive, they are always roles having a common function.

This means that if one role is economic in function, the other will also always be economic; if one is power oriented, the other will also always be power oriented. Consider, for instance, the following role relationships, together with their associated institutional functions.

Bilateral Role Relationships

Role Relationship	Institutional Function
Provider—Dependent	Economic
Cashier—Customer	Economic
Teller—Depositor	Economic
Lecturer—Auditor	Educational
Teacher—Student	Educational
Supervisor—Subordinate	Political
Disciplinarian—Offender	Political
Priest—Penitent	Religious
Mistress—Maid	Domestic

Whenever two roles are paired in a complementary relationship, they are, as this list shows, always part of the same functional subsystem. It is intuitively clear that this will also have to be true of reflexive relationships. For example, the provider role in the family is economic in nature and logically a part of the network of roles that constitute the economic institution of society. It is also an extramural role—that is, it cannot be performed unless the person to whom it is assigned participates in an external group from which he obtains the necessary resources to perform that role. Since the role is economic, the resources needed are economic; therefore, the extramural provider role must be linked reflexively to external economic roles which provide the needed inputs. In our society, the external role is most usually that of employee in an organization.

The employee role is a dependent economic role in a work group or organization, and is one role among many that make up the occupational situs of the actor who is also provider in the family. The school teacher, for example, has an employee role contained in his occupational situs. It contains expectations which specify the conditions of pay, leave, fringe benefits, and other economic considerations with respect to the actor. Through this role the teacher is paid, and it is with this role and not the others making up his situs that the family provider role is linked.

Figure 18-1 shows Mr. Doe as father-husband in a family with the extramural provider role assigned to his position. This provider role is

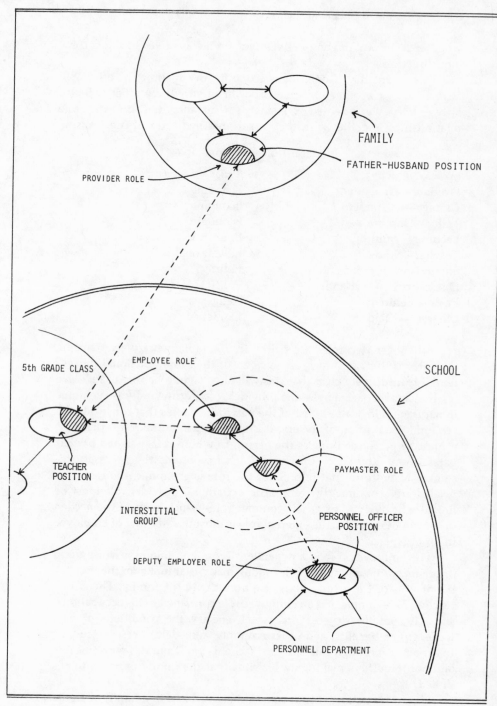

Figure 18–1 A Fragment of the Economic Institution

linked by a reflexive relationship to his employee role, which is in turn linked to a role in a position occupied by a member of the school system's personnel office, the deputy employer. This deputy employer role, the representative of the employing school system, is in turn connected to a paymaster role in the personnel group. Through this chain of role relationships, which of course may actually become quite elaborate, the necessary economic resources for performing the provider role flow from the school organization, in which Doe's occupational situs is located, into the family.

Only a part of Doe's occupational situs is connected to the provider role directly. The other parts are connected indirectly by virtue of being located either in the same position that contains the employee role, or by being in other positions connected to the one containing the employee role. Furthermore, the other roles contained in the occupational situs are here described as being noneconomic. Since we are talking about a school teacher, some of them will obviously be educational. When Doe is acting out one of his teaching roles—for example, lecturing to his class—he is performing as part of the educational institution. When he is lecturing he is not acting as an employee, but as a lecturer. Nor can it be said that he is providing for his family while he is lecturing. Providing is linked to lecturing only indirectly. Lecturing is linked to an employee role in the situs structure of the actor, and simultaneously to the structure of the organization, but lecturing socializes or educates—it does not provide.

Because both bilateral and reflexive relationships are invariably unifunctional, if we traced the entire chain through which any given role relationship is attached directly or indirectly, we would eventually encounter every role in the structure of the entire society with a given type of function. If we start with a political relationship, say, and follow every bilateral and reflexive relationship wherever it leads us, we will eventually end by tracing a path through the entire political institution of society. In the process we will never encounter an economic role, or an educational, religious, or domestic role except as parallel roles contained within the boundaries of the same positions that contain political roles. If an economic role appears in our analysis, it will be there because we made the mistake of not staying with bilateral or reflexive relationships, and jumped instead to another kind of relationship among the roles that comprise the same position.

One important implication of this view is that the things people do for a living are only partially economic in nature. If the school teacher while he is actually engaged in one of his teaching roles is performing as a part of the educational institution, then obviously teaching is not an economic activity, even though people, through their employee roles, are paid for it. Preachers while preaching, governors while governing, or housewives while housekeeping are performing noneconomic roles.

Let us define the five major social institutions in terms of the roles or role behavior of which they are comprised.

1. *Domestic Institution:* All those roles devoted to the maintenance of the group situation; to the maintenance of group members through satisfying the need for food, shelter, clothing, protection, health care, and sexual gratification; and to the recruitment or biological reproduction of members.

2. *Political Institution:* All those roles devoted to the control of behavior in the group, through the exercise of power to co-ordinate group activities, enforce group norms, or formulate rules and goals for group activities.

3. *Educational Institution:* All those roles devoted to the socialization or training of group members in the culture of the group or other groups; or to the transmission of information or attitudes to group members.

4. *Religious Institution:* All those roles devoted to the creation and maintenance of belief systems which serve to justify the norms, values, and transmitted attitudes of the group.

5. *Economic Institution:* All those roles devoted to the acquisition, control over, and exchange or transfer of property, including land, goods, money, stocks, bonds, franchises; or to the creation or manufacture of property or goods for exchange outside the group or organization producing the property.

Given these definitions, let us take Mr. Jones, the president of the Ajax Black Box Factory, and look at some of his roles in terms of their institutional affiliation. One subset of his roles is management roles, involving such activities as giving orders and instructions, making rules, setting goals for the organization, and enforcing organizational rules. These roles are, by our definition, clearly political, and therefore part of the political institution. It matters not that they have the effect of directing economic activity. Such activity, along with religious, educational, and domestic activities are always directed by political role behavior. The control over group activities through the use of power is the function of the political institution everywhere it occurs.

Jones also has a set of roles related to training junior executives, supervisors, and office workers in the procedures associated with their roles. This set of roles is obviously educational in nature, and a part of the educational institution.

Among Jones' remaining roles is a set having to do with the acquisition and control over property. For example, he has a role of financier for the organization. This role requires him to acquire money through relationships with banks and investors. It is economic in nature, and part of the economic institution. It is only when he is acting out one of these property-oriented roles that he is actually performing economic behavior. When he is exercising power in any of its multiple forms, he is acting politically; when he is engaged in socialization behavior, he is acting educationally. It follows therefore that only part of his set of positions that constitute his occupational situs is economic, although he heads an organization built around an economic function, the acquisition of profits through the exchange of a product in a market.

Take another set of roles—those we have classified as domestic. Among them are roles related to the providing of food for people in groups. If we consider a restaurant as a group, or perhaps an organization, then the roles of the cook in preparing food, of the waitress in serving it, and of the dishwasher and bus boy are domestic, rather than economic. The economic roles involved in restaurant structure are things like the cashier role, through which money is obtained in exchange for a domestic service; the employee roles of restaurant workers, through which an income is obtained for playing domestic roles; or the purchasing-agent roles of the manager, through which food and other resources are obtained in exchange for money.

The fact that we view occupations, regardless of their behavioral content, as being economic in nature—since people are paid for their services—means we classify almost all of the behavior in society as economic. But if it is all economic, it cannot simultaneously be political and religious. However, there is a way to resolve the dilemma this raises about the economic institution. That is, to keep in mind how roles are performed in action.

Recall that we defined behavior as occurring in action streams. Acts and sets of acts which constitute parts of roles flow through time and space in linear progressions. The progression in which roles, or, more properly, parts of the total behavior that constitutes a role, occur may be diagrammed as:

$$\text{Time O } R_1\ R_2\ R_3\ R_1\ R_3\ R_2\ R_1. \ldots \text{ Time N}$$

The structure of society places roles with different functions at particular points along the role progression in an action stream in such a way that the performance of one role is contingent upon the performance of another at some earlier point in the action stream. This statement also holds true for linear progressions representing person-centered or system-centered units.

Thus, the performance of the provider role, R_2, is dependent upon the performance of the employee role, R_1, at some previous point in the action stream. This is essentially what is meant by an extramural role. If we let R_X represent any other role, than we have: $R_X\ R_2\ R_X\ R_X\ R_1$.

A point may be reached such that R_2, the provider role, cannot again be performed until another performance of R_1, the employee role, has taken place.

This contingency among roles is true not only for extramural roles, but also for intramural roles that are a part of the same position. For example, we can say that the cook role in the wife's position in the family cannot be performed unless (1) the provider role of husband is first performed; and (2) her dependent role is performed through which she receives the wherewithal to activate the cook role. In other words, the cook role, a domestic institutional function, is contingent upon the performance of economic roles like provider and dependent before it can be performed.

If R_X=any role; R_D=dependent role; R_P=provider role interaction; R_E=employee role; and R_X=cook role interaction; then this may be diagrammed as:

T_O T_N
Wife: R_X R_X R_D R_X R_C. . . .
Husband: R_X R_E R_P R_X R_X. . . .

This example can be extended to the cook's role in a restaurant. The performance of the role of cook is contingent upon the performance of the employee role in the future. That is to say, the domestic role of cook is placed in a linear progression that contains the economic employee role. As long as the person performing the cook role anticipates performing the employee role, and thus anticipates being paid, he continues to perform the role. If the linear sequence is disrupted by the nonperformance of the employee role, then cooking will no longer take place. The employee role contains norms that specify when and where it will be performed, and what kinds of exchange of money or property the person occupying the position of cook can anticipate. These expectations place an economic role, or perhaps a set of roles, in a linear progression organized around performing a noneconomic function. This has the effect of linking this linear progression to another linear progression organized primarily around the economic function, but containing other noneconomic elements.

Roles which perform a given function occur in sets that contain roles which perform entirely different functions. For example, an economic role will occur in a set that contains a political role and a domestic role. These sets constitute social positions in groups, and are combined into larger sets of both a person-centered and system-centered sort. The person-centered sets form situses and stations, and the system-centered sets form group structures and organizational structures.

These spatial sets are so constituted that their activity-latency cycles place them in temporal progressions—what may be called *role se-*

quences. Members of the spatial sets are dependent for their performance on the occurrence of role sequences at a certain point in the temporal sets. If certain roles are not preceded by or followed by the performance of other roles in the set, they themselves cannot be performed. This contingency within the temporal and spatial ordering of behavior is what is meant by *vital function* or *functional prerequisite.* The performance of one function is requisite for the performance of the other, and there must be a certain periodicity in a certain sequence in order for the social system to continue to operate or the members of the society to survive as actors.

In other words, differentiated institutional functions are integrated as parts of functioning social systems by (1) being placed together spatially as parts of the same social systems at the level of functioning groups and organizations; and (2) by being arranged in temporal orders within such systems so that each becomes contingent upon the other.

CHAPTER 19 SOCIAL STRUCTURE AND THE DISTRIBUTION OF POWER, HONOR, AND WEALTH: SOCIAL STRATIFICATION

Dimensions of Social Structure

The habit of referring to social relations in spatial terms is deeply embedded in the culture of Western society (1). English is replete with expressions that use spatial terms to describe social relationships. We speak of people holding high positions, being distant in their relationships with one another, belonging to the lower class. In ascribing vertical and horizontal dimensions to society, therefore, sociologists merely adopt a generally held view of its structure.

When sociologists talk about the vertical dimension of society, they are referring to the phenomenon of social rank and its many manifestations in the behavior which constitutes the social system. The horizontal dimension of society refers to differences in social role, occupation, or position at the level of the individual; or to the differentiation of group functions and organizational missions at the level of the group and organization. Thus, the horizontal dimension of society is an expression of the division of labor, which grows out of social differentiation. In contrast, the distribution of social rank in society is viewed as a result of the social stratification that accompanies the differentiation and produces a vertical ordering of differentiated roles in society.

In this chapter we will analyze the vertical dimension of society in terms of system-centered and person-centered analysis. To do this, we must first identify and define certain variables associated with social ranking.

Social Rank Variables

Three variables, or dimensions, of social rank are usually employed in discussions of social stratification: power, honor, and wealth. These attributes are possessed by individuals, and can be used to categorize them in terms of their positions or locations in the stratification system of society.

Power, Authority, and Influence

Power is defined many ways in sociology and political science, but its most usual definition is that it is the ability of one person to control or determine the behavior of another according to the controller's desires. One man has power over another man if he is able to call forth in him the behavior he desires, regardless of the other's objections (2).

We have to distinguish power from the general notion of social interaction. In social interaction, every individual determines and controls the behavior of every other to some extent. Roles involve reciprocal and conjunctive responses: when ego performs a given act, he elicits a response on the part of alter, and thereby determines alter's behavior insofar as alter's role definitions become active and operate as a result of ego's behavior. Interaction thus involves a mutual stimulation and response through which ego and alter determine each other's behavior, given the fact that other variables are also operating. What, then, of power?

The difference lies in the type of interaction between ego and alter. Out of all those acts that ego performs, power behavior specifically consists of one of the following types of actions: (1) the giving of orders, directions, instructions, commands, or directives; (2) the deliberate application of recognized punishments and penalties, withdrawal of legitimate privileges and rewards, or the application of recognized rewards and privileges to gain conformity to norms or to directives; and (3) the stating of new rules, norms, role definitions, procedures, schedules, and so on, which are binding upon alter.

These types of behavior constitute power behavior; but ego has power only when one of two conditions prevails. First, he has power if members of the group in which this behavior is performed recognize his right to engage in this kind of behavior with respect to given alters, and his behavior is defined as legitimate. Second, he has power if, even though no right to this kind of behavior exists, he can engage in such behavior and alters have no alternative but to accept it and conform to his desires.

These two conditions are used as a basis for differentiating two forms of power—authority, and influence. Kingsley Davis, in *Human Society*, defines *authority* as positional power (3), by which he means that it is power lodged in the role structure of the positions occupied by ego, and is therefore legitimate. In other words, authority exists when ego has the right to perform power roles with respect to alter. In contrast, *influence* stems not from the structure of the system, but from the characteristics (including the behavior) of the actor. According to Davis's reasoning, a person can add to or detract from the total amount of power he has, which stems from authority, through positive or negative influence. Positive influence is ego's ability to go beyond the rights lodged in the norms of his roles, and to give additional orders, directions, instructions, punishments, rewards, or to enforce additional rules beyond the limits of his authority norms. Negative influence, in contrast, means that due to his behavior or his character he is unable to utilize all of the power lodged in the position that he occupies (4).

Essentially, the distinction between authority and influence rests on a distinction between sources of power. Authority has its source in the structure of the system, and in our view, stems from the cultural structure variable. In contrast, influence has its source in the actor, and stems from the personality variable.

All platoon sergeants in army infantry companies, for instance, occupy identical positions that contain authority roles which specify the rights and the duties of the sergeants in infantry companies. They can all give orders, directions, and instructions, enforce rules, and form norms. These rights and duties determine the amount of authority that goes with the positions of platoon sergeants. There are complementary subordinate roles and positions for the other platoon members, reciprocal roles containing sets of rights and duties that define the authority relations between the platoon sergeant and his men. The sergeant's power stems from the role definitions lodged in the positions occupied by the actors constituting the platoon.

Each individual, however, has a unique personality. Some platoon sergeants have what Max Weber called *charisma*, while others lack it (5). Some platoon sergeants will be able to induce their men to follow them willingly, and as a consequence, will be able to exercise power over them beyond that actually lodged in the positions they occupy. This additional increment of power is influence; it stems not from the positions that they occupy, but from their personal characteristics and behavior. In contrast, some platoon leaders may be so hated by their men that even their legitimate orders are ignored. These individuals have negative influence.

Power, then, is a generic term referring to the ability of one individual to control or direct the behavior of another, regardless of source. Authority refers to a particular type of power that stems from the cultural structure which defines the roles that people play in relation to one another. Influence is wielded on the basis of the character of the actor, rather than the structure of the group.

Authority, then, is found in the structure of society, lodged at particular points in social systems, and authority roles are parts of the positions that people occupy in social groups. In the Ajax Black Box Factory, the supervisor of the box shop occupies a position which contains one or more authority roles. These roles include norms that call for behavior controlling the actions of other actors within the group. Authority roles give the supervisor the right to issue orders, directions, and instructions to other people, and to exercise social controls over their behavior in the form of rewards and punishments. Authority roles also place an obligation on the actor to engage in such behavior in order to perform a function for the group. In other words, the actor has both the right and the duty, according to normative expectations, to engage in power behavior, and through it to control the activities of other members of the group. Similarly, reciprocal roles exist within other positions that comprise the group structure, requiring the position occupants to take orders, directions, and instructions, and to accept controls from the supervisor. All of these authority roles are located at particular places in the structure of the system.

There are other authority roles located at other points in the structure of the same system. These roles may be performed by the same actors discussed above. For example, the supervisor of the Box Shop occupies a position in an interstitial group which is comprised of him, the supervisors of the other shops in the factory, and the president of the company. In this group, he is assigned the supervisee, or subordinate, role. His obligation is to take orders rather than give them. He has the right to expect directions to be given to him, and is in almost an opposite power position from that which he occupies within his own shop.

The same individual also occupies other positions in other groups within society. For example, he is a father-husband in a family. His position in this group also contains authority roles. These roles give him the right to engage in authority behavior regarding his children and wife, and obligate him to engage in such behavior within this system of relationships. It can be seen from this example that one individual may, by virtue of his participation in various groups, learn various authority roles, and such roles may be stored in the form of latent behavior in his personality.

The various positions which make up the station structure contain authority roles. Some positions in a given station contain roles that give the individual a large amount of power within the group in which the position exists, although the same individual may also occupy positions in other groups where he is the object of power behavior on the part of someone else. Evaluating the total amount of power that someone has is equivalent to evaluating the amount of power contained within a given station. It is a complex task. In order to be able to control the behavior of specific others, the individual has to be involved in the kind of relationship where power is exercised. But authority is divided up and allocated throughout social systems, which means it is also divided up and allocated to various positions comprising the structure of a given person's station. There will be, in other words, a certain amount of authority contained in each position comprising the station of a person. In order to evaluate the person's total power in society, we have to estimate the authority associated with each position, and relate it to the social system in which the position is located.

It seems reasonable to say that a person who has power over another by virtue of an authority position in the structure of the social system has more power if he controls a person who also has authority within that system, than if he controls someone who is powerless. If ego has authority over an alter who himself has authority over many others, he has more power than he would have if the alter whom he controls has no power. In order to evaluate the total power contained in a station, we therefore must place that station in the context of the social system within which it exists. When this is done, of course, the individual as a functioning system becomes fragmented by virtue of the allocation of his behavior to the various positions he occupies at different locations in social space.

The same comments hold true for an individual's influence. Each position that he occupies in the structure of society represents an opportunity to exercise influence. In terms of real behavior, a certain amount of influence will be associated with each position that the person occupies. To speak about his total influence in society, we have to relate him to the social system at the particular points where he participates in social behavior.

The points where authority and influence occur in social space can be described in terms of positions and roles. Authority takes the form of role definitions that normatively define the behavior appropriate to performing one or another power function within a group. Power behavior consists of acts directed at achieving or performing these same functions.

A system may have either highly specialized or highly generalized power roles within it. There are at least five different kinds of power functions around which authority may be organized in the structure of social systems. The first function is directing group activities by giving orders, directions, instructions, and suggestions. The second is making the rules with respect to members of the group. The third is setting goals and objectives, determining standards of performance and adequacy of role fulfillment. The fourth is selecting the personnel to occupy the position which makes up the group structure by recruiting, hiring, or otherwise admitting members, and by firing, replacing, or ejecting group members. The fifth is enforcing the rules by using sanctions, or by controlling the allocation and use of rewards and punishments.

In undifferentiated power structures within organizations and groups, all of these behaviors may be combined into a single role. In highly differentiated group and organizational structures, they may be divided into particular roles which are assigned to different people, and can even be subdivided according to the part of each subfunction performed by a given individual. In other words, one power role may be organized around the actual supervision of the behavior of people within the group and assigned to a particular person, who becomes the director of group activities. A totally different person may be assigned the responsibility of enforcing the rules which apply to the behavior of members of the group.

The point is that power in the form of either authority or influence is highly specific to social relationships. It is not a general phenomenon in the sense that an individual who has power in one group will always have power wherever he participates in the social system. Power is attached to particular groups and assigned to particular people. It is exercised at that point in social space. In another group the same individual still has latent power, in the sense that he occupies the first position, but he cannot exercise that power in the second group. The General of the Armies may have tremendous power that he can exercise in relationship to particular people in the organizations within which that power exists in the form of authority and influence. This does not mean that he will command authority over his wife or children, his butcher, baker, or next door neighbor. However, his authority within the army may supply him with a source of influence in these other contexts.

To sum up, both power and influence are highly specific to social relationships. One does not have power over communities or societies or physical objects. One has power over specific people.

Honor, Prestige, and Esteem

The second variable used in ranking people in society is *honor,* a concept that refers to deferential behavior. In social relationships, individuals pay deference or homage to one another. Some individuals are given greater amounts of respect than others and are looked up to. Protocol in society codifies the deferential honor that each individual is entitled to.

Deference is expressed in a number of ways that amount to a display of a human pecking order. Titles of respect like *sir* or *ma'am,* seating order at the dinner table, bowing, tipping the hat, allowing a person to go first through a door, ways of dressing, and other signs of social rank are forms of behavior that express varying degrees of honor within society.

Like power, honor may be described in terms of its source. *Prestige* is honor that is lodged in the position a person occupies in a group. By virtue of occupying a position, a person may be entitled to a certain degree of respect and deference. All company commanders in the army, for instance, regardless of who they are, are entitled to a salute. This is a sign of deference that is lodged in their position rather than in themselves as individuals. In contrast to this, as Kingsley Davis points out, there are signs of deference paid to individuals in terms of their personal character; some individuals are afforded more respect than others, even though they occupy the same position (6). Honorific behavior lodged in character is called *esteem.*

Prestige, then, is parallel to authority; esteem is parallel to influence. *Status* is a concept that today means something closely akin to honor. An individual who has high status usually occupies a position of high prestige, or is much esteemed by members of society. Vance Packard's phrase, *status seeker,* means someone interested in achieving honor or perhaps, more generally, high rank (7).

Prestige is a measure of the amount of deference and respect that is defined as appropriate for a person by the norms that govern particular social relationship. There are no prestige roles; that is, there are no roles lodged in the structure of groups organized around performing a prestige function. There are authority roles, but prestige is measured in terms of the kind of deference due individuals in performing other roles. Some norms calling for deferential behavior may be found within an authority role. For example, saluting in a military situation may be closely associated with the performance of the authority role of command. Deferential norms for behavior in teacher-student relationships, for example, may demand that a student address the instructors by titles of deference—to say "Yes, sir" or "Yes, ma'am," or to call them Mr., Mrs., or Miss, Doctor, Professor, or Dean, rather than by their first names. In other words, the norms that call for prestige behavior are distributed throughout the role structure of social groups, rather than being collected at one point around the performance of a prestige function.

Esteem refers to the amount of actual deference realized in ongoing social behavior. In other words, esteem refers to the honor a person receives in social organizational terms, while prestige refers to honor with respect to sociocultural structure.

As in the case of power, it is possible to assess the amount of honor received by a person by virtue of occupying each and every one of the positions he holds in society. In some positions, he is paid deference by members of the group, and has a high standing in that group relative to other members. In other groups, if his standing is lower than other members of the group, he may be expected to pay deference to them. His total social honor can be estimated by adding up the amounts from the various positions that he occupies. As with power, a person has a higher honorific standing in society if he receives deference from others who are highly honored, than if he receives deference from those who are not. Therefore, we have to know his station in relation to the social system in order to assess his standing with respect to honor. The amount of power or honor associated with the station is a function of accumulating positional increments.

Situses can also be evaluated in terms of power and honor. We can evaluate Mr. Brown's power score with respect to his occupational or work situs by assessing the amount of power he realizes through his behavior in each position in his work situs. When we do this, we are assessing the amount of influence contained within his work-related behavior. Similarly, we can evaluate the total amount of authority contained within the various authority roles related to his work or occupational situs, and evaluate his prestige and esteem with respect to either occupation or kinship.

When we speak of honor or power with respect to such structural units as a station or situs, remember that we have artificially created this evaluation by imagining that we can add up increments of these two variables that exist within the positions and roles that comprise group structures. Positions and roles actually contain the norms or the behavior about which we have generalized. That is, positions have power or honor; but stations, in reality, do not have these attributes. Stations do not function as unitary systems within the structure of society. The power and honor of a person are not located within the structure of society at one and only one point where the power and honor can be exercised in a meaningful fashion. To exercise power or receive honor, a person must be in a relationship to other specific individuals who either grant the honor, or act as the recipients or the wielders of power. These relationships involve positions and roles, not whole stations or situses.

In this discussion of social rank we must tie the concepts about rank in with those that define the structure of social systems and person-centered analysis. For example, it is essential for us to relate power and honor to the positions that people occupy in groups, and furthermore, associate them with the roles and norms that form these positions. Honorific roles do not exist in the structure of every group. Instead, individual norms, lodged in the various roles that comprise the group structure, are apt to define norms of deferential behavior among members of the group. That is, the norms which call for behavior expressing differential amounts of honor are diffused among the various roles forming a given position, and are specific expectations associated with individual roles. An individual may be expected to call his supervisor by the honorific title "Mr. Jones" whenever he addresses him, regardless of the role he is performing. He is, in other words, expected to show a certain degree of deference or respect for the supervisor in every role that he performs. Honor, then, is a way of analyzing the content of roles that comprise a given position, but it is not itself a central function around which a role is formed in a given group.

A person's station consists of all the positions he occupies in society, and its power and honor, taken as an entity, amounts to the sum of the power ratings contained in the various positions that comprise it. When we say that an individual is a powerful man, we are saying essentially that he occupies positions in the structure of society that contain authority roles, or in which he has great influence over others. It is only in these positions that he exercises such power over others. A similar statement can be made with respect to honor. The total prestige associated with a given person's station in society is a function of the prestige lodged in the individual positions that he occupies, or the amount of esteem he has acquired through the occupancy of such positions.

Wealth, Property, and Income

When it comes to wealth, we are dealing with concepts that are basically person-centered. But if we refer to the amount of wealth associated with each position that a person occupies in the structure of society, or to the amount of income he receives by virtue of occupying each position and the amount of property that he controls, then we can treat the three variables of social rank—power, honor, and wealth—in equivalent ways. We can use system-centered analysis most easily with respect to the wealth of adult males in our society, especially if we apply it to their occupations. Income, for example, is easily related to the occupational situs of an individual. Within the occupational situs, however, an individual occupies numerous positions, and it is difficult to associate income in the form of money with any given one of the positions forming the occupational situs. We can only apply the concept of income to the over-all occupational situs. How, then, can we deal with the variable of wealth with respect to the kinship situs, or the educational situs, or other situses that go into composition of a person's station in society?

A system of rewards does exist within our society that induces individuals to occupy positions in various groups, and to perform the roles they perform in such groups. Each position, let us say, yields a certain level of rewards, or income, to the actor who occupies the position and performs the role. This income may take varying forms. In some cases it consists of psychological gratifications received by the individual when he interacts with others. In other cases, it consists of tangible rewards—money or property. If we intend to apply the concept to both system and person-centered analysis, we will therefore have to define wealth very broadly as the rewards received by an individual, both tangible and intangible, by virtue of occupying all the positions that he occupies within society.

The concept of *property*, which is important for social rank, must also be defined broadly. On the one hand, property consists of the ownership of tangible objects—land, buildings, tools, machinery, livestock, clothing, jewelry—and other items of tangible property valued by members of society. On the other, it consists of the ownership of ritual privileges, and even of ideas.

How can we employ the concept of property in conjunction with the positional approach? The western concept of ownership of property largely rests on the idea that the individual as a significant social unit owns the property. In terms of person-centered analysis, therefore, property ownership is a quality lodged in the structure of the individual's station, rather than in the particular positions that comprise it. It is possible, however, to consider ownership also to be the control over property—that is, what we may call social, rather than legal ownership.

Social ownership of property, then, is the individual's right to use it in the performance of his various roles. The secretary working in an office owned by the Ajax Black Box Factory exercises social ownership over her desk, her typewriter, and the other office equipment she uses. Social ownership of property is associated with each position that a person occupies, and perhaps even with the various roles that comprise that position. In virtually every group, each individual uses material objects in the performance of his roles, and therefore exercises at least temporary social ownership over property. This point of view allows us to deal with property in the same way that we deal with prestige.

In dealing with the wealth dimension of social rank, sociologists often employ three concepts: level of living, standard of living, and style of life. Essentially, all three refer to a total individual, or perhaps the family. Level of living, which was first measured by Chapin (8), and later by Sewell (9) and Belcher (10), usually refers to the economic circumstances of a family in terms of its physical surroundings and the property that it owns and controls as a family. Standard of living refers to the ideals of property ownership and physical surroundings, either of the individual or the family. Level of living, then, describes the actual circumstances of life as measured by the physical objects in the home, while standard of living refers to the desires or the aspirations of the individual with respect to level of living. Style of life is a broader term than either of the other two; it includes not only the physical surroundings of the individual at home, but also the kinds of activities he participates in in society. It covers such things as his recreational activities, his work activities, and his participation in civic and religious groups. Style of life thus encompasses level of living, plus an additional component, social participation. All three terms, however, refer to the individual or to his family, and not to the constituent positions he occupies in the various groups that he belongs to in society.

A measure comparable to level of living at home might be employed to measure level of living at work or at school, so that characteristics of the work situation that society evaluates positively and negatively are employed to construct a scale. For example, an estimate of level of living at work for bureaucratic occupations in a government agency might be based on such items as the size of a person's desk, the presence or absence of a rug on the floor, the size of the office, and the type of office equipment used on the job. The fact is, that with respect to each position a person occupies in each group he participates in, he exists in a situation whose elements can be used to construct a level of living scale for his participation in that particular group. A person's total level of living associated with his station in society is, like power and honor, measurable only if we add up the individual levels from each of the groups he participates in. Such a score must be weighted in terms of the amount of time spent in each type of situation, so that each group receives its proper weight in the total score.

The trouble with using the individual or the family as the point of reference for wealth and income, as most sociologists tend to do, is that the individual's participation in society consists of far more than his involvement in family relations. As a matter of fact, in modern urban industrial society far more time is spent by the individual in performing roles in other groups than in performing family roles. As a consequence, if we tie the concepts of wealth and property and income to the individual and his family, we overlook the fact that these variables are actually located in the social structure.

There are two questions concerning the distribution of social rank which are confused in the sociological literature on social stratification. The first question is, "How is social rank distributed within the groups and organizations comprising the social system?" The second question amounts to asking, "How is social rank distributed among individuals and categories of individuals?" The first question can only be answered in terms of system analysis, and the second, only in terms of person-centered analysis. The answers to the two questions will be quite different.

When analyzing the distribution of social rank within the social system, we are concerned with the location of power, honor, and wealth in the structure of groups and organizations, communities and societies. We wish to know how much power each position in the group structure contains. In asking, "How is social rank distributed among individuals and social categories?" we are not concerned with the location of social rank within specific groups, organizations, and community structures, but with how much power, honor, and wealth various categories of individuals have: the social rank of females as opposed to males, or blacks as opposed to whites, or blue-collar workers as opposed to white-collar workers. Questions about the distribution of power, honor, and wealth among social categories are essentially person-centered questions rather than system-centered questions; and social strata, whether they be classes, castes, or estates, amount to categories of individuals, not of structural elements of social systems.

In social systems, power, honor, and wealth are distributed among the various groups that form the component parts of complex structures within society. Each group has its own power structure, its own honor structure, and its own wealth structure, in which positions corresponding to the participation of actors in the group enjoy different amounts of power, honor, and wealth. The same individual who ranks relatively high in power in one group may rank lower in the power structure of another group. Every member of every group in society is thus a part of the total power structure of society and the total prestige structure, as well as the total wealth structure; but he does not occupy one homogeneous and specific point. Instead, his participation is distributed throughout the structures, depending on the number of groups and organizations to which he belongs.

The supervisor of the Ajax Factory Box Shop occupies a position of relatively high power within the context of that shop with respect to the activities of other individuals within it. When he participates in the interstitial group which includes the other supervisors as well as the company president, he occupies a subordinate position, and one of relatively low power. In this group, the president of the company occupies a position of relatively high power.

Power is distributed throughout the organization in a hierarchial arrangement, so that individuals occupy several points within the structure of the system, depending upon the group in which they are participating. In other words, power as a social-rank variable is distributed throughout the social system, and lies within the structure of groups. It is reasonable to assume that a person such as the president of the factory, who stands high in the power hierarchy, has power over the supervisors of other groups in the organization. So, the distribution of power within the structure of society includes not only direct power exercised in interaction, but also indirect power exercised through indirect interactions involving interstitial group relations.

Power, therefore, is distributed throughout social systems, and is located within particular positions contained in exact locations in that structure, just as honor and wealth are. This means that each position comprising a station will contain part, but not all, of the power, honor, or wealth pertaining to a given actor. The structural distance between two positions contained in a station structure is identical with the structural distance between the same positions in the social system; in other words, the distribution of positions in a station in social space will be determined by the distribution of the same position within the social system. But these positions cannot be distributed in such a way that all positions in a given station fall within the boundaries of an arbitrarily established stratum within the structure of a social system. The system is simply not put together that way. There are no strata in the structure of society. If there were, we would have to locate parts of groups and organizations within a given stratum, and other parts in other strata, which would be contrary to the nature of positions and roles. We cannot, therefore, classify an entire individual as part of one or another class or caste within the structure of the system, because to do so denies the organic structure of organizations and groups, and limits the entire station of the individual to simply a matter of social rank.

Stratiflcation as a System of Allocation

Stratification is a method of allocating individuals to positions in the social system; it is not a characteristic of the structure of society. A social class, caste, or estate system constitutes one way in which individuals come to participate in the various groups in society that they belong to. In a sense, a class, caste, or estate system is a system by which the station structure of an individual is built; and social classes, castes, or estates amount to categories of individuals who, through the process of stratification, have been allocated to positions that form similar station structures.

There are two ways of allocating people to positions within the social structure. One is through ascription; the other through achievement. Ascription relies on the automatic assignment of an individual to positions within the structure of society on the basis of real or imagined personal characteristics which are beyond the power of the individual to change. Achievement, on the other hand, refers to the allocation of the individuals to positions in the structure of society on the basis of their performance as actors, or on the basis of their achievement of personality characteristics that are not fixed at birth, but depend upon the individual's life experience.

Ascription of positions within the social structure is most frequently based on such biologically derived characteristics as sex, age, race, or ethnic background. Achievement is usually based on learning, education, individual abilities, or other characteristics that relate to the performance of the individual in society. Most societies utilize both principles for allocating individuals to positions in the social structure, although some rely more on one than the other.

A society that relies heavily on ascription limits admission to groups on the basis of ascribed characteristics, by requiring that an individual with certain personal characteristics occupy a given position, and excluding other individuals lacking these characteristics. An extreme example is royalty and the positions occupied by a king. Only an individual who comes from a certain family, and is born in a certain birth order is permitted to occupy the royal positions. Another example of positional ascription related to occupation used to occur in the medical profession. At one time, only a male Caucasian could enter medical school in the United States. Since medical school is a prerequisite for occupying the various positions associated with being a doctor, this effectively ascribed such positions to one category of people and excluded other categories from occupying them.

There are two forms of ascription, structural and functional. Structural ascription exists when a given position contains within its role requirements the specification of the personal biological characteristics of the individual who is to perform the role. Thus, if a position specifies that the occupant be a male adult Caucasian between the ages of 30 and 60, it is a structural ascription. The allocating mechanism is built into the structure of the position, and therefore is a part of the structure of the social system. Functional ascription exists when certain achieved characteristics are required for occupying a position or set of positions, but access to the necessary resources to achieve the characteristics are limited and unequally distributed. For example, a four-year college education is required to become a practicing engineer. There are individuals who lack the necessary financial resources to get through four years of education. This is a functional ascription within the system; an entire category of individuals is excluded from the possibility of achieving the necessary prerequisites to enter a given profession. Thus, the unequal distribution of wealth, power, and honor among categories of human beings becomes a self-perpetuating, functional ascription system within society.

The caste system, such as used to exist in India, depends heavily on structural ascription. A person must be a member of a given kin group in order to occupy certain positions. Being a member of the kin group classifies him as a member of a category of individuals called a caste. Being a member of the caste determines what positions he has access to in the structure of society. The class system of the United States relies heavily on functional ascription to allocate people to positions in society. Existing inequalities in social rank are perpetuated through a complex system of requirements for entering various occupations. Since the occupations require different degrees of education, and education depends greatly on preschool training as well as on family income, individuals tend to be ascribed to station structures similar to those of their parents. Thus, functional ascription amounts to a system whose values favor achievement, but which lacks the structural means to allow achievement to function as the allocating principle.

The distribution of power, honor, and wealth within the structure of a social system is one thing; the assignment of individuals to positions within that structure is quite a different matter. Because of the way groups and organizations form complex systems, it is probably inevitable that inequalities in power will exist. It may be true that inequalities in income and honor do supply needed motivation for performance; but given a certain distribution of power, honor, and wealth within the structure of a system, it cannot be argued logically that a given system for allocating people to these positions of differential rank is structurally required.

There are inherent advantages for the survival of society in both ascription and achievement systems of stratification. Ascription allows the socialization process to be highly specialized, and focused upon the specific requirements for role performance of a given group of people. If it is known that a given individual will eventually become king, his training for kingship can begin at birth, and be highly specific, focused, and intensive, insuring that when he eventually does come to the throne, he will know the roles he will perform. The disadvantages of ascription are that individuals with low abilities, aptitudes, or interests in occupying given positions may be trained for them. If the eldest son of the king is a moron, no amount of training will help.

The advantage of achievement systems is that individuals with high levels of motivation and ability with respect to the positions that they occupy are probably more likely to occupy them than with ascription. However, training or socialization becomes much more difficult. It is impossible to predict at birth, or for many years thereafter, what roles individuals will perform within the structure of society when they reach adulthood. As a consequence, training must be general, and there is some risk that highly motivated but ill-trained people will occupy critical positions in the social system.

Sociologists have not had an adequate conceptual scheme to deal with the microstructure of society in terms of social groups and complex organizations, and so have not been able to specify accurately the nature of the person's relationship to the social system. In this book, we have said that the individual as a participant in society is comprised of those positions that he occupies in the various groups he belongs to, which is the opposite of the usual point of view. Instead of seeing society as consisting of units called individuals, we consider individuals to consist of parts of society called positions and roles. These positions exist independent of given individuals, and are distributed throughout the social system according to the structure of that system. Hence, the organization of the person-centered system, called the station, is a function of the structure of the social system, rather than the other way around; and our concept of the person is constructed out of our concept of society, instead of the other way around. But a conception of society constructed out of an already-defined conception of the person as a system leads to confusion in trying to formulate any adequate notion of the vertical dimension of society.

If we start by assuming that individuals constitute a unitary system, and that they in turn constitute the units out of which the social system is comprised, then it is reasonable to say that the structure of society contains strata comprised of individuals of similar social rank. If whole persons make up the structure of society, and it can be demonstrated that people vary in power, honor and wealth, then we have to conclude that the vertical dimension of society consists of categories of persons called classes, castes and estates. But this conception ignores the existence of specific groups and organizations that are intricately linked together to form organically-functioning social systems smaller than a total society. In other words, we can only entertain the traditional notion of stratification if we are satisfied with a notion of society that includes no specific conception of its internal structure in terms of subsystems and sub-subsystems.

In our view, society is not an amorphous mass of ill-defined relationships, but a highly organized system of specific relationships. It is not possible to conceive of strata as part of the structure of that system. Instead, we are obliged to think of strata as categories of persons, and to regard stratification as a system for building individual station structures that fit these categories.

Dimensions of Station Structure

The structure of stations may be examined in terms of two dimensions: composition and rank. Composition refers to the contents of the station in terms of the positions and roles that make it up. Each station consists of a number of specific positions that contain repertoires of roles. These positions are, in turn, organized into situses. The composition of a station describes the number and type of positions and roles that comprise the various situses in its structure. The composition of stations varies in: (1) the number of positions comprising the various situses; (2) the number and complexity of the roles that make up the various positions; (3) the type or content of roles that comprise the structure; and (4) the structural linkage and distance between the various positions comprising the various situses.

The composition of the stations of the members of a given society varies. Some people occupy more positions, with more complex roles separated by greater amounts of structural distance, than others occupy. The contents of their various roles also differ. Male stations, for instance, contain a different complement of positions and roles in most societies than do female stations. Similarly, the stations of children differ from those of older people, and the stations of doctors differ in composition from the stations of mail carriers or carpenters. Some stations are comprised of a few positions containing a small complement of relatively simple roles, while others will be comprised of a very large number of positions containing many complex roles.

In most known societies, individual stations vary in the amount of social rank associated with them. The amount of power, honor, and wealth associated with each position can be evaluated, and a measure of the total amount of social rank ascertained by the accumulation of individual positional increments.

Station Distribution

If we could examine every station stemming from the structure of society in terms of rank and composition, we could create a series of frequency distributions showing how rank and composition vary along one or more of their subdimensions. One distribution might show station composition as measured by the number of positions comprising the various stations; another might represent composition in terms of some measure of role complexity, and still others for other dimensions of composition. Similar families of distributions may be created for subdimensions of social rank such as power, honor, and wealth.

In our opinion, these distributions would approximate a Poisson distribution, so that for a characteristic such as the number of positions included in the station structure for all members of a society like ours, the distribution would look somewhat like this:

Figure 19–1   Distribution of Stations
with Varying Degrees of Complexity

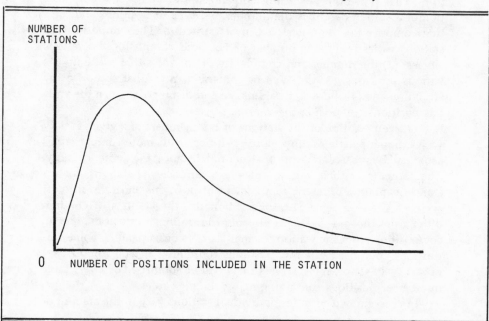

NUMBER OF
STATIONS

0   NUMBER OF POSITIONS INCLUDED IN THE STATION

At the upper end of the distribution are those individuals whose occupations and community involvements, generated by their occupation, produce a very large number of group memberships. We believe that these individuals would also tend to fall high in the distribution of social rank. Corporation executives, high-ranking government officials, and professionals like doctors and lawyers would probably fall at this end of the distribution.

At the lower end of the distribution are those individuals who lead a solitary life with few social contacts. An extreme case is a hermit who has virtually no social contacts. The majority of the members of society fall in the middle of the distribution. Because most people are involved in kinship relations and in certain other community relations, regardless of occupation, it will probably prove true that the occupational situs will make the greatest difference in composition of stations in society, discounting the effect of age and sex.

If many different societies were compared with respect to these distributions, it is likely that they would vary significantly in the characteristics of their distributions of both rank and composition. Some societies will have a low mean number of positions included in the stations of their members, and a low variance around that mean, while others will have the opposite characteristics.

We can conceive of two theoretical extremes for variation in station composition. At one extreme is the theoretical possibility that every station in society will have exactly the same composition, and therefore there will be no variance in any characteristic of composition. For example, each station will contain the same number of positions, and each position the same roles. At the other theoretical extreme, every station will be different in composition from every other one. They will contain different numbers of positions, which contain different combinations of roles of different levels of complexity, and so on.

These two extremes represent the two ends of a theoretical continuum. In between are distributions that vary in the amount of variance in station structure. This continuum measures the amount of replication in station structure. Complete replication occurs when every station is like every other one, and there is no variance in the distributions of either rank or composition. Replication, therefore, refers to the relative number of times a given station structure is repeated in a given distribution, and the standard deviation of such distributions would be a measure of replication. A zero standard deviation would be equivalent to complete replication of the characteristic being considered. A very large standard deviation approaching the size of the largest number in the distribution would be complete nonreplication. We visualize a family of distributions such as in Figure 19–2.

The following four-celled table shows station replication for station rank and composition treated as separate variables for adult males only.

The rank and composition of the stations of adult males are shown classified by the degree of replication in these characteristics. Cell 1 represents societies in which there is very little variability in either station composition or rank; that is, societies with a very low level of social differentiation. In such systems virtually all adult males perform the same roles, and have similar social rank. Examples are the societies of Eskimos, and those of some other preliterate people such as the Australian Aborigines. In such societies the structure of the social system is so simple that station structures which are extracted from it are simple, and tend to be identical in content.

In Cell 2 are those societies in which the roles assigned to adult males are virtually identical, but in which a system of social rank based on excellence of performance exists. In these societies, adult males all have the same repertoires of roles and the same sets of positions; but they have different amounts of power, honor, and wealth based on how well they perform these roles. The Indians of the American Plains had a system like this. Virtually all Sioux Indian males were hunters and warriors, and their involvements in kinship and other affairs of the

Figure 19–2   Distribution of Station Complexity
for Various Societies

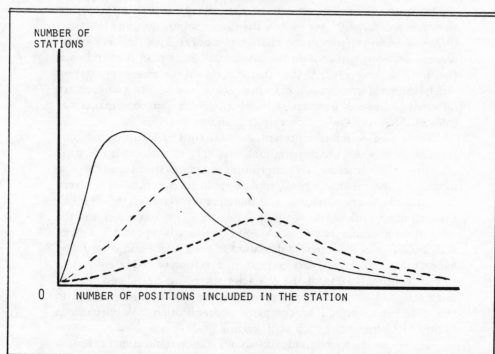

NUMBER OF
STATIONS

0   NUMBER OF POSITIONS INCLUDED IN THE STATION

society were virtually identical. They varied in social standing or rank, however, on the basis of how well they performed the various roles of hunter and warrior, and they had a complex system for keeping track of standing in a kind of ritual competition for prestige.

Such societies are only slightly more differentiated than those of Cell 1. The difference is due not so much to technology, as to the size of the human community that the technology will support in the environment in which the society exists. It is possible that warfare and external aggression are the elements that add the complexity of the social system. Societies that fall in Cell 1 usually are at the edge of subsistence, are small, and have no organized system of military activities.

In Cell 3 are those societies, real or ideal, that attempt to hold social rank constant while allowing the composition of stations to vary. This is, of course, the objective of ideal communism. Such societies allow considerable variation in the composition of stations, for example, in the variety of occupations and professions. These differences in roles, and in the complexity, size, and other compositional attributes, however, cannot be associated with differences in social rank. Differences in power, honor, and wealth are held to a minimum, and in theory, if not in absolute fact, all stations are equal in rank.

Theoretically, when it comes to stations in a relatively complex differentiated social system, it would be easier to maintain equality in honor and wealth, than in power. A highly differentiated system, and

TABLE 19-1

Replication of Composition	Replication of Rank	
	High	Low
High	1)Societies with simple social structures having little variation in composition and rank *Example:* Eskimo	2)Societies where adult males all have basically same types of group memberships and perform same roles, but rank varies according to role performance. *Examples:* American Plains Indians
Low	3)Societies in which considerable variation exists in composition, but in which station rank is held to a minimum. *Examples:* Marxian model, kibbutz	4)Societies in which both rank and composition vary considerably. *Examples:* Modern industrial societies—USA, Japan, USSR, and societies which tie rank to composition, as in Indian caste system and medieval estates

thus a wide variation in the composition of stations, presumes complex organizational structures. Complex organizational structures presume differentiation in the power structure. As a consequence, stations inevitably differ in power. If power is the key to amassing wealth and prestige, complex societies that want to hold rank constant will have a difficult, if not impossible, task; and the ideal will remain more a fiction about the structure of the system than a reality. Both Americans and Russians hold that all citizens are equal—but as George Orwell has suggested, some are more equal than others (11).

Cell 4 displays societies with high degrees of differentiation in both composition and rank. These are the societies that tie social rank to the composition of the station, and in which rank depends upon what roles a person performs.

The Davis-Moore hypothesis that social rank is associated with the functional importance of the occupation performed by an adult male fits these societies nicely (12), as do other theories that say that the social value placed on a role accounts for its rank. The point is that social rank is tied to, or made dependent upon, composition in such a way that for every variation in composition there is a variation in social rank. It is logically possible for there to be complete independence of rank and composition; however, all known societies where both rank and composition vary widely involve covariation of these attributes.

What is extremely interesting is the fact that all three of the classical sociological stratification systems fall into this category. Class, caste, and estate systems all tie social rank to station composition. In each of the three, occupational category is the key to differences in social rank. Furthermore, in each system the kinds of positions that people occupy in other areas of social life are tied to occupations, and both are tied to social rank. We tend to oversimplify such systems, especially caste and estate, but each involves minute graduations in rank, as station composition varies. In other words, all Brahmins are equal, but some are more equal than others. This was also true for the nobility or clergy of the estate system, and it is true today for the middle class of the class system.

These considerations suggest that the structures of the societies that have caste, class, and estate systems are alike, in that they have highly differentiated occupational, governmental, and religious structures, in which social rank and station composition are tied to each other. With respect to station replication, the three systems are quite similar.

The Transmission of Station Structure

How is station structure transmitted from one generation to the next? Let us compare the station structures of fathers with sons at comparable points in their lives—that is, the father's station structure in childhood with the son's station structure in childhood, and the father's station in young adulthood or old age with the son's station structure at these same stages. We can compare the rank of each station at comparable periods, as well as the composition.

Measures of difference in rank and composition can be related to such subvariables as power, honor, and wealth; or complexity, size, structural distance, and role content. Comparisons of this sort may be called "cross-generational duplication" of station structure. If a son's station is quite like the father's at similar points of their lives, station duplication has occurred. When they deviate drastically from one another, there is no duplication. The amount of duplication will thus depend on how similar or different stations are with respect to measures of rank and composition. As in the case of replication, theoretically rank may be duplicated without duplication in composition, and vice versa. We can thus generate a four-celled table of duplication in station structure similar to the one for replication.

The most interesting cells in Table 2 are 1 and 4. These represent the extremes in duplication, one representing high duplication in both

TABLE 19-2

Duplication of Composition	Duplication of Rank	
	High	Low
High	1) Societies in which the son's station structure is like the father's in both rank and composition at various points along life progression. *Examples* Highly undifferentiated societies, such as Eskimo; caste systems; ascription oriented societies	2) Societies with little or no variation in composition, but in which rank varies according to role performance to a considerable degree. *Examples:* Plains Indians of U.S.; any relatively simple but achievement-oriented society; possibly early Norse tribes and Saxons
Low	3) Societies in which there is little or no variation in rank permitted, but where greater variations in composition or the roles performed by people exist. *Examples:* Communes; Communistic utopias; democratic utopias; experimental communities—kibbutzim	4) Societies which do not in any way ascribe station structure on the basis of kinship or family origin. Both rank and composition vary from father to son. *Examples* USSR today—ideal; USA and Western Europe—ideal; achievement-oriented societies

rank and composition, and the other representing low duplication on both attributes. They also represent the two principles of station transmission discussed earlier, ascription and achievement.

The high duplication cell, 1, represents societies in which the son's station structure is ascribed, and therefore duplicates the father's. In extreme cases, this would be true at all points of possible comparisons along the life progression. Caste systems fit in this cell, and very complex societies may be in this class. As a matter of fact, nothing logically prevents highly industrialized and urbanized societies such as ours from fitting into this cell.

For this cell, the principle by which people are allocated to group membership in society, and thereby achieve station rank and composition, is ascription. Sons assume the positions and roles of their fathers. The roles a child will be expected to perform as an adult and as an aged person are known at birth, so that socialization is systematically and intensively directed toward preparing him to occupy his various positions and perform his various roles. A parental training system or an apprenticeship system bound to kinship usually handles most of the training for adult roles.

The achievement cell in the lower right hand corner has opposite weaknesses and strengths in terms of allocation. Here, chances of matching ability and motivation with station composition are maximal; but there is a risk of having badly prepared or inadequately socialized persons occupy positions. In this kind of society, socialization and education are carried on outside the family in institutions; every newborn infant is given equal treatment, and the difference in what is learned becomes a function of performance based on motivation and capacity. Any efforts to classify children or adults on the basis of what type of future training they should have, or any effort to start specialized training, would move the system closer to the ascription model and away from the achievement model. Only absolute equality of opportunity, coupled with a laissez-faire policy with respect to what and how much is learned, or which positions people occupy, would prevent the growth of a functional ascription of future station structure. Indeed, societies of the complex urban and industrial sort are inevitably pressed toward a mixture of ascription and achievement, by a clash between the necessity that the system prepare people to occupy complex positions, and the need for a reasonable match between motivation, ability, and the positions people occupy.

The United States, the Soviet Union, and most societies of Europe fall somewhere in the achievement cell, but are by no means near the ideal extreme. In all of these societies, family origin determines to a large degree the structure of a person's station, and there is a general similarity in rank and composition between the stations of fathers and sons. Therefore, both ascription and achievement are operating. That is why *social class* is an appropriate designation for the broad categories of station structures found in these societies. These categories are reasonable ways of describing such systems only insofar as duplication in station structure occurs across generations. If it does not, then classes of stations of similar structures, by using discrete categories of variables of rank and composition that vary continuously and independently, merely take note of the class origin of the class members.

Stratification systems allocate people through the processes of socialization and station building to the structure of society, but they do not describe the structure of the society itself. A society with a structure that has a high degree of differentiation in the ranks and composition of stations may at the same time lack people who have inherited their station structure. Societies with highly differentiated systems of power, honor, and wealth distributed to positions in groups in their structure may lack replication of station structure, and so are not describable in terms of concepts like class, caste, or estate.

To sum up: castes, classes, and estates are not units, or parts, or even strata in the structure of social systems. Instead, they are categories used in systems involving varying degrees of ascription as a principle for allocating people to that structure. They are, therefore, categories of people and person-centered in nature; they are not features of social structure. Not now and never have there been social strata in the structure of any society. Castes, classes, and estates are ways of categorizing people for the ascription of station structure. The difference among types of stratification systems lies primarily in the degree to which structural or functional ascription operates to determine station structure of members of society, by allocating them to participation in varying sets of groups and organizations.

CHAPTER 20

The question of how social systems change and adapt
is among the most difficult that social scientists face.
The reality of change is indisputable; in fact, it is so apparent that it is
puzzling how we can fail to understand the processes that produce it.
At a certain level of generality, we do have a crude understanding—as,
for instance, in the classical statement by anthropologists that societies
change either because inventions or innovations occur within the society, or because they borrow patterns from other societies that surround
them. Inventions and borrowed items of culture are diffused throughout
the system, being adapted and altered to fit already existing patterns (1).
As these new items become a part of the culture of a society, they set
off a sociocultural chain reaction which produces changes in other parts
of the system.

This explanation has face validity and is hardly disputable, but of
what real value is it? What we really need to understand is the process
whereby inventions occur and diffusions take place. The really significant questions are: How can we predict when and where an invention
will occur? What factors or variables operate to produce an invention?
Why do some inventions spread and supplant older patterns, while
others disappear? Of all the possible parts of other cultures that could
be borrowed and diffused, why are certain ones selected and others not?
If there are chain reactions of change, what are the mechanisms that
operate to transmit the influence of a change in one part of a system to
an entirely different part of the system?

To answer some of these questions, we need a conceptual model
that can be used to describe and analyze change. The model to be
presented here is based on the models of the social system and of the
person as a participant in the system that have been presented in previous chapters.

Some Propositions Concerning Change

Societies, according to our model, consist of communities of various orders, organizations, and groups. Each of these parts of society is articulated with others at particular definite points in time and space. As a system, society with its various parts consists of behavior, active and latent, and is more like a series of events occurring in time and space than like an edifice that persists through time and occupies space. It is a pulsating, living system of action and behavior, and is constantly emerging as it proceeds through time.

From this perspective, it is more sensible to ask why behavior remains unchanged, rather than to ask why it changes. At each moment the actions that constitute a society are different from those that occurred during the last moment. Yet over the days and years, the events of comparable time periods bear remarkable resemblances to one another. If societies consist of behavior, and behavior is recurrent but never constant, what mechanisms join past, present, and future to permit the system of behavior to persist as a recurrent and recognizable entity? The remarkable thing is not so much that societies change, but that they persist with so little change.

Social scientists consider that culture and socialization serve to transmit behavior patterns, and account for the recurrence of the same type of behavior at different times within the same society. Culture explains why every Monday morning millions of people get up, and through highly repetitive behavior patterns prepare themselves to face another week of highly repetitive work behavior. Culture—that is, norms organized into roles that are then organized into positions, groups, and multigroup structures—exists through time, and links past, present, and future. Culture is latent behavior: it consists of a very large set of learned and stored behavior patterns that exists in the personalities of society's members even when they are performing only a small portion of the total cultural repertoire at any given time.

In addition to culture, there are at least three other factors that influence learned and stored behavior: personality, situation, and social interaction. Culture accounts for the persistence and recurrence of behavior; these other three are the sources of variability and change. For change in behavior can only be produced by the variables that produce behavior itself.

Before we can examine how culture, personality, situation, and interaction combine not only to maintain, but also to change social systems, we need to discuss some general assumptions.

The first one is that whole societies do not change in all of their parts at one time. Instead, change begins at one particular point or set of points within the system. If the whole system changed simultaneously, and every part were altered in form and relationship to all others, there would be no way to recognize the changed society as the same object as the unchanged society; and instead of thinking in terms of change, we would have to think of two different societies. *Change* implies that an object or entity persists through time and can be recognized as the same object at successive time periods—otherwise we could not recognize that it is different now from the way it was before. At least one element in the system must remain stable for us to be able to identify and recognize the system as changing.

Societies do not change all at once, even in the case of revolutions. They are not like butterflies whose adult form is totally unlike the pupa. Societies change one part at a time, while the other parts remain at least temporarily unchanged. Many changes may occur rapidly or simultaneously; but there is no over-all master change that produces a set of co-ordinated and interdependent changes. Each change has a definite point of origin in the structure of the system. Simultaneously, different changes can begin at different points independently of each other. Ultimately, of course, such independent changes, since they affect the same system, will affect each other; and in this sense, their effects on the system are interdependent.

We approach change by trying to identify the location or locations in the structure of the system where it is introduced. This location is a role or part of a role, located in a position that is part of a given group structure that is located at a certain point in a multigroup system. We need a definite location; otherwise, we will not be able to identify the part undergoing change, or describe the process of change itself. Nor will we be able to assess the operation of the variables which act to produce change.

When we say that change starts at a particular location, we mean exactly that. If we talk about change in a particular role contained within the housewife's position, for example, the role of laundress, we mean a particular family and a particular housewife, not families in general or housewives in general. Each family exists at a different location in social space, and this particular location or set of locations is where change begins. A number of similar locations, structurally linked to some common point in the system of which they are a part, may be influenced simultaneously by the same change-inducing variables. Many housewife laundress roles are simultaneously affected by influences emanating from the larger social system—for example, the invention and commercial production of washing machines. But influences which simultaneously affect many housewives have definite starting points in the social system from which their influence radiates.

Secondly, although changes must have some starting point, they are spread or transmitted from this point of origin to other parts of the system. This presumes a definite path or set of linkages over which the change travels, which are formed by the patterns of role relationships. In other words, change can spread only over bilateral and reflexive reciprocal and conjunctive relationships from one position to another, and from one group and organization to another. Where there is no linkage between units, spread or diffusion of change is impossible.

There are two kinds of diffusions involved here. The first is the spread of a change to similar units of structure—for example, from one housewife's laundress role in one family to another housewife's role of laundress in another family. The second kind is the spread of a change to dissimilar units—for example, from the housewife's role as laundress to the soap sales manager's role as advertiser, or from the housewife's role as laundress to her role as cook or sex partner.

In other words, there are two kinds of chain reactions that can occur when change is introduced into a system at a given point. The change can spread to other points in the system where similar substructures exist; or, because systems are systems and their parts interdependent, the change can set off adaptive changes in other parts of the same system which are unlike the one originally affected, but in some respect dependent upon it. For either type to occur, a definite path must exist over which the change influence can travel and have its effect.

Thirdly, change must be regarded as a constant and continual process. It does not start and stop, with periods of change alternating with periods of nonchange. Because society is comprised of behavior, and behavior is constantly being altered to fit the situation in which it is occurring, the personalities of people performing it, and the exact interaction which is taking place, society must of necessity always be in a state of flux. The real questions about social change, therefore, can only be questions about the degree, rate, direction, and permanence of the changes occurring in the system. Every deviant or innovative act, every mistake or error in the performance of a role, must be regarded as at least a temporary and perhaps at first insignificant change in the social system. What we want to know is whether these innovations will persist and spread, rather than whether they are changes or not.

Societies are open, morphogenic systems whose parts are also open morphogenic systems. The most important characteristic of such systems is that they tend to alter or adapt their behavior in response to information fed back into them with respect to the effects of their behavior or their environment, feedback that is measured by the intent or orientation of that behavior as defined by the system. An open

morphogenic system and change are one and the same. Change is therefore a constant phenomenon, the process by which the open morphogenic system survives as a system.

The argument between the functionalists and the conflict theorists
over the equilibrium or integration issue, therefore, is spurious. Change
is not the antithesis of equilibrium, but instead the very process of
equilibration; it is the means through which social systems adapt and
survive, and also the process through which they break down and
disintegrate. Whether a society moves in the direction of survival or
away from it is not a matter of change; it is a question of the adaptive
or maladaptive characteristics of the changes that occur. Survival of
social systems is impossible without change, but change does not insure
survival. Equilibrium, if indeed such a thing ever exists, must be defined
not in terms of the stability of a system's internal structure, but in terms
of the system's relationship to its environment. And indeed, the social
system and its environment themselves form an ecosystem, in which the
parts interact and mutually affect one another. For a social system to
survive, it must maintain balance or equilibrium with respect to its
environment. Since its behavior affects the environment, and these
effects are fed back into the social system, it follows that the social
system must continually change and adapt in order to maintain a relatively constant survival relationship to its environment. For it is only by
achieving a form of equilibrium with the environment that longterm
survival can be assured.

One popular theoretical approach to change has been to assume a
system in which all of the various parts are in perfect adjustment, so that
unless some influence enters from the environment the system remains
unchanged. This assumption of perfect internal adjustment eliminates
internal sources of change, a condition that does not exist in social
systems. Of the four factors—culture, personality, situation, and interaction—that influence behavior, none is ever stable enough for persistent internal adjustment. Take culture, for instance. It consists of
norms learned or invented by individuals in ways that are imprecise and
unstable, and subject to considerable variation. This means that considerable variability in behavior will always be characteristic of social
systems, and any perfect adjustment among all the parts of a social
system could exist for only an instant. External influences from the
environment are therefore not required to produce change. It is a constant state; for although some parts of society may remain more or less
stable, others are always in the process of changing.

Forms of Social Change

What are the manifestations of change in social systems? If change is always with us, how shall we recognize it as being different from nonchange?

Change can take three interdependent forms, occurring along different dimensions of the structure of social systems. They are: growth or decline; elaboration or simplification; differentiation or consolidation.

Growth or Decline

The simplest and most easily understood manifestation of change is a growth or decline in the size of the social system. Societies or their constituent parts or subsystems become larger or smaller.

Growth or decline in a society means an increase or decrease in the amount of behavior included within the system. Societies increase in size only by adding new members, either through an excess of births over deaths, or through greater immigration than emigration—that is, by increasing their populations. But since societies consist of behavior, not of people, from our point of view what happens is that the birth of a new member of society adds behavior to the system, and the death of a member subtracts behavior from it.

An act is the smallest particle of behavior performed by actors. At any given instant, there will be one act occurring for every person who is a member of the society. Increasing the population of actors by one person means that the number of acts occurring at any given time has also increased by one. The number of acts can also, of course, be decreased. Essentially, then, the size of a society is measured by the number of acts in the process of occurring at any given moment, which is a function of the number of people participating in the system.

The variety of actions that constitute society may also grow or diminish. Change in variety does not necessarily affect the size of the system; what it does affect is its differentiation or its level of elaboration. New members can be added to society without changing the way the society is organized. If they occupy positions and play roles like those already occupied by others, there is merely more behavior of the same type. For example, the number of families in a given society may increase, but these additional families fit into society in the same way as those that already exist, and perform behavior like theirs.

Growth or Decline in Parts of Society

Parts of societies can increase in size without an accompanying increase in the size of the whole society, if some other part of society simultaneously decreases in size. For example, work groups may expand by creating new positions and increasing the number of workers performing behavior within the group. The Ajax Box Factory, for instance, may add several new painters to the paint shop. This growth occurs without other manifestations of change, if these new workers play roles identical to those already included in other positions in the group. On the other hand, if entirely new positions with new roles are added to the group, along with new actors to play them, then growth occurs together with an increase in the division of labor.

A second way that the size of a work group may increase is for the span of time during which group roles are active to increase. We could increase the size of the group by increasing the work day from eight to ten hours, so that a greater amount of behavior would occur and the group would take up a greater portion of the society's total behavior supply. If a work group expands by increasing its span of activity, its members will have to participate in other groups for shorter periods. Other groups would decline in size or scale as the work group increased.

The size of a social unit is thus measured by the number of acts performed by the actors that make it up. Size is measured in both time and space. There are two ways to expand a part of a society. The number of positions (members) can be increased; the amount of time these positions are active as opposed to latent can be increased. Decreases in size occur for opposite reasons.

Society, however, can only be increased by adding stations to its structure. The station of a person represents his total behavior, and is entirely included within the structure of a single society. Shifting the amount of behavior contained in one position within the same station does not increase the size of the society. It merely affects the allocation of behavior within it, and implies a change in the division of labor.

We have to measure group size in terms of the volume of behavior that takes place in the group, rather than by the number of members, because each person in society belongs to many groups. To give equal weight to group membership by saying that any group containing five members is the same size as any other group with five members is wrong, because it ignores the fact that a person may perform more behavior in one group than another. The size of a group should be measured by the amount of social space it occupies, rather than by the number of biological bodies who perform behavior in that space.

Aside from this, defining group size by the volume of behavior which takes place within it allows us to deal with the expansion and contraction of groups in social space more precisely and effectively. For example, a family may remain relatively constant in the number of its members; but if the amount of behavior that occurs within it declines, the total amount of social space it occupies in society also shrinks.

The Origin and Spread of the Growth Process

We said above that each change must have a point of origin, and that for change to spread there must be a structural path over which the change can travel. Let us see how these statements apply to the phenomenon of growth in the social system. It will be easiest to illustrate with respect to the birth of new members of society. Let us assume that the birth is not compensated for by a death, and so represents an increase in society's members.

The total amount of behavior that must be integrated into the social system increases with the birth of a child—that is, twenty-four hours worth of action each day must be fitted into the social system at particular real locations in social space. Our particular newborn infant occupies positions and plays roles in the kinship network where the growth is first registered. This set of locations in the structure of an exact set of kinship groups is where the added behavior is located, and therefore where the expansion of society first takes place. This kinship network is located in a particular neighborhood and community, and has connections through extramural roles in interstitial groups that link it to other groups and organizations in these systems.

The newborn infant represents an increase in the population of these entities. As a child, it begins to occupy positions and play roles in groups other than the family; and then these groups too will increase in size if they have not lost members. As the child begins school, the school as a social system grows. If this child is multiplied many times, the school will be forced to expand by the influx, and a secondary-order expansion will occur as new teachers and new administrators are added to the staff. Ultimately, growth is affected in the firms that publish school textbooks, and that manufacture school equipment. Each of the expansions may be traced through a series of structural linkages to multiple points in the structures of families where growth in the social system first occurred. In this example, of course, some of the growth in groups and organizations manifests a shift of behavior from one part of society to others—that is, people may shift their training from engineering, say, to education.

Social systems routinely maintain the size of social units by compensating for additions of behavior to the system by subtractions of behavior in another part of the system. Thus, schools move children through a system of grades, with new first graders replacing older ones who have gone into the second grade. Some participants are always entering the system as others are leaving; so it is only when a new member increases the volume of behavior in the system that growth occurs.

As the people in different age groups reach various points in their life cycle, and changes take place in their station structure, changes in the new reproduction rate produce expansion and contraction in various parts of the social system. Not only is the size of the society as a whole affected, but the relative size of its various parts expands and contracts as birth, death, migration, and immigration-emigration rates vary. This variation in relative size of various parts requires a constant reallocation of activities among the various substructures of society.

Growth may also occur for a totally different set of reasons from those having to do with birthrate. The Ajax Black Box Factory, for instance, may increase in size when the size of the society remains constant. We will assume there has been an increased demand for black boxes, without any improvement in technology, so that a greater number of black boxes must be manufactured by increasing the amount of work activity devoted to their production. There are three possible ways to meet these conditions, each of which is a type of growth.

In order to produce more boxes, the work day may be extended, so that the same workers put in more hours of work behavior than previously. This means the Ajax Black Box Company takes up more social space than before, because it incorporates within its boundaries a greater share of the total behavior making up the society. But society has not grown, even if the factory has; so some other parts of the society must, of necessity, occupy less of the total space of the society than before. It is obvious that positions that the workers occupy in other groups must constitute the parts of the system that have grown smaller. In other words, growth or decline in one part of a social system sets off a chain reaction that inevitably affects other parts of the same system by producing compensating declines or growths.

A second way to handle growth of the Ajax Black Box Factory is to add new workers to the work groups instead of expanding the working hours. When a worker is added to the Ajax Black Box Factory, the behavior he was performing in other groups during that time interval is subtracted from other social units, and a decline in size must take place somewhere in the society to compensate for it. This decline may turn into a game of musical chairs: Ajax hires a worker formerly employed by Acme, which then hires a worker away from Eureka, which then hires someone from Alliance, and so on. At the end of the chain, however, some set of activities in some part of the social system will go unperformed, and the social unit affected will decline in size. Again, if all work expanded in this manner simultaneously, then some groups, families, for example, would necessarily decrease; and perhaps housewives, or children, or elderly people who performed nonwork roles in families would be employed in work groups.

A third possibility for Ajax is to organize itself into a two-shift operation, and become a company with two cohorts of actors who occupy the same positions but at different times. If Smith is foreman of the Paint Shop during the day shift, and Brown, Jones, Black, and Adams are painters, at night, Grey would be foreman, and White, Green, Kelly, and Williams the painters. These men would occupy the same positions and play similar roles, but at different hours. This increased behavior, too, has to come from some other place in the social system where it previously occurred.

An opposite, countergrowth process occurs when the demand for black boxes is constant, growth in the total society is constant, but laborsaving technology has been introduced that allows the same number of boxes to be produced with less human behavior being expended. Under these circumstances, either the Ajax Black Box Company declines in size, or the reduction in labor is compensated for internally by the expansion of nonproductive work activities. In a reversal of the three alternatives outlined above, the work day could be shortened; workers in each work group reduced; or a second shift eliminated. In all these cases, behavior would become available that would have to occur in other parts of the social system, which would have to expand to take up the slack. There is no possibility of the reduction being turned into nonbehavior. If the amount of time spent at work is reduced, and therefore the relative size of work groups declines, then the amount of time spent in nonwork groups must increase and nonwork groups must expand.

Thus, it is clear that growth as a process inevitably affects different parts of the social system unequally, and that alterations in the relative size of social units are an important aspect of change.

Elaboration and Simplification

The size of a society or one of its parts is measured by the amount of behavior taking place within it during an interval of time. Roughly speaking, therefore, the size of a social unit is measured by the number of acts included within it. We can analyze the action constituting a social system in terms of the variety of acts which make it up, as well as in terms of the total number, because each act constitutes a definite kind of behavior with a recognizable content and form. Ploughing is different from planting, egg-cooking is different from sewing, speech-making is different from reading. Some societies show a much greater variety of behavior than do others, even when the size of the society is controlled. In advanced technological societies, for instance, there are many times as many different kinds of acts performed in work groups alone as there are in very simple tribal societies.

Elaboration or simplification of behavior within a social unit is therefore a dimension of change different from growth or decline. Elaboration and growth are frequently associated with each other, as are simplification and decline. Let us see how a social system can increase the variety of behavior taking place within it without necessarily growing or declining in size.

Elaboration involves the total repertoire of behavior that constitutes the social system. We may focus at the level of the act, or at higher levels of scale in the social structure, and measure variety in terms of the number of different kinds of roles, or positions, or groups, or organizations in a society. In larger units of structure, it is difficult to distinguish elaboration from social differentiation; for this reason we will discuss elaboration at the level of the social act, and focus on a single role assigned to a single person, examining the variety of behavior that goes into the performance of the role. Let us take the wife-mother's role as cook, and see how it has changed over the centuries.

Several hundred years ago, the cook role in the family in western societies involved the use of a relatively simple technology— open fires or fireplaces; a few simple cooking utensils; and a small variety of foods always prepared in the same way. As time passed, the number and variety of cooking utensils increased, as did also the variety of food. Stoves, ovens, refrigeration units, and other ways to preserve and prepare food were introduced. Each new aspect of technology demanded a new set of behaviors expressing the technology. Eventually, a generation ago, the housewife's role as cook reached an apex of elaboration when such devices as electric mixers and blenders, freezers, toasters, electric frying pans, self-timing ovens, dishwashers, and microranges were introduced. Then came pre-cooked meals, specialty fast-foods restaurants, and premixed, packaged, and instant foods. Today the cook role seems to be in a period of simplification. The cook role thus illustrates how a given role becomes more and more elaborate as new types of behavior are added to the repertoire of acts constituting the role. It also illustrates the fact that a role may become more elaborate and then grow simpler.

The simplification of the cook role within the family in our society is probably the outcome of a change in the division of labor in other parts of society. With respect to an entire society, an elaboration of behavior patterns may take place without a significant change in the division of labor. In traditional terms, as the culture base expands by the addition of new items to the culture of the society, and as the variety of different types of behavior in the society thereby increases, the society is undergoing a process of elaboration. But elaboration cannot proceed very far without a change in the relative size of social units making up the society, or a change in the division of labor. If the cook role increases in the variety of behavior performed by the cook, almost certainly the size of the cook role will change. It doesn't necessarily have to increase in size, however. If the greater variety of behavior employs an advanced technology, it may decrease in size, because the technology saves labor.

If the variety of behavior in the cook role increases by employing a more advanced technology, almost certainly a division of labor in society has occurred to support the advanced technology; for growth, elaboration, and differentiation are interacting processes. The advantage in viewing them separately is that it enables us to trace change to its origin, to locate the points in the social system that are changing, and to deal with changes in part of the social systems without knowing everything else that is happening in the entire system. Take, for example, change in family structure. All of the following things may occur within the family simultaneously with other conditions in the entire society.

A family may grow or decline in size, measured by the volume of behavior taking place within it, even when the society is growing or declining in opposite directions.

It is possible for the variety of behaviors performed within a family to increase or decrease even as the variety of behavior in society is moving in opposite directions.

It is possible for the divisions of labor in a family to increase or decrease, even as the division of labor in society is moving in opposite directions.

Furthermore, in terms of the internal family system, the family may grow or decline without the variety of behavior or the division of labor within it changing. Increase or decrease in the variety of behavior may occur within it, without growing or declining or changing the division of labor. The division of labor can increase or decline, without growth or elaboration being changed.

Given all these possibilities, it is necessary to separate growth, elaboration, and differentiation from each other conceptually. Each can occur without the other, especially with respect to given parts of large social systems. Since the group is the part of the system that we can most readily observe, it is at this level that we can most easily check out our theories of change.

Elaboration, Invention, and Diffusion

The traditional anthropological concepts of invention and diffusion are most useful in dealing with elaboration, because they explain that a cultural base is widened by increasing the variety of behavior patterns that are practiced in society. Each item of culture becomes a part of the culture at some particular time, when it is either borrowed from outside the system or arises internally within it. The item of culture may be a relatively complex behavior pattern consisting of many acts and therefore, in the latent state, of many norms; or it may consist of a single act or norm. Furthermore, new items of culture may involve behavior which requires a new way of interacting between people in groups; or it may affect the behavior of a single actor.

Invention and diffusion imply that culture is a system of shared behavior patterns. Most students of diffusion believe that for an item to become a part of culture, it has to be adopted as a standard part of the behavioral repertoire of most persons in a certain category in society. To say that the use of horses for transportation became a part of the culture of the American Indian means we are speaking of horses and American Indians as categories that are tied together.

Research on the diffusion of agricultural practices has demonstrated that new items of behavior enter the behavioral repertoire of people in a given community at particular points, and that they spread from this point in certain patterns. That is, the elaboration of behavior first occurs in some definite part of the social system, and not in the entire system at one time. Items of culture are diffused into a society from outside over linkages that connect the society with other systems in its environment. For this reason, elaboration occurs unequally.

Inventions or innovations arising within the system also arise at definite points, and then spread to and affect other parts of the system through processes of diffusion. Like borrowed culture, natively invented culture results in the unequal elaboration of parts of the social system. In our society, for example, both invention and diffusion have elaborated those parts of the social system associated with material goods and their manufacture, distribution, and consumption; they have not produced elaboration to the same degree in our religious or family life. Indeed, kinship relations and religious activities seem to have been simplified. This simplification is probably associated with changes in the division of labor in society, through which nonfamily and nonreligious groups have assumed functions formerly performed by these groups. Nevertheless, it is apparent that our economic institution has been becoming more and more elaborate, and our kinship and religious institutions have been becoming less and less so.

Differentiation and the Division of Labor

Social differentiation is a process whereby behavior patterns are re-allocated within the structure of society, so that behavior formerly performed in one social unit is allocated to other social units. Differentiation does not amount to dividing up the behavior once assigned to one person among two or more people, who then specialize in the performance of some particular set of related behavior taken from the original repertoire. Actually, the division of labor that results from differentiation is among social units, such as social positions or groups or organizations, and not among the actors who happen to occupy the positions, or perform the behavior constituting the group or organization at a particular time.

We can illustrate this point by examining social differentiation at the group level, say, the managerial group in the Ajax Black Box Factory. The group contains four social positions: company president, accountant, chief secretary, and assistant secretary. A division of labor exists in the group, so that the roles to be performed in the group are assigned to four distinct social positions. The president has supervisory and management roles. The accountant keeps the books, makes out the payroll, pays the bills, and receives the income of the company from sales. The chief secretary works for the company president, types, acts as receptionist, and takes dictation. The assistant secretary types, runs the mimeograph machine, does the filing, and assists in taking dictation. The roles performed by the actors are differentiated in that there is a different set of behaviors—a different set of roles—associated with each position.

Suppose the volume of work required of this group increases due to a phenomenal increase in the demand for black boxes. There is too much work for the company accountant to do, and he begins to fall behind. To solve the problem, a bookkeeper is hired, and parts of the duties formerly assigned to the accountant are assigned to a new position. The person occupying the new position is made responsible for acting as paymaster and personnel officer for the company. The accountant retains the roles associated with receiving money from sales, distributing funds for purchases, and keeping cost-accounting records. The accountant's position has been differentiated into two separate positions by assigning some of the roles formerly associated with that position to a new one.

In this example, both growth and differentiation have occurred simultaneously. However, growth would occur without differentiation if an extra secretary were hired and assigned exactly the same duties as the secretary already employed in the office. For differentiation to occur, a re-allocation or restructuring of the system must take place. Adding another, but identical position does not increase the differentiation within the group unless a re-allocation of roles also takes place.

What is true for the positions in a group also applies to entire groups within an organization. A single group in an organization may be split into two groups, each with a specialized part of the total function of the first assigned to it. The Box Shop could be split into two groups, for instance, one responsible for forming the box from sheet metal, and the second for welding the seams and drilling the holes for wires to be fed into it. At the organizational level, a single organization may grow and split into separate specialized suborganizations. Even at the community level, differentiation may occur if the communities become specialized in products produced within them.

Pure and Synthetic Differentiation

Differentiation can occur in two ways. One is pure, and the other synthetic. Pure differentiation occurs when some part of an existing system splits into separate, specialized social units. In pure differentiation, an existing real social system splits or divides; or conversely, two existing real systems merge or consolidate.

In synthetic differentiation, an elaboration of the social system itself introduces a new specialized social unit into the system which produces a product or output previously produced by more generalized social units. Such an innovation might arise when an organization begins to specialize only in producing and selling fried chicken. The fried-chicken restaurant did not differentiate out of an already existing restaurant, an organization, let us say, that produced hamburgers, fried chicken, pizza, and roast beef, and then split into individual parts specialized in the production and sale of a single food. Instead, a specialized restaurant, a fried-chicken establishment, was organized in competition with other existing groups of generalized restaurants. Actually, synthetic differentiation probably occurs as frequently as pure. Innovations introduce brand new, specialized, and differentiated structures alongside and in competition with older, more generalized ones.

Whole specialized social units may be introduced into the social system by either invention or diffusion, and the elaboration process may also produce differentiation. Thus, a developing society that is relatively undifferentiated may borrow highly differentiated parts from more technologically advanced societies. For example, a gasoline station is a highly specialized social unit—a group of people specialized in the dispensing of a single product or small group of products. Yet, there are occasional gasoline stations in relatively underdeveloped societies. These gasoline stations did not differentiate out of existing structures within the society. Instead, a specialized social unit was introduced as a unit already differentiated.

Growth, Elaboration, and Differentiation

The factors that produce pure differentiation may be quite unlike those which produce synthetic differentiation, as the relationship between growth, elaboration, and differentiation demonstrates. Growth consists of an increase in the amount of behavior occurring in a given part of the social system. When growth occurs under conditions in which no new members are added to society, behavior must be subtracted from activities in one part of the system as it is added to other parts. This may mean that whole sets of group activities disappear. As the behavior required in work groups or in groups associated with the production and distribution of goods increases, for instance, the behavior performed in families may decrease. As it decreases, certain roles, for example, recreational roles, may become less and less active until they have virtually disappeared, and the variety of behavior in families will have undergone simplification.

In other words, differential rates of growth in parts of the social system may simultaneously produce elaborations and simplifications in different parts of the system. Elaboration of the behavior occurring in a given group will, in most cases, result in growth of that group. Similarly, simplification will produce shrinkage.

Differentiation will also produce differences in the relative growth of parts of the social system. As specialized groups and organizations emerge to perform functions once performed by families, the family will almost inevitably go through a process of simultaneous shrinkage in size and decrease in elaboration. As more differentiation takes place in a society, interstitial groups that link specialized parts to one another will grow both in number and in magnitude. The courts, for example, are interstitial groups designed to settle disputes among social units that normally stand in a conjunctive relationship. As the number and variety of specialized social units in a community increases, more and more interstitial groups will be required to facilitate exchanges among them, and to co-ordinate their functioning. Since these interstitial groups will contain conjunctive relationships, and such relationships are essentially conflicting, we might expect more and more litigation would be needed to settle disputes. As a consequence, courts would expand to handle an ever greater volume of conflict among specialized parts of society. Differentiation would thus produce growth in a part of the social system.

On the other hand, growth might also force differentiation. If the courts have to handle a high volume of litigation, differentiation may be expected to occur, and the general court split into Juvenile Court, Traffic Court, Family Court, Small Claims Court, Criminal Court, and Civil Court—as has actually happened in our judicial system.

Thus, growth, elaboration, and differentiation are interacting processes. As one occurs, the others follow. Social change amounts to the simultaneous, interacting transformations that alter the structure of the system.

The foregoing discussion defines social change, and discusses the various forms that change takes. It does not account for change, and leaves certain important questions unanswered. How for instance, are change processes set in motion? What mechanisms transmit change occurring in one part of the system to other parts? What effects does change have on the functioning of the social system? In the next chapter, a theory of change designed to deal with these questions at the micro level will be presented. We shall leave the explanation of change processes on the macro level to the students of social movements and revolution.

PART VI

A GENERAL ASSESSMENT

CHAPTER 21

**STRESS, STRAIN, DEVIANCE
AND SOCIAL CHANGE**

Societies, even the smallest and least developed, are relatively complex open systems, made up of many intricately related parts. It would indeed be surprising if all of these parts were ever to adjust perfectly to one another. The very openness and complexity of social systems almost certainly assures both an imperfect internal integration and a continual change and need for adaptation.

Societies are open all along their boundaries at every point where an actor or system of actors encounters the system's environment. The environment does not present these actors only with internally consistent inputs; almost certainly, at any given moment the various parts of societies are receiving bits of contradictory or inconsistent information. These inconsistent inputs, when processed, result in diverging changes in the various parts of the society. And as the parts of society diverge in response to diverse inputs, they will almost certainly become maladjusted to one another.

Two concepts—*stress* and *strain*—will be used in discussing this maladjustment and its consequences for social change and adaptation. *Stress* is defined as a condition that arises in a social system when two or more of its parts become inconsistent with or dysfunctional for one another. *Dysfunctional* means that two parts of the system impair each other's functioning in some way; when this happens, they either cease to produce their outputs for the larger system and for its members, or else the cost or effort needed to produce these outputs is increased above the minimum that is theoretically necessary. In either case, the amount of output of various system parts is reduced or changed in a way that affects other parts of the system negatively.

Strain is defined as the psychological consequences for those actors who perform the behavior that makes up the parts of the system under stress. Stress therefore is a system-centered concept, and refers to the consequences of maladjustment among parts of social systems. Strain is a person-centered concept, and refers to the consequences of maladjustment among parts for an actor. Strain, as a person-centered concept, refers to maladjustments involving station structure as it relates to personality.

Sources of Stress and Strain

In order for all parts of a social system to achieve adjustment to one another, the four groups of variables that produce the behavior constituting the parts of the social system must be in adjustment to one another and mutually supportive. This means that the culture, personality, situation, and interaction variables must be so related to one another that if the content of each were left unchanged, the form and organization of the behavior making up the society would itself remain unchanged and stress free. When we say that these variables must be adjusted to one another and mutually consistent, we mean, for example, that the culture that defines the roles played by an actor must be compatible with the personality traits of the actor required to perform them, with the elements of the situation in which they must be performed, and with the interaction patterns that they are performed in.

Forms of Stress

It is possible to derive a large number of forms of stress from our four-factor model. Let us assume, for instance, that the elements that make up each variable must be internally consistent if that variable is to produce stress-free behavior. That gives us four forms of within-factor stress: (1) stress arising out of inconsistency between two or more parts of the same culture; (2) stress arising out of inconsistency between two or more parts of the same personality; (3) stress arising out of inconsistency between two or more parts of the same situation; and (4) stress arising out of inconsistency between the acts performed by two or more persons in interaction. Each variable or group of variables may thus be viewed as a potential source of stress, providing that (1) the variable can be broken down into smaller parts, and (2) that those parts may vary in the degree to which they are internally consistent and mutually supportive with respect to one another.

We could also say that any one factor must be in adjustment with each of the others for stress to be absent from the system. In this case, there are six possible two-factor sources of stress built into our model.

Two-factor Stress Sources

1. Culture inconsistent with Personality
2. Culture inconsistent with Situation
3. Culture inconsistent with Interaction
4. Personality inconsistent with Situation
5. Personality inconsistent with Interaction
6. Situation inconsistent with Interaction

By the same reasoning, we can arrive at three possible forms of three-factor stresses, and one form of four-factor stress.

Three-Factor Stress Sources

1. Culture—Personality—Situation
2. Culture—Personality—Interaction
3. Personality—Situation—Interaction

Four-Factor Stress

Culture—Personality—Situation—Interaction

For the behavior that makes up the social system to occur without stress, then, it is necessary for each of the four factors contributing an influence over behavior to be internally consistent, and for each factor to be externally consistent with each other one. If these conditions do not exist, then the behavior produced by the combination of the four variables in interaction with each other will become inconsistent, and display self-defeating or conflicting patterns to the degree that these variables are internally and externally inconsistent.

If there were such a thing as a system in a state of perfect internal consistency among and within its various parts and elements, and we introduced into it one of the fourteen forms of stress listed above, the various outputs of the system in the form of any of its products, tangible or intangible, would be reduced, providing that no additional expenditure of energy or effort occurred. Either that, or it would cost the system more in energy expenditure to produce the same amount of output. In other words, as stress is introduced into the system, some of the behavior and effort expended in the system must be used in dealing with the stress. The cost in effort or energy to deal with the stress results in lowered efficiency of production, and therefore ultimately in lower output.

This is all very abstract. Let us therefore be more specific, and consider only stresses that involve the culture variable and one other of the four variables, so that we can illustrate them with relatively concrete examples. Table 21–1 shows the various forms of stress involving the cultural variable, and gives the source of each.

TABLE 21-1
Role Stresses Between Culture and Other Factors

Variables	Source	Types of Stress
Culture	Two parts of culture	Role conflict
Personality	Culture—Personality	Role inadequacy
Situation	Culture—Situation	Role frustration
Interaction	Culture—Interaction	Role non-reciprocity

Role Conflict

The term *role conflict* refers to an inconsistency between two or more roles performed by the same actor. Several other forms of stress have also been called role conflict, but we will give these other designations (1).

Roles, at least in their latent state, consist of sets of norms that are organized so as to provide a guide to an actor for performing a function in a group. Since they consist of norms, and norms are the elements of culture, then roles in their latent state are parts of culture. If two roles assigned to the same actor are in conflict, it means that two parts of culture are inconsistent. Role conflict, therefore, is a stress arising out of some internal inconsistency in the culture, as it applies to one member of the social system in which the roles are located.

Earlier, when we defined roles as consisting of the norms held by the actors who perform the roles, we avoided the kind of mistake made by sociologists who say, for instance, that the supervisor role for Mr. Jones, president of the Ajax Black Box Factory, consists of norms "defined by the culture of his society." Instead, it is our view that Mr. Jones' role as supervisor is defined by Mr. Jones' norms. These norms may or may not correspond to those of others in the society. They were probably, but not necessarily, learned from others, and probably more or less correspond in content to supervisor norms found throughout the society. Furthermore, Mr. Jones' role as supervisor is located at one exact position in social space, and constitutes an entity occupying that space. Other roles with similar functions, such as Mr. Smith's supervisory role in the Acme Instrument Company, are located at different positions in social space, and are therefore quite different entities, even though similar or perhaps identical in content and function.

Since we define roles in this way, we must restrict *role conflict* to inconsistencies among the norms defining different roles assigned to the same actor. Since roles assigned to the same actor are all defined by that actor, the norms contained in one personality are the source of role conflict. Traditionally, sociologists have used this term to refer to at least two different kinds of normative inconsistency. The first is when ego has two roles, supervisor and friend, both performed toward alter. The supervisor role calls for ego to give orders to alter. The friend role calls for democratic decision-making. These norms are contradictory. Both sets of norms are held by ego (2).

The second kind of situation occurs when ego has a role, supervisor, which his boss defines one way, but his subordinates define another. He is expected to do one thing by his boss (one set of norms), and another by his subordinates (another set of norms). These norms are contradictory; however, they are not held by ego, but by two different alter actors to whom ego relates (3).

In our view only the first situation should be called *role conflict*. The second, in our view, is *role-nonreciprocity*, and involves the dual variables of culture and interaction. Role conflict, then, refers only to inconsistencies between or among the contents of roles that are all defined and performed by the same actor. The norms that are inconsistent must all be contained within the station structure of one person, and therefore must be latent behavior in the same personality system. By defining role conflict in this way we can discuss the conflict among norms using station structure to keep track of the relationship among the parts in conflict.

Distance and Role Conflict

Let us now consider the distance variable, and the probability of role conflicts developing among roles separated by differing amounts of structural distance. We can measure structural distance within a station by counting the number of boundaries among parts. Our distance scale is given in Table 21–2.

It is not necessary to assume an interval scale for these distances. It is better to regard this way of calculating distance for the time being as ordinal. It is also possible to extend this reasoning by conceiving of subsets and supersets of sizes in between the units of structure presented above. For example, we have defined orders of communities and orders of organizations. It is therefore possible to say that two positions in different situses in the same first-order community are closer together than two positions in two different situses in different first-order communities.

Where are role conflicts most likely to develop? and what are the mechanisms are that are likely to lead to their development? We can answer the first question by saying that: *The greater the distance separating two roles, the greater the probability that they will be in conflict with each other.*

This is the same as saying that two roles that are part of entirely different situses, for example, one's occupational and one's kinship situses, are more likely to develop conflicts than are two roles that are a part of the same situs—two kinship roles, for example. The reasoning behind this statement is as follows.

Each role is contained in a position, and each position is a part of a different group structure. Groups are open systems, subject to influence from their structural environment as well as their situations. Furthermore, the positions making up a situs are each a part of a different group, which itself may be a part of an organization that is also an open system. Open systems receive and process information from their environments, and then utilize that information to change their internal behavior so that their relationship to their environment is altered— hopefully, in an adaptive direction. This is accomplished through a closed loop involving feedback of information, that records the effects of a system's output on its environment and evaluates that effect in terms of the system's original orientation or intention.

The Ajax Black Box Factory sends salesmen, let us say, into the environment to dispose of black boxes. They establish conjunctive relationships with representatives of other organizations in interstitial groups. In these groups they attempt to sell the company's product. Let us assume they are successful, and obtain many orders for black boxes. These orders enter the Black Box Factory as feedback information from the environment, that reinforces or reconfirms behavior patterns going on within the system. If orders drop off, or are not received, this negative feedback means that eventually the internal structure of the Black Box Factory will begin to change. These changes are not necessarily based solely on rational decision making.

UNITS OF DISTANCE	BASIS FOR CALCULATING STRUCTURAL DISTANCE	SCHEMATIC REPRESENTATION
1	TWO NORMS OR SUB-SETS OF NORMS IN THE SAME ROLE PERFORMED TO-WARD THE SAME ACTOR	
2	TWO NORMS OR SUB-SETS OF NORMS IN DIFFERENT ROLES PERFORMED TOWARD THE SAME ACTOR (PART OF THE SAME STATUS)	
3	TWO NORMS OR SUB-SETS OF NORMS IN DIFFERENT ROLES IN DIFFERENT STATUSES IN THE SAME POSITION (ROLES ARE PERFORMED TOWARD DIFFERENT ACTORS)	
4	TWO NORMS OR SUB-SETS OF NORMS IN DIFFERENT ROLES IN DIFFERENT POSITIONS OCCUPIED BY THE SAME ACTOR BUT IN THE SAME SITUS	
5	TWO NORMS OR SUB-SETS OF NORMS IN DIFFERENT ROLES IN DIFFERENT POSITIONS IN DIFFERENT SITUSES BELONGING TO THE SAME ACTOR	

Table 21–2   The Scale of Structural Distance

The point is that open systems, such as the Ajax Black Box Factory, are subject to change through the feedback process from the environment in which they operate. In the same way, all social systems are open to an environment that includes those other parts of the larger social system to which they are structurally attached, and also the surrounding set of circumstances or situations in which they operate. In some systems, such as families, the feedback process may be less clear and considerably more varied than in others, such as business establishments; but this merely means that families make less conscious and rational adaptive decisions, and that feedback usually results in a welter of small and sometimes confusing changes, rather than significant organizational change.

In order for a system to change the pattern of its output to the environment, the norms that define roles, and therefore relationships, must change, since norms ultimately give form to behavior within the system. If norms are not changing in response to already existing stresses, the fact that they are changing will in itself create inconsistency with other existing norms, and as a consequence, stress will be introduced into the system, and result in other norms changing. Thus stress can only be reduced if the original change is negated, and things return to the way they were; or other changes occur in parts not related to the source of change in such a way that stress is reduced.

The important point there is that two positions in different situses in the same person's station are subject to entirely different and virtually independent environments. As a consequence, feedback from these independent environments will tend to produce change in independent directions. The norms in these separated parts of the social system may therefore diverge greatly. As a matter of fact, the division of labor that produced these separations created open systems that are only dependent on each other through long chains of indirect relationships.

Because of this structural separation, stress must operate very indirectly over great structural distance. At the same time, it will inevitably meet stress from another direction that is the result of other processes of change set in motion by the environment of a far-off part of the same society.

To illustrate: both families and factories change in response to their environments. As a consequence, the roles of Mr. Jones contained within his position as foreman of the paint shop in the Ajax Black Box Factory change in one direction, and the norms governing his family roles change in an entirely different one. He finds that there is a conflict between family expectations and work expectations. Since his roles are parts of different group structures, each of which is a part of different organizations located in different parts of the social system, he finds himself constrained by separate forces operating on different aspects of his behavior. The only connection between these parts of society is Mr. Jones himself, and the reflexive-conjunctive link created by his dual membership in the two systems. If the conflict is to be resolved, it will be resolved only by a change produced through this linkage.

Since two parts of the same role are subject to feedback processes from similar, if not identical, environments, feedback is more likely to produce changes in similar or compatible directions within roles than between them. An actor, for example, the housewife, performs her role as cook in a given situation which includes her kitchen and the various people and paraphernalia associated with cookery. The various norms comprising this role call for behavior toward a relatively homogeneous set of objects. This means that feedback processes are less apt to present her with contradictory or inconsistent information than feedback from widely divergent situations.

Feedback is provided, among other things, by interaction with alter actors toward whom role behavior is directed. It may take the form of complementary responses that confirm the appropriateness of ego's behavior; noncomplementary responses that question the appropriateness of that behavior; or positive or negative sanctions that reward or punish ego and thus reinforce or undermine his behavior. Feedback may also be obtained from the physical situation. If ego's behavior produces on his environment the effect ego desired or predicted, he receives positive feedback. If an unexpected or undesired effect is perceived, he receives negative feedback.

Since ego's choice of actions is a function of the norms that provide guides to behavior, along with the variables of personality, situation, and interaction, these feedbacks from the environment function either to reinforce or to modify the norms. In the case of one particular role, ego receives all of these feedbacks from a single alter actor, or a small group of alter actors who themselves interact directly with each other; consequently, the likelihood of contradictory feedbacks is less than when ego plays two entirely different roles toward different sets of actors who do not themselves interact.

We must now consider the consequences of role conflict. Feedback from the environment of the system provides the mechanism for change, and produces stress in the system. But what happens as a result of stress?

Stress occurs when two parts of a system work against each other, so that one impairs or negates the functioning of the other. In essence, this means that behavior being produced in one part of the system undermines, interferes with, impairs, negates, reverses, or reduces the effectiveness of behavior being produced in another part of the system. By so doing, the functions being performed by the behavior are similarly affected—and as Merton might say, one part of the system becomes dysfunctional for the other (4).

In the case of role conflict, norms located in one part of the social system in a particular role assigned to a particular actor conflict with norms in a particular role in another part of the social system which is also performed by the same actor. The interference of one role with the other takes place because the same actor must perform the two roles. For one role to interfere with another, there has to be some path over which the conflict or interference travels. In the case of role conflict, this path is provided by reflexive relationships that link together parts of a particular person's station structure.

There are at least two ways that the effect can be transmitted over this route. The first is directly, although the actor involved never experiences strain and is never aware of the conflict. The second involves an intrapersonal strain that magnifies the stress on the social system.

As an example of the first way that stress is transmitted, consider Mr. Brown, sales manager for the Ajax Black Box Factory, who is married and has two children. His occupational situs contains a set of roles associated with the various positions contained in the salesman situs. He also occupies a kinship situs containing roles associated with the father-husband position. In order to fulfill his roles as sales manager, he is required to travel constantly, and therefore to spend most of every week away from his wife and children. Brown is an old-fashioned man, and defines his roles as father-husband in a traditional fashion. He thinks the man should be head of the household, and that the father should be shown respect by the children and given instant obedience. Brown, however, is never home except on weekends. During the week he cannot act out his disciplinarian roles. When he is at home and attempts to play his role as disciplinarian, he meets with unexpected, and, for him, surprising resistance from the children. He never really understands that his definition of the disciplinarian role is in conflict with his occupation. It never occurs to him that his continually being away from home interferes with the performance of the disciplinarian role. Instead, he blames his difficulties on the degeneration of society, or perhaps on his wife's tendency to be more permissive than himself.

In this case, the performance of occupational roles reduces or impairs the performance of a family role, because the work role must be active at a time when family roles are normally in force. A person cannot be in two places at the same time. Roles may therefore create conflict when their activity-latency periods overlap or compete. The actor may never perceive the conflict, and yet the roles may still interfere with one another.

The second type of role conflict involves strain—the actor's psychological perception of the inconsistency. Let us assume that Mr. Brown defines his roles with respect to the other salesmen in his organization as containing both the role of boss and the role of friend. His interpretation of the boss role is much like his definition of his father roles. He believes that he should exercise firm and authoritative control over his subordinates. He furthermore believes that he should give them orders regularly and closely supervise their work; and that they in turn should accept this authoritarian interpretation without questioning his right to act this way.

At the same time, he also thinks that co-workers should be friends, both on the job and off, and that he ought to be a buddy to his men when he is not giving them orders. He furthermore feels that his men should accept him as a friend, and reciprocate with the appropriate behavior.

Brown finds himself continually faced with situations in which he feels that he must give unpopular orders, or distribute rewards, such as pay increases, unevenly. Each time he faces such a situation, he has to choose between conformity to his norms of friendship and conformity to his norms for being a boss. If he acts the way he thinks he ought to as a boss, he goes against his norms of friendship. If he acts like a friend, he goes against his norms for being a boss. Each time he makes this kind of choice, he wonders whether he has done the right thing. He feels guilty and anxious; he worries about whether his choice has been wrong. In other words, he feels strain because stress exists between the norms defining two of his roles.

Brown thus experiences the strain produced by the role conflict as guilt, anxiety, and fear of sanctions from alter actors whose expectations have not been met. All these emotions are unpleasant, and he would like to avoid them if he could. There are two ways out. One is for Brown to abandon one or the other of his roles—either quit being boss and become one of the boys, or quit being one of the boys and become all boss. The other route is to redefine one or both of the roles involved in the conflict by fashioning a new set of norms—for example, he could redefine the role of boss in much more democratic terms, and come closer to the role requirements of friendship, acting more like a chairman than an autocrat.

We believe that the strain Brown experiences will lead to behavior modifications in one of these two directions. Other pressures, arising from the interactions between Brown and the other members of the group, will also act to force a redefinition of roles. If the men in the group accept the friendship role as part of their positions, as well as Brown's, when he deviates from it by acting the boss they will use sanctions to try to force him into conformity with friendship norms. These sanctions will add to Brown's internal strain, and provide greater stimulus for him to redefine roles or to withdraw from them. In other words, both internal and external pressures or strains operate to modify behavior, and consequently modify the norms defining roles. Thus, strain gives the impetus for change in a small corner of the social system.

Role conflict is more likely to occur among roles that are separated by great structural distance within the station of a given person. Because members of a society generally learn their roles from each other through processes of socialization, and because whole classes of individuals share similar situations, whole categories of people may experience similar role conflicts. It is also possible, through communication and interaction among members of the same society, for solutions to the conflict problem to spread, and for a common role redefinition to emerge.

It is apparent that the more differentiated a society becomes and the greater its division of labor, the greater will be the average structured distance contained within the stations of the society's members. Distance is a function of the division of labor, and varies directly with it. This means, of course, that large, more complex societies are much more likely to generate role conflicts than smaller, less differentiated ones. It also means the greater the division of labor, and consequently the greater the mean structural distance within stations, the greater the tendency for change to occur in roles as a consequence of attempts to resolve role conflicts.

Even in the most complex societies, individuals will vary in the complexity of their stations. The level of the division of labor dictates the average complexity of stations, and sets the range within which complexity can vary. However, considerable variance around the mean within that range can occur. In our society, for example, a night watchman at an industrial plant who is single and a recluse will have a much less complex station than the president of the company who is married, a member of a large number of civic and social clubs, and an elder in his church.

We can sum up the relationship between station complexity and role conflict by saying that: *The greater the complexity of a person's station, the greater the likelihood that the station will contain role conflicts.*

This statement reflects the fact that the more parts (roles) there are in a station, the more chances there are for role conflicts to develop. Since each role is joined to the structures of the social system at a different point, and exposed to influences stemming from these unique locations, it seems reasonable to expect divergent changes to produce role conflicts.

Social Rank and Exposure to Stress

In our society it appears that complexity of station structure varies roughly with social rank. This statement is most easily illustrated with respect to the occupations. Low-ranking occupations require their practitioners to participate in few groups, and within these groups to perform only a few simple roles. The occupational situses of low-ranking occupations therefore contain only a few positions with relatively simple structures—for instance, those of night watchmen, day laborers, custodians, garbage collectors, and farm laborers.

At the upper end of the occupational income and prestige hierarchy are occupations with relatively complex situses containing numerous positions, each with complex repertoires of roles. Physicians, for example, in order to practice their professions must participate in many groups, for each of which there will be a different position in the doctor's occupational situs. Furthermore, each position will contain a large number of roles, each of which in itself is relatively complex. The same thing is true with respect to the other professions, and also with respect to managerial and supervisory jobs.

Outside the world of work, participation in community affairs seems to follow occupational rank to a certain extent. Higher-ranking occupations involve their practitioners in greater numbers of community, civic, social and occupational groups, as well as in affairs associated with politics and religion. Hollingshead and Warner found community participation to be greatest in the upper middle or lower-upper classes. The very rich old families in their studies did not participate to the extent expected, given their rank (5).

It would appear from this discussion that station complexity increases with social rank. The relationship, of course, cannot be perfect, since numerous exceptions to the rule no doubt exist; nevertheless, persons of relatively high social rank seem to be exposed to a greater risk of role conflict. They have a greater number of roles which are parts of a larger number of positions, and as a result, there are more chances for role inconsistencies to develop. It is possible, therefore, that differences in occupational prestige and income can be explained in another way than that suggested by Davis and Moore (6). If occupations vary in complexity, and complexity is associated with exposure to stress, then perhaps high prestige and income are necessary rewards that induce people to expose themselves to stress. That is, the more complex an occupation, the more likely it is to produce stress. If its rewards are not high enough to compensate for the stress, the occupation will not recruit practitioners, nor will it retain those recruited. Therefore, a society containing highly complex, stress-prone occupations will tend to evolve a system of rewards that relates prestige and income to the degree of exposure to stress associated with occupations. As a consequence, occupational ranking will tend to vary directly with the exposure to stress, and both will tend to vary with the complexity of the occupational situs structure.

Role conflict is only one of the social stresses to which this statement applies. As we shall see, role-inadequacy, role frustration, reciprocity, and saturation also seem to be associated with both occupational complexity and with occupational rank.

Role Inadequacy

A second stress arising out of culture results from a mismatching between the roles assigned a person and his personality. Each role consists of a set of norm-defined behaviors executed in group situations. The behavior required by a given role, for example, the supervisor role in a work group, fits certain personality types better than others. As a matter of fact, for each role there is a set of personality characteristics that fit the role best—that is to say, certain personality traits will facilitate or support the performance of the role, while others will interfere with or undermine the performance of the role. When the requirements of the role and the characteristics of the personality performing the role are mismatched or in conflict, a stress arises in the social system. This is *role inadequacy*. This stress produces faulty or inadequate performance of the role, so that the function around which the role is organized either goes unperformed, or is misperformed in some manner which affects the operation of the system in which the role is located.

Role inadequacy occurs at the level of the individual role; it also exists with respect to larger units of structure. For example, positions consist of role clusters, and situses of position clusters. Just as role and personality may be mismatched, so may personality and position, or situs, or for that matter, an entire station. The clusters of roles making up the father-husband position in a family places certain behavioral requirements on the actor occupying the position. In turn, these requirements demand a certain range of personality characteristics for their adequate performance. If the person occupying the position has a personality that falls outside this range, then role inadequacy will occur in several if not in all of the roles making up the position. Similarly, a mismatch may occur between personality and situs requirements. For example, only a certain range of personality characteristics may fit the occupation of brain surgeon.

We are justified in applying the concept of role inadequacy to these larger units of structure on the assumption that larger units, such as positions and situses, consist of sets of roles that operate as a system, and through such operation achieve some degree of internal consistency. If they have not achieved internal consistency, then role conflict is present, and the stress and strain it engenders is operating to force the system toward consistency. The mechanism of role conflict operating over a long period of time on many position and situs occupants will continually move these role clusters in the direction of internal consistency. It is probable, therefore, that if a given personality type is in conflict with a certain role in a given position in a particular situs, it is likely that it is also in conflict with other roles in the same structural unit.

We may approach this point from a different direction. All the roles that comprise the positions that make up a given situs are, by definition, performed by the same person. This means that they must be in adjustment to the same personality. If there is maladjustment, stress will arise, and the person will experience strain. Both stress and strain will operate to produce behavior directed toward reducing them. There are only three alternative ways to do this: (1) The roles may be changed, or redefined in the direction consistent with the personality of the actor assigned to perform them. There will, of course, be pressures from alter actors which resist this alternative. (2) The personality of the actor performing the role may be changed, either by replacing the actor assigned the roles with another actor whose personality fits, or by actually changing the personality of the actor through resocialization—which is, of course, very difficult to do. (3) Changes may be made simultaneously in role content and in personality structure, so that the two converge. All these alternatives are directed at making the position or situs consistent with the personality of the actor occupying them.

If an actor redefines a role to fit his own personality, he comes up against two powerful deterrents. The first is resistance on the part of alter actors. Ego is not completely free to define his role as he sees fit. His roles are performed toward alter actors who stand in complementary relationships to him. Their alter role definitions prepare them to respond to ego's behavior only insofar as that behavior conforms to what they expect and understand. If ego redefines his role, then alter will have difficulty responding unless he also redefines his role. Alter may not be willing or able to do this. If ego changes his role, and alter does not change his, role noncomplementarity arises. This stress will be discussed at length below; at present, we may say that noncomplementarity tends to produce one of three conditions: (1) Alter will resist ego's role definitions, and try to force him to accept his (alter's) role definition; (2) alter will be forced to redefine his own role in a direction that establishes complementarity with ego's expectations; or (3) a combination of these two will occur.

The second deterrent to changing role definitions is the role conflict that arises when one role in a set is redefined without redefining others. If ego changes his definition of one of his roles, he will almost inevitably find that he has created a role conflict for himself with another one of his roles. Since one way to resolve role conflict is to return to the old role definition, role conflict does constitute a deterrent to role redefinition as a solution to the role inadequacy problem.

It is probably true that the usual way to solve role inadequacy situations is for actors to give up the positions or situses containing the source of the conflict, and to seek positions and situses more suited to their personalities. To the extent that this does happen, it amounts to a sorting out process by which people seek roles that do not make them suffer the stress of role inadequacy—a kind of reverse Peter Principle (7).

One form of role inadequacy occurs when a role or cluster of roles assigned to a person requires certain character traits for its performance, but the actor assigned the role simply does not have them. The position of Platoon Sergeant in an infantry company contains roles which require an actor to give orders to subordinates. These orders often require that men expose themselves to danger, or perform behavior which is unpopular, dirty, physically difficult, or otherwise unpleasant. Suppose that the person assigned the position of Platoon Sergeant were extremely sensitive, lacked self-confidence, and had a deep yearning to be loved by his associates. Each time he has to give an unpopular order and his men begin to gripe and resist, he will feel personally threatened, and greatly anxious about whether his men approve of him. As a consequence, he will hesitate, or perhaps even refuse, to give unpopular orders, and the performance of his roles will suffer. At the same time, he will be anxious, guilty and fearful because he cannot perform behavior defined by the norms of his position.

Our hypothetical sergeant illustrates that if the character of a person does not fit the roles assigned him, he will be unable to fulfill some of the requirements of the role, and will suffer strain manifested as anxiety, fear, guilt, and depression. Timid people have no business becoming professional prize fighters, and extremely aggressive people should not train to be nurses.

Another manifestation of role inadequacy occurs when the actor assigned a role lacks the training, experience, physical strength or size, intelligence, or dexterity to fulfill the role requirements. In these cases character traits are not the problem, but physical or mental skills. One example of this kind of role inadequacy would be the stupid son who inherits a position as president of a large company. He lacks the mental ability to perform the roles assigned to a corporation president, and cannot learn the necessary skills. Or, let us say, a high-school football coach makes his clumsy son quarterback on the high-school team.

Since roles are learned, and learning often takes place after the actor is assigned the role, it follows that role inadequacy may often arise in the early stages of socialization when persons are learning assigned roles. Formal socialization or education never completely prepares actors to fulfill all of the role expectations associated with positions they come to occupy in various groups. This kind of role inadequacy is most likely to occur where role requirements for a position or situs are extremely specialized or complex. There is likely to be a scarcity of people prepared to perform extremely specialized roles, and it is difficult for the social system to allocate proper role performers to these locations. Moreover, extremely complex role requirements usually require such a mixture of personality characteristics, that it is rare for any one person to possess all the required traits. Any occupation that requires a high level of education for adequate role performance, or a complex background experience, is therefore more apt to be associated with role inadequacy than an occupation that demands less from its practitioners.

The more complex an occupation, therefore, or the more specialized and rare its roles, the more likely those who are in it will suffer the strain of role inadequacy. Again, the prestige and income associated with such occupations will tend to be high. A person may continue to be occupationally mobile, therefore, until he reaches a position where he experiences this stress, although it seems to be true that some occupations are much more likely to produce stress of this sort than others.

So far we have discussed cases in which the person is underqualified for his roles because he lacks some personality component required for their performance. The opposite possibility also exists. That is, an actor may be overprepared or overqualified for his roles. Such an actor will experience role inadequacy as boredom or monotony, and may resent a lack of opportunity to use his talents or abilities. The literature on industrial sociology suggests that workers may experience strain when their jobs are too simple, routine, or repetitive to challenge their interest, or to motivate them to strive for adequate role performance. Thus, some roles may seem meaningless, demeaning, boring, monotonous, and intrinsically unrewarding.

Role Frustration

Every role is performed in a situational context that provides the actor with the stage upon which he performs his role behavior. The situation contains objects, conditions, and, frequently, other actors. These situational elements provide the objects upon which or toward which action is performed. The situation therefore must be matched with the role that is to be performed before the performance of role behavior can take place without disruption or stress.

In other words, every role requires certain situational elements for its performance. If some of these elements are not present, or if the elements themselves do not function properly, role behavior is disrupted or impaired. When this happens, we have *role frustration*. This stress results from a lack of correspondence between role requirements, some part of culture, and the situational variable.

Role frustration is most easily illustrated with respect to occupational roles, but applies to all roles that require structured or semistructured situations. In order for a secretary to perform her occupational roles, she must be provided with a situation containing certain equipment and certain conditions, as well as certain alter actors who perform certain actions toward her. She must have a typewriter in working condition, a desk, chair, paper, and erasers. There must be sufficient space, light, heat, and privacy to perform the role. Furthermore, there must be someone to assign work and to receive and use it when it is complete. If any of these and numerous other conditions are not met, then the roles of the secretary will be disrupted. If the typewriter breaks down, or if the light goes out, her role performance will be disrupted, her functions will not be performed, and the behavior of other group members will be affected.

In role frustration, behavior is blocked or impaired by the situation. The personal consequence for the actor is frustration, rather than guilt or anxiety. The emotional response is more likely to be anger or irritation than self blame, or anxious anticipation of sanctions from alter actors.

The more complex the situation required by a role, the more likely role frustration will occur. Occupations requiring highly complex equipment, and highly specialized facilities difficult to maintain are exposed to role frustration to a greater extent than occupations dependent on simple situations. Similarly, occupations dependent on situations beyond the control of the practitioner, or of others upon whom he can depend, are subject to maximum role frustration—for instance, farmers who are dependent on weather conditions in areas where the weather is highly problematic.

Most roles depend on other people's performing behavior. The boss in an office needs to have his secretary present and performing her roles before he can perform his. If the secretary is ill and does not come to work, his role behavior is frustrated. Of, if the secretary resolves a role conflict by choosing to conform to family norms that require her to attend a relative's funeral, his role behavior is frustrated. If alter actors for any reason fail to perform complementary behavior required by ego's role, then ego's role performance will be frustrated.

The situations in which some roles are performed may be subject to change when events occur in the social system far removed from the group whose situation is being considered. Take technological change, for instance. Its effects on situations in which roles are performed may be either positive or negative. It may facilitate the performance of the function around which the role is organized, or it may hamper or even eliminate the role altogether, thus permanently inhibiting its performance.

As an example of how technological change can affect role performance, let us consider the laundress role, which is included in most housewife positions. A generation ago this role was comprised of norms related to the use of zinc tubs, washboards, hand-operated wringers, clothes lines, and clothes pins. The behavior required to perform the role consumed much time. The introduction of the washing machine and clothes drier completely and positively changed the norms of the laundress role. The function around which the role is organized is now much more easily performed, and requires a great deal less time. Thus, these technological improvements changed the situation in which the role of laundress was performed by facilitating it and reducing the amount and form of behavior necessary to perform it. In a sense this is the opposite of role frustration. However, in both cases, situational elements interfere with the performance of behavior called for by norms.

Technological change may also block role performance, sometimes when the role performer still wants to perform the roles. This is what is meant by technological unemployment. A man spends a lifetime learning the trade of blacksmith, let us say. Along comes the automobile, and fewer and fewer horses show up at the blacksmith shop. There the blacksmith stands, with all the paraphenalia of his trade, and all the skill necessary to perform his occupational roles, but without one essential ingredient—a horse that needs his services.

Both war and natural disasters are sources of role frustration, since either may deprive role players of access to situations in which to perform their roles, or may destroy part or all of those situations. One of the major tasks after wars and disasters is to restore situations to their previous conditions so that normal role playing may proceed.

Nonviolent and also violent demonstrations are designed to produce role frustration in certain publics, and thus dramatize real or imagined injustices. Demonstrations are staged to frustrate the performance of roles defined as illegitimate by the demonstrators, who disrupt the situation required for their performance in order to gain concessions from those affected. Street demonstrations that interrupt the flow of traffic and keep people from getting to work, or from getting to various destinations where role performances are pending, are intended to, and do, arouse the anger of those whose passage is blocked. The demonstrators know their cause is just, and believe there is no reasonable justification for not giving in to their demands. They also believe that once their targets grow tired of being disrupted, they will give in in order to be able to perform their normal roles. Industrial strikes also use role frustration in this same way. Both strikes and demonstrations are effective insofar as they succeed in frustrating the performance of some valued roles on the part of the target group, especially where their demands are regarded as less valuable by the target group than the regained role performance.

Role frustration is thus most likely to occur when the role requires a complex set of situational elements for its performance, when it depends on inputs from other actors whose behavior is subject to disruption, or when it is located in a part of the social system which is undergoing rapid change.

Still another source of role frustration occurs when a person has learned a role or set of roles, is motivated to perform them, but has no access to a position in the social structure where the roles can be activated. Three examples in particular need further sociological study. The first is involuntary and voluntary retirement, in which a person, who has learned and practiced occupational roles for a lifetime is separated from the positions in the social structure where the roles may be legitimately performed. The second occurs at the beginning of an occupational career, when the lack of a job that matches the learned roles may frustrate role performance. Young people who have been trained for given occupations but who cannot find positions in the social structure where the roles may be performed are subject to role frustration in much the same way as are the technologically unemployed or the retired.

Events that prevent access to the alter actors necessary to the performance of a role are the third major source of role frustration: the death of alter actors, for instance, or divorce or separation. If family roles are learned, and people are motivated to perform them, and then family members migrate or leave, a degree of role frustration will ensue. Hospitalization, institutionalization, or being drafted produce role frustration for those left behind, as well as for the person himself.

Whenever a person cannot gain access to the alter actors he needs to perform a role, or to the physical or social conditions which support such performance, he will experience role frustration. Even being caught in a traffic jam that prevents access to the situation in which role performance is desired will produce role frustration. So will a bureaucratic run around with red tape which keeps someone away from the situation or the people required for performing a role or set of roles.

Role Noncomplementarity

Another form of role stress arises when complementary roles assigned to different actors do not correspond. Remember, roles usually come in complementary pairs or larger sets, and for each ego role there is normally an alter role containing complementary behavior expectations. Role noncomplementarity occurs when the norms held by ego for the relationship do not correspond or agree with the norms held by alter. Consequently, when ego and alter interact using the normative definitions of their respective roles as guides to their actions, they come into conflict with one another.

In noncomplementarity, the norms in conflict are held by two different actors, but define the same interactional transaction. In role conflict, in contrast, the norms in question are both held by the same actor, and apply to his behavior in different interactional transactions.

Noncomplementarity amounts to a mismatch between the cultural variable and the requirements of social interactions as a process. It is only in interaction that the norms in question produce stress by making interaction between ego and alter noncomplementary. Ego performs a given act, expecting a certain response to that act on the part of alter. Instead, alter responds with an unanticipated action, one which does not complement the action performed by ego. Ego is thereupon forced to do one of four things. He can repeat his behavior, on the assumption that alter misperceived its meaning or content. He can change his behavior to some other action to which alter is able to respond as expected. He can withdraw from the situation; or he can negatively sanction alter's behavior in the hope of producing the desired response. In each of these cases, stress has occurred, since the normal flow of behavior has been disrupted.

There are at least two ways in which noncomplementarity can occur. First, it can occur when ego's role, as defined by ego, and alter's role, as defined by alter, fail to correspond and therefore make complementary interaction impossible. Second, it can occur when ego's definitions of his own role, and alter's definition of ego's role are incongruent. In either case, when the actors attempt to interact their behavior becomes disorganized, and a form of interpersonal conflict occurs.

Noncomplementarity is characteristic of newly formed groups, and of interaction between new and old members of established groups. It is also characteristic of interaction among people who represent different cultures or subcultures. Its importance as a process lies in the fact that the stress is felt by the members of the system primarily as interpersonal conflict.

Actually, a great deal of the conflict in society is over the norms that apply to the interactions among people who occupy positions in the same group. Husbands and wives, for example, often quarrel over the way in which they define their roles in relation to one another. Members of work groups fight among themselves over who is supposed to do what, when. Neighbors disagree over their obligations to one another. So, in a sense, many problems that have been attributed to normlessness, or anomie, stem not from the lack of norms to regulate interaction among people, but from an overabundance of norms.

The strain produced on actors by role noncomplementarity originates first because ego, when his role is not defined in a complementary fashion to alter's role, cannot predict the response he will receive from alter when he acts. He may therefore become confused or angry, and respond to alter with aggressive, sanctioning behavior. Secondly, when ego performs an act that is not anticipated by alter, ego may be the recipient of the same sort of negative sanctions. Both of these situations will be experienced as punishing by ego.

Resolving problems of nonreciprocity requires that either or both actors involved in the role relationship redefine their roles, or else withdraw from the relationship and seek compatible alters elsewhere. But as actors are changed, and a new person occupies a position formerly occupied by someone else, the definitions of the roles in those positions will also change. Hence, noncomplementarity may be resolved, or it may be exacerbated, when the actors change. A husband-wife relationship between two particular actors, for instance, that involves noncomplementarity may lead to divorce. If the two then remarry, they may establish role complementarity by changing mates; or, if they are not more careful than the first time, they may make their situations worse.

There are two situations that allow for predictability in behavior. In one of them, the members of a group learn what to expect from each other in response to their own behavior. In learning what to expect, they learn each other's norms. If this process is continued long enough, group members know how to respond to each other in order to produce the desired output of the group. This is complementarity.

In the second situation, ego may have a set of role definitions different from alter's. He may learn what alter's expectations are, so that he can predict how alter will react. Even though he may disagree with alter's norms, and he still does not change his own expectations, he does know what to do to get alter to respond in a certain way. In order to produce this behavior, he may then act that way, even though it means deviating from his own norms. Noncomplementarity continues to exist, but when ego uses information concerning alter's expectations to guide his behavior, rather than his own norms, interaction becomes complementary although the norms remain in conflict. Such a resolution, however, is apt to result in ego's feeling guilty or resentful.

There is one remaining role stress we need to consider. Stress may occur because an actor is assigned too many roles to perform, and is therefore overloaded with role expectations. Given fewer roles, he would be able to function without experiencing strain, and the system would be stress free. This excess of roles is *role superfluity* or oversaturation. In this condition, an actor must leave some role expectations unfulfilled because he does not have enough time in which to do everything expected of him. Given more time, he could perform the behavior without stress.

When some expectations go unfulfilled because of superfluity, something goes undone, and other members of the group experience role frustration. The actor experiencing superfluity is apt to feel guilty, anxious, irritable, harried, and set upon by others through no fault of his own, and therefore to feel extreme strain.

Superfluity is characteristic of occupations and jobs at the higher end of the occupational hierarchy. The President of the United States is a classic example. Superfluity usually precedes differentiation among positions or occupations in a society. In other words, superfluity is apt to produce a further division of labor in the part of the social system in which it occurs. In a sense it represents a case of so much growth in a part of the system that the actors, given limitations of time and energy, are unable to handle it.

At the other end of the scale is role poverty, when an actor has so few roles to perform in society, and these roles are so simple, that they do not take his full energy or capacity. But every actor is *always* in a state of activity; this means that a person's time is always filled with behavior even if it consists of watching television, rocking on the porch, or sleeping. Role poverty results in boredom or monotony, and under these conditions actors are apt to invent ways to spend their time. Such innovations may produce new forms of behavior that elaborate some activities of the social system to the point where they fill the time and consume the energy of the actors located there.

Deviance and Stress

Deviant behavior is one of the most important, yet foggiest aspects of the behavioral sciences. Traditionally, a person is regarded as a deviant if he violates the norms of society. But we do not believe there are norms of society from which deviance can occur. How, then, can we deal with behavior like crime, delinquency, insanity, and neurosis?

We must redefine *deviance* to fit our concept of norms. From our point of view, there are three ways in which an actor may deviate from norms: he can deviate from his own norms—intrapersonal deviance; he can deviate from the norms of others; or he may do both simultaneously. The causes, consequences, and meaning of these different forms of deviance are quite different.

An actor who deviates from his own norms must necessarily do something he does not define as right, proper, intelligent, or efficient. Usually he will do this to conform to the expectations of others, or to manipulate others by catering to their wishes even against his own moral judgment. Under these conditions, ego is apt to experience guilt, or to resent alter's power over him. He has performed behavior he defines as wrong, either to keep peace between himself and alter, or because alter is more powerful than he and he is forced to do so.

There are many reasons ego may deviate from alter's role expectations. Probably the most common is that he is conforming to his own norms in a situation of nonreciprocity. Or, ego may not be aware of alter's expectations, and defines the situation quite differently from alter. At any rate, ego may, in deviating from alter's norms, actually be conforming to his own.

Furthermore, ego may be perceived by tangential actors as deviating from their norms in his behavior with respect to alter. For example, a parent may treat his children in a way the neighbors consider deviant. In this case too, he may be, and usually is, conforming to his own norms and sometimes also to alter's. Indeed, we submit that interpersonal deviance is not deviance at all, in the sense that the norms that define the roles being performed are being violated. Alter's norms, and the norms of tangential actors simply do not operate on ego's behavior as norms. They operate only on the person holding them as norms, and in the case of alter actors or tangential actors these norms shape behavior for *them,* not for ego. A tangential actor, let us say, observes that his nextdoor neighbor beats his children with a rubber hose. He perceives this behavior as being deviant because, according to his norms, such behavior is defined as wrong. In other words, his perception of the act of childbeating is shaped by his norms. The norms operating on the neighbor doing the beating are his own, to which he may be conforming by engaging in such action. For that matter, he may even be conforming to the norms held by the child and by the child's mother.

What this means is that a person perceived as "crazy" by others may only be perceived that way because he has different norms, and the observers consequently do not understand his behavior. Similarly, persons defined as criminals may and usually are conforming to some set of norms, even though these deviate from the norms of others.

It would be far too great a simplification to say that people are always conforming to norms when they act. A criminal may commit a crime, and at the same time feel that it is wrong to do it. A person may do what is expected of him by others and be perceived by them as a hero, and at the same time feel that he has done something wrong. People are capable of both conforming to and deviating from their own norms, and when they do, they may be perceived as either conforming to or deviating from the norms of others.

One reason an actor may deviate from his own expectations may be that he faces various role stresses. Role conflict typically requires an actor to choose between several norms; deviance is a natural consequence, since if he conforms to one, he deviates from the others. Jean Valjean in *Les Miserables* illustrates this situation (8). As a matter of fact, we must conclude that all actors at some time are forced to deviate from their own norms, and/or deviate from the norms of others. Otherwise human actors would be automatons guided entirely by internally consistent norms. As a matter of fact, deviance seems to be a natural and inevitable part of the operation of human behavior systems, a necessary condition for social change, and the invariable companion of social adaptation.

Change and Stress

The various forms of stress enumerated above produce changes in the parts of the system in which they occur, because human actors react to the strain they produce by redefining and reallocating their behavior. Role conflict is the transmitter of change from one part of the system to another. As one part of the system changes and the other parts do not, actors experience role conflict; as role conflicts are resolved for ego, nonreciprocity or role frustration are introduced for alter actors, and thus the stress is transmitted from one actor to the other. Through waves of change, and the intervening periods of stress for the system and strain for the actors occupying positions in it, changes are transmitted throughout the social system.

As actors experience strain, or as stress disrupts the operation of social systems, new behavior patterns emerge to reduce stress and strain. When they are lowered, perception of this condition amounts to positive feedback, which confirms and supports the survival of the new behavioral adaptation. Such solutions are temporary, since new stress and strains will inevitably produce new periods of change.

Of course, all this ignores the origin of change itself. Why do role conflicts develop or other forms of stress arise? We can only answer this by saying that human inventiveness is continually at work in behavior systems. Furthermore, the process through which persons acquire norms, and thereby adaptive behavior patterns, is subject to considerable variability and error at all times. Human actors, as morphogenic systems, are continually learning new modes of adapting to problems posed by their environments; and invention or innovation are continual natural processes.

An explanation of invention itself is beyond the scope of this book, and must be left to theorists of social change or perhaps to the behavioral psychologists to devise. All we can say here is that stress and strain lead to innovation, as actors attempt to reduce the cost of performing their behavior in relation to one another, and to increase the predictability of the responses they receive from their environments as they act in relation to it.

CHAPTER 22

A REVIEW OF BASIC ASSUMPTIONS

Our primary objective in this book has been to create a conceptual model for describing and analyzing societies and their various parts, and to tie this model to various aspects of human behavior. A second objective has been to create a related model for dealing with the individual actor in his relationship to social systems, and to co-ordinate the sets of concepts used to describe society with the concepts used to describe the individual. A third objective has been to relate our conceptual models of society and of the individual to social institutions, social stratification and social change. In trying to create a set of logically interrelated and consistently defined concepts, we have, where necessary, redefined traditional terminology. At this point, we think it will be useful if we state (1) what we think we have done; (2) how we have done it; (3) how it differs from the usual sociologal conceptions; and finally, (4) what we think are the advantages or disadvantages of our perspective.

Guiding Principles and Assumptions

We have made a number of definite assumptions in building our model. The first is that: *Society and its various parts, such as communities, organizations, and groups, are real entities, and not merely intellectual constructs or abstractions based on real phenomena.*

That is, we have assumed that a society and its parts are real objects which occupy space and transpire in time; they can be observed directly through the senses, like any other objects in nature, and they can be described using first-order abstractions. Actually, whole societies are so large that they cannot be observed as a totality at one time; also, they are so long-lived that only a small segment of their life span can be examined by any small number of observers. Nonetheless, they are objects which do exist, and therefore can be observed at least in part.

It may seem strange to stress the reality of societies, since sociology exists to observe and describe them. The point is meaningful, however, because the problem of scale does preclude the sociological observer's seeing a whole society at once. It therefore becomes reasonable to debate the questions of whether indeed society does exist at all. Our unaided senses allow us to observe only small fragments of a society; indeed, we can only observe part of the phenomena that constitute a small group. Organizations and communities are beyond our reach through direct and total observation. This being true, is it not reasonable to say that groups are real, but that societies are abstractions?

But this question confuses levels of scale and levels of abstractions. Real objects may be observed at various levels of scale, and in various degrees of completeness and accuracy. An ecosystem such as a forest, for example, may be observed at the level of a single cell in a single tree; or at the level of part of a tree, such as its bark or leaves; or at the level of the relationship of whole trees and other bio-organisms in a grove in the entire forest. The cell is certainly as real as the whole tree; similarly, the entire forest, viewed as an ecosystem, is as real as the single cell. What we see will depend on the focus or scale of our observations. In one case, we are paying attention to a very small part of a larger entity; in the other, we are ignoring the small parts and observing larger ones. The point is, our senses simply cannot operate simultaneously at all levels of focus. Nevertheless, each of these objects, regardless of size, exists at a particular place in space through a particular period of time.

The problem of abstraction does not involve the scale of the object being observed, but instead, involves generalizing about many real objects of similar scale. We can, for instance, talk about cells of a certain class—leaf cells as opposed to root cells. Or, we can generalize about plant cells as opposed to animal cells. There is no referent in the real world for the words "plant cells." We cannot point to an object that corresponds to these words. There are only real, particular, individual cells located in real time and space. When we talk in abstractions, we remove things from time and space, and group together real objects in terms of some shared qualities. Because this grouping together precludes the possibility of being able to directly observe an object of reference, in order to observe a referent object, we operate in real time and space—that is, return to the first level of abstraction.

What is the point of all of this for sociology? The concepts of act, group, organization, community, and society, when applied to particular times and places, refer to different scales of real objects, and are in no sense anything more than first-order abstractions. There are particular, real acts, groups, organizations, communities, and societies. The concept of society is no different. Even though its scale is larger, it is still only a first-order abstraction.

When we speak of a society, therefore, we are not thinking of it as a kind of statistical summary of all of the groups that make it up, or of all of the actors that comprise it. Instead, we consider society as a system in which the various parts, at whatever level of scale, are articulated with one another to form an entity which has a boundary. If the parts were not really parts—that is, if they were not connected into a larger whole—then we would have created an abstraction at a different level from that of, say, a group. In other words, we regard society as being comprised of groups which are articulated with each other to form an organized whole. Society is a larger entity than the groups that comprise it, but as concepts, group and society are at the same first level of abstraction. Furthermore, these real objects, called societies, are describable, on the basis of observation, as social systems.

It is true that each scale of social object may be viewed at increasingly abstract levels. Between the real world and the first level of abstraction, where we are forever trapped by the nature of our senses, our minds, and the world of nature, the operation is observation, where the senses are employed directly upon some object in nature. Instruments may be used to augment our senses, and to allow us to change the scale or speed at which our senses operate, but the instruments may not themselves employ a different level of abstraction from the unaided senses. That is, they may not legitimately accumulate, average, or statistically summarize sets of observations, and create a "measure" on the basis of sampling from real units. If they collect a number of observations, and then summarize these in some way, they are operating at higher than the first level of abstraction.

Between the first and second levels of abstraction, and between each successive two levels a summarizing or averaging process goes on. The process may be merely mental, as when we speak of "work groups" in general, rather than a particular work group. Or, it can be statistical and rigorous, as when we subject to statistical procedures a set of observations taken on real groups, and work out summary measures of central tendency, dispersion, relationship, and so on.

Such rigorous statistical or quasi-statistical procedures cannot operationally define a phenomenon without simultaneously raising the level of abstraction. Obviously they cannot improve upon the individual observations on which they are based. Nothing is gained in terms of accuracy by such statistical processes. Instead, something is inevitably lost at each step, since it moves us further and further away from the reality for which our concepts ultimately are supposed to stand.

Sociologists collect most of the data they employ in studying society by asking questions of members of society, either through interviewing, or by questionnaire procedures. We are fond of calling our interview schedules and questionnaires "instruments," implying that they are the sociological equivalent of a microscope or a voltmeter. We have to ask, however, whether such instruments obtain data which can be employed in connection with concepts at the first level of abstraction, or whether they inevitably move us to a different level of abstraction, and thereby isolate us from the objects we are attempting to understand?

The answer to this question lies in the nature of the items used in such instruments. Questions presented to subjects can be stated so that they require the subject to answer at a given level of abstraction. "Who washed the dishes at your house last night?" calls for a particular response, concerning an exact set of dishes in a given condition at a given time. It asks the subject to recall observations made directly on a set of specific stimuli. "Who usually washes the dishes at your house?" calls for an answer at a different level of abstraction. Here the subject has to group observations together and base his statements on a mental summation of many particular observations. Obviously, questions like "How do you feel about crime on the streets?" or "What is your feeling toward labor unions?" require even more abstracted answers. And questions that employ high-level abstractions beg for high-level abstractions as answers. "Are people in society today politically freer than they were in the past?" implies many ideas, all highly abstract.

Questions asked and answers given at a certain level of abstraction can never be broken down into lower-level abstractions. We can only climb upward on the ladder of abstraction. It is impossible, therefore, to create a scale which measures the dimensions of a real phenomenon at the first order of abstraction by using second or third order abstractions as parts of the scale. However, almost all questionnaire and interview data do use questions of a high order of abstraction. They can therefore never be used to accurately describe real social objects. Perhaps it is for this reason that so many sociologists seem to regard society and its various parts as mere abstractions. But since we believe societies are real, we also believe we should observe them directly, and ask questions that can be answered at the first level of abstraction. That is why we have created a set of concepts usable at the first level of abstraction to deal with real societies and their various real parts.

Our second basic assumption is that: *Society is comprised of the interrelated behavior of human actors who act as members of groups, organizations and communities.*

If society is real, then we must be able to specify what real ingredients or parts comprise the whole. It is furthermore essential that we specify parts or particles that can be defined at the first level of abstraction, and observed directly. To our view, societies are large complex systems of behavior; and behavior performed by human beings in relation to one another is the ingredient or element out of which society is formed.

Behavior, however, is a high-level abstraction. It refers to an extremely large variety of actions which differ in form, content, duration, and frequency. Therefore, we must identify and define units of behavior which can be pointed to and directly observed. We have chosen to use an *act*—a particular bit of behavior occurring at a particular time and place—as the smallest particle of society which is capable of being observed.

What are the implications of the view that societies are behavior systems, as opposed, for example, to the view that societies are collections of people? Behavior is a fluid, pulsating, almost ephemeral phenomenon. It is neither matter nor energy in the classical sense, but instead, is more akin to the movement of matter and energy in time and space. Behavior is more like process than structure. Yet it is nonetheless real, because it is observable in the same sense that matter and energy are observable. A society comprised of behavior is therefore a fluid, changing, pulsating, ever-moving object whose dimensions and structure are constantly in a state of flux. Parts of society are always in the process of operating or transpiring, while other parts are dormant or latent.

It follows that if society at the micro level is comprised of behavior, then its parts must also be made up of behavior. Thus, groups and organizations are also behavior systems, and as such, they turn on and off. They seem to appear, disappear, and reappear, only to disappear again. How is the continuity of the behavior system maintained, given the apparent on-again-off-again nature of its parts? The answer is that because it *is* a behavior system, it persists beyond the life of its individual members. Society, like life, goes on as members come and go.

Each actor as an organism or as a personality is a contributor to behavior in the sense that his individual characteristics figure into the actions he performs; but if we focus on his actions as part of a larger system of actions, we can conceive of a different actor performing behavior which fits into the system at the same place that behavior performed by another actor previously fitted in. True, the new actor may act differently than the old one; but the *system* of behavior persists. This point of view demands that we suppress those cultural values that say that the individual man is the most important thing. But we are sociologists, after all—not humanists or psychologists, philosophers, or political ideologists. Society, the social system, is our object of study; and the fact remains that the behavior system called society goes on even as individual personalities come and go.

Our concern is with the problem of how complex behavior systems, such as societies, are put together and maintained, and how they operate through time. This task demands that we climb inside the black box of human personality, and devise means of dealing with its contents. Thus, in contrast to the behaviorists, we regard thought and feeling as behavior. Our ideas are also in sharp contrast to those of rationalists like the action theorists and symbolic interactionists. Action theorists, beginning with Weber and continuing through the Parsonian tradition, treat thought in general, and choice-making in particular, as the master processes that guide or shape behavior. Action theorists see thought process, and the will of the actor as the real controlling force over behavior. To them, actors are "motivated" or "oriented" toward ends or goals. They choose alternative means, and act in response to these choices. But choice, if it is the guide for actions, can only be a disguise for rational or irrational thought, especially if we allow motivation—which is essentially irrational—to be pursued by rational means.

We consider thought and feeling, as well as overt behavior, as dependent variables—things to be explained, not as explanations themselves. Thought is not seen as preceding action and in control of it; rather, it is a form of action, itself to be explained. Thoughts and feelings are real, and occur in real time and space. Thoughts and feelings, like overt actions, occur at particular locations in social space, and are therefore parts of the social system. This means that thought and feeling, like overt muscular activity, are social processes. They occur in interaction, and are produced by the interplay of culture, personality, and situation. We would rather not say that thought and feeling guide behavior and are the master processes, because we see no compelling evidence to justify such a position. It is as logical to say that what an actor is doing determines what he is thinking and feeling, as it is to say that what he is thinking and feeling determines what he is doing. It is true that, like Skinner, we reject the notion that what goes on inside the black box controls what goes on outside; but we are equally unwilling to ignore what is happening within the individual, since thought and feeling are as much a type of behavior as overt action, and are therefore legitimately to be regarded as parts of society.

The symbolic interactionists, along with the action theorists, are inclined to attribute to the individual actor more control over his own behavior than we think is necessary in order to explain society. They make the mind the master of the man, which means that society

becomes a kind of meeting of independent minds. Some symbolic interactionists put the "self" or the "I" at the controls of the human
behavior system, and make thought and feeling, rational or irrational,
the independent variables in human behavior. In an elaborate disguise
made up of a modicum of culture, a bit of socialization, and a lot of
symbolism, will, in the form of the self, becomes the ultimate explanation for everything. Men act as they do because, using their symbolic
equipment, they choose to act that way. If they did not choose to do
so, they would act differently.

We prefer to examine choice, perception, and symbolization as
behavior to be explained and incorporated into a model of social systems, rather than as explanations for the systems. How men perceive
things and define them symbolically, how they perceive and define
situations, how they choose to act—these are all behaviors subject to
explanation, and therefore cannot be themselves used as explanations.

We believe that if we observe and record where and when people
think certain thoughts, feel certain emotions, and do certain things, and
if we accurately record the surrounding circumstances, then we can
begin to perceive the way the phenomenon called social behavior operates as a system. It is true that at present we cannot observe thought and
feeling as readily as we can overt behavior; but it seems reasonable to
assume that thoughts and feelings occur at particular locations in real
time and space, and that there are configurations of interconnected and
interacting thought and feeling patterns which form parts of systems
larger than the single actor. This is not to say that there is anything like
the group mind or collective emotions. Rather, we are saying that the
things that one man is thinking or feeling in a group situation are related
through interaction processes to what others in the group are simultaneously thinking and feeling. This being true, then thought and feeling are
as much a part of the social process and thereby of the social system as
are the overt actions which are observable directly by the unaided
senses.

Like the symbolic interactionists, however, we do believe that the
acts of human beings that comprise the society obviously have meaning
to the actors who perform them. This meaning is probably the key to
understanding how social interaction remains organized, and hangs together as a system. But the attribution of meaning is itself a social
process, and therefore must itself be explained. We wish to account for
the attribution of meaning and the occurrence of symbolic reactions, not
to merely use the concept as an ultimate explanation for all behavior.

To say that society is comprised of behavior means that society
consists of the feelings, thoughts, and overt actions of human beings in
relationship to one another. The person as a behavior subsystem, and

the society as a behavior supersystem are not separate. What a person thinks, feels, and does occurs as a part of the social system. This system is comprised of the same exact behaviors that comprise the actors as subsystems. The person does not act toward the society or the group. He is a part of the society or the group. He is in no sense independent of the system of which he is a part. Being a part and being dependent are one and the same thing. Thus, except for hermits, a person feels, thinks, and acts as a part of the social system in which his behavior is occurring. To place thought and feeling outside this system, and to place overt behavior within it is to separate one aspect of the person from another on a completely arbitrary basis. It is also to ignore the demonstrable fact that a person's thoughts and feeling depend upon the group he is involved with, and what is happening within that group.

It will be said that since we cannot observe the thoughts or feelings occurring in people's minds, we cannot collect data on them. Consequently to incorporate them into a conceptual model may seem foolhardy. But available methodology should not be the determinant of our models or our theories; instead, our models and theories should stimulate us to create new methodology. We need to devise ways of observing thought and feeling. We should not ignore them simply because we cannot now contend with them. It is a poor science, indeed, whose efforts conform to the methods available at the moment. The creative scientist designs his methodology to suit his problem, not his problem to suit his methodology.

One last word on including thought as part of behavior. Thought, in our view, is real. It is an electrochemical event transpiring in an organism at a particular time or place, and as such is as real as the movement of an arm or leg. The fact that we cannot at the moment observe a thought only reflects the present state of the art.

The assumption that societies are behavior systems thus leads to the statement that it is the human act, in the form of feeling, thought, or overt behavior, which is the basic particle out of which images of larger and larger entities are built. Larger units are organized systems comprised of the smaller units as parts; and society is ultimately a very large and complex system formed of subsystems and sub-subsystems, each constituting an organized configuration of smaller parts, all of which consist of behavior.

Our third basic assumption is that: *Society is an open morphogenic system comprised of open morphogenic systems as parts.*

In what respect are social systems open? How are social systems morphogenic? What implications do these characteristics have for our understanding of society?

Essentially, open systems are entities that can and do alter their behavior in response to feedback from the impact of their own behavior with respect to an environment. To be open, a system has to have a means of receiving, processing, and responding to information. Not only is society as a whole an open system, but it is comprised of open systems as parts—that is, the groups that comprise an organization, and the organizations themselves, are open systems. As such they obtain information inputs from each other, and adjust or adapt their behavior in response to these inputs. Society is not like a machine, a clock, let us say, in which the parts cannot and do not alter their behavior in response to the behavior of other parts through feedback information. Instead, a society is comprised of parts that themselves can and do alter their outputs and their internal operation, in response to external events and the information fed back to them from their environment, which itself contains other open systems. The fit or linkage among the parts of the social system is relatively loose; it is maintained through information flow rather than through a mechanically precise direct linkage. The parts of society, through feedback from the environment, can speed up or slow down in response to external information. They interact, rather than acting and reacting as do the parts of a machine.

Furthermore, societies are not like systems which, although open in a limited sense, consist of parts which themselves are not open. A home heating system, for example, while open to information on the temperatures of its environment, consists of parts which themselves act in conjunction with each other much as do the parts of a clock. A heating system is on or off. While on, the parts act as a closed system with respect to the other parts to which they are connected.

Societies are much more complex than this. Virtually every part is itself an open system which reacts to feedback information from the other parts of the system to which it is attached. Interdependence among the parts is maintained through constantly operating information flow among them. Societies as systems, then, are continually in the process of having their parts move into and out of adjustment to one another, as mutual feedbacks produce adaptive reactions which oscillate around some very temporary and tenuous steady state.

If societies are open systems, we must be able to explain the mechanisms through which information can flow into and out of its parts, and also the mechanisms through which the behavior of the part may be altered in response to feedback from the environment.

It is our view that groups are open systems with mechanisms for processing information primarily because their members are animals, specifically human beings, and therefore possess sensory equipment enabling them to receive and process information. The senses of the members are therefore the senses of the group. Furthermore, a group is open to its social environment because its members are all involved in a system of reflexive relationships based on extramural roles. In other words, groups contain positions occupied by people who themselves are capable of obtaining, storing, processing and passing on information. These positions contain extramural roles, which require members to participate in external groups from which inputs are required, or to which outputs must be transferred. This participation creates reflexive relationships through which information can flow into and out of the group. Members, while acting outside the group, are acted upon by external events, and bring back with them the effects of these external events. Such effects can act as information and affect internal events.

If a group is a part of a larger system, then all its members will also occupy positions and play roles in other groups which are a part of the same system. Through this multiple group membership, groups are open to the influence of other groups in their environment. Some of the influences will enter through reflexive reciprocal linkages, and others through reflexive conjunctive linkages. All information travels over a linkage of some sort, carried by an actor who provides the sensory and decision-making equipment to interpret, or to transmit and react to it.

Interstitial groups are the points in the structure of society where multiple open systems simultaneously receive and transmit information that has important consequences for adaptation to social environments. Some of these interstitial groups merely serve as the equivalents of switching points or junction boxes, through which inputs and outputs are exchanged and feedback obtained. Others serve as places where the input/output relations among systems are co-ordinated by altering the rules of the game, or by providing needed information to adjust internal and external operation.

It is virtually impossible to separate mere openness in social systems from the process Buckley calls morphogenesis. Morphogenesis amounts to alteration in the nature of the parts themselves, rather than in their input/output relations to the environment. Obviously, in co-ordinative interstitial groups, morphogenesis is perhaps the main target of behavior. In such groups behavior is either directed at preventing a change in structure from occurring, or toward producing such change. Nevertheless, both exchange and co-ordinative interstitial groups are critical points in large open systems comprised of open systems as parts. It is here that the information processes that provide feedback and ultimately produce change in structure are most concentrated. They are like sociological synapses in the neurological system of society.

When objects and events are perceived, recognized, and converted into information they have an impact on behavior. The internal and external actions of society and its parts, such as groups, are all guided by information. Inputs into a group, which itself is a behavior system, can only be in the form of information. Even when raw materials like sheet steel, nuts, and bolts flow into a work group, they affect this behavior system only because, through perception and cognition, they are perceived as information. Similarly, as money from sales flows back into the organization, it serves as feedback only when the flow is perceived as information. What is not sensed or perceived cannot guide or alter behavior. The flow of money may be inadequate to pay for raw materials, so that eventually the operation of the factory may be threatened by bankruptcy; but this circumstance will not affect behavior until this inadequate flow of money is perceived as information.

It is also true that open systems, like closed ones, are directly affected by external conditions even when they have no means of treating these conditions as information. The effects of external events may flow over the linkages between groups and their environment and affect the group. Thus social systems, like all systems, are only partially open to their environments. To be completely open, a system would have to sense all events and conditions which affect it, and respond adaptively to every one. No system is capable of such complete environmental monitoring, and absolute equilibrium is therefore impossible. However, even though all inputs into a system are not necessarily converted into usable feedback, all inputs will have some effect on the system. What kind of effect depends on whether the inputs received are converted into information by the actors who are a part of the system. Inputs may affect behavior indirectly after affecting other things, without being immediately perceived and reacted to as information.

Some open systems are capable of changing their own internal structure and the mechanisms through which they relate to their environments in response to feedback. Such systems, in effect, learn from their experience. Animals, and especially human beings, are morphogenic behavior systems. Human actors acquire their patterns of adaptive behavior through learning. They receive information from their environment, store and interpret it, and on the basis of such information processes, form normative and attitudinally guided patterns of response. These patterns of response are continually updated by further experience, which supplies additional information to the actor.

As actors behave toward their environment, they receive either positive or negative feedback from it. Positive feedback reinforces the behavior, while negative feedback undermines the normative and attitudinal patterns that have generated it. In the absence of positive feedback, or in the presence of negative feedback, exploratory behavior is encouraged. When exploratory behavior hits upon a response pattern yielding positive feedback, a new patterned response is likely to arise if sufficient repetitions occur. When and if it does, morphogenesis has taken place. If we multiply this individual experience many times, so that large segments of the social system are involved, then morphogenesis in a social system sense becomes perceptible. All new patterns of behavior, like all changes in the social system, begin at some point, and always involve the adoption of some new behavior pattern by some actor or a group of actors.

Some morphogenic changes may be seen as the accumulation, over time, of many small changes occurring in many parts of the social system. Such changes are a kind of morphogenic drift, rather than planned or intentional change. Other changes may come about by more dramatic and more deliberate processes. A scientific, technological, religious, moral, or political revolution may substitute new forms of action for old ones. But any such revolution comes about through processes of learning and conditioning: patterns arising in response to positive and negative feedback are at some point in the social system reinforced through successful trials, and become a part of the social system for long or perhaps short periods of time.

When morphogenisis occurs, roles are redefined, group structures are altered, and the patterns of linkage among the parts of the system are changed. They are changed, however, in response to the information processes that reinforce or undermine established behavior patterns. As people perform behavior in various parts of the social system, and play roles oriented toward performing various functions, their behavior is subject to change by information processes which impinge upon it. Positive and negative feedback are defined by the orientation of the behavior being performed. If the behavior accomplishes the function it is oriented toward, it is reinforced; if it does not, it is undermined. Thus the behavior system is always in the process of being altered in the direction of adaptation and survival. This is not to say that morphogenic changes are themselves always adaptive in the long run. Many small morphogenic changes which are adaptive in the short run, or in terms of a small corner of a complex system, may be maladaptive in the long run, or in terms of larger aspects of the system.

Morphogenic changes, being based on learning, are more or less immediate, short run, local adaptations. That is, the actor who is acting out a role in a situation receives feedback from that situation. It is this feedback which produces change or stability. He cannot receive feedback, at least in an information sense, from the long run or indirect effects of his behavior.

The social system does not have a mind, nor does it have perception mechanisms. The social system does not learn. Its members learn and change. Changes in them may be perceived by the sociologist, in the long run, as changes in the patterns of behavior in the larger social system. The system, however, changes and adapts because its members change and adapt. Since the behavior of members is interdependent, and social interaction transmits the effects of behavior of one actor to the behavior of another, a morphogenic change in the behavior of one actor will produce changes in the behavior of others. It is through such complex processes that complex morphogenic changes can and do occur in large parts of social systems.

In this book, we started at the micro level with units of
behavior called acts and norms, and described large
social systems in terms of their smaller component parts. At each level
beyond the act, we defined the way smaller parts are organized to make
up larger units, and showed how their boundaries could be identified.
Let us review the way these units of structure are organized.

Acts and Norms

The smallest particle of behavior performed by an actor as a member of the social system is an *act*. The size of an act, and therefore its
boundaries, are established by its meaning. An act is the smallest particle of behavior performed by an actor that has meaning to the actor or
to alter actors toward whom it is performed. Acts are therefore viewed
as symbolic, in the sense that, as behavior, they are recognizable by
actors in terms of the significance or meaning they have for or within
the continuing action of the actors in the social situation. An actor
performs a behavior; other actors recognize, or comprehend what he is
doing, and respond with another act whose meaning is related to the
first.

Acts are the units out of which all social behavior is comprised. Like
words in language, they are units in a behavioral dialogue among actors.
Their boundaries are established by the symbolic, or meaningful, nature
of behavior. The boundaries of an act are also established by its changing behavioral context in terms of the preceding and following acts, the
surrounding situation, and the response acts occurring in conjunction
with them.

Norms are acts in a state of storage or latency. Because the same kind of act occurs over and over again in the social system, there must be some way in which the pattern of the action is stored and kept available for recurrence. Norms perform this function. They store not only the content, form, or pattern of an act, but also its meaning.

Acts have meaning because they are associated with norms which themselves contain learned meanings for behavior. Thus, norms are like a learned behavioral vocabulary; they constitute a basic behavioral repertoire of possible meaningful acts which are stored in the memory of actors. Once learned, or otherwise acquired by an actor, norms, through giving form and meaning to behavior, also function to establish boundaries for the act. As the smallest units of behavior which have meaning, acts are also the smallest particles of behavior that convey information among actors in interaction. That means they are the smallest units that can furnish feedback in social interaction. Nevertheless, acts themselves are made up of smaller observable events: the movement of individual muscles, or the various parts of the electrochemical process that constitutes thought. These smaller particles, however, do not, themselves, convey meaning. It is when they combine in temporal sequences with one another in a more or less stable pattern, that the pattern itself becomes recognizable as having meaning. Obviously, acts vary in size or duration, as well as in the complexity of their individual parts. So, therefore, will the norms which constitute the acts in storage.

Norms and acts are the smallest units of social structure with which we have been concerned. We regard a particular act or a particular norm of a single actor in a real time-space situation as a first-order abstraction. We view norms at the first level of abstraction in order to be able to point to a particular real norm acting on real behavior. Therefore, we define them as ideas of a certain sort contained in the minds of real particular people. A norm, in our view, is therefore a conscious or unconscious conception held by an actor about how to act in response to certain events occurring within himself or in his environment. As a real phenomenon, a norm is a particular sort of memory pattern which exists in a particular biological organism and functions as a stored guide to the behavior of that actor.

All norms are acquired by human actors through their experience in living situations, and are therefore, in a sense, all learned. But not all are shared with others, nor are all learned through the transmission of already existing norms from other actors. Each real norm is a particular idea located in a particular mind. But some of these particular norms are like others in other minds. They are shared, therefore, in the same sense that blue-eyed people share a gene for eye color. There is no supraorganic blue-eyed gene that exists as an external entity in biological hyperspace, zapping people with big blue eyes. Similarly, there is no handshaking norm that exists in sociocultural hyperspace, sending cultural messages from without to produce handshaking behavior when people are introduced. Norms, like genes, operate from within the organisms that contain them. They may be transmitted from one person to another, but when they are, there are definite processes for the transmission.

This view of norms allows us to deal with social change, conflict, and deviant behavior in a realistic manner. If norms are regarded as real things, and we can define them at the first level of abstraction, then we can also define how they spread or diminish, how they are transmitted, and how people with different norms come into conflict.

Furthermore, since we have defined norms and acts, we can form some ideas about sharing and consensus. In interaction, actors guide their behaviors through using norms. Norms allow them to recognize what other actors are doing, and what they expect in response. If an actor invents a norm which shapes his own action and gives it a personal meaning, but others cannot recognize his actions as having meaning, then they will not respond with a meaningful or predictable response. This means that the actor is constrained to innovate or invent behaviors that others will be able to understand and relate to. The very process of meaningful interaction thus imposes a degree of sharing or at least understanding of others' norms. This does not mean it imposes agreement. Two actors may understand the meaning of each other's behavior, but not agree on the appropriateness of it. The idiosyncratic invention of behavioral norms therefore is constrained by the same factors that constrain the idiosyncratic invention of words. People are capable of creating private symbols or words, but such symbols are usable in interaction with others only when others can understand what they mean.

Although norms are themselves first-order abstractions, the idea that constitutes a norm as a real entity may be an idea at any level of abstraction. That is, a particular human being has the normative idea that "People should never lie." This is an abstract concept; nonetheless the idea itself is real, and located in the normative storage of a particular real actor. It is the location of the idea as an entity in real time and space that makes it real, not the nature of its content. Norms with an abstract content operate on behavior as abstractions; but since behavior is real, and abstract norms are quite general, some intervening processes must occur to translate an abstract norm into a form which affects real behavior. If the norm is, "Always be honest," the idea of honesty has to be translated into a form that can be acted out as real behavior. One cannot be honest in general—there is no such thing as "acting honestly." Acts are particular real behaviors in particular real situations.

Theoretically, the norm's most important function is to provide a mechanism for the storage of patterns of behavior. This allows us eventually to think of larger parts of society in storage, for example, latent groups, and lets us deal with the pulsating, recurrent nature of activity in human societies. This conception also makes it possible to explain the continuity of the social system under conditions of intermittent rather than constant activity, and also to explain the relationship of culture and society. Culture, from this point of view, is the pattern of society's structure or organization in storage, distributed among members of society, and keyed to the division of labor among groups, organizations, and communities, and within these, to particular time-space specifications.

Roles, Statuses, and Positions

Acts and norms, as particles of social behavior, form clusters or sets, called *roles,* which themselves are combined into sets called *statuses* and *positions.*

Roles may be discussed either in terms of acts or norms, depending on whether we are concerned with active or latent behavior. In the latent state, roles consist of a set of norms contained within an actor that, as a set, define the appropriate behavior for performing a given function in a given group. Stored roles are systems of norms clustered around a function that one actor performs toward another in a given group.

In active behavior, the role is observable as a set or sequence of acts performed by one actor toward other actors or objects in order to fulfill some specialized function in a group situation. At any given instant, an actor can be in the process of performing only a single act, which is a part of a single role he has learned to perform. The remainder of the role he is in the process of performing, along with all other roles associated with the positions he occupies in society, are in a latent state. In this latent state, the role consists of a set of norms which define the kinds of acts expected of the actor by himself and others under a given set of circumstances. The internalized role is a product of the actor's experience in previous situations where his behavior has been shaped and molded by the feedback he has received from his environment.

Roles are important parts of two types of open morphogenic systems, *personalities* and *group structures.* As parts of personalities, roles operate as a set of internalized instructions to the organism that provide the organism as an actor with a set of contingent response patterns. A norm is a stored idea that "says" to the organism, "If so-and-so occurs, then respond with such and such a behavior." Of course the norm may not operate at the conscious level; but nevertheless, it is a learned response pattern to a set of stimuli which themselves are stimulus representations of events to which the organism must respond. In other words, a role is a set of instructions that operates from within an actor on a contingency basis. Depending on what the actor perceives in his situation, a certain norm will be activated out of the complex set of norms constituting the whole role. In systems terms, the norms forming the latent role operate as a set of instructions to the actor much as does the thermostatic setting on a heating system, or the program in a computer. However, roles are complex sets of contingency instructions. Which exact instruction operates to shape or guide behavior depends on what the actor perceives as occurring in his situation. The actor's perception process leaves his behavior open to influence by his environment; and through this process, various possible alternative response patterns defined by the norms that comprise roles are selected. Furthermore, normative role definitions exist alongside a system of stored information and a system of attitudes, each of which may act to modify behavior away from the normative model.

Roles are not fixed, unchanging entities. They are subject to change and adaptation through the very processes which produce the behavior of the actor. As the individual selects a response pattern from among the various norms contained in one of his roles, and puts it into effect as real behavior, he receives feedback information from his environment, this either reinforces or undermines that response pattern, or produces exploratory behavior in search of an adaptive response. If the act performed by the actor produces positive feedback, the response pattern is strengthened and is more likely to occur in the future, given the same perceived situational requirements. If feedback is negative, then the response pattern is weakened and the likelihood of its future occurrence reduced. If negative feedback is received frequently enough, or more properly, if no positive feedback is forthcoming to a given response pattern, the actor will attempt alternative response behaviors. When these exploratory responses are rewarded by positive feedback a sufficient number of times, a new norm will have been formed. In this manner, role content, in terms of norms which define acts appropriate in response to environmental conditions, will change. This change is the essence of morphogenesis in the personality, as well as in the social system. In other words, morphogenesis occurs in roles as actors are conditioned by their experiences in performing the role to respond in a different fashion than previously.

Roles are not only located in the minds or personalities of individual real actors; they are also located in the structure of real groups in social space. Social space is defined as the location occupied in space by the acts performed by different actors simultaneously and by the same actor on different occasions.

The behavior performed by an actor in a group thus occupies a region of social space. This region of space is called a *position*, and contains the roles and therefore the norms and acts associated with that actor in that group. The location of the region of space occupied by one actor is determined by its relationship to regions of space occupied by other actors, and to other regions of space occupied by the same actor in other groups where he occupies other positions. When two people are interacting, they occupy tangent or contiguous regions of social space. By definition, when they are interacting they must also be occupying positions and playing roles in the same group.

Groups, in the latent sense, consist of a set of positions, each position being occupied by a different actor, and each being joined to the others by complementary relationships. The existence of such relationships is equivalent, on the one hand, to the expectation that interaction will occur, and on the other to contiguity in social space. The social positions and the roles that comprise them, which themselves are occupied by actors in specific groups, are located sociologically in given regions of social space, and located biologically in the organism of a given actor. The actor may move around in physical space independent of movement in social space. He may change locations in physical space, and remain in the same region of social space; or he may change regions in social space and not move in physical space.

The real object called a role, therefore, while located in physical space within the organism of a particular actor, is located in social space where that role fits into a system of other roles, some played by the same, and others by other actors. In social space the role is located as a part of a social position. The position consists of a set of roles all performed by a single actor toward a set of other actors who perform complementary roles. This complementary relationship establishes the contiguous location of the various positions forming the group.

Complementary role responses also constitute feedback among the positions and roles forming a group structure. When complementary responses received in social interaction constitute favorable feedback, as noted above, they maintain the role definitions; and when they are not favorable, they tend to change the role.

Obviously the role is changed only as a real actor learns new response patterns. The role cannot change in social space if it does not change in the minds of the actor or actors involved. The reverse is, of course, also true. One cannot change the way an actor defines his role

within his own personality, and not simultaneously change the definitions of the role in social space. The real roles in the minds of real men
are the same roles that are located in the structure of the group at
particular locations in social space. Therefore, as morphogenesis occurs
within the actor as a biological behavior system, it simultaneously occurs in the region of social space occupied by the role in question.

When we raise the scale of role morphogenesis to the level of the
entire group structure of which the role is a part, we must deal with
simultaneous and mutually interacting changes in role definitions of the
several actors who occupy contiguous regions of social space, and who
thereby constitute, through their actions, parts of a larger system, the
group.

Complementary role relationships require two different actors to
interact. The acts performed by one actor are thereby contingent upon
the acts performed by the other. Each, as he acts, receives feedback from
the reaction of the other. As a consequence, alterations in the role
performance of ego will necessarily produce alterations in the response
behavior of alter. As ego performs an unexpected or innovative act, alter
is forced to respond, and through his response, to furnish ego with
feedback for his behavior. While ego and alter are interacting, there is
no possibility that if ego acts, alter will not act. An actor cannot shut
off and go through a period of nonaction. Hesitating, withdrawing,
thinking, asking a question about what ego means by his behavior, are
all responses with feedback significance.

Given the fact that interaction involves morphogenic systems acting
and reacting in relationship to one another, it is reasonable to assume
that the changes in role content which represent morphogenesis in ego
and alter are not independent of each other. Instead, changes in the roles
of ego and alter are highly interdependent, and as a consequence the
structure of the group, as represented by the role definitions comprising
its component positions, constitutes morphogenic change at the level of
the whole group.

How are the parts of roles joined to form the whole role? and how
can one role be distinguished from another in terms of boundaries?
Roles, in their latent state, consist of norms in storage in the memories
of actors as learned behavioral prescriptions. The individual norms
comprising a role form a bounded set which can be identified in a
number of different ways. First, all of the norms comprising a single role
call for behavior that is related to the performance of a single function
or related set of functions in one group. Therefore, function is one
criterion for establishing role boundaries. In addition, the norms comprising a role call for behavior which is usually performed in a common
situation toward a given exact set of alter actors. Thus, the individual

norm comprising a role usually prescribes acts which occur close to one another in both physical time and space. As a consequence, situational elements also establish role boundaries.

The manner in which individual normative elements are related to form a whole role can best be described in spatial terms. It is our contention that they occur close to each other, in a common region of social space. Whenever two actors are interacting, the acts they perform toward each other are tangent in social space. This rule holds for all acts in a series of acts performed by two actors in interaction. If, for example, a series of acts, such as $A_xA_yA_z$, in the action stream of ego, are tangent to (performed in interaction with) a series of acts such as $A_aA_bA_c$ in the action stream of alter, then A_x must be close in social space to A_y, since both A_x and A_y are tangent to acts in alter's action stream. However, since ego and alter may shift the roles they are performing in a given interval of time, a second criterion, such as that of function, is required to establish role boundaries.

A third criterion for setting role boundaries and defining the relationship of normative elements may be derived from the fact that the norms associated with acts are in mental storage as a set. The evidence for this lies in the fact that the behaviors called for by a role are learned and performed as sets or sequences of acts that become mentally associated with one another. Thus, if one norm in the set is activated, other norms in the same set, being associated with one another, are also likely to be activated. This, of course, assumes that no additional factors intervene to trigger a new and different set of norms.

The norms forming a role are stored close to each other in the memories of the actors holding the role—that is, there are mental associational links among the elements of the set. It seems reasonable to argue that these norms are not only associated mentally with one another, but are also associated mentally with a given function in a group, a certain configuration of situational elements, and a certain set of behaviors on the part of given alter actors. Since the norms forming a role are associated mentally with each other and with common external referents, we are justified in thinking of a role as a bounded entity whose parts, norms, or acts are linked to one another.

Statuses form larger sets, which are comprised of roles as parts. The various roles forming a status are related to one another by the fact that they are all performed by a given actor (ego) toward a single alter actor or set of identical alter actors. This means that the roles comprising a status are all related to a common region in social space occupied by another person in the same group, and must themselves occupy a common region of social space. Again, mental storage and association may be used to describe relationships. All of the roles in a set called a status are associated with a given particular alter actor or type of alter actors.

Positions are formed of all of the roles, and therefore of all the statuses, held by a single actor in a single group. Their boundaries are established by the rule that each position in a group is occupied by a different actor, and by the rule that the position contains all of the behavior performed by the actor in a single group. As a consequence, positions are sets of roles whose parts are related because they are stored in or acted out by a given ego actor; they are defined by the criteria that establish group boundaries.

Groups, Organizations, and Communities

Act, norm, role, status, and position refer to the microstructure of social systems—the small parts of the behavior system called society. They furnish us with conceptual elements that allow us to describe and analyze social systems of enormous scale. In order to use them for this purpose, we have to conceive of a way that they can be combined to furnish concepts that refer to larger and larger parts of the social system. The key to solving this problem lies in devising concepts which refer, not to the parts of social systems themselves, but to their relationships.

We must, at any given level of system, above the smallest and below the largest scale, be able to move in either direction, and say how one particular part of that scale is made up of smaller parts, and is, itself, a part in a larger whole. Unless we are able to do this, we cannot check out what we know at one level against what seems to be true at another.

The secret to distinguishing the qualities and behavior of objects of different scale lies in understanding how they are organized or put together. The organization of the parts or elements in the whole creates qualities and processes not found in the parts considered separately. The group displays characteristics and processes which are different from the positions that make it up, or, in more imprecise terms, the actors who participate in it. This difference stems from the way the elements making up the group are combined into an organized whole. Since the key to climbing the ladder of scale is in understanding relationships among parts, and since this is also the key to understanding how large parts can be so different from their individual small elements, we must examine the problems of relationships.

Relationship Concepts

The basic concept of social relationship in our scheme is the idea of complementary roles. Complementarity in roles refers to a structural linkage between or among the roles played by two different actors, who habitually interact with one another in a repetitive or patterned fashion. That is to say, ego learns and performs a set of behaviors toward an alter actor, who has learned and performs matching or complementary response behavior. Thus, ego performs behavior which has meaning for alter, who responds in return with behavior that has meaning for ego. In the process, each is able to predict and understand and respond to the behavior of the other because they have learned complementary role expectations.

Complementary relationships therefore refer both to the stored pattern of interaction (complementary norms) and the performance of real interactive behaviors in a live on-going situation (complementary acts). Thus the relationship may exist in both an active and a latent state. Since complementarity exists between or among expectations, as well as among live actions, relationships among roles exist even when the roles are not being performed. The linkage among roles therefore does not disappear when behavior ceases, but continues as long as the expectations exist.

Complementary relationships thus operate to link roles which are a part of different positions; in behavior, they function as a guide to interaction. Potential or real interaction is basic to complementarity, and furnishes the cement which binds the parts of larger systems together.

The positions which form a group are linked by complementary role relationships that join a role in one position to a role in another. In examining these internal linkages, we found that such relationships vary in their span of activity, and in the complexity of their linkage to other roles in other positions. Nevertheless, we are able to define groups as systems in which every position is linked directly to every other one by one or more complementary role relationships. Such a definition makes a group a bounded entity, which, in almost every case, will be part of a larger system that also contains other groups. How are groups joined to one another across their boundaries to form these larger systems? Every group which is a part of a larger system must, by definition, be specialized in the functions it performs in the larger system. In other words, it must be a part of a division of labor, and depend upon other groups or larger social entities for things that it needs to operate.

In examining groups, we identified roles which were so constructed that the role player was forced to leave the group and occupy positions and play roles elsewhere, in order to be able to perform the behavior required of him inside the group. These extramural roles are a product of the division of labor, and are the key to how groups are linked to one another to form larger systems. An extramural role requires an actor who occupies a position in Group A also to occupy a position in another group, Group B. The fact that the same actor occupies positions in Groups A and B links these two groups to each other.

The extramural role in the position occupied by ego in Group A, his provider role, let us say, is linked specifically to a role he performs in Group B, his employee role. It is the role in Group B through which the output of that group leaves it and enters Group A as an input directly related to the extramural role. Let us say the actor is a welder, and fills a number of technical intramural roles in a work group. These roles are indirectly, not directly, related to his provider role. It is in his role as employee, through which he receives his pay envelope, and therefore through which the output of one group enters the other group as input, that the linkage exists.

There are two forms of complementarity—bilateral and reflexive. Bilateral relationships exist among roles performed by different actors occupying different positions in the same group. Reflexive relationships exist between positions occupied by the same actor in different groups. Once an actor, through his reflexive relationship, has externally obtained the necessary resources to perform his extramural role within the group, that role—for example, provider—is performed in bilateral relationships with others inside the group.

Groups are joined to their sociological environments through networks of reflexive relationships. These networks may be very complex, and the group may be included in a web of intricate input-output relations with other groups upon which it depends for various resources. The networks can also be quite simple. Every group which itself is not an entire society, however, will always contain extramural roles, and be linked to other groups through reflexive relationships.

Our criterion for group boundaries precludes one group's interacting as a whole with another, or one member of the group's acting as a representative for it and interacting with another group. If one person represents a group, and interacts with another person or persons who represent other groups, then this configuration of representatives forms a group in and of itself. On this basis, we identified two types of groups: elemental and interstitial.

Interstitial groups are comprised of people who represent elemental groups, in the sense that they have extramural roles in those groups that require them to obtain some resource or input from outside, but which they cannot do by becoming a member of the group which itself has the resource. The family needs groceries, but the housewife does not become an employee of the grocery store, and thus a member of that work group, to obtain them. Instead, she interacts with someone who represents that group in an interstitial group.

Two mechanisms are thus provided for joining elemental groups together to form larger systems. Groups A and B may be joined by sharing a member, as in the case of a family being joined through a reflexive relationship to the work group which employs the provider. A second way is for a representative of elemental Group A and a representative of elemental Group B to participate in a third or interstitial Group C. Between A and C there is direct member sharing, and therefore a reflexive relationship. Between B and C the same situation exists. Within all groups, A, B, and C, whether elemental or interstitial, the relationships are bilateral.

In each case extramural roles and reflexive relationships form the basis of the linkage, and create a network of real or potential interaction over which inputs and outputs flow among parts of the system. The actors, as open systems, occupying positions in groups which are open through extramural roles and reflexive relationships, provide the links that allow us to view groups and systems of groups as open morphogenic systems.

Complex Systems

Multigroup systems, in and of themselves, vary in size and complexity. Two types of multigroup systems are apparent in the real world. They are referred to by sociologists as "organizations" and "communities." They themselves are joined to form even larger entities through two forms of complementary relationships: reciprocal and conjunctive.

Reciprocal relationships exist among social units when those units are operating together to produce some common output, or set of outputs, which are exchanged with other social systems in their environment. They are like the ties which exist among the members of a team who are playing a game with another team. It is the team which wins or loses relatively or absolutely, and the members are expected by the natures of their roles to co-operate with one another. A conjunctive relationship is more like the relationship among two teams who are in a contest, except that it is not one of zero sum. That is, the teams may each win or lose relatively, but their successes or failures are not joint. In a conjunctive relationship each team needs something the other has in order to keep on playing its own game. The grocery store needs customers, the customers need food. Customers and grocers do not play as a common team, but must interact in order to obtain resources needed for their own operation.

What makes a relationship conjunctive or reciprocal is not the presence or absence of behavior called conflict or co-operation. The real interaction that takes place in either form of relationship may be of either sort. The differentiating factor lies in the nature of the division of labor among the units thus related. Reciprocal relationships exist among social units that are producing a common output using a set of common inputs. Structurally they are parts of a common subsystem, in which each part has a specific and more or less permanent linkage to specific other parts that are obligated to furnish it with inputs, and to receive outputs from it. Furthermore, in reciprocal relationships all units thus joined are subject to the same authority structure. In a sense they all report to the same boss. Of course, some reciprocally-related parts may form a system in which the authority structure is quite hierarchical and bureaucratic, while others may be parts of a system with a more diffuse and democratic authority structure. Nevertheless, in reciprocal relationships, the parts are so related that they are more or less permanently bound together by specific linkages, oriented toward producing common outputs, and co-ordinated in their behavior by a common authority structure.

In conjunctive relationships, the units are more autonomous in the sense that they are producing separate and distinct functions. They are interdependent, however, in the sense that they need inputs and outputs furnished by the other social unit which is different in function from themselves. Furthermore, in conjunctive relationships one unit is only temporarily and voluntarily associated with the other. There is no mandatory, permanent linkage that requires one unit to accept inputs only from the other, and to send outputs only to that other group. In addition, the authority structures that regulate and coordinate the behaviors of members of the two social units are separate and distinct.

Organizations, which may be either traditional or formal, are systems comprised of groups joined by reciprocal relationships. Communities are systems whose parts are joined by conjunctive relationships. Conflict and co-operation, as forms of real social interaction, may take place in either type of system. In reciprocal relationships, conflict will usually take place over whether or not one person is performing his behavior properly in relation to the common effort, or over what means should be pursued to accomplish the common end, or over what the common output should be. In conjunctive relationships, the conflict usually involves disputes over the fairness or unfairness of the exchange that is taking place among systems, or over the rules which may give advantage to one system over another. Both conflict and co-operation are possible and even likely in both kinds of relationships. However, in reciprocal relationships the role definitions and group structures are designed to produce co-operation in the production of a common output; in conjunctive relationships, they are designed to control conflict in the interest of permitting an exchange to take place.

Reciprocal relationships are a product of the division of labor within a group or organization. Conjunctive relationships are the product of the division of labor in the community or society that separates groups and organizations from each other, and makes them more or less autonomous. The division of labor in society specializes social units in the functions they perform, and at the same time creates a linkage system that joins them together through a system of exchange relationships. In such a system of relationships the various specialized units are interdependent, but they are not specifically linked to one another in a fixed system of structural linkage. Thus, families need grocery stores and are dependent on them for needed inputs. But a given family is not permanently and exclusively linked to one and only one store. Instead, a system of alternative linkages, which are conjunctive in nature, exists which may potentially satisfy the family's need for inputs.

Communities are systems whose parts are linked exclusively by conjunctive relationships. This means that between and among parts of varying sizes, both bilateral and reflexive conjunctive relationships among persons at the level of the social relationship form the linking mechanisms. Interstitial groups exist both within organizations, and between organizations and groups in the community. However, within organizations the bilateral relationships among members of interstitial groups are reciprocal, and within interstitial groups between organizations in the community the relationships are all conjunctive.

Summary

It can be seen that we need only a very limited number of parts and relationship to conceive of an entire society. A society, to us, is an nth-order community, that is, a community that contains long chains of indirect conjunctive linkages among parts. In form, society is therefore like a community, except that it is a community of maximum size, given the boundaries reached by conjunctive relationships. There is really only one society today on the planet Earth, made up of all nations as communities of a lower order, which themselves contain even smaller communities.

The parts of social systems of societal size vary in scale from the micro units of act and norm, to the macro units of society or culture.

Each unit is defined as based on the next smaller unit as elements* which are joined by a relationship system to form the whole. These units are shown in the table below.

Social Units

Active State	*Latent State*
Act	Norm
Role	Role definition
Status	Status definition
Position	Position definition
Group	Group subculture
Organization	Organization subculture
Community	Community subculture
Society	Culture

Complementary relationships in the system are of two distinct types—reciprocal and conjunctive. The first explains how roles, statuses, and positions are joined to form social units. The second explains how positions, groups, organizations, and communities are joined to form social units of ever-increasing scale. The reciprocal relationships are essentially social-psychological, in that the norms or acts that form a role are joined as a unit within the personalities of the actors who contain the role or occupy the position. Ultimately it is the fact that the behaviors are learned as a set, and are therefore stored and recalled as a set, and also are performed in sequences which correspond to the set, that justifies thinking of the parts of roles, statuses, and positions as being joined to or related to one another.

The relationship concepts used for social systems of varying orders of scale all involve forms of social relationships. To date, we have found it necessary to define only four different kinds.

Forms of Complementary Social Relationships

1. Reciprocal
   a. Bilateral
   b. Reflexive
2. Conjunctive
   a. Bilateral
   b. Reflexive

Classes of social units are what generate various forms of relationships. Thus, reflexive relationships involve extramural and intramural roles. To maintain a conception of group boundaries we need two forms of social groups, elemental and interstitial; the interstitial group is what

*The exception is a community of less than nth-order. In such communities, parts of organizations, rather than whole organizations, may be regarded as units or parts.

links elemental groups into larger systems. Two types of interstitial groups exist—exchange and coordinative interstitial groups. When elemental groups and these types of interstitial groups are cross-classified with the forms of social relationships, we have a list of five types of groups out of which whole societies may be constructed.

Type of Group	Where Found
1. Elemental groups	Alone, or within organizations
2. Reciprocal co-ordinative interstitial groups	Within organizations, or between elemental groups
3. Reciprocal exchange interstitial groups	Within organizations, or between elemental groups
4. Conjunctive co-ordinative interstitial groups	Between organizations, or independent elemental groups within a community of x-order
5. Conjunctive exchange interstitial groups	Between organizations, or independent elemental groups within a community of x-order

Of course, any one of the above group forms, when combined with a particular behavioral content and classified by the type of function performed by the behavior, can be further subdivided into subclasses. Thus, it can be argued that there are four types of elemental groups found in organizations: (1) management or supervisory groups; (2) production groups; (3) service groups, and (4) maintenance groups. Or, it could be argued in more traditional terms that there are line and staff subtypes.

These subclassifications of groups do not help us understand how a large system is put together out of smaller parts, and in this sense, they are unnecessary to the task of building a structural model. What they do do for us is to flesh out the model in terms of content, for they are more related to the way the system functions than to the way it is put together.

Our primary purpose in this book was to provide a systematic means of conceiving of whole societies using concepts which could be defined at the first level of abstraction and checked against observation. A secondary objective was to co-ordinate these concepts with the conception of the person as an actor, and thereby to provide a means of conceiving of how people fit into societies. This involved introducing two concepts that relate to the person's participation in organizations and in society as a whole—situs and station.

Situs refers to the set of positions occupied by an actor in an organization. It is, in Merton's terms, a position-set—but of a particular sort. The parts of a situs, the positions, are joined by reflexive reciprocal relationships, and its boundaries are established by the criteria which establish boundaries for an organization.

Stations consist of situses as parts. These parts are joined by reflexive conjunctive relationships. As a whole, the station consists of all of the latent and active behavior performed by one person in society. It corresponds to the total person as an actor in the largest social system in which he participates.

The person does not fit into society as a unit which can be located at one and only one point in the social system. Instead, the person is distributed among groups, a part of him or his behavior belonging to each. It is therefore incorrect to think of whole people as belonging to groups or organizations, or of whole people interacting with one another. Furthermore, it is immediately apparent that the whole person, as represented by his station, is an object of larger scale and duration than the acts observed to occur at one point in social space. To conceive of the whole person, it is therefore necessary to construct a model which stands for that person in our thought about him.

What then of social stratification? We conclude that stratification systems constitute the mechanisms through which a person's station structure is built as he progresses through the life cycle. Societies and their constituent parts do not contain strata, but instead they relate people in complementary relationships which afford varying amounts of honor, wealth, and power. Stratification systems limit or control access to such relationships, and determine the processes whereby stations are constructed. This is the same thing as saying they allocate people to positions and roles in the structure of groups and organizations in society. The allocative mechanisms that constitute the stratification system are inherent in the way the whole social system is organized, and in the norms that are distributed unevenly in that organization. This, however, is a far cry from conceiving of the structure of the system as containing social strata.

As for institutions, we define them as functional subsystems which are comprised of the same content as the content which comprises the whole society. We reject the notion that whole groups and organizations can be viewed as parts of institutions. Instead, we view institutions and their structure as systems comprised of roles as parts, where every role is related to the performance of one homogeneous requisite function for society. Furthermore, every organization and detached group in society must have a part of each institution contained within it. Thus each such unit receives inputs and produces outputs related to each vital function for the society.

CHAPTER 24   EPILOGUE

Since the time of Comte and Spencer, sociologists have focused their interest on society, which they have defined as being made up of groups, organizations, and communities linked in an intricate network of relationships. But sociologists have always lacked a systematic way to explain how social units like groups, organizations, and communities are constructed out of smaller parts, and how they are linked to one another to form a larger whole. Vague general statements about parts and linkages are inadequate. The model presented in this book is admittedly not perfect; nevertheless, it does clarify some of the problems we face in conceiving of society as a system. These are to identify social units; state how they are constructed out of smaller parts; denote how they are joined together to form larger units; and explain how feedback and morphogenesis operate. These tasks are essential to sociology, and our model is one way to meet them.

The strength of a structural model such as ours lies in its general applicability to all forms of social systems, no matter what their content or level of complexity. It also has the advantage of defining the structure of large and complex systems in terms of an observable scale. Using our model, one may observe portions of society, or portions of organizations and set these observations in a structural context with other observations made on the same system.

A structural model also makes it possible to think systematically about the structure of society and about the individual's participation in it. It furnishes a basis for testing and evaluating the probable accuracy of other theories and models, for it allows us to say that if it accurately represents the way societies are put together and the way they function, then certain things must be true and other things untrue, and that some theories and concepts work, and others do not.

Our model, furthermore, refutes the idea that society is a static, architectural system of social relationships; instead, we perceive it as a system of pulsating, moving, ever-changing behavior patterns that flow through the system, co-ordinated with time and space.

Yet another strength of the model is that it integrates systems theory and the symbolic interactionist perspective, using one to support and supplement the other. It accounts for interpersonal conflict and deviance in behavior without having to introduce contradictory assumptions, and without having to ignore conflict and deviation on the basis that social systems are configurations of integrated co-operating individuals.

Because the model defines larger complex systems using concepts that are amenable to direct observation, it does have a number of weaknesses—especially when it comes to mass phenomena like political and social movements, conflicts, and audience behavior and public opinion. Furthermore, since we regard all behavior as the product of a combination of simultaneously operating, mutually interacting influences, we are hard put to deal with such phenomena as decision making and choice, at least in a manner which will satisfy humanists.

Although we consider both thought and feeling are forms of behavior, our model is much more efficient and more easily applied to overt action. The major problem is that there is not an adequate methodology for making direct observations of human behavior in live, natural settings. What methodology there is is most highly developed in the areas of interviews and questionnaires, and in the manipulation of verbal responses to these instruments to create scales and measures. Even statistical methods designed to test hypotheses are oriented toward this type of data, and are rarely used on observational material. Because of this fact, we seem to have created a model for which an adequate methodology does not exist. Our defense is to reply that our model reveals the glaring weaknesses in current methodology and theory, which we think have been and are being used to answer the wrong questions about society. Sociology needs to move more in the direction of ethnological research, perhaps even toward "ethnomethodology." Sociologists cannot hope to understand what they have not observed directly, personally, and rigorously. We must become more like naturalists in our approach to our subject matter, and less like political pollsters content to predict behavior, or to reduce the unexplained variance in our secondary source material.

Our model requires great attention to detailed observation, and therefore great labor. To describe a whole society in its terms is virtually impossible, and so is describing even one group in all of its richness of detail. No one should ever attempt to apply this model at once to social objects even on a small scale. Instead, it should be used to derive hypotheses to test critical aspects of the model. Testing a series of hypotheses about the way extramural roles operate, for instance, would permit us to learn more about how groups are linked together to form larger systems. Or, carefully examining interstitial groups in communities and comparing them to interstitial groups in organizations on one or more carefully selected dimensions would test the validity of the distinction between conjunctive and reciprocal relationships, and simultaneously reveal a good deal about how organizations and communities are alike or different.

Whether or not our model is superior to others is ultimately a matter of usefulness, and that question will remain unanswered for some time to come. It certainly ought not to be rejected simply because it defines concepts in a new way, or because its assumptions are morally or ethically repugnant to individual sociologists. It is undoubtedly defective, because it is based on complex logical processes and limited empirical evidence. Nonetheless, it does show the need for a series of detailed models of social systems defined so that they show the interrelationships between social objects of all scales and contents are both logical and consistent.

REFERENCES

Chapter 1

1. Miriam Glucksmann. *Structuralist Analysis in Contemporary Social Thought, A Comparison of the Theories of Claude Levi-Strauss and Louis Althusser.* London: Routledge and Kegan Paul, 1974, 8.

2. Edmund Leach. *Claude Levi-Strauss.* New York: The Viking Press, 1970; Claude Levi-Strauss, *Structural Anthropology.* Garden City, New York: Anchor Press, 1967.

3. Talcott Parsons. *The Social System.* New York: The Free Press, 1951, pp. 132–53.

4. George Homans, *The Nature of Social Science.* New York: Harcourt, Brace, 1967.

5. Thomas S. Kuhn, *The Structure of Scientific Revolutions.* Chicago: The University of Chicago Press, 1970.

6. Kuhn, 1970, 15.

7. Robert W. Friedrichs. *A Sociology of Sociology.* New York: The Free Press, 1972, 11–56.

8. Herbert Blumer. *Symbolic Interactionism: Perspective and Method.* Englewood Cliffs, New Jersey: Prentice-Hall, 1969.

9. Lewis A. Coser, *The Functions of Social Conflict.* Glencoe, Illinois: The Free Press, 1956; Ralf Dahrendorf, "Out of Utopia: Toward a Reorientation of Sociological Analysis," *The American Journal of Sociology* 44 (1958), 115–27.

10. Glucksmann, 1974.

11. Parsons, 1951.

12. Robert K. Merton, *Social Theory and Social Structure.* New York: The Free Press, 1949, 21–81.

13. Lee Freese. "Cumulative Sociological Knowledge," *American Sociological Review,* 37 (1972), 472–82.

14. Walter Buckley. *Sociology and Modern Systems Theory.* Englewood Cliffs, New Jersey: Prentice-Hall, Inc., 1967, 42–45; George C. Homans. "Bringing Men Back In," *American Sociological Review,* 29 (1964), 809–18.

15. W. I. Thomas. *Primitive Behavior.* New York: McGraw-Hill, 1937, 8.

16. Edward E. Sampson. *Social Psychology and Contemporary Society,* New York: John Wiley and Sons, Inc., 1971, 14, 112, 114.

Calvin S. Hall and Gardner Lindzey. *Theories of Personality.* New York: John Wiley and Sons, Inc., 1957, 480, 488, 498.

Arthur W. Combs and Donald Snygg. *Individual Behavior: A Perceptual Approach to Behavior.* New York: Harper and Row, 1959, 21.

17. James G. Miller, "Toward a General Theory for the Behavioral Sciences," *American Psychologist,* 10 (1955), 513–531.

Talcott Parsons. "The Prospects of Sociological Theory," *Essays in Sociological Theory*, Rev. Ed. New York: The Free Press, 1964, 348–369.

Alex Inkeles. *What Is Sociology?* Englewood Cliffs, New Jersey: Prentice-Hall, Inc., 1964, 28–46.

David Willer, *Scientific Sociology: Theory and Method.* Englewood Cliffs, New Jersey: Prentice-Hall, Inc., 1967, 15–21.

Chapter 2

1. Richard and Fernande DeGeorge (eds.). *The Structuralists From Marx to Levi-Strauss.* New York: Doubleday and Company, Inc., 1972, xxv–xxvi.

Jacques Ehrmann (ed.). *Structuralism.* New York: Doubleday and Company, Inc., 1970, 1–4.

Marion J. Levy. *The Structure of Society.* Princeton, New Jersey: Princeton University Press, 1952, 57–58, 114–15.

Siegfried F. Nadel. *The Theory of Social Structure.* London: Cohen and West, 1957, 149–50, 7.

2. John Rex, *Key Problems of Sociological Theory.* London: Routledge and Kegan Paul, 1961, 60–77.

Kingsley Davis, "The Myth of Functional Analysis as a Special Method in Sociology and Anthropology," *American Sociological Review,* 24 (December, 1959), 757.

Ralf Dahrendorf. *Essays in the Theory of Society.* Stanford, California: Stanford University Press, 1968, 118 ff.

3. Walter Buckley, *Sociology and Modern Systems Theory.* 1967, 58–66. Englewood Cliffs, New Jersey: Prentice-Hall, Inc., 1967, 58–66.

4. Talcott Parsons and Edward A. Shils (ed.). *Toward a General Theory of Action.* Cambridge, Mass.: Harvard University Press, 1951.

5. Roland J. Pellegrin. "The Nature and Characteristics of Sociology," in R. W. O'Brien, C. C. Schrag and W. T. Martin, *Readings in General Sociology,* Boston: Houghton Mifflin Company, 1964, 7–11.

6. Nadel, 1957, 128–29, 145.

Carl G. Hempel. "The Logic of Functional Analysis," *Symposium on Sociological Theory,* ed. Liewellyn Gross. Evanston, Ill.: Row, Peterson and Co., 1959, 278.

7. Lester F. Ward. *Outlines of Sociology.* New York: The MacMillan Company, 1913, 168–79.

Nicholas S. Timasheff, *Sociological Theory: Its Nature and Growth.* New York: Doubleday and Company, Inc., 1955, 22–23.

8. Buckley, 1967, 17–23; Nadel, 1957, 128–34.

Chapter 3

1. Wsevolod W. Isajiw. *Causation and Functionalism in Sociology.* New York: Schocken Books, 1968, 125–29; Buckley, 1967, 66–80; Robert K. Merton. *Social Theory and Social Structure.* New York: The Free Press, 1957, 21; Parsons, 1951, 537.

2. F. Kenneth Berrien. *General and Social Systems.* New Brunswick, N.J.: The Rutgers University Press, 1968, 14–15; Buckley, 1967, 41; Claude Levi-Strauss. *Structural Anthropology.* New York: Doubleday, 1967, 271–72; Charles P. Loomis and Zona K. Loomis. *Modern Social Theories.* New York: Van Nostrand, 1961, 444; Charles P. Loomis, *Social System.* New York: Van Nostrand, 1960, 4; Parsons and Shils, 1951, 107.

3. Buckley, 1967, 68, 78, 36–40.

4. Parsons, 1951, 68.

5. Buckley, 1967, 68; Robert M. MacIver. *Social Causation.* New York: Ginn, 1942.

6. Blumer, 1969, 6–7.

7. John J. Honigmann. *Understanding Culture*. New York: Harper and Row, 1963, 2–3; Pitirim A. Sorokin. *Society, Culture and Personality*. New York: American Book, 1941, 313; Eli Chinoy. *Society*. New York: Random House, 1967, 26; Ralph Linton. *The Study of Man*. New York: Appleton-Century, 1936, 275.

8. Raymond Firth. *Elements of Social Organization*. London: Watts and Co., 1961, 35–40; Robin M. Williams. *American Society*. New York: Knopf, 1960, 20.

9. W.I. Thomas. *Primitive Behavior*. New York: McGraw-Hill, 1937, 8.

Chapter 4

1. Talcott Parsons. *The Structure of Social Action*. Glencoe, Ill.: The Free Press, 1949, 43ff; 731; 737–38; 749; 769.

2. Homans, 1964, 809–18.

3. Roger G. Barker. *The Stream of Behavior*. New York: Appleton-Century-Crofts, 1963; Roger G. Barker and Herbert F. Wright. *One Boy's Day*. New York: Harper and Brothers Publishers, 1951.

4. Barker and Wright, 1951, 9–10; William G. Sumner. *Folkways*. Boston: Ginn and Co., 1913, 34–35.

5. Jacques Ehrmann (ed.). *Structuralism*. Garden City, New York: Doubleday and Company, Inc., 1970, 1–9.

6. John Rex, *Key Problems of Sociological Theory*. London: Routledge and Kegan Paul, 1961, 65–70.

Isajiw, 1968, p. 14; 72–73; pp. 87–88.

Marion J. Levy. *The Structure of Society*. Princeton, N.J.: Princeton University Press, 1952, quoted in Don Martindale, *The Nature and Types of Sociological Theory*. Boston: Houghton Mifflin Company, 1960, 490.

Bronislaw Malinowski. *A Scientific Theory of Culture and Other Essays*. Chapel Hill, N. C.: The University of North Carolina Press, 1944, 83; 48; 53–54.

A. R. Radcliff-Brown. *A Natural Science of Society*. Glencoe, Ill.: Free Press, 1951, 85.

A. R. Radcliff-Brown. "Functionalism: A Protest," *American Anthropologist*, 51 (1949) 32; Kingsley Davis. "The Myth of Functional Analysis as a Special Method in Sociology and Anthropology," *American Sociological Review*, 24 (December) 1959).

7. Merton, 1957, 23–25; Isajiw, 1968, 27–28, 74;

A. R. Radcliff-Brown, "On the Concept of Function in Social Science." Bobbs-Merrill Reprint Series in the Social Sciences, No. 227, 304–402.

Chapter 5

1. W. G. Sumner, 1913, 17–114.

George A. Lundberg, Clarence C. Schrag, et al. *Sociology* (4th ed.). New York: Harper and Row, Publishers, 1968, 67.

Russell Middleton and Snell Putney. "Religion, Normative Standards and Behavior," *Sociometry*, 25 (1962), 141–52.

Leonard Broom and Philip Selznick. *Principles of Sociology*. New York: Harper and Row, 1970, 54–55.

2. Elihu Katz and Paul Lazarsfeld. *Personal Influence: The Part Played by People in the Flow of Mass Communications*. New York: The Free Press, 1955, 60–65.

International Encyclopedia of the Social Sciences, David Sills (ed.). New York: MacMillan, 1968, Vol. 11, 205.

3. Linton, 1936, 271–87.

4. Linton, 1936, Chapter 16.

5. E. T. Hiller. *Social Relations and Structure*. New York: Harper and Brothers, 1947, 87–88, 93, 95; Sorokin, 1962, 539.

6. Ralf Dahrendorf. "Out of Utopia: Toward a Reorientation of Sociological Analysis," *Essays in the Theory of Society*. Stanford, California: Stanford University Press, 1968, 122–25.

7. B. F. Skinner. *Beyond Freedom and Dignity*. New York: Alfred A. Knopf, 1971.

8. B. F. Skinner. *The Behavior of Organisms*. New York: Appleton-Century, 1938.

9. Gerald R. Leslie, Richard F. Larson, and Benjamin L. Gorman. *Order and Change*. New York: Oxford University Press, 1973, 250.

F. J. Roethlisberger and W. J. Dickson. *Management and the Worker*. Cambridge, Mass.: Harvard University Press, 1939, 423.

Chapter 6

1. Sorokin, 1962, 359–60.

2. Pitirim Sorokin. *Social and Cultural Mobility*. Glencoe, Ill. Free Press, 1959, 4–6; Kingsley Davis. *Human Society*, New York: The MacMillan Company, 1948, 94.

3. Judson R. Landis. *Sociology: Concepts and Characteristics*. Belmont, California: Wadsworth Publishing Co., Inc., 1971; Robert Bierstedt. *The Social Order*. New York: McGraw-Hill Book Company, Inc., 1957, 175; Lundberg, Schrag, *et al.*, 1968, 12; Ronald G. Cowin. *A Sociology of Education*. New York: Appleton-Century-Crofts, 1965, 64; Alan F. Jansen. *Sociology: Concepts and Concerns*. Chicago: Rand McNally, 1971, 106; Everett K. Wilson. *Sociology: Rules, Roles, and Relationships*. Homewood, Ill.: The Dorsey Press, 1966, 63.

4. Ragnar Rommetveit. *Social Norms and Roles*. Minneapolis: University of Minnesota Press, 1954, 65–78.

5. Linton, 1936, 113–14; Hiller, 1947. Rights, 224, 243; duties, 2, 11, 24, 48, 56, 81, 84, 97, 108, 115, 128, 157, 186, 196, 199.

6. Bronislaw Malinowski. *Crime and Custom in Savage Society*. London: Routledge and Kegan Paul, Ltd., 39–45.

7. Rommeteit, 1954, 21.

8. Hiller, 1947, 331–34; Linton, 1936, 113–14; Logan Wilson and William L. Kolb (eds.). *Sociological Analysis*. New York: Harcourt, Brace and Company, 1949, 208.

9. We have chosen not to present an historical analysis of the concepts of position, status, and role, and we have also not discussed how our formulations differ from those of others, in order to present our own conceptual scheme without diverting the reader's attention. However, we do refer the interested reader to the several reviews of role theory available in the literature. Theodore R. Sarbin and Ralph H. Turner present an excellent overview in Volume 13 of the *International Encyclopedia of the Social Sciences*. An exhaustive treatment of role theory may be found in Bruce J. Biddle and Edwin J. Thomas, *Role Theory: Concepts and Research* (Wiley, 1966.) Another excellent discussion of problems in role theory is given in Michael Banton, *Roles: An Introduction to the Study of Social Relations* (Basic Books, 1965).

The usages of the three terms *role, status,* and *position* vary a great deal. The ones closest to ours are Robert K. Merton—see Chapter IX of the revised edition of *Social Theory and Social Structure* (The Free Press, 1957)—and those in Neal Gross, Ward S. Mason, and Alexander W. McEachern, *Explorations in Role Analysis* (Wiley, 1958). These two sources may be compared with Frederick L. Bates, "Position, Role and Status: A Reformulation of Concepts," *Social Forces*, 34 (1956), 313–21.

Each of the three approaches defines these concepts slightly differently, but all recognize the necessity of dealing with the multiplicity of roles associated with a single position in the structure of a social system. This multiple-role approach makes it possible to deal with complex systems of relationships, so that we are no longer restricted to analyzing dyads, as we were by the traditional definitions of these concepts.

Chapter 7

1. Bruce J. Biddle and Edwin J. Thomas (eds.). *Role Theory: Concepts and Research*. New York: Wiley, 1966, 29–32; Parsons, 1951, 38–39; Linton, 1936, 113; Leonard S. Cottrell, Jr. "The Adjustment of the Individual to His Age and Sex Roles," *American Sociological Review*, 7(1942), 617, reprinted in Theodore M. Newcomb and Eugene L. Hartley (eds.). *Readings in Social Psychology*. New York: Holt and Co., 1947; Theodore R. Sarbin, "Role Theory," in Gardner Lindzey (ed.). *Handbook of Social Psychology*. Cambridge, Mass: Addison-Wesley, 1954, I, 225; Loomis, 1969, 19; Hiller, 1947, 224; Merton, 1957, 368–69; Nadel, 1957, 23; Leslie, Larson, and Gorman, 1973, 121–22; Florian Znaniecki. *Social Relations and Social Roles*. San Francisco: Chandler Publishing Company, 1965, 201–06.

2. Linton, 1936, 104.

3. Ralph Linton. *The Cultural Background of Personality*. New York: Appleton-Century, 1945, 113; Hiller, 1947, *passim;* Davis, 1948, 90–91; Sumner, 1960, 85–87.

4. Nadel, 1957, 23–31; Neal Gross, Ward S. Mason, and Alexander W. McEachern. *Explorations in Role Analysis*. New York: Wiley and Sons, 1958, 62, 67.

5. C. Wright Mills. *White Collar*. New York: Oxford University Press, 1956, 207.

6. Nadel, 1957, 35; Merton, 1957, 64–66.

Chapter 8

1. Earle A. Eubank. *The Concepts of Sociology*. Boston: D. C. Heath, 1932, 116–17; Charles Cooley. *Social Organization*. Glencoe, Ill.: Free Press, 1956, 23, 26–27; Leonard Broom and Philip Selznick. *Sociology*. New York: Harper and Row, 1968, 124–25; Bierstedt, 1957, 129–54; C. K. Warriner. *The Emergence of Society*. Ill.: The Dorsey Press, 1970, 15.

2. Frederick L. Bates. "A Conceptual Analysis of Group Structure, *Social Forces* (December, 1957), 103–11.

3. Merton, 1957, 368–84; Biddle and Thomas, 1966, 4, 65; Nadel, 1957, 70–71; Hiller, 1947, 340–41.

4. Sheila Cunnison. *Wages of Work Allocation*. London: Tavistock Publications, 1966.

5. Frederick L. Bates, "Institutions, Organizations, and Communities: A General Theory of Complex Structures," *The Pacific Sociological Review*, III (Fall, 1960), 59–70.

6. Bates, 1960.

7. George C. Homans. *The Human Group*. New York: Harcourt, Brace and World, 1950, Chapter 4, and 109; Roethlisberger and Dickson, 1939, 422–23.

8. Sorokin, 1959, 3–5.

9. Roger Barker (ed.). *The Stream of Behavior*. New York: Appleton-Century-Crofts, 1963.

Chapter 10

1. H. H. Gerth and C. Wright Mills (eds.). *From Max Weber: Essays in Sociology*. New York: Oxford University Press, 1946, 196–204; James Thompson and F. L. Bates, "Technology, Organization and Administration," *Administrative Science Quarterly*, 2 (December, 1959), 325–43.

2. *Situs* was first used by Emile Benoit-Smullyan, "Status, Status Types, and Status Interrelations," *American Sociological Review*, 9 (1944), 152–54. He used the term to refer to a person's membership in a social category or reference group, and not as a cluster of social positions. We took the word from Smullyan and changed its meaning. The dictionary defines it as "the place where something exists or originates."

3. Both situs and station refer to types of "status-sets"; see Merton, 1957, 369–81. In a sense, *station* is like the total status-set of an individual, and *situs* is like the status-set of an individual in a single organization.

Chapter 11

1. James D. Thompson. *Organizations in Action,* New York: McGraw-Hill Book Company, 1967; Thompson and Bates, 1959.

2. George C. Homans. *Social Behavior: Its Elementary Forms.* New York: Harcourt, Brace, 1961; Peter M. Blau. *Exchange and Power in Social Life.* New York: John Wiley and Sons, Inc., 1964; Alvin W. Gouldner. "The Norm of Reciprocity: A Preliminary Statement," *American Sociological Review,* 25 (1960), 161–78.

3. Peter Singelmann. "Exchange as Symbolic Interaction: Convergences Between Two Theoretical Perspectives," *American Sociological Review,* 37 (1972), 414–24.

4. Blau, 1964.

5. Gerth and Mills, 1946, 51–55, 196–244; Leslie, Larson, and Gorman, 1973, 308–11.

6. Charles J. Dudley and Dennis R. Keefe. *The Transformation of Family Behavior Systems.* Mimeographed, 1973.

7. Elizabeth Bott. *Family and Social Network.* London: Tavistock Publications, 1957.

8. Rudolf Heberle, "The Normative Element in Neighborhood Relations," *The Pacific Sociological Review,* 3 (Spring 1960) 3–11.

9. Bott, 1957, 58–61.

10. Gerth and Mills 1946, Chapter 8;

Peter M. Blau. *The Dynamics of Bureaucracy.* Chicago: The University of Chicago Press, 1955.

Chapter 12

1. Thompson and Bates, 1959.

Frederick L. Bates. "The Impact of Automation on Organization of Society," in Ellis Scott and Roger Bolz, *Automation and Society,* Athens, Georgia: The Center for the Study of Automation and Society, 1969.

2. Charles J. Dudley, Frederick L. Bates and Harold L. Nix. "Community Power Structure: A Structural Approach," presented at the Southern Sociological Society, 1966.

3. Blau, 1964; Homans, 1961.

4. Thompson, 1967.

5. Davis, 1948, 48–49, 94–95.

Chapter 13

1. George A. Hillery, Jr. "Definitions of Community: Areas of Agreement," *Rural Sociology,* 20 (June, 1955).

2. Ferdinand Tonnies. *Community and Society (Gemeinschaft und Gesellschaft).* Charles P. Loomis (ed.). New York: Harper and Row, Publishers, 1957.

3. Irwin T. Sanders. *The Community.* New York: The Ronald Press Company, 1966. Sanders defines a community "as a territorially organized system coextensive with a settlement pattern in which (1) an effective communication network operates, (2) people share common facilities and services distributed within this settlement pattern, and (3) people develop a psychological identification with the 'locality symbol' (the name)."

Dorothy and Curtis Mial, "Ways of Looking at the Community," in *Our Community* New York: New York University Press, 1960. "A community is *a geographic area* where people cluster together and have more to do with each other than with people outside the cluster."

4. Eugene P. Odum. *Ecology.* New York: Holt, Rinehart and Winston, 1963.

5. Amos H. Hawley. *Human Ecology: A Theory of Community Structure.* The Ronald Press Company, 1950, 3, 33–36, 41, 55; Amos H. Hawley, in Roderick D. McKenzie's *On Human Ecology.* Chicago: The University of Chicago Press, 1968. The whole idea of metropolitan

dominance and subdominance is similar to the ideas presented in this chapter on orders of communities.

6. Harold F. Kaufman. "Toward an Interactional Conception of Community," *Social Forces*, 38 (October, 1959). "The community is a set of locality-oriented interactions: as goal-directed processes engendered by the fact of people's common residence in a locality."

Joseph Bensman and Bernard Rosenberg. *Mass, Class, and Bureaucracy*. Englewood Cliffs, New Jersey: Prentice-Hall, 1963. "The community is a relatively permanent grouping of individuals, families, and institutions, occupying a given territory, and bound by legal or customary ties, and all that they imply."

7. Merton, 1957. Community: "collectivities—people who have a sense of solidarity by virtue of sharing common values and who have acquired an attendant sense of moral obligation to fulfill role expectations."

Chapter 15

1. Merton, 1957, 369.
2. Benoit-Smullyan, 1944, 151–61;
Frederick L. Bates. *The Structure of Occupations: A Role Theory Approach*. Raleigh, North Carolina: Center for Occupational Education at North Carolina State University at Raleigh, 1968, 59–78.
3. Hiller, 1947, 341; Davis, 1948, 91.

Chapter 16

1. Henry A. Murray and Clyde Kluckhohn. "Outline of a Conception of Personality," in Clyde Kluckhohn and H. A. Murray (eds.). *Personality in Nature, Society and Culture*. New York: Alfred A. Knopf, 1949, 7–12.
2. Linton, 1936, 464.
3. Merton, 1957, 282–83.
4. Charles H. Cooley. *Human Nature and the Social Order*. New York: Charles Scribner's Sons, 1902, 152; George H. Mead. *Mind, Self, and Society*. Charles W. Morris (ed.). Chicago: University of Chicago Press, 1934.
5. Seymour M. Berger and William W. Lambert, "Stimulus-Response Theory in Contemporary Social Psychology," in Gardner Lindzey and Elliot Aronson (eds.). *The Hand Book of Social Psychology*, 1968, I, 81–177.
6. Melvin H. Marx and William A. Hillis. *System and Theories in Psychology*. New York: McGraw-Hill Book Company, Inc., 1963, 171–200.
7. Skinner, 1965, 53.
8. Skinner, 1965, 65.
9. Sigmund Freud, *The Basic Writings of Sigmund Freud*, translated and edited by Dr. A. A. Brill. New York: Random House, Inc., 1938, 228, 536, 121.
10. Vernon L. Allen, "Role Theory and Consistency Theory", in Robert P. Abelson *et al.* (eds.). *Theories of Cognitive Consistency: A Sourcebook*. Chicago: Rand McNally and Company, 1968, 201–09.
11. Herbert A. Simon. *The Sciences of the Artificial*. Cambridge, Mass.: The M.I.T. Press, 34 ff.

Chapter 17

1. August B. Hollingshead. *Elmtown's Youth.* New York: John Wiley and Sons, Inc., 1949, 288–325.
2. W. Lloyd Warner. *Social Life of a Modern Community.* New Haven: Yale University Press, 1941.

Chapter 18

1. Robert F. Winch. *The Modern Family.* New York: Holt, Rinehart and Winston, Inc., 1963, 17–26.
2. Talcott Parsons. *Structure and Process in Modern Societies.* Glencoe, Illinois: The Free Press, 1960, 98–131.
3. Bronislaw Malinowski. "The Group and the Individual in Functional Analysis," *American Journal of Sociology,* 39 (1944), 938–64.
4. D. F. Aberle *et al.* "The Functional Requisites of a Society," *Ethics,* 60 (1950), 100–11.
5. W. F. Ogburn. *Social Change.* New York: B. W. Huebsch, Inc., 1922, 200–01.
6. Ira L. Reiss. *The Family System in America.* New York: Holt Rinehart and Winston, Inc., 1971, 195.
Bernard Farber. *Family Organization and Interaction.* San Francisco: Chandler Publishing Company, 1964, 8.

Chapter 19

1. Sorokin, 1959, 3–6.
2. Gerth and Mills, 1946, 180.
3. Davis, 1948, 95.
4. Davis, 1948, 95.
5. Gerth and Mills, 1946, 245–52.
6. Davis, 1948, 93.
7. Vance Packard. *The Status Seekers.* New York: David McKay Company, 1959, 6.
8. F. Stuart Chapin. *Measurement of Social Status.* Minneapolis: University of Minnesota Press, 1933.
9. William H. Sewell. *The Construction and Standardization of a Scale for the Measurement of the Socio-economic Status of Oklahoma Farm Families.* Oklahoma AESTB 9, Stillwater, 1940.
10. John C. Belcher. "Evaluation of and Restandardization of Sewell's Socio-economic Scale," *Rural Sociology,* 16 (1951), 246–55.
11. George Orwell. *Animal Farm.* New York: Harcourt, Brace and World, Inc., 1954, 148.
12. Kingsley Davis and W. E. Moore, "Some Principles of Stratification," *American Sociological Review,* 10 (1945), 242–49.
13. Frederick L. Bates and John D. Kelley, "A Station-centered Approach to the Study of Social Stratification," *LSU Journal of Sociology,* 2 (1972), 22–47.

Chapter 20

1. A. L. Kroeber. *Anthropology.* New York: Harcourt, Brace 1948, 412; W. F. Ogburn. *Social Change.* New York: The Viking Press, 1950, 377.

Chapter 21

1. Harold L. Nix and F. L. Bates. "Occupational Role Stresses: A Structural Approach," *Rural Sociology,* 27 (1962), 7–17.

2. F. L. Bates, "Some Observations Concerning the Structural Aspects of Role Conflict," *Pacific Sociological Review,* 5 (1962); F. L. Bates, "Social Disorganization at the Group Level: A Role Theory Approach," *The United College Journal,* The Chinese University of Hong Kong, 3 (1964).

3. Bruce J. Biddle and Edwin J. Thomas, *Role Theory; Concepts and Research,* New York: John Wiley and Sons, Inc., 1966, 273–274; Ralph Turner, "Role: Sociological Aspects," *International Encyclopedia of the Social Sciences,* 13 (1968), 556.

4. Robert K. Merton, 1957, 60–64.

5. August B. Hollingshead, *Elmtown's Youth* (New York, John Wiley and Sons, 1949) and W. L. Warner, Marcia Meeker and Kenneth Eells, *Social Class in America* (Chicago, Science Research Associates, Inc., 1949).

6. Kingsley Davis and W. E. Moore, "Some Principles of Stratification," *American Sociological Review,* Vol. 10, April 1945, pp. 242–249.

7. Laurence J. Peter and Raymond Hull, *The Peter Principle* (New York: William Morrow and Co., Inc. 1969).

8. Victor Hugo, *Les Miserables,* (New York: Fawcett World, 1961).

INDEX